THREE STRIKES

CAN'T TAKE ME OUT

HALEY MAZANEC

ISBN: 978-1-966798-37-8

Life doesn't play fair. But neither does she.

Haley Mazanec has faced more than her share of heartbreak, betrayal, and loss. From her small-town beginnings in Northern California to the chaotic allure of Los Angeles, every chapter of her life has tested her in ways she never could have imagined. A fractured family. A romance that left deep scars. A tragedy that nearly consumed her. Every chapter of her life has tested her strength—but every time, she's fought to rise again.

But this isn't just a story about survival—it's about transformation. With raw honesty, dark humor, and a spirit that refuses to quit, Haley peels back the layers of her past, revealing the choices that shaped her, the wounds that nearly broke her, and the unrelenting fight to reclaim her life.

But when the third and final strike comes crashing down, one question remains: **Can she rise once more, or has life already written her off?**

Gritty, gripping, and impossible to forget, Three Strikes Can't Take Me Out is a story of resilience, reinvention, and the power of rewriting your own story—even when the world counts you out.

Table of Contents

Acknowledgments 7

Chapter 1: Fertilizer for the Soul 10

Chapter 2: A Love So Loud the Neighbors Complained 23

Chapter 3: Negative Nancy and the Gaslight Chronicles 45

Chapter 4: Dancing with Shadows 58

Chapter 5: Powdered Promises 65

Chapter 6: The Devil's Carousel 77

Chapter 7: Grey Knight's Last Ride 88

Chapter 8: A Toast to Trouble 96

Chapter 9: Till Jail Do Us Part 101

Chapter 10: Cold Turkey in the Foothills 114

Chapter 11: Confessions at a Speakeasy 121

Chapter 12: Drama Ditch 125

Chapter 13: King's Cup Karma 135

Chapter 14: Secrets in the Sun 146

Chapter 15: A Lotus in the Mud 161

Chapter 16: Red Flags Wrapped in Glitter 174

Chapter 17: Meet Meatball 192

Chapter 18: Diagnosis: WTF 214

Chapter 19: Breadcrumbs & Bullsh*t 225

Chapter 20: How to Lose 10 Pounds in Two Weeks 242

Chapter 21: Italy, Interrupted 258

Chapter 22: Escape Room: Italian edition 279

Chapter 23: Excuse My French 305

Chapter 24: Pain Has a Passport... 326

Chapter 25: Plot Twist Mayhem.. 353

Chapter 26: Whispers from the Universe 376

Chapter 27: Spiritual Wi-Fi... 398

Chapter 28: Sparks Fly 422

King Shit's Rule.. 452

Grey Knight.. 463

About the Author 467

Acknowledgments

To my family—thank you for bringing me into this world and, more importantly, for not disowning me after all the chaos I've caused. For every lesson, every tough-love moment, every time you shook your head but still showed up for me—I'm endlessly grateful. No relationship is perfect, but what we have now? It's real, it's strong, and that's what matters most. Thank you for standing by me when I stumbled and for cheering me on as I found my way back. I wouldn't trade this imperfectly beautiful bond for anything.

Oh, my wild, wonderful, irreplaceable friends—what did I do to deserve you? Through laughter that shook the walls, heartbreak that nearly broke me, questionable decisions, and victories that felt like lifetimes in the making, you've been there. You've seen me in my brilliance and in my disasters, and somehow, you stayed—for that, I am endlessly grateful. And to those who have drifted away, I still hold space for you, too. No matter how our story ended, good or bad, I choose to cherish what was, because every connection meant something, and every moment mattered.

Some people leave footprints in your life, and then there are those who shape the entire path. Grey Knight is the latter. A name I once gave him, never realizing how perfectly it would come to define him—a presence too powerful to fade, too woven into my story to be unwritten. If not for him, this book wouldn't exist. Our wild, complicated, unforgettable love story is the reason these pages were born.

I won't use his real name, but Grey Knight is who he has always been to me—an undeniable force, a turning point, a chapter that refused to end. He didn't just influence my life; he changed its course, set it ablaze, and made sure I'd never see the world the same way again. So, to him—thank you. For the memories, the madness, and for giving me a story that demanded to be told.

Our story is not one of perfect fairy-tale endings, and yet, it's one I cherish with all its imperfect, jagged edges. It's a story of growth, of heartbreak, of laughter that carried us through storms, and silence that nearly drowned us. Despite everything, I look back and see two souls who have come so far, who weathered their storms and made it to the shore—changed, but better for it. I couldn't be prouder of the person he's become, of the person I've become. Truly. I wish him nothing but boundless joy, fulfillment, and all the things you didn't even know your heart longed for.

To all of you—thank you. You are the threads that weave this tapestry of my life, and I wouldn't change a single stitch.

ACT I

Beneath the Mud

Before beauty, there was burial.
Before bloom, there was the breaking.
She wasn't planted—she was buried beneath shame,
silence, and the weight of everyone else's stories.
This is where the goddess slept, aching in the dark,
not because she was weak—
but because she was gathering roots

Chapter 1

Fertilizer for the Soul

Before I dive into the heart of my story, let me first take you back—just for a moment. I believe it's important to give you a glimpse into my childhood. Not just the sugar-coated version we tend to tell ourselves, but the raw, sometimes messy, often beautiful beginnings that shape us. After all, childhood is where it all starts, isn't it? It's where the foundation of who we are gets built, brick by brick, memory by memory. And just like you, I've been carrying my own set of stories, stories that have begged to be told for years. But here's the kicker—every time I thought I had the final chapter, life threw another plot twist my way. More drama, more revelations, more... juicy material, if I'm being honest. And now, I'm finally in a place where I can share it all, with a heart full of both gratitude and vulnerability. It's not just the act of writing that excites me; it's the thought that maybe, just maybe, you'll see a part of yourself in my story. That you'll resonate with the ups and downs, feel empowered, or be inspired to make a change, big or small. Maybe even laugh or cry alongside me. If I can offer you that, then every moment of reliving these experiences will be worth it. So buckle up—because we're just getting started.

I was raised in the Bay Area, Northern California—specifically in Brentwood. No, not the LA Brentwood with the glitz and glam, but the smaller, humbler town with cornfields as far as the eye could see. It's the kind of place where the summers are long, the air smells of fresh earth, and kids grow up playing in the neighborhood until the sun dips below the horizon. My parents were happily married—until they weren't. When I was nine, they got divorced. A classic tale, right? But I'll admit, the details are hazy. I don't have one of those sharp-as-a-tack childhood memories. Nope, mine's a bit blurry around the edges. What I do know is that I was a full-blown daddy's girl, and my mom... Well, let's just say she wasn't exactly present. It's hard to admit that, even now. It's like admitting the sky isn't really blue, something you've convinced yourself of your whole life.

My dad used to say, "Your mom neglected you." It wasn't whispered in a quiet moment of reflection. No, it impressed into my head, over and over. She was off shopping, partying, and doing her thing, while we were left in his capable hands. And as much as I hate to admit it, I believed him. I let that narrative take root, and naturally, I resented her. I became the quintessential daddy's girl, while my brother—who's a year younger—sided with Mom.

And as if the divorce wasn't enough, my parents couldn't stand each other so much that they avoided all communication. Guess who got to play a messenger? That's right—me. I became the delivery girl, shuttling messages between two people who should've been doing the talking themselves. Looking back now, I realize how twisted that was, but at the time, it felt normal. It was my job, my responsibility as the older sibling.

We split our time evenly—fifty-fifty. Every other week was a back-and-forth between my dad's house and my mom's. I favored my dad, of course. We were close, maybe too close, if I'm being honest. I held his hand, kissed it with all the love a little girl could muster, and felt joy just being by his side. It's one of the few memories from my early childhood that stands out, like a snapshot from an old photo album. But then there was the anger. My dad's anger. Towards my mom, towards the world, and sometimes, it felt, towards me.

He vented—a lot. And when he vented, there was no stopping him. I'd try to get a word in, but he'd barrel right past me, like a freight train of frustration and bitterness. I felt like his punching bag at times, absorbing every word, every ounce of negativity. You know that feeling, when the air around someone is so thick with negativity, it feels like it's sucking the life right out of you? Yeah, that's what it was like. And yet, I was happy to be close to him. Isn't that strange? How we cling to the people we love, even when they hurt us? I started shutting down, retreating inward, like a crab crawling back into its shell. It became safer to be silent than to try and fight for space in the conversation.

When my dad moved into a two-story house, my mom was waiting for her new place to be built. In the meantime, we lived with my grandma— Cookie Grandma Rita, as we called her. Let me tell you, she was a character!

Think Lucille Ball but with a tough-cookie attitude that could stop you in your tracks. She was everything I didn't know I needed—a mother figure, a role model, a friend. Even though we only lived with her for about six months, she left an indelible mark on my heart. She had COPD, then lung cancer, and then, as if the universe decided to really pile it on, a brain tumor. The doctors gave her one to two months to live, but Grandma Rita was a fighter. She surpassed the odds, staying with us for another eight months.

In those months, we grew closer than ever. She taught me how to bake, and we spent countless hours laughing, eating ice cream (yes, sometimes for breakfast), and watching old *I Love Lucy* reruns. She told me stories about her life and shared memories that I treasure to this day. I'll never forget the day she bought me a charm with an angel on it and said, "I'll be your guardian angel when I'm gone." It was a promise that still comforts me, even now.

One of the most poignant moments came when she confided in me and my mom about something she had never shared with anyone else—a baby boy she gave up for adoption after being roofied and assaulted. It was a secret she had held close her entire life. And somehow, she chose me to hear it. Me, her favorite granddaughter. I felt special, yes, but more than that, I felt the weight of her trust, the enormity of her pain.

I watched her deteriorate, bit by bit, until the vibrant woman I knew was a shadow of herself. And yet, even in her final days, she kept her humor, playing with her dentures and wig, cracking jokes like only Grandma Rita could. The morning she passed, I kissed her cold cheek and whispered my final goodbye, a moment that still haunts me, still grips my heart in a way I can't fully explain.

The worst part? I felt it before it happened. The night before she passed, I crawled into bed wearing one of her big kitty night shirts, like some kind of magic armor that might keep her here. Instead, I woke up screaming, shaking from a dream that she was gone. My heart was pounding, but my mom calmed me down, *Relax. It's just a dream.* Then morning came. I opened my eyes to find my family huddled together, their silence louder than words, and just like that—I realized my nightmare wasn't just a dream. It was real.

Writing this now, I realize how much of an impact she had on me, not just in the eighteen months we lived together, but in the years that followed. She taught me resilience, humor in the face of hardship, and the importance of cherishing every moment. And yes, she also left me with a deep-seated fear of cancer, a fear that has loomed over me for years. Watching someone you love fade away, bit by bit, has a way of sticking with you. It changes you. But it also teaches you. It teaches you the fragility of life, and the strength we have to carry on, even when the weight feels unbearable.

So, as I continue to write this book, I remind myself that memory is a tricky thing. We hold on to some moments tightly, while others slip away. Sometimes, we even misremember, convincing ourselves of a timeline that doesn't quite add up. But that's the beauty of stories, isn't it? They evolve, just like we do. And I'm here to share mine, as honestly and vulnerably as I can, hoping that in my words, you might find a piece of your own.

Once we moved into Mom's new house, it was as though the quiet resentment I had buried deep inside began to unfurl, slowly, like an unwelcome vine creeping its way into every moment. I had hoped that maybe, with the new house, things would change—that Mom would change. But life has a funny way of revealing truths you don't want to face. Her grueling two-hour commute to and from work left her exhausted beyond belief. By the time she got home, she'd collapse onto the couch, her body seemingly glued to it, and her eyes would shut faster than I could say, "Welcome home." I tried waking her once, but it was like trying to rouse a statue. The fear became a steady hum in my chest, growing louder as I watched her fall asleep at the wheel when we drove, the roads blurring into a potential disaster at every turn. I talked nonstop, desperate to keep her awake, feeling like I was carrying her safety in my words.

It wasn't just on the road that terrified me. If I left her in the bathtub too long, she'd nod off and slip into unconsciousness. The fear I had of losing her, or worse, being the one to find her like that, struck me in ways I hadn't expected. So, I did what anyone would do when their world spins out of control—I became the parent. I took care of my little brother, cooked meals, cleaned the house, and tucked them both into bed, as if that might somehow fix what was broken. The resentment simmered underneath all that responsibility, but I buried it deep enough, opting instead for rebellion. I took advantage of my "adult role" to sneak out and see my boyfriend—the older bad influence that everyone warned me about. I believed he was my first puppy love, the kind that swallows you whole. But he wasn't the Romeo I thought he was—no, he cheated on me for eight months, breaking my heart like it was a cheap toy. And yet, I had to break my own heart even more by walking away, even though I thought I'd found the one.

My brother—just fourteen months behind me in birth, but lightyears away in experience—was once my sidekick. We shared the kind of childhood closeness that felt unspoken, seamless... until it wasn't. Everything shifted when he was diagnosed with ADHD and ADD. The doctors scribbled out prescriptions, promising focus and control. Maybe they worked in invisible ways, but what I did see was a sharp, chilling divide form between us. Our playful bond twisted into something darker, meaner. We didn't just argue like typical siblings—we brawled. And somewhere in that chaos, he transformed. It was like a shadow slipped into him overnight—he became someone I didn't recognize. Someone who seemed to carry a secret vendetta against me.

The worst of it happened when no one was watching. He'd corner me, waving knives and scissors with a haunting calm, like we were reenacting some deranged thriller. I fought him off more than once. My bedroom—my sacred escape—was no longer mine, even after I bought a lock. Fear became my new bedtime ritual. At school, he sketched drawings that mirrored the movie The Ring, counting down my so-called final days. Seven. Six. Five... twisted child's play that felt anything but innocent.

I begged my parents to believe me. Pleaded. But it was like screaming underwater. Mom—predictably—coddled him. Her baby boy. Either she couldn't see what was happening, or worse... she wouldn't. And I wasn't just battling him. I was battling the silence in my home, the chaos in my heart, the deep loneliness that crept in when no one seemed to care enough to look closer. The weight of it all—my brother's rage, my mother's denial, the isolation that wrapped around me like a straitjacket—became unbearable.

One day, it all cracked. I didn't break in one dramatic moment—I had been unraveling quietly for months. But that night, it felt like the walls finally closed in. I found a bottle of my grandmother's German liquor and drank it like a potion, hoping it would dull the ache. Then came the pills—thirty in total. Tylenol. Grandma's cancer meds. Anything I could get my hands on. I wasn't trying to be dramatic. I was trying to make it stop. The terror. The helplessness. The feeling that no one saw me drowning.

Mom found me—alive, somehow. The doctors couldn't explain it. My kidneys should've failed. My body should've shut down. But it didn't. I survived. Barely. And even though no one said it outright, something shifted.

Eventually, with enough pushing from both Mom and Joey, they took him off the medication. A silent admission that maybe, just maybe, I hadn't been making it all up. And that's when the wildest thing happened. He changed. Almost overnight. Grew out of the rage. Out of the pills. Out of that angry 5'5" kid and into a 6'4" gentle giant who remembered nothing. Poof—like the darkness had been a ghost that only haunted me. I was young, but I could see it clearly: those pills had warped him into something unrecognizable. They didn't just stunt his body—they hijacked his mind. He was a victim, too. Of chemistry. Of carelessness.

Still… he never apologized. Not once. And I don't throw the word "hate" around lightly, but for years, I hated him. I hated what he became. What I had to survive. What nobody saw. And even now, the apology never came. So how do you forgive someone who doesn't even remember what they did?

Healing from something like that is lonely work. But I've done it. At least, most of it. He's still my brother—the only one I've got. And a part of me holds onto this stubborn little hope that one day, maybe, we'll find our way back. For now, that hope stays quiet. But the beauty in all of this? The pills are gone. The darkness has lifted. And my brother—the real one—is still in there somewhere. I see him now. A good man. A kind soul. And me? I'm no longer the girl afraid of the hallway shadows. I'm the woman who walked through them and came out whole.

Despite all that, the heavy weight of depression lingered over me like a dark cloud. I couldn't bring myself to talk about it with anyone—not even a therapist. I had a close-knit group of girlfriends, about seven of us. We were all carrying our own wounds, sharing them like battle scars, and leaning on each other through the chaos of adolescence. We were bound by both laughter and darkness. But somewhere along the way, we picked up a dangerous habit—wrist-cutting. We thought it gave us control over our pain, but really, it just pulled us deeper into the void. The drama between us became suffocating, absorbing all of my energy. It interfered with school, with life, with everything.

My dad tried to help me through it, though. He found me crying more times than I can count, always stressing over some ridiculous drama. He'd sit with me, telling me over and over again, "Love yourself! You're all you have." I'd nod, but I didn't really get it. What did that even mean? Love myself? I didn't know how to. But his comfort meant everything, even if I didn't fully understand his words at the time.

Then there was the rage I had during the weeks I spent at Mom's. I would lock myself away in my room, writing hate-filled letters about her, pouring out all my resentment. It felt toxic, like I was feeding my anger just to survive. The final straw came when my friends betrayed me—one by one, they stabbed me in the back. So, I cut them all off. No conversation, no closure, just gone. It was the first real boundary I set for myself. No more drama. No more cutting. I had to change. I *wanted* to love my life, even if I didn't know where to start.

That was the beginning of my journey—my promise to myself to stop letting the past define me and start figuring out what it means to truly love myself. And from that moment on, I began walking toward the life I knew I deserved.

My mom met her perfect match in the most unexpected way, and suddenly, Joey was in our lives, right on the heels of Grandma Rita's passing. It was almost like fate decided that one firecracker was leaving, so it had to send another in her place. Joey, though? He was a different breed of dynamite. He called himself "The Clairol," as if he were some walking, talking brand of charm and humor. He was hard-working, fun-loving, and a man who knew how to make you laugh when you least expected it. I could see how much my mom treasured him—it was in the way her eyes lit up whenever he was around. My brother, of course, adored him instantly. He finally had a father figure he could look up to, someone who genuinely cared.

But me? Oh, I let my tangled-up feelings toward my mom get in the way of ever letting Joey in. For three long years, I barely spoke a word to him, too wrapped up in my own walls and adolescent rebellion to see the good right in front of me. But eventually, I cracked. The silence broke, and once I started talking to Joey, our relationship blossomed into something that felt as effortless as it was unexpected. He became a friend I could talk to about anything, his joyful spirit and endless humor a balm for all the hurt I'd carried. Over time, he wasn't just Joey anymore; he was a father figure, a stepdad I never knew I needed. And man, I'm blessed to have him in my life.

Now, let's get one thing straight: I grew up a *daddy's girl* through and through, and with that came my very firm policy of a drama-free zone. If there was one thing I learned from my early years, it was that male friendships felt far less toxic than the tornado of emotions that seemed to swirl around my female friendships. The drama that came with girls? No thanks! I had had enough. I shut that door and bolted it shut. Male energy was my safe haven. Easy-going, light-hearted, fun vibes were my jam, and I gravitated toward them like a moth to a flame.

But here's the catch. While I enjoyed the simplicity of male friendships, my subconscious was on a whole different level. It craved attention, validation, and the sense of being seen—not just as a friend, but as something more. The problem was that I kept finding myself viewed as nothing more than *the girl next door*, my inner beauty invisible behind the surface. I became a people-pleaser, addicted to making others happy, terrified of angering anyone. And yet, ironically, I gravitated toward the exact opposite when it came to boyfriends. I dated the bad boys. The ones with anger management issues. The type your mom warned you about. You know how they say, "You always date someone like your father"? Well, I took that a bit too literally. My childhood was a carousel of these guys—angry, troubled, but with enough good qualities to keep me hooked. It wasn't all bad, though. There were moments of love, growth, and connection, especially with two of my longer relationships.

The first was Rob, my "puppy love" in freshman year. He was everything my teenage heart thought it wanted, but also everything it didn't need. He cheated on me for eight months, and it shattered my trust in ways I didn't fully understand at the time. I held on for too long, convinced I could fix him, that love would somehow be enough to drag him out of his bad habits—gangs, drugs, the whole shady package. It wasn't, and I ended things, but not without a lingering pain that followed me into my next relationship.

Then, there was Chris. Oh, Chris. He was the best friend who unexpectedly became the boyfriend after three years of just being there for each other. It was one of the healthier relationships in my life, and for that, I'll always be grateful. Chris was already a wonderful person, but like all of us, he had his inner battles. Watching him grow, watching both him and Rob express how much I'd influenced them for the better, filled my heart in a way that words can't quite capture. Rob quit his toxic friend group. Chris clawed his way out of his mental gutter. I was there for it all, front row, as they stepped into their light. And honestly? It was beautiful.

But, as it often goes, wonderful friendships with men hit a wall. Time and again, I'd get hit with the same bombshell—these friends, these guys who I thought were on the same page, would suddenly confess their love for me. Every. Single. Time. And I didn't want that. I never wanted that. My intuition was like a compass, always pointing me in the right direction. I knew when something was just a friendship, and I never had those deeper feelings for them. So I'd have to turn them down, break their hearts a little, and eventually cut them out of my life. Each rejection hurt me as much as it hurt them, but I couldn't fake feelings I didn't have.

And as more and more of these friendships crumbled, my heart took the hits, one after another. I became hyper-aware of how sensitive I was, of how deeply I felt everything. My self-esteem took blow after blow, and eventually, I spiraled into a phase that I'm not proud of—bulimia. I ate my feelings until I couldn't anymore, and then I purged them, hoping that somehow losing weight would fill the void inside. Of course, it didn't. It never does.

I trusted too easily, let people in too quickly, and then wondered why I was left feeling used and discarded. I became a magnet for toxic people, a sponge for their negativity. Until, one day, I just couldn't anymore. I shut myself off. I built walls so high and thick that no one could get in. I developed mad trust issues—turned into someone so fiercely independent, I refused to let anyone do anything for me. Especially men. If they offered, I'd question their motives. What did they want in return?

And with that, my femininity—the softness, the vulnerability—took a backseat. I wrapped myself in a tough, masculine energy, an armor that protected me from the world. I became the warrior, shield in hand, blocking out everything and everyone that could hurt me. But in doing so, I also blocked out the love, the care, the connection I so desperately needed.

By the time I hit fifteen, there was only one thing on my mind: freedom. And to me, freedom meant money—my own money—so I could finally do whatever I wanted. I wasn't going to beg for an allowance, and I sure as hell wasn't going to rely on anyone else. But when the universe offered up my first job opportunity, it was at Baskin Robbins, of all places. Really? Ice cream? I mean, I love a good scoop as much as the next person, but working there? I had visions of myself rolling out the door with a belly full of World Class Chocolate and Cookie Dough. Nope. Not happening. That was a hard pass. Ice cream and a teenage metabolism are a dangerous combination.

So, I waited until I turned sixteen, and the moment the clock struck midnight on my birthday, I had a hostess job lined up at Mimi's Café. Glamorous? Absolutely not. But it was something. And I was determined to make it work.

Growing up, I was obsessed with supermodels—the likes of Gisele Bündchen, Tyra Banks, Heidi Klum, and Naomi Campbell. I'd watch them strut down the runway, and it was like a lightbulb flicked on in my head. That's what I wanted—to be the one walking down the catwalk, commanding the world's attention. Sixteen wasn't too young to start chasing dreams, right? So, I dove headfirst into the modeling world, building a portfolio and learning how to pose like my life depended on it.

Independence was in my DNA. I didn't need anyone else to push me forward—I was my own engine, full speed ahead. The truth was, I felt like I grew up overnight. After everything I'd been through, self-sufficiency wasn't just a choice; it was my reality. I had learned to depend on no one but myself.

But, as life would have it, just as I was finding my rhythm, my dad's second marriage crumbled. Honestly, part of me wasn't surprised. I'd secretly suspected it wasn't built to last, but then came Lois. She wasn't just another girlfriend. She was different—magnificent, even. I watched in awe as my father transformed before my eyes. The anger that once seemed permanently etched into his face evaporated. He was softer now, more tender. I had never seen him like this, and for the first time, he was genuinely happy. He was so wrapped up in Lois that he stopped clinging to me like he used to. I should've been happy for him, and I was… at least on the surface. But deep down? I was devastated.

See, I never had a relationship with my mom, and now my dad, the one person I had left, was drifting away, too, swept up in the tide of his newfound love. I was proud of him—really, I was—but that didn't stop the ache of feeling neglected. It wasn't long before a wedge formed between me and Lois. How could I let myself get close to her when I already felt like an outsider in my own family? And yet, once upon a time, I would brag about my dad to anyone who'd listen. When he dated after my mom, I was his biggest cheerleader, parading him around like the catch of the century. But now? Now it felt like I was the one being left behind. Neglected by both parents, I was fiercely independent but so very alone.

There was only one solution: I had to get out of that town. There was an entire world out there that I hadn't even begun to explore, and I couldn't waste any more time feeling stuck. So, I did what I do best—I hustled. I saved every penny I could, working late shifts, sacrificing weekends, all with one goal in mind: escape. And when the opportunity came to transfer from my community college to a four-year university, I set my sights on Los Angeles. The city of dreams, where ambition never sleeps.

I thought distance might be the cure. Maybe, just maybe, if I wasn't so close, I could mend the broken threads of my relationships with my family.

Maybe with space, we could all breathe easier. So, at twenty-one, with a few suitcases and big dreams, I moved to LA. I didn't know a soul in the city. It was terrifying and exhilarating all at once.

But I was ready. Ready to build something new. Ready to finally live for me.

Let me be real with you—I have to share some of my past and give you a peek into where I come from, or this whole book is going to feel like one giant trauma dump. And let's face it, nobody wants to read a hundred pages of someone else's messy, unfiltered baggage. I promise you, though, this isn't just a story about me wallowing in all the crap life threw at me. No, this is about how I took that crap and turned it into fertilizer. Yep, you heard me—fertilizer. Kind of like how a lotus flower grows from the mud.

Now, if you're asking yourself, "Why a lotus flower?" Well, buckle up, because there's some symbolism coming your way. See, lotuses are these gorgeous, delicate flowers that literally rise out of the filthiest, murkiest waters you can imagine. And when they bloom, they're immaculate—not a single stain on them. It's like they've never even touched the mud. They're seen as symbols of purity for that very reason. But the magic doesn't stop there. Each evening, the lotus sinks back into that same murky water, only to rise again, fresh and new, when the sun breaks the next day. How amazing is that? There's something so beautiful, almost magical, about how they pull themselves up and bloom despite their surroundings. That, to me, is the definition of strength, resilience, and rebirth.

I'm not saying I'm some perfect, pristine lotus flower floating above the chaos of life. Far from it. I've been deep in the mud, trust me. But over time, I've learned how to rise from it, how to let it shape me without letting it define me. Like the lotus, I've been in the murkiest of waters, but each time, I've found a way to come back up, a little stronger, a little wiser. And I think that's something worth sharing. Life hands us mud—sometimes buckets of it—but what matters is how we deal with it. Do we let it swallow us, or do we rise above it and bloom despite it?

So, yes, this book might take you through some tough, muddy moments. But don't be fooled. It's not a pile of shit for the sake of wallowing in it. It's about learning to cultivate growth in the middle of the mess. Because here's the thing: Life is messy. But in the mess, in the grime and the dirt, that's where real beauty takes root. It's where strength is forged. So no, this isn't just a sad story. It's a story of resilience, of figuring out how to thrive even when you feel like you're drowning in it all.

And while my lotus moment didn't happen overnight—it's a slow process, trust me—it happened. I found my way to the surface. So, stick with me through the mud, because the bloom is coming. And I promise, it's worth it. And that, my dear reader, is something I can't wait to share with you. Because if I've learned one thing, it's that we all have a little lotus flower in us, waiting to rise above the muck and bloom in our own way.

Chapter 2

A Love So Loud the Neighbors Complained

I remember it like it was yesterday. Not the kind of yesterday where the details blur into a foggy memory, but the kind that feels imprinted on my soul. That day at BOA Steakhouse—the epitome of fine dining in Los Angeles, a place where stars align under candlelight over plates of Wagyu and decanters of wine. I was walking up to the front door for my interview, barely able to contain my excitement. The world felt lighter, like the breeze itself was pushing me toward some grand destiny. The place wasn't even open yet, and there I was, full of hope, with my nerves bubbling just beneath my skin.

Then the door swung open, and standing there was a man—no, not just any man—a tall, six-foot vision of perfection. His green eyes were the kind you could drown in, deep and bright, and that smile… Oh, that smile. It could melt glaciers. He was dressed in slacks and a white button-up, with a vest that hugged his frame just right. Muscular but elegant, with that effortless charm of a Midwestern boy who just happened to stroll into a Hollywood romance. He greeted me with the kind of hospitality that made me question whether I was at a restaurant or a dream. I remember thinking, Is it possible to fall in love at first sight? because that's exactly what it felt like. My breath caught in my throat, and suddenly, the stakes of this interview seemed trivial compared to the overwhelming wave of attraction I felt for him. Forget the job—*What if I get to see this man again?*

When the manager arrived, I somehow snapped back to reality, reminding myself why I was there. The interview itself? Oh, it went great! My nerves had smoothed out, and even though I'd never set foot in a fine dining establishment like this, I held my own. But let's be honest—half my mind was still on the handsome stranger who had stolen my breath the moment he opened that door. Two weeks. They told me it would take two weeks before I'd hear back, and I spent every one of those days not just praying for the job, but praying to see him again. It was as if getting the position became secondary to the chance of connecting with him. I wanted more than just a paycheck—I wanted the possibility of something extraordinary.

And then, the call came. The moment that changed everything. I got the job! At just 22 years old, I was stepping into the world of fine dining, and let me tell you, I was ecstatic. I mean, steak is practically my love language, so you can imagine how excited I was. But let's be real—what I was *really* looking forward to was seeing him again. The beautiful stranger who had made my heart skip a beat. Training began, and every shift with him was like a new chapter in a romance novel I couldn't stop reading.

At first, it was just the usual small talk, nothing too deep, but oh, was there chemistry. We laughed, we flirted, and every time we locked eyes, it was like the universe was giving us a nudge. One day, we even had one of those magical moments that only happens in movies. We both quoted *Step Brothers* at the exact same time—"Did we just become best friends?!" It was goofy, hilarious, and perfect, like something out of a rom-com. And in that moment, I knew. I wasn't just attracted to him. I *wanted* him. Badly. He was magnetic, and every time I was around him, I felt like the air itself was buzzing with possibility.

But, as life often does, there was a complication. Just as my heart was getting tangled up in fantasies about this man, there was this other guy. Let's call him Mr. Wrong—a total party animal, a walking red flag, and someone I was clearly wasting my time with. I didn't even know why I was interested, but there I was. Until one night, my green-eyed knight sent me a text asking if I wanted to grab a drink. I'd already made plans with Mr. Wrong, but in that moment, I realized something important: I didn't care. So, I ditched the loser and said yes to the man who made my heart race.

We ended up at an Irish pub, sitting at the bar, chatting like old friends who had known each other for years. The conversation flowed effortlessly— about life, our hometowns, our dreams. It was like peeling back the layers of someone you were always meant to know. As we sat there, something shifted inside me. It wasn't just attraction anymore; it was recognition. My intuition, that gut feeling I've always trusted, screamed at me: *This man is going to be in your life forever.* And in that moment, I believed it. There were no butterflies—

no, that's too small a word. There was a zoo inside me, a wild stampede of emotions. I had met my soulmate, my person.

We kept hanging out, slowly, and yet somehow, every time we were together, it felt like a firework show inside me. But then came the gut punch. One night, at a work party, I saw him walk in with another woman on his arm. My heart sank like a stone in water. He was taken. I tried to smile, tried to swallow the disappointment, and told myself, *Fine. It's okay. You'll just be friends.* But deep down, I knew that wasn't true. I couldn't just be friends with him. My heart was already too far gone.

Fast forward a bit, and I took a risk. I invited him out to a club with my friends. You better believe I dressed to kill, hoping to make him sweat a little. And it worked. Oh, did it work. When he saw me, his eyes lit up like Christmas morning. The night went on in a blur of music, laughter, and drinks, and before I knew it, we were dancing, lost in our own little world. And then it happened—our first kiss. Right there on the dance floor. It was electric, the kind of kiss that makes the world fade away until all that exists is the two of you.

Back at my apartment that night, everything seemed to blur into a dazzling mix of heat, passion, and a dash of delightful absurdity. As our encounter unfolded, the intensity of our chemistry escalated into an unexpected climax of vulnerability. In the midst of our steamy entanglement, he fixed me with those stunning green eyes and, with a raw burst of sincerity that caught us both off guard, declared, "You're so beautiful… I love you." And here's the kicker—it was only our second time hanging out!

For a split second, I was caught in a whirlwind of emotions: should I laugh, cry, or dash for the door? The timing was ludicrous—two meetings in and suddenly, love was on the table. It was as if the universe had hit the fast-forward button on our budding romance, thrusting us into a scene that was equal parts crazy and hilarious. I couldn't help but marvel at the absurdity of it all; who ever thought that the words "I love you" could tumble out so recklessly, so early in the game? And yet, there they were, spilling out in a moment that was as much a comedy of errors as it was a confession of raw emotion.

I was well aware that he was more than a little intoxicated, the alcohol loosening his tongue and blurring the lines between reality and a particularly vivid dream. In that moment of heated intimacy, I couldn't keep my incredulity to myself any longer. I blurted out, "I'm not a homewrecker!" In a mixture of jest and a genuine need to reclaim some sanity. It was a spontaneous verbal riposte that perfectly captured the surreal hilarity of the situation—his drunken love declaration met with my unfiltered, public rebuttal. And just when I thought the script couldn't get any more outlandish, he nonchalantly added that he'd just broken up with her.

That revelation dissolved the last of my reservations. As if by magic, my defenses crumbled, and I found myself leaning into the chaos, allowing a spark of trust to kindle amid the madness. The night unfolded into an unexpected blend of passion and laughter, a reminder that sometimes life's most memorable moments are born from utter unpredictability.

Over time, that night evolved into a cherished memory, a quirky hallmark of our unconventional beginning. Once his sobriety returned, I found endless amusement in teasing him about his impromptu love declaration. It became our running joke, a light-hearted reminder of that wonderfully insane moment when logic took a backseat to passion. Every teasing quip was laced with affectionate laughter, a nod to the surreal experience of hearing "I love you" so early on—a line that, while utterly premature, perfectly encapsulated the wild, unpredictable energy of our connection.

Looking back, that moment remains a testament to the beautiful madness of new love. It reminds me that sometimes, the most memorable parts of our stories are those that defy convention—a hilariously premature confession that turns into the glue binding us together. It's crazy, it's risky, and above all, it's undeniably human. And isn't that a little bit magical?

The next morning, I was half-expecting things to be awkward. I mean, how could they not be after a night like that? But instead, he asked me to breakfast. And just like that, the spell wasn't broken. We laughed our way through our hangovers, blowing latte foam out of my nose and being told by strangers how cute we were together. It was like the universe was whispering, *This is it. This is the one.*

There's one thing I forgot to mention, and it's a big one. The same day we had planned to go to the club was also the day my car got towed. And not just a casual "oops, I parked in the wrong spot" kind of tow—oh no, life had bigger plans for me. I got pulled over for driving 10 miles over the speed limit on my way home from the grocery store. Innocent enough, right? Except it wasn't. A month prior, I'd been slapped with a DUI, which meant my license had been suspended. Worse, it was set to officially expire just days after my car was towed away, like the universe was trying to see how much chaos I could handle in a single day.

In that moment, I felt like my guts had been ripped out and put through a blender. What was I going to do without a car in this sprawling, insane city of Los Angeles? I had college classes, a job to get to, and the kind of commute that made public transportation seem like a joke. Ubers? Out of the question—I wasn't made of money. But instead of dealing with this enormous, life-altering problem, I decided to shove it aside. Why? Because that night, I was seeing *him*—my Grey Knight. And somehow, in the middle of my internal meltdown, the idea of spending time with him was enough to make me push this disaster to the back burner.

After brunch, when we returned to my place, I confessed. I told him everything—the speeding ticket, the DUI, the fact that my car was gone and my life was now spiraling into logistical chaos. I was mortified. But instead of reacting with judgment or shock, he opened his arms and held me, like it was the most natural thing in the world. Who was this man? How did I get so lucky to find someone so kind, so effortlessly supportive? I swear, in that moment, I wondered if God had sent me an angel. Better yet, was this you, Cookie Grandma Rita?!

And then, something I never would have expected happened. He lent me his car. I mean, yes, it was kind of naughty on both our parts. I didn't technically have a license anymore, but my commute was much longer than his, and he insisted. Just like that, my nerves vanished.

He made sure we planned out our routes, so both of us could manage our busy lives with just one car. It wasn't easy, but it worked. I was beyond grateful. In fact, I'd never experienced anyone showing up for me like that before. He became my hero at a time when I was at one of the lowest points in my life. He helped me juggle everything—my DUI classes, my college courses, my job. He made me feel like I wasn't alone, like I had someone in my corner, holding me up when I thought I might fall apart. And yes, by then, we were definitely dating, though it all happened so fast that I almost missed the moment when it became official.

We threw ourselves into our relationship. We went on dates that felt like scenes from a rom-com—hiking adventures, country line dancing, you name it. We were both fitness fanatics, so naturally, we became that gym couple. He even offered to train me, and we spent the next year sweating it out together. Somewhere between the squats and the deadlifts, I realized just how much fun we had together. He brought out the childlike joy in me that I didn't even know I still had.

We tried shrooms for the first time together, sprinting around like giddy kids under the influence of psychedelics. I'll never forget the sunset at the beach—I was dancing barefoot on the shoreline, high on life (and, well, mushrooms), when I saw a whale breach the water. I screamed, dropped to my knees in the sand, and totally lost it. Whales are my spirit animal. I'd never seen anything like it, and now that memory is seared into my brain as one of the happiest moments of my life.

The adventures never stopped. Valentine's Day in Santa Barbara. The laughter was so contagious, it felt endless. Marilyn Monroe once said, "If you can make a girl laugh, you can make her do anything." Well, I was *that* woman. He made me laugh so much that my cheeks hurt, and I never wanted it to end.

He opened up to me, too. One day, we were at the beach, soaking up the sun, when he looked at me and said, "I'm an addict." He wasn't confessing it like it was a burden, more like he was sharing a part of himself that he needed me to know. He'd been to rehab not once, not twice, but four times. He told me it never worked because he never wanted it for himself.

What was I supposed to do with that information? I'd never been close to an addict before. I didn't know how to react or what it meant for us. But somehow, I couldn't bring myself to care in that moment. Our connection was flawless—his energy matched mine in ways I couldn't explain. He brought out all the best parts of me. He felt like my mirror, the male version of myself. Could it get any better than this?

For the astrology fans out there, I'm a Gemini, and he's an Aries. A match made in heaven, right? Two rare souls that had found each other. I fell under the spell of his green eyes and his smile that seemed to light up the whole room. No one had ever looked at me like that before, like I was the center of their universe. He touched my soul in a way that felt permanent, like I was branded for life.

When I was with him, every fear, every disappointment, every painful memory melted away. We were inseparable. We couldn't keep our hands off each other, like two magnets drawn together by a force bigger than us. We kissed at every stoplight, so intensely that people would honk at us. It became a running joke. And the fire between us? Let's just say we couldn't contain it. Our chemistry was overwhelming and beautiful—a thousand times over.

From that moment on, we were inseparable. The ups, the downs, the highs, the lows—they all blurred together into this whirlwind romance that felt like it was destined. He was my Grey Knight, and I? I was hopelessly, wildly in love.

My heart was wide open, like a blooming flower in the first warm light of spring, ready to pour all my love onto him. No reservations, no fear, just raw, unfiltered love. The first time I laid eyes on him, it was like a rom-com cliché brought to life—love at first sight. I believed in it instantly, like I'd been struck by some cosmic thunderbolt. And, in *The Notebook* fashion, two weeks into our whirlwind romance, my intuition screamed with wild certainty: *This is the one*. The Grey Knight, the man who would rewrite the ending of my story. The one I was destined to be with, forever.

I had never been the kind of woman who planned her future around someone else. The idea of picturing a life, a home, a forever with a single person? It had always seemed like a fairy tale—charming, but distant. But with him, oh, it was different. I didn't just see it; I felt it in every cell of my being. I could see the life we would build together, the adventures, the quiet moments, the messy, beautiful chaos of us. And I had zero shame in telling him that, either. Why hide what feels so right? To my delight, he felt the exact same way. Madly, head-over-heels for each other. It was game over. There was no hesitation, no second-guessing. We knew—*we knew*—we were the real deal. We knew in-between.

In our excitement, we started dreaming out loud. We talked about rings. Yes, already. Couldn't help ourselves. I was practically floating on a cloud when he mentioned he wanted to design the ring himself. *Be still, my heart.* But that didn't stop me from sending him little hints, playful suggestions like, "How about this one? Or this one?" It was fun, giddy fun. The kind of joy that makes your heart race, knowing that it's not just me anymore. *It's we.* No matter how fast we were moving, it didn't feel reckless. It felt right.

Three months in, we decided to go on a road trip—just the two of us, the wind in our hair and the road stretching out like the promise of an endless future. We drove to the Bay, my hometown. I showed him around San Francisco, the streets where I grew up, and introduced him to my dad and stepmom. And wouldn't you know it? They adored him. Of course, they did! Who wouldn't? He's charming and warm, the kind of person who lights up a room just by walking in.

But life has a way of throwing curveballs, doesn't it? A month later, in my search for a new apartment, my naïve, young self fell for a scam. I lost a chunk of money, and with my notice already submitted, I was scrambling. Enter my hero—*Grey Knight*, the nickname I'd given him because, well, he saved me more than once. "Move in with me and my roommate," he said. *Of course, I said yes. Of course!* I wanted to be with him every second of every day. The apartment was tiny, so small that three people felt like a crowd. But I didn't care. I was so blissfully happy just to be near him. And, bonus, I became fast friends with his roommate, Jason—a laid-back, free-spirited guy from the Midwest who fit right into our little trio.

Living together brought us even closer, as if we weren't already inseparable. And Jason? He was like a divine little sidekick, always down for fun, but never getting in the way. A road trip later to meet my mom and stepdad? Strike out! Grey Knight wins again. They loved him, too. I mean, how could they not? The man is a walking ray of sunshine.

My birthday was creeping up, and let me tell you, I had been dropping *all* the hints. Over the last couple of months, I'd been sending him pictures of engagement rings I had my eye on, favorite styles saved like little treasure maps to my dream proposal. I teased him. I antagonized him, maybe a little too much. Every time we talked about it, I could practically see the wheels turning in his head. How incredible would it be to get proposed to on my birthday? I mean, come on, it's like the ultimate gift, right? I had convinced myself that it was going to happen. The anticipation was intoxicating, almost dangerous. So much so that I took a step into territory I had no business stepping into—I snooped.

Naughty me, I even went full Nancy Drew, rummaging through his stuff, looking for that telltale small, square box. And yes, cliché or not, I found it. Was I ruining my own surprise? I couldn't help it! Curiosity took the wheel and floored it. And as the universe would have it, I felt like I'd doomed myself to bad luck. I confessed, nervous as hell, but he surprised me. He was *relieved*! The sweetest man. He'd been so unsure about the ring design, and now he was glad to get my opinion before the big day. I looked at it… and as much as it pained me to say it, it wasn't *the* ring. I told him. I was honest. It didn't feel right. And without hesitation, he returned it. Just like that. What a guy, right?

Fast forward to my 23rd birthday. It's here! And when I woke up that morning, he was like a little schoolgirl, practically bouncing on the bed, teasing me about some grand surprise. "Get up! Get up! It's your birthday!" he chirped. Before I knew it, I was being whisked away, barely awake, straight to a spa. But not just any spa—*the spa*. I had never experienced anything like this in my life. Head-to-toe massages, salt scrubs, deep cleansing facials—I was pampered into oblivion. For four hours, I drifted into another dimension, floating somewhere between bliss and nirvana. My body was softer than a baby's bottom, and my face was glowing… or maybe just strawberry red from the facials, but I didn't care. I was in heaven.

When he picked me up, I was barely coherent. He immediately insisted, "We're going to Ben & Jerry's!" And normally, I'd be the first one out of the door. I mean, ice cream is practically my religion. But for some bizarre reason—maybe because I was still floating in a post-spa haze—I said no. I actually turned down *ice cream*. Who was I? Even he was shocked. "You never say no to ice cream!" And he wasn't wrong. Ice cream for breakfast? Hell yes! Just like my Cookie Grandma Rita always taught me. But that day? I wanted to curl up in bed and relive my spa-induced euphoria. Still, he insisted. Jason's meeting us there, and he wouldn't take no for an answer. Fine, I thought. I dragged myself along, messy hair and all, feeling like a hot mess wrapped in sweats, but still game for my favorite guilty pleasure.

We arrived at Ben & Jerry's, and naturally, I ordered two scoops of my favorite flavors, in a cone, of course—because is there any other way to eat ice cream? As I reached out for my cone, dazed and lost in my spa day hangover, I barely registered what was happening. The employee handed me the cone, but something was off. He turned it around slowly—*too slowly*—and there, written on an edible chocolate piece, were the words: "Will you marry me?"

Time stopped. I snapped back to reality, and the air felt thick, electric. I turned around, and there he was—my Grey Knight, down on one knee. I screamed. Like, actually screamed. Like a hyena who had just won the lottery. My body danced around like a penguin on caffeine, and in that moment, I was the happiest woman on the planet. He was tearing up as he expressed his love, every word as sweet as the ice cream melting in my hand, and then came the moment I'd been waiting for—he asked me to marry him. My heart felt like it would explode from my chest.

And Jason? Oh, Jason wasn't just there for ice cream. He was there to capture the whole thing on film, fulfilling yet another of my little wishes. Despite all my teasing, all my hints, I was genuinely surprised. I giggled through the whirlwind of emotions, barely able to process what was happening. I was floating again, but this time from pure joy. And the ring? Oh, the ring. Over a carat-sized oval set on a delicate band covered in diamonds. It was *perfect*—the kind of ring you don't just dream of, but a ring that feels like it was made for your finger.

That night, we celebrated in style. Dinner was at one of the most romantic Italian restaurants in LA—all glowing lights and dreamy decor. We dressed to the nines and toasted to not only my birthday but to *us,* to our engagement. This was the beginning of our future. My future. The one I'd always hoped for but never truly believed would come. Yet, here I was, on the precipice of something extraordinary.

It felt like a fairy tale, but not the kind you read about in books. No, this was real. This was *my* fairy tale, and it was only just beginning.

The congratulations poured in, and our passion blazed hotter than ever. We were on fire—chemistry off the charts, our connection palpable in every look, every touch. And let's just say, we weren't exactly quiet about it. Poor Jason. Living in that tiny apartment, with walls as thin as paper, hearing our wild, uninhibited love? Yeah, the neighbors heard it, too. One night, we even got a shout from someone outside: "Shut the fuck up!" Priceless. But it did come with consequences. I was two weeks late. My body felt strange, my mind racing.

I took the test, secretly, while we were in the middle of an argument. Positive. Two lines. My jaw hit the floor. I walked out, heart pounding, and told him. His face lit up like fireworks on the Fourth of July. Twenty-three, pregnant, and barely five months into our relationship. And yet, there it was on the ultrasound—a tiny little peanut growing inside me.

Thank goodness for small miracles! Morning sickness was a distant concept for me; instead, I marveled at my body's transformation, like a sunflower opening to the sun. Hormones were swirling through me like a tempest, leaving me frazzled and frantically questioning every change I saw in the mirror. I was on the edge of a precipice, stressing myself sick. So sick, in fact, that the notion of "eating for two" became a far-off fantasy. I was barely able to eat for myself. The little peanut—my growing baby—was becoming more real, while I felt my identity shift into something undeniably maternal.

In a spontaneous burst of creativity, Grey Knight, my fiancé, proposed an idea that caught me off guard: he wanted a tattoo about me, to symbolize our bond.

He's a passionate devotee of tattoos, with each new design adding another layer to the living canvas of his arms, gradually building from scattered pieces into full-fledged sleeves. It was this evolving masterpiece—a boldness I found irresistibly attractive—that captured my attention and shifted my perspective on allure. Every swirling line and vibrant hue tells a tender memoir of his life, a humorous, vulnerable, and utterly captivating declaration of a man who wears his heart on his skin.

His choice? An ice cream cone! The thought made me chuckle but also sparked something deep within me. "What if we get matching tattoos?" I exclaimed, grinning from ear to ear. He wanted his in grey scale to fit his aesthetic; I, on the other hand, envisioned a riot of color dancing across my skin. Who would have thought I'd ever consider getting a tattoo? A permanent commitment seemed daunting, yet here I was, leaping into the abyss of ink with my beloved. We were about to mark our love on our bodies—what a thrilling prospect!

Freshly engaged and fueled by the excitement of impending parenthood, he was eager to introduce me to his parents. So, with our doctor's blessing, we packed our bags and flew to the Midwest. Touching down in Chicago felt like a warm embrace, and the drive to his hometown in Wisconsin unveiled landscapes I had never truly appreciated before. For someone who hadn't traveled much, the Midwest was a revelation, a breath of fresh air. I found myself entranced by the vibrant hues of fall foliage and the lush greens that stretched as far as the eye could see. The charming brick homes were like something out of a storybook, each one a testament to a life filled with warmth and love. I soaked in every detail, every moment, relishing my surroundings. Meeting his family was an experience I would treasure forever; they welcomed me into their fold with open arms, showering me with kindness. My heart swelled with joy at the thought of becoming their daughter-in-law.

Returning to Los Angeles brought with it another ultrasound appointment. At two months pregnant, my heart was filled with hope, yet it quickly turned to stone when the doctor's news pierced my soul.

The doctor's words hit me like a landslide. "The peanut… it's just a peanut." It had stopped growing, ceased becoming. In that sterile, too-bright room, time stood still, and suddenly, it was as though the earth had shifted beneath my feet. Tears flowed, hot and relentless, like bullets that refused to miss their mark. My heart—my poor, already bruised heart—plummeted into a deep, cold place. It was as if the grief had come alive, clawing its way out of me with every sob, every tear that escaped.

I thought I had been prepared for anything. I thought I could handle whatever came my way—hadn't I always? But the weight of those few words, of losing something I hadn't even realized I wanted so desperately until it was slipping through my fingers, left me reeling. I fell into a pit of sadness so deep, so overwhelming, that it took every ounce of strength I had not to disappear into it completely. The miscarriage was inevitable, the doctor said, and so they gave me the pills—the abortion pills, to drain what was left of the peanut from my body. The words were clinical, the process necessary, but none of it made the hollow ache in my chest any easier to bear.

It's one thing to experience the devastating loss of a miscarriage, but to be handed a prescription for abortion pills—well, that twist in the narrative shattered me in a way I hadn't prepared for. The mental jolt of having to take pills, rather than letting nature take its course, etched a scar on my psyche—an unsettling intrusion that tainted my ability to process grief. In those quiet, private moments, the heaviness haunted me, making it that much harder to reconcile what I thought I knew about loss—and what I was now forced to endure.

I went into survival mode. I did what I had to do. I loaded up on anything I thought would make the process less terrible—heat pads, painkillers, even my favorite snacks. As if anything could actually comfort me in a time like that. And yet, amid all the heartbreak, a small glimmer of hope surfaced.

Grey Knight and I, despite everything, decided to take the plunge and move in together. The lease on the Venice beach apartment was about to expire, and with an engagement ring on my finger, it felt like the right move. We found a cute little one-bedroom apartment, still near the beach—because, let's be honest, the beach is the one thing that keeps me sane some days—and close to work, too. The stars seemed to align in a small, practical way, a small win in a season where wins felt impossible.

But moving day... oh, moving day was something else entirely. I was in bed, writhing in pain that defied explanation, my body in the throes of the miscarriage. No amount of ibuprofen could dull it, no heating pad could soothe the agony that pulsed through me. It was a kind of pain that cut deeper than physical, though the physical was unbearable enough on its own. And yet, in that moment of vulnerability and weakness, my Grey Knight transformed into the hero I always believed he could be. With a kind of quiet, determined strength, he moved every single box, every piece of furniture into our new apartment—all by himself. What a beast!

I could barely move, but I watched him, in awe of his perseverance, his tenderness, his drive. He never once complained. Not about the boxes, not about the weight of it all—both physical and emotional. Instead, he'd pause every so often to check on me, his hand gently brushing a tear from my cheek or adjusting my blanket, whispering words of comfort as though he were the only thing holding me together.

In that moment, I realized just how much he meant to me. How much we meant to each other. Sure, life wasn't perfect—far from it. But we were in this together, fighting through the pain, the heartache, the uncertainty. And in a way, that made the future seem a little brighter, even on the darkest of days.

With our new home came a shared love for dogs, and we eagerly set out to adopt a puppy. Our hearts were captured by the enchanting Australian shepherd breed. We dove into research, marveling at their intelligence and striking beauty. Our first encounter was with a half-German, half-Australian shepherd puppy, but the universe had other plans, and we had to let her go when the asking price skyrocketed. Disappointed yet undeterred, Grey Knight scoured Craigslist, and just like that, we stumbled upon a litter of Australian shepherd puppies! My heart raced as I dialed the number on the ad. "We're coming now!" I exclaimed. "Please send me photos!"

Two hours later, we arrived at the breeder's home, excitement buzzing in the air. The moment I laid eyes on the litter, I felt like a kid in a candy store, overwhelmed by the cuteness around me. One puppy, in particular, stood out—a little fluffball with a twisted nose and a propensity for sniffing her rear. I couldn't contain my excitement as I spotted her—pure white with scattered grey and black spots and one striking blue eye. "This is our baby!" I screamed with joy.

Finally cradling my new fur baby, I felt an overwhelming rush of love. But as I turned to leave, the puppy's mother approached, her gaze piercing right through me. I could almost hear her heart breaking. "Please don't look at me like that," I whispered, feeling guilty. "I promise to love her fiercely and give her the best life ever!"

And just like that, we became a family. My post-pregnancy blues melted away in the presence of our adorable Australian shepherd, whom we named Mocha. All eyes turned to her, basking in her charm as she quickly became the star of our lives. I know I'm biased, but she truly is a rarity—a blue merle with a coat of mostly white, black, and grey spotting, adorned with splashes of brown around her face and feet. Mocha was not just beautiful; she was enchanting.

Her personality began to blossom, revealing one ear that stood tall while the other flopped adorably, a quirk we cherished. As new puppy parents, we were committed to giving her the best life possible, which meant hiring a trainer to help us along the way. But our journey wasn't without its challenges. Mocha arrived home with ticks and fleas—oh, the horror! With determination, we set to work, battling these pesky invaders day in and day out. It felt like a military operation—armed with combs and boiling pots of water, we combated the little fiends that dared to invade our lives. After what felt like an eternity, we triumphed for a solid month, emerging victorious against the onslaught of pests.

In the early glow of our newfound connection, every shared moment felt like the opening lines of an epic, unscripted romance. We found ourselves effortlessly working together—even in the delightfully absurd ritual of flea-picking—which revealed our uncanny ability to turn the mundane into something magical. With each tiny victory, our hearts whispered that we were meant to be, a playful promise of what our future might hold. The way we laughed together in the face of life's little challenges was a testament to our unique, blossoming synergy. And as we navigated those early days hand in hand, I couldn't help but marvel at how perfectly we worked together, each quirky moment deepening the spark between us.

Just when we thought we were in the clear, we discovered ticks, and panic set in. My heart raced every time I spotted one latched onto Mocha's delicate skin. I remember the night Grey Knight woke up in a frenzy, a tick crawling on him. I couldn't help but chuckle despite our predicament—it was a comical twist in our chaotic lives. Armed with tweezers and determination, we eradicated the ticks, cleaning our home from top to bottom in our mission to keep Mocha safe and healthy. Eventually, our efforts paid off; she thrived, her coat becoming a silky masterpiece after we introduced coconut oil into her diet. She was a shining star, a puppy destined to fill our lives with joy.

We were blissfully living together in our first apartment, that magical time when everything felt new and thrilling, as if the universe conspired just for the two of us. We had rushed into things, sure, but we couldn't resist the pull toward each other. Like gravity, it was strong and undeniable. Jumping in headfirst into this whirlwind relationship, so naturally, we were still figuring each other out, learning the intricacies of our habits, quirks, and the unspoken rhythms that came with cohabiting. But every day felt like another page in a novel we were writing together, each adventure adding another chapter, another cherished memory. And Mocha, our fur baby, was the center of it all. She was our pride and joy, our little mischief-maker with those big, soulful eyes that melted both of us on sight.

We merged who we were—our routines, our belongings, our dreams. And then, there was Mocha. Sweet, wide-eyed Mocha, the glue that bound us in the beginning. She wasn't just a pet; she was our pride and joy, our little heartbeat that connected us. We adored her so much that we paid sixty dollars on some sketchy website to register her as a service dog. We got a shiny certificate in the mail, complete with an official-looking ID card. Was it fake? Absolutely. Did it work? Every single time.

We took Mocha everywhere. Yes, *everywhere.* She'd come with us on dates, strolling into restaurants like she owned the place. We even smuggled her into movie theaters. I still remember sneaking in her favorite bone to keep her busy, and when she finally fell asleep, we'd hear her little paws twitching as she dreamed, and we'd laugh quietly in the dark, feeling like rebels. Grocery stores? Okay, that was where we drew the line. Or rather, they drew it for us when we got kicked out. Fair enough—no more grocery store escapades for Mocha.

Our Friday nights weren't filled with the typical booze and bar hopping—nah, we were healthnuts through and through. Our indulgence was finding the next trendy fine-dining spot to blow our hard-earned cash. It was our thing—our way of celebrating life. Cooking at home was its own kind of ritual, a dance in the kitchen where we'd whip up meals for each other without a second thought. No questions asked, just love on a plate, nourishing each other, quite literally.

When we weren't in the kitchen, we were binge-watching shows, tucked away in our little bubble of comfort. Then there were the nights we'd smoke weed to unwind. Just a casual, chill habit before bed. Funny how, back then, the idea of him being an "addict" never crossed my mind. It was just another thing we did together, like sharing a blanket or a quiet moment.

And let's talk about the gym. Oh, the gym was our sanctuary. His influence, his relentless commitment to strength-training, transformed not just my body but also my mindset and knowledge. We were there every single day, and had to force ourselves and remind ourselves that we have to have rest days as well. It was an intoxicating addiction for us. Like gym rats we were swinging from machine to machine, our love for fitness another thing that bound us. We'd push each other, sweat pouring down, sometimes collapsing on the floor, grinning ear to ear, knowing we were in this together. Like athletes training for a marathon, we took care of each other and massaged each other's sore muscles afterwards. Two hours a day, six days a week—our dedication to fitness mirrored our dedication to each other.

But there was always more. We were playful, too. Pranks were our love language. He had this wicked trick where he'd sneak into the bathroom while

I was showering and dump a cup of ice-cold water on me. My shrieks echoed through the apartment, and he'd stand there, smug as ever. I got him back, though, every time, when he least expected it. We were like children in love— full of light and laughter, never taking life too seriously.

And, of course, Mocha was always there, our little mascot, joining us on walks and trips to the dog park where she'd run wild with the other dogs. We trained her together, a team in every sense of the word. She was the reflection of our life—happy, free, a little chaotic, but full of love.

When I had to take a break from college to handle my DUI situation, I used that time to pursue acting. It wasn't my proudest moment, but it gave me space to focus on other dreams. Film had always been a love of mine, ever since high school when I got a taste of what it was like working both in front of and behind the camera. It felt like a natural transition—modeling had already given me confidence in front of a lens. Deep down, I knew I belonged *in front* of it. Modeling had already given me a taste of the spotlight, so acting felt like the natural next step. And, naturally, I roped Grey Knight into it, too.

It wasn't hard to convince him—he had that larger-than-life charisma. So, we both jumped into the film industry together, taking acting classes, getting headshots, the whole hustle. It was exhilarating, and having each other made it feel like we were unstoppable. We'd help each other with auditions, jet from audition to audition while the other played the curbside driver, read lines together, and cheer each other on. It was another layer to our bond.

But then, there was football. Oh, football. If there was one thing we couldn't see eye-to-eye on, it was our teams. Grey Knight, with his midwestern roots, was a die-hard Packers fan—a "fucking cheesehead," as I loved to tease him. Meanwhile, I'm a 49ers girl to the core. Born and raised in the Bay Area, I practically grew up in Candlestick Park, surrounded by red and gold. Game days were a battlefield, playful but fierce. Despite our rivalry, I couldn't help but love how passionate he was. No matter how heated the banter got, it was all in good fun. We'd always end up laughing, even if it was over who had to buy the next pint of ice cream.

Ah, ice cream. That was my vice. I was obsessed with it—pints of it lined our freezer like little treasures, but I was notoriously stingy about sharing. It was a cute war of spoonfuls, and before I knew it, I was somehow learning to share. I wanted to because it wasn't just about sharing dessert. I was giving him all of me.

And then, things changed. We spent every waking moment together, and what felt like bliss at first slowly turned into a slow suffocation. My mind never stops—it's always racing, always moving at a hundred miles an hour. I found myself consumed by an internal struggle, racing at breakneck speed in my mind. Blame my Gemini nature, but I thrive on motion. The shadow of the miscarriage loomed over me like a dark cloud, and my once steadfast independence felt like a distant memory. It wasn't just the emotional grief; it was the hormonal chaos that followed. I felt ripped open, like a part of me was missing. I'd always prided myself on being fiercely independent, but when my car was taken away, I had no choice but to rely on Grey Knight. He told me it was okay to lean on him, that I could. We were engaged, after all— partners for life, right? He was my home, my comfort, yet the weight of financial stress loomed large, a constant reminder of my DUI debt and the struggles that lay ahead. I was lonely, longing for genuine friendships, yet the few I had felt more like chains than bonds.

Communication, my lifeline, became tangled in a web of frustration. I craved profound conversations that stretched into the night, moments where time stood still and our souls connected. Grey Knight had such potential, and I wanted to guide him toward his own greatness. Yet, as I delved deeper into his layers, insecurities bubbled to the surface. Instead of open dialogue, anger was his armor, and I found myself in a war of wills. I was drawn to the fire within him, eager to learn how to dance with it rather than flee.

But finances weighed heavily on me. I wasn't working enough to cover my bills, let alone chip away at my DUI debt. I didn't have many friends—at least, not the kind you could call when things went to hell. Forget about girlfriends—I've witnessed more than enough melodramatic chaos in my past to swear off that negative energy. I've come to detest the incessant whirlwind of drama, and over time, I've learned that many women, burdened by insecurities, often let jealousy render them intimidated by my very presence—

a humbling truth that's as bittersweet as it is real. As a result, forging genuine female friendships has become a delicate dance of vulnerability and self-preservation, a challenge that leaves me both wryly amused and poignantly aware of life's ironic twists. I'd always gotten along better with guys—less drama, more fun. But it all added up, the pressure mounting until I couldn't breathe.

I became ensnared in a labyrinth of overthinking, trapped in the echo chamber of my own head. At first, I didn't even notice the shift—engagement news had swept me away, inflating my mind with impossibly high expectations of him. I began to see him not only as my newly engaged fiancé but as my person, my best friend—the one soul I truly believed could complete me. I craved long, vulnerable conversations where I could spill out every fear and anxiety, dissecting the chaos until it all made sense, even as I wondered, was it too much to ask? And when our tender exchanges morphed into a slow-burning tension that left him retreating behind layers of silence, I found myself clinging desperately to the only connection that still made me feel close—our bittersweet, physical refuge in the intimacy of sex.

Our physical connection had always been electric, but now, it became my lifeline. It was like I needed that intimacy to feel like we were still connected, still in this together. But something shifted for him. He didn't like cuddling and said it made him sweat, made him anxious. I needed that touch, that closeness, but the more I asked for it, the more he pulled away. One day, after trying to jump his bones, he looked at me and said, "Sex with you is like a job." The words sliced through me. Sex was our glue—our bond—and now it felt like it was falling apart, too.

I wanted to get closer, to peel back the layers of his soul and understand what was going on, but every time I tried, I hit a wall. His insecurities came out like a fire I couldn't put out, and instead of cooling things down, I found myself playing with the flames, trying to control them. I thought I could be his gold miner, dig deep enough to find that heart of gold I knew was in there. But instead of finding treasure, I ended up dodging the coals he threw at me, each one burning deeper than the last.

We were stuck, both of us, in this cycle of hurt and frustration. He thought tough love was the answer, that pushing me would somehow make me stronger. But all it did was break me down. Each argument, each moment of rejection, cut deeper, and before long, I felt like a shell of myself. We were supposed to be partners, soulmates, but instead, we were unraveling. And I was desperate—desperate to rekindle the fire we once had.

However, my attempts to dig deeper often led to misunderstandings, and I became a target of his frustration. It was a tumultuous cycle that left me feeling increasingly vulnerable. I clung to the intimacy we shared, often relying on physical closeness to bridge the emotional distance.

It was time to hit the reset button. To pack up the chaos, the miscommunications, and the routines we'd become trapped in, and trade them for palm trees, sunshine, and a little bit of tequila. We needed an escape, not just from the LA grind but from ourselves—the version of us that had grown tired, frayed around the edges. So, we booked a trip to Playa del Carmen, Mexico, and set our sights on an all-inclusive resort that promised no distractions, no Mocha (sorry, fur baby), and no demanding schedules. Just us.

The plane ride felt like the first deep breath we'd taken in months. As the city disappeared beneath the clouds, so did the stress, the laundry lists of things left undone. We weren't just flying to Mexico; we were flying back to each other. I had this image of us—laughing like we used to, talking without the undercurrent of stress tugging at every word. Was it too much to hope for? I wasn't sure, but I was damn well willing to try.

Our days were an adventure buffet, filled with zip-lining through forests that seemed to swallow us whole, paddling canoes in the serene ocean, and kicking up mud on four-wheelers that made us feel wild and reckless again. At one point, just before a zip-line plunge into the cenotes, we found ourselves chanting some old lovers' phrase—a silly, traditional incantation meant to bind our souls and bless the jump. I don't know if it worked, but in that moment, suspended above the crystalline water, I felt closer to him than I had in a long time. Maybe magic exists in the moments we choose to believe in it. Or maybe it was the tequila. Either way, we were back.

Speaking of tequila, we drank a lot of it. And by a lot, I mean the kind that comes with mid-day naps, the kind that has you waking up at sunset, groggy but happy, ready to rally and see where the night might take you. No plans, no pressures—just us, following the breeze to wherever felt right. The weight of everything back home melted away. There was no room for worry in that little paradise we'd carved out. Just joy. Pure, unfiltered joy. We were like kids again, giddy and in awe of everything around us—each other, the place, the freedom we hadn't realized we so desperately needed. It was like someone had refilled our spirits, like we were standing at the candy counter of life, and everything we wanted was suddenly within reach.

Every day felt like a new memory in the making. There were no big, earth-shattering moments—just a series of small, perfect ones that reminded me why we were doing this in the first place. The adventures we had—whether plunging through a jungle or just lying in the sun—weren't the kind you can measure by how epic they were. They were measured by how much we smiled, by how much we held onto each other.

And then, as quickly as it had begun, it ended. We landed back in Los Angeles, greeted by the familiar grey haze of reality, and it hit us. All the stuff we'd left behind—the issues, the struggles, the "pile of shit," as we so lovingly referred to it—was waiting for us, as if we hadn't been gone at all.

But something had shifted. We had shifted. The magic didn't evaporate as soon as our feet touched the tarmac; it lingered, a reminder that no matter how deep we might sink into the everyday grind, we could still find our way back to each other.

Chapter 3

Negative Nancy and the Gaslight Chronicles

Returning to Los Angeles felt like stepping into a tempest that swept me off my feet and slammed me against a wall. My thoughts swirled like leaves caught in a cyclone, filled with endless worries that piled up like laundry waiting to be folded—so many pieces crumpled and wrinkled, unable to fit neatly into my life. I was drowning in a torrent of stress, its weight too immense to bear alone. My mind whirled uncontrollably, fixated on every worry while every part of my life crumbled—except for my love life, the sole island of calm. It was a wildly absurd time, where chaos reigned and even the simplest moment felt like a battle.

I sought connection, reaching out to him, yearning for dialogue, but instead found myself in a battle of words where he called me "Negative Nancy," dismissing my concerns as nothing but a drizzle of pessimism. It was as if my worries dripped from my mouth like poison, infecting the air between us. I couldn't help but fixate on the chaos around me, the tidal wave of stressors crashing over my head like relentless ocean waves, pulling me under.

All I wanted was to confide in him, to share my burdens so they wouldn't feel so crushing. Maybe I did dwell on the negative a bit too much; that's fair. But feeling alone in my struggle was a fate I couldn't accept. It was as if I was trying to lift a boulder, and each time I reached for help, it felt like he added another layer of weight. The pressure from his reactions made me feel like I was losing my grip on reality, as if I were spiraling down a rabbit hole of self-doubt and anxiety. My thoughts raced, frantic like a hamster on a wheel, desperately seeking a shred of calm in the storm of emotions.

In an attempt to untangle the mess in my mind, I sought therapy. A Groupon deal led me to a nearby therapist, and each session felt like releasing a dam of pent-up emotions. I would spill my heart out, tears streaming down my face like a river, finally feeling like I wasn't alone in my turmoil. In those sacred hours, I could speak freely, the weight of my worries lifting just a fraction as I poured out my thoughts to someone who wouldn't judge me. But three sessions weren't nearly enough; I was still adrift in a sea of loneliness, even with my fiancé by my side. So, I turned to my mom, calling her more frequently, letting her in on the chaos swirling around me. Surprisingly, as the darkness closed in, we began to rebuild our relationship, brick by brick, through the rubble of my struggles.

I can't pinpoint the exact moment our love transformed into something unrecognizable. It's as if my memories of those times have been shrouded in fog. What I do recall is the overwhelming weight of our different agendas colliding. I was a whirlwind of emotion, a sponge soaking up empathy, while he seemed to operate on a different frequency, responding to my turmoil with tough love that felt more like a fist than a hand. My cries for affection and understanding were met with indifference; I was met with coldness when I sought warmth. Whenever I dared to challenge his perspective, he wore his stubbornness like armor, refusing to yield or even acknowledge my feelings. I was cast as the villain in my own story, the scapegoat for his frustrations. Day by day, my confidence withered, and I morphed into a shadow of my former self, a fragile figure craving his affection while also feeling the sting of his unyielding criticism.

Stubbornly, I refused to take full accountability, instead seeing his actions as bullying, and with each encounter, I became smaller and weaker, retreating into a shell that once held vibrant laughter. Our exchanges became a twisted dance of passive aggression, each jab thrown felt more like a dagger, cutting deeper with every word. We were locked in a brutal cycle, the air thick with tension and unspoken grievances. As the tender-hearted person I was, I struggled to break through the walls. I found myself trapped in a victim narrative, falling deeper into the abyss of self-pity.

Then the layers began to peel back, revealing a core I didn't recognize. He transformed into an enraged stranger, one who wielded emotional and verbal abuse like weapons, inflicting wounds that ran deep. The words he hurled at me were dehumanizing, crafted to shatter my spirit. Yet, I'd rather not relive the exact phrases that dripped with venom; who would want to remember that? I fought with every ounce of my being, desperate to salvage what remained of our relationship. But he had conditioned me, groomed me to accept his manipulation, filling my heart with confusion and self-doubt. He flirted with others, orchestrating scenarios designed to elicit the reaction he craved, reveling in my pain. When I reacted, he twisted it around, labeling me as jealous, as the one causing all the drama. "Haley's always the Negative Nancy," he would say, a refrain that echoed in my mind like a haunting melody. I felt my sanity unraveling, the happy, confident soul I once was slipping away, leaving behind a hollow shell struggling to survive in a relationship that felt like a prison.

In the haze of my past, I was blind to my own truths, yet Grey Knight saw me—really saw me—as if he knew me better than I knew myself. There's a rare blessing in being with someone who can strip away your façades and gaze into the very core of your being. Back then, I wasn't cloaked in confidence, but he embraced every facet of me with startling clarity. His intimate understanding, however, became a double-edged sword; he wielded my flaws like weapons, each revelation chipping away at my already fragile self-esteem as I navigated an inner storm. In the end, all these forces converged into a perfect storm of emotional chaos, leaving me both humbled and, in a bittersweet twist of humor, oddly grateful for the raw truth of it all.

Every day with him was like existing in a horror film, a nightmare from which I couldn't wake. His rage was a wildfire, consuming everything in its path. I became mute, my feelings trapped under layers of fear, waving a white flag in a desperate plea for help. Each threat, each explosive outburst chipped away at my spirit.

In one explosive moment, he hurled my phone across the room, leaving me scrambling to salvage even a fragment of self-care amid the wreckage. His fury didn't stop there; in a fit of rage, he flung my clothes out the front door in a humiliating spectacle that not only exposed my vulnerability but also escalated quickly. In the madness, I fought back, resisting his anger, my thumb crushed between the door in a brutal slam of irony. The pain was a constant reminder, a thumb so battered that it eventually fell off–a painful but honest symbol of my struggle. Each visceral act became a stark testament to the chaos he unleashed—a wild ballet of fury and absurdity that left me both mortified and, in a twisted way, oddly amused.

I recoiled from him, the once gentle touch now felt like shards of glass cutting into my skin. I spent sleepless nights curled up on the couch, fearing the very person I had loved deeply. And the sight of my beloved Mocha hiding from his anger was unbearable. The way she cowered, those sad puppy eyes begging for safety, mirrored my own devastation. She'd curl up in my lap, offering comfort as I wept for the love we both deserved but rarely received.

As if the emotional turmoil wasn't enough, he pushed me to the edge, declaring with casual malice, "Get the fuck out!" each time he felt cornered. I was shaking now, realization dawning heavy upon me: this was real, and I was trapped in a burning building with no escape. The flames of our relationship had reached an inferno, consuming everything I held dear, leaving only ash and despair in their wake. It was my wake-up call, the moment I recognized that those torturous months of emotional warfare had eroded the very core of who I was.

In my desperation, I turned to my mother, needing her support and understanding. But even then, I feared burdening her with the truth of my life, knowing it might spark disappointment. My social circle had dwindled— Grey Knight felt threatened by my male friends and cut them out, leaving me isolated. I was a lost puppy seeking a path home, and the only light came from my mom, who listened patiently, absorbing my anguish without judgment. She created a safe space for me, letting me cry and vent, offering the unconditional love I desperately craved. Despite my predicament, she persisted in wrapping me in compassion, reminding me of the beauty that still existed in the world. I even confided in my dad about the toxicity of my home life, knowing that sharing such intimate details might seal my fiancé's fate in my father's eyes. But I was beyond caring; I had lost myself entirely, and I needed to be seen, even if that meant dragging my truth into the light. The journey toward rediscovery had begun, with my family as my lifeline.

On a bright note, stepping into the role of a first-time dog mom was like being swept up in a whirlwind of joy and chaos! Bringing home my angelic little furball, Mocha, at just seven weeks old, was like watching a sunrise after a long, dark night—my heart exploded with a love I never knew existed. Sure, I had dogs around me throughout my childhood, but this was different; I finally had one of my own. Nothing, and I mean nothing, could prepare me for the rush of motherhood that came with puppy parenting. I felt like a wide-eyed explorer setting foot on uncharted territory.

Embracing my role as Mocha's mom was the most incredible blessing I could have ever received. My fiance, Grey Knight, wasn't exactly the snuggly type—no warm, fuzzy cuddles from him. So, I took it upon myself to train Mocha to be my little spoon each night. There's simply nothing more comforting than sinking into slumber, enveloped in her silky fur and puppy smells. At first, I didn't fully grasp how profound this bond would grow as I watched her blossom into her spirited self. Mocha, like most puppies, ballooned in size seemingly overnight. The energy of a young Aussie was like a supernova, bursting with enthusiasm as she bounded around the house, eager to sniff out every nook and cranny.

Oh, those teething days were a trial—she devoured more pairs of my shoes than I care to admit, each chewed morsel a testament to her determination and my growing frustration. But let me tell you, even amidst the destruction, there was an undeniable charm to her antics. Each day, we fell deeper into the rabbit hole of love. Mocha was no ordinary pup; she possessed a dazzling intellect that often left me in awe. From her cleverness in rolling down the car window to her adventurous spirit—like the time she leapt from the car, chased by the tantalizing sight of the dog park just a heartbeat away.

By the time we screeched to a halt and I leaped out to rescue her, our tiny darling had taken a fall, leaving a bloody cut beneath her chin—our poor baby! At just a few months old, that chaotic moment sparked an overwhelming surge of maternal love—only you, crazy Mocha girl, always keeping me on my toes.

The second time she jumped out was nothing short of a heart-stopping moment. And I mean, *literally*. I still remember that day, the wind whipping through my hair as I drove down a busy six-lane road, only to glance in the rearview mirror and see nothing but her harness dangling from the window. Panic surged through me as I pulled over, praying she hadn't darted into the chaos. Thankfully, she miraculously crossed five lanes unscathed, and as I scooped her up in my arms, I felt a wave of relief wash over me. Grey Knight and I quickly learned to be hyper-aware of her newfound leaps and bounds, but there was a unique joy in this wild journey of dog parenting.

As evenings settled in, Grey Knight and I would unwind with some marijuana—a cozy escape from the day's pressures. I fondly remember the euphoric sensation of sinking into the couch, feeling like a marshmallow floating on a cloud. Of course, there were times when I miscalculated my dose, hitting that blissful edge where my body felt both heavy and light, like I was a rag doll in a feel-good frenzy. I recall one memorable day when we splurged on a veritable treasure trove of edibles—Rice Krispy treats, cookies, gummies, brownies—all totaling a staggering 500mg of THC. A feast fit for stoners! We never intended to devour it all at once; instead, we rationed the deliciousness to make it last.

I vividly remember the first time I dared to consume 25 mg of THC. It felt like an overdose, plunging me into a state of blissful paralysis. Fast forward to our glorious stash, neatly placed at the center of our round dining room table—out of reach, we thought, from our furry little Houdini. But low and behold, two hours later, after a gym session filled with endorphins, we opened the door to absolute chaos. The brown bag lay shredded on the floor, its contents scattered like confetti. Our eyes darted to Mocha, who was perched on the couch, swaying back and forth like a drunken weeble wobble, her excitement palpable. My heart raced; I burst into tears, envisioning the worst.

Grey Knight was equally horrified, caught between laughter and sheer panic. How could this happen? How did she reach that high? It was a terrifying yet hilarious realization that we'd underestimated her reach. I rushed to check on her, but she sat still, wide-eyed, and seemingly clueless, her innocence on full display. My heart ached for her as I showered her with gentle love and attention. Meanwhile, Grey Knight was frantically Googling what to do when your dog gets high—because, let's be real, there's a world of difference between being "high" and "stoned." Mocha had devoured every morsel of those edibles, and there was no denying it: She was stoned out of her mind!

The internet revealed that we had to treat her like a human—calm her down, reassure her, and keep her from spiraling into paranoia. So, we nestled her in bed with me, cocooning her in love as I stroked her fur, whispering sweet nothings to keep her grounded. We couldn't resist the urge to see how she'd fare on the floor. But when we set her down, she could barely lift a paw, stumbling in her attempt to navigate this altered state. We couldn't help but chuckle, but deep down, we worried for her well-being.

As we cuddled together, something shifted. Grey Knight loomed over her, and Mocha suddenly went into a frenzy, her anxiety palpable. He feared she was having a seizure, but I suspected he was just spooking her further. Time to jet to the Vet.

Our visit to the vet was nothing short of harrowing. I paced the waiting room, tears streaming down my cheeks as Grey Knight continued his frantic research. The looming presence of potential vet bills hung over us, an ominous specter. Thankfully, a receptionist reassured us that she'd seen much worse—dogs who had indulged in far more dangerous substances. It offered a sliver of comfort amid the storm.

When the doctor finally returned, relief flooded through me. Most of the edibles had come back up, and Mocha was a healthy pup once again. He suggested keeping her overnight for observation due to the milk chocolate content, but we scoffed at the idea. No way was I letting them drain our wallets further; I would watch over her myself. Back to bed, we went, a patchwork of comfort as I kept a watchful eye. Time felt endless as I stroked her fur, ensuring she remained calm. After what felt like an eternity, Mocha surprised me by leaping off the bed, full of life after ten hours, as if the whole ordeal had been nothing more than a fleeting dream.

What a rollercoaster ride it had been! Looking back, I can't help but laugh at the absurdity of it all, though it was terrifying in the moment. A few years later, marijuana was legalized, and dog-friendly edibles became a thing. How far we've come!

But back to the reality of my life.

The beat-downs from Grey Knight—emotional, psychological, and the sheer weight of his anger—took a toll on me, to say the least. It's funny, isn't it? How a love so high, a love that once felt untouchable, can plummet to depths you didn't even know existed. Our home life was spiraling into a mess—no, a hurricane—and I was caught right in the eye of it, powerless and paralyzed. This was my first time living with a boyfriend, and there's a first for everything, right? First apartment, first love, first heartbreak so raw it felt like shards of glass beneath my skin.

We'd gone from the dizzying highs of passionate, reckless love to the kind of lows that steal the air from your lungs. I just needed a break—a little space to *breathe*, but the walls were closing in, and the tension at home became suffocating. Every step I took, every word I said, felt like stepping on a landmine, unsure if it would trigger another explosion of his temper. So, when we didn't work together, I'd start pushing back the clock on my "arrival" time. Not by hours, just enough. Just enough to pretend I was still stuck at the restaurant, when really, I was across the street at Misfits in Santa Monica, sipping on a cocktail and stealing a moment to myself. A stolen moment to clear my head, to reset.

Misfits became my little sanctuary, my escape. I'd order a glass of wine or, if I was feeling adventurous, a cocktail. Then, one night, the bartender introduced me to something new—a smooth egg white martini that made my eyes pop. One sip and I was hooked. It was a small delight, but it was something. Something to look forward to, a reason to return, to delay the inevitable.

There was one night in particular. I remember it vividly, because it felt like a turning point, though I didn't know it at the time. I was walking at the bar, ready to nurse a cocktail, trying to digest the swirling storm of emotions. The heartbreak. The suffocating feeling that had become my constant companion. And then, out of nowhere, this guy—Troy—taps me on the shoulder. "Excuse me, you took my seat," he says. I was ready to move, to apologize, but he smiled and waved it off and told me to stay.

We started talking, and for the first time in what felt like forever, I didn't feel weighed down by the chaos of my life. The conversation was light, effortless, like stepping out into fresh air after being stuck in a room with no windows. Troy was kind, funny even, and before I knew it, we exchanged numbers. It felt innocent enough—a new friendship, a much-needed distraction from the nightmare I was living in.

But I knew Grey Knight would never understand. He had this belief— no, an obsession—that men and women couldn't *just* be friends. He sincerely believed that every one of my guy friends was harboring secret, ulterior motives, as if they were covert Casanovas plotting beyond the bounds of mere camaraderie. I, however, remained utterly incredulous, steadfast in my conviction that my male friendships were built on unyielding boundaries that ensured no lines were ever blurred. In that poignant clash of perspectives, his raw suspicions collided with my unwavering trust, revealing a humorously tender vulnerability in the way we navigated love and loyalty.

It was a constant battle between us, a wall we could never climb over. So, I did what I always did when I was scared. I hid. I didn't tell him about Troy. How could I? I knew in my heart it was purely friendship, but Grey Knight's jealousy was a force I wasn't willing to reckon with. Not then, not when I was already fragile, already feeling like I was walking on eggshells.

Still, nothing went unnoticed with Grey Knight. He had this sixth sense when it came to me, always one step ahead. And, of course, when he found out about Troy, it was as if the universe had handed him a grenade, and he pulled the pin without a second thought. Another eruption. Another storm. Another night when the walls felt like they were closing in, and I was left standing in the wreckage, trying to make sense of it all.

What was I supposed to do? I wanted to tell him it was nothing, that I just needed a little space, a sliver of normalcy outside the madness of our relationship. But his insecurities wouldn't allow that. And so, I stayed silent, taking the blows, feeling the cracks deepen between us. The rift widened, but all I wanted was for things to go back to the way they were, back to when our love was effortless and free.

But once that trust is gone, once the seeds of jealousy and fear take root, everything changes. And I was standing there, caught between wanting to hold on to what we had and knowing deep down that we were slipping away from each other.

How on earth do I escape the fire that seems to consume me? My financial situation was dire, small enough to make survival feel like an impossible dream. I worked tirelessly to pay off my DUI debt, with no car and only one job. Los Angeles, the city of dreams, was one of the most expensive places to call home! I found myself growing increasingly codependent on Grey Knight, desperate for a way out. There had to be a solution, I told myself. I couldn't let fear keep me trapped; I deserved so much more than this cycle of abuse. It was time to stop being a victim and kick myself into fifth gear.

I started hunting for a new living situation—anything, really. A roommate, a spare room, a cozy corner anywhere but here! The only thing that mattered was shifting my mental gears and taking decisive action to reclaim my independence.

As threats of eviction started flying, the conversation about Mocha's custody came up. Grey Knight could sense the distance growing between us. Once the light switched on in my head, I stopped fighting him. He insisted we share her in a fifty-fifty split, alternating our time like divorced parents. Seriously? She's not a child! She's a dog! I needed to flee—far away from him and his grasp. The thought of sharing Mocha felt suffocating; I wanted to escape, not remain tethered to him.

I shut down the conversation every time it came up. In my eyes, Mocha was a mama's girl—there was no contest. Every friend I confided in echoed that sentiment. She favored me, plain and simple. I lavished her with love and care in a way he never did. Mocha always sought solace in my presence whenever his anger surged; the idea of losing her made my heart drop. I couldn't let that happen, not after all I'd endured. In a moment of impulsiveness, I decided to secretly get her microchipped—she would forever be my dog, my companion.

Yeah, it was impulsive and, admittedly, not fair to him—but in that moment, under the weight of everything I was facing, all I wanted was to protect her as my own. In my mind, he was the villain, and villains don't get happy endings. So, I did what any flight-risk with a bruised heart would do—I ran, fast and far, with Mocha by my side, claiming her as mine before the dust had even settled.

The search for a new home was relentless. I felt trapped, thwarted by exorbitant prices, restrictions on dogs, and potential roommates who felt off. Then, on a random day, I confided in a generous, laid-back friend who offered me a lifeline. "You and Mocha are welcome to live in my spare bedroom until you get back on your feet," he said. Relief washed over me like a wave of warmth; this was my ticket out!

I loaded up on boxes—big ones, small ones—because, apparently, over the years, I had turned into a borderline hoarder of things I couldn't part with. And, naturally, I owned the bulk of the big-ticket items, too. The couch, the TV, the furniture that filled our apartment—a solid chunk was mine. It felt oddly empowering, realizing I was the one taking everything that made our home a home. I was like a secret agent, or maybe more like a squirrel, stockpiling all the bits and pieces of my life into boxes while he remained unaware. I kept my plans to myself, letting his mind wander, wondering why things were starting to look... sparse.

I spent an entire day packing, cramming a huge chunk of my life into cardboard containers. Every box felt like another piece of me reclaiming my freedom, but I didn't pack everything. No, that would've been too obvious. I left certain things out intentionally, like little breadcrumbs, allowing his curiosity to flicker without giving him anything concrete to latch onto. Of course, he noticed. He wasn't entirely oblivious. He asked questions, trying to poke and prod, hoping for a fight, but I wasn't giving him anything. No drama. No fuel for the fire. If I was going to do this, I had to do it right. I had to leave quietly, swiftly—like a whisper in the night.

The next morning, it was game time. I needed backup, a couple of strong, capable hands to help me escape from that apartment. I had already recruited my new roommate and my new friend Troy—both in on the plan, both fully aware of the nightmare I'd been living in. They had no hesitation. They were ready to help me execute the great escape. I was grateful, almost overwhelmed with relief. My plan was in motion. I just needed the final piece: his absence.

I knew his schedule like the back of my hand. Grey Knight, as I affectionately called him, had a lunch shift that day. I knew exactly when he'd be walking out that door, off to work, clueless about what was about to go down. The moment the door closed behind him, I texted my guys. "Green light." It's go time. Thirty minutes later, they arrived, and the three of us switched into beast mode.

We moved fast, fueled by adrenaline and the knowledge that this was my one shot at freedom. Troy and my new roommate handled the heavy lifting—the couch, the TV, the boxes, and all the kitchen necessities that was technically mine. Meanwhile, I was a whirlwind, shoving everything into boxes like a woman possessed. It didn't matter if things were packed neatly or if clothes were spilling out—just as long as it all made it into the truck. There was no time for perfection. Only survival.

The apartment was alive with movement, sweat dripping down our faces as we hustled to get everything out in record time. But despite the chaos, we were having fun. Somehow, amidst the urgency, we found ourselves laughing, cracking jokes as we worked. There was this electric energy, this thrill of knowing I was getting out, that my life was about to change for the better. I could never forget that day—the animation in our movements, the unspoken camaraderie as we packed up the last traces of my old life and loaded it into the back of the truck.

An hour and a half. That's all it took to dismantle the life we had built together. As I walked through the stripped-down apartment, the space that had once been filled with love, laughter, and far too many fights, I felt a pang of something I couldn't quite name. Sadness? Maybe. Regret? Definitely not. A part of me was devastated, walking through the rooms that suddenly felt foreign and hollow, but another part of me—let's call it the vengeful side—couldn't help but smile at the thought of him coming home to this. To nothing. No fiancée. No dog. No home that felt like home anymore. Just an empty shell of what used to be. It wasn't nice of me, I know, but I secretly hoped he'd feel it, too. The loss. The absence of everything we'd shared.

Almost a year and a half together, and all of it unraveled in the blink of an eye. There were still a few months left on our lease, but I didn't care. Let that be his problem. Let that be his consequence for the bullshit he put me through. I grinned ear-to-ear as we drove away, the wind in my hair and my life in the back of that pickup truck. Off to a new home. A better one. One that didn't reek of toxicity.

We pulled up to Venice, my new paradise. I felt like I'd floated right into heaven: a peaceful neighborhood, great walking spots, and the beach practically on my doorstep. I was about to live my best life. And the relief—oh, the sweet, sweet relief—washed over me in waves. I was free.

The first morning in Venice, I woke up early, Mocha and my new roommate by my side. We took a long walk to the beach, watching the sunrise paint the sky in soft pinks and oranges. The air smelled fresh, like possibilities and new beginnings. Mocha was in her element, sprinting across the sand, chasing her frisbee with wild abandon. And I stood there, watching her, feeling the warmth of the sun on my face, and thought, *I finally did it*. I had closed that toxic chapter of my life, even though my heart still felt a little bruised from it all. But in that moment, as peace settled over me, I knew I was where I was supposed to be.

My dear friend welcomed us with open arms, making us feel at home immediately. Mocha never left my side as we explored the town together, walking from the gym to the grocery store to the beach, our little routine forming like it had always been there. And with time, I started saving money again, preparing for whatever came next. I had my calm after the storm, and in Venice, I had found my new favorite place to live. It wasn't just a location. It was a new life, a fresh start, and for the first time in a long time, I felt whole.

Chapter 4

Dancing with Shadows

My friend welcomed us into his home with an effortless grace that made my heart swell. It was like stepping into a cozy sanctuary—there was a spare bedroom waiting just for me, complete with a closet that could hold all my whims and a pristine shower and bathtub that felt like a luxurious retreat. The entire space had been lovingly renovated, looking as spotless as a freshly polished diamond. A delightful little balcony overlooked the neighborhood, inviting me to sip coffee and soak in the morning sun, while a charming backyard with a barbecue awaited lazy afternoons and gatherings. Gratitude washed over me in waves as I settled into this newfound comfort, where every corner exuded a friendly warmth that made me feel at home.

And then there was Mocha, my ever-shedding furball, who had her own royal treatment with a weekly maid service that eased my worries about pet hair flying everywhere. Every necessity was just a stone's throw away—the grocery store, the gym, the beach, and an array of shops in downtown Venice where I could leisurely stroll. My only concern became those brief Uber rides to work, but even that felt like a small price to pay for this idyllic setup. It was as if I had stumbled into a serene haven, a sanctuary nestled between the chaos of life and the gentle rhythm of a peaceful neighborhood. Mocha thrived in this environment; she walked alongside me on our daily adventures, her tail wagging as if she understood just how spoiled we both were. Our escapades lasted for hours, to the point where I worried about her developing separation anxiety. The absence of Grey Knight lingered in the air, casting a shadow that Mocha had to navigate. It was a new dance for both of us—her adjusting to life without the presence of her former companion, and me learning to be her sole caregiver. I had never heard her cry or howl before, but now, every time I left for work, my heart broke a little more with each sound that escaped her lips.

Routine, as my friend continually reminded me, would train her out of it, and slowly but surely, we found our rhythm. Together, we forged a bond in this new chapter. My friend and I shared delightful moments that glimmered—grabbing bites to eat, taking Mocha out for sunrise strolls along the beach, and hanging out for a movie night. Each day felt like a gift, and I reveled in the freedom to be myself. My heart, mind, and body were finally beginning to experience a sensation of rest that had eluded me for far too long. The weight that had anchored me down for months lifted, leaving behind a lightness that made me feel almost buoyant.

But amidst this newfound joy, shadows lingered. The only hiccups in my blissful existence were the moments when I encountered Grey Knight at the gym or work. I would carefully sidestep the hours I knew he would be there, my heart racing as I kept my head on a swivel, scanning every corner for a glimpse of him. With every rep I completed and every machine I moved to, I felt the flutter of anxiety in my chest, a tremor of apprehension whispering that he might appear. The thought terrified me.

At work, I donned my mask of cheerfulness, floating through the restaurant with smiles plastered across my face, determined not to let him see the cracks beneath my facade. Deep down, I felt a surge of defiance. Sadness was a ghost I had danced with for too long, and now that I had escaped its grasp, I was determined to embrace my liberation. I could feel the joy radiating from me, the lightness in my heart illuminating the darkest corners of my past. I had finally broken free from the chains of heartache and abuse, and the fact that my friend had gifted me this haven felt like the universe smiling down on me.

It was amusing to witness the expressions on Grey Knight's face whenever I crossed paths with him. It was as if he were the one who had lost a piece of himself—his brows knitted together in disbelief at how I could be so inexplicably happy. How dare she find joy in her newfound freedom! The thought brought a wry smile to my lips; I felt a sense of vindication as his irritation became my secret source of amusement.

It was as if a light switch had flicked in my heart, casting a gentle glow upon the hidden recesses that had long been cloaked in sorrow. All the pain I had endured daily felt like it had been washed away, flowing down the drain the moment I walked out. The weight of his toxicity had drained me for so long that the moment I tasted freedom, it felt like oxygen to starving lungs—a high I never wanted to come down from. I had been starved of happiness, deprived of joy, and stripped of even the simplest thing—a reason to smile.

I wasn't heartless—I understood that healing takes time, that grieving a relationship is a process. Yet, at that moment, I reveled in the joy of rediscovery. I craved the experience of being treated like a queen, longing for the romance that had been lacking for so long.

In a moment of daring clarity, I decided to take the plunge into the world of dating—enter Bumble. The app where women wield the power to choose their suitors, swiping right on those who catch their eye. I approached it with clarity and resolve: I wanted to go on dates, to explore what kinds of men were out there, but with no expectations of anything beyond that. Keeping it rated PG-13, of course. I knew that I wasn't ready to let anyone into my heart just yet, but I was ready to embrace the thrill of casual encounters.

I quickly morphed into a serial dater, embarking on ten first dates with ten different men. Each outing was an adventure—some casual chats at the dog park, others elegant dinners where I allowed these gentlemen to cater to me, showering me with the romance I had longed for. It was refreshing, like a gust of wind on a sweltering day. Each encounter opened my eyes to the kind of attention I craved and deserved. It was fun meeting new faces, some of whom even morphed into casual friendships. With my shield firmly in place, I kept them at arm's length, refusing to let anyone breach my defenses.

But soon enough, the texts from Grey Knight began trickling in, like rain on a clear day. He missed Mocha, he said, and wanted to spend time with her. Initially, I found it sweet, yet guilt crept in, gnawing at my insides for taking her away from him. The messages continued—persistent, like a haunting melody that wouldn't fade. It felt like he was trying to find a way back into my life, to gauge where I had taken refuge. There was no way I would let him in.

I firmly expressed that Mocha wasn't a child; there was no need for parental-type custody that would have us sending her back and forth. How long could we sustain that ridiculousness? I had witnessed his patterns in past relationships, the way he had navigated breakups with a calculated nonchalance. I would not allow that chaos into my life again. It was evident that Mocha had chosen her side—she was a mama's girl, and I was her devoted caretaker. No amount of coaxing would change that fact.

Grey Knight's persistence escalated to an unsettling level when he pulled the "I know where you live" card. A shiver ran down my spine. I didn't want to admit it, but I felt the rush of fear that bubbled beneath the surface. He had no idea about my friend's character—gentle, kind, and an absolute gentleman. Yet, if Grey Knight learned the details of my life now, it would likely ignite a firestorm of drama that I had no interest in inviting into my new sanctuary. I was determined to shield my peace from any negativity.

Grey Knight finally stopped asking about seeing our baby girl. It was like the silence before a storm, the kind that makes your skin prickle because you know something is coming, even if you can't quite place it. I didn't expect what came next. Out of nowhere, he poured his heart out, words tumbling from his mouth that I never thought I'd hear again. He said he missed me. Not just missed me in passing, but deeply, profoundly. He asked for another chance. He even asked me on a date. I stared at my phone, reading and re-reading his messages like they were written in a foreign language. *Was this real?* The Grey Knight, the man who had shattered my heart into a million jagged little pieces, was now asking to put them back together.

My heart sank. I wasn't sure what to think, honestly. Could he be sincere? Or was this some twisted game? Was I really about to consider going back to the same man who broke me in ways I never thought I could break? My mind was screaming, warning me to be careful, to protect myself, but my heart—oh, my poor heart—was already galloping ahead, racing towards the idea of a rekindled love. Could I trust him again? Was it even safe to step back into that fire? He had burned me so badly before, leaving scars that hadn't even begun to start healing.

I made him wait. Of course, I did. I wasn't about to let him waltz back in and act like everything was fine. But deep down, there was a part of me that still wanted it. I wanted him. Despite everything. Despite the abuse, despite the pain, all I ever wanted was his love—his true, unconditional love.

Is that so much to ask? To wish for someone to love you the way you've loved them?

And oh, those damn butterflies. They fluttered in my chest, wild and uncontrollable, like they didn't know whether to take flight or hide away. I was a mess of contradictions. One part of me knew going back could mean stepping into the same old patterns, falling into the same toxic cycle. But another part of me, the part that still ached for him, couldn't help but hope. What if this time was different? What if he had changed? What if…?

So, I caved. I let him back in. My heart still belonged to him, whether I wanted to admit it or not. Everyone deserves a second chance, right? I wanted to believe that so badly. Even though, deep down, I knew the truth. Second chances have never worked out for me. Not once. They always end up worse than the first time around, like I'm destined to repeat the same mistakes until I finally learn. But this time—*this time*—I convinced myself it would be different. He is the *exception* to my rule. Grey Knight had to be different. Now, he just had to prove it.

We spent the next three months slowly rebuilding, like tentative steps on fragile ground. I made him work for it, made him earn my trust back little by little. But the time came when I had to make a decision. Venice had been my sanctuary, but the moment had arrived for me to leave that peaceful bubble behind. Grey Knight and I decided to move in together again. I was nervous, but also weirdly hopeful. A friend of mine wanted to be roommates, so I suggested we share the apartment—with Grey Knight secretly living there, too, splitting the rent three ways to make it more affordable. It was risky, but it felt right in the moment.

We found the perfect place. A Spanish-style oasis in the heart of Hollywood, tucked away behind big trees that wrapped the building in shade, hiding it from the chaotic energy of the city. Walking through the front door felt like entering another world—a peaceful one, far removed from the hustle and bustle of LA. The apartment was charming, with its arched walkways, rounded pillars, and quirky, colorful shower tiles. The kitchen was modern, though, with blinking lights under the cabinets that gave it a rave vibe I didn't know I needed. But the real magic was on the balcony. A small, narrow door led out to it, where two chairs and a little table fit perfectly. From there, I could look down at the world below, feeling like a princess in her castle, while the trees shielded me from the craziness of LA. To this day, it's still my favorite place I've ever lived.

But just as I was settling into this new chapter, I learned about Grey Knight's "freedom" during our time apart. He had made a new friend—a fun guy from work, the kind who parties hard, drinks like there's no tomorrow, and always seems to be blown out of his mind. There were drugs, of course. And Grey Knight? He partied right alongside him. I wasn't naive. I knew the kind of wild nights they were having. I even met the guy—super cool, sure, but he reminded me of someone who peaked in high school and never quite grew up.

It made me feel… uneasy. Like a teenage girlfriend hearing about a party her boyfriend went to without her. My stomach twisted with jealousy and suspicion, even though I had no right to be mad. After all, I hadn't exactly spent my time apart sitting at home knitting. I went on dates, too—plenty of them, for fun, for distraction, for the experience. And I hadn't told him about any of it. Why would I? Nothing serious happened, but I kept my shield up just the same. We both had our own ways of coping with the separation. He had his wild nights, and I had my serial dates. What mattered now was moving forward, not backward.

But could we? That was the question I wasn't ready to answer.

ACT II
Petals Under Pressure

✦ ✦ ✦

Growth is not delicate.
It's a fight through the dirt,
a stretch toward light that may never come.
This is the ache of becoming—messy, magnificent, and
maddening.
She cracked open under pressure,
watered by grief, pulled by longing.
This is the part where she doesn't wait to be saved—
this is where she dares to bloom anyway

Chapter 5

Powdered Promises

Soon after Grey Knight and I moved in together, the universe whispered to me, softly at first, like a faint tug at the edges of my consciousness. My intuition, that sneaky little voice we all try to drown out, spoke words I didn't want to hear. Grey Knight was not meant to be my "forever after." It was a truth that shattered me. I wasn't ready to accept it, so I did what any stubborn heart does—I ignored it. I fought tooth and nail against the grain, clinging to the hope that maybe, just maybe, this second chance would be different. That he would prove me wrong, and we'd somehow craft a better, more beautiful version of the love we once had.

It didn't take long for reality to creep in, though, like it always does. One night, early into our cohabitation, we found ourselves blissfully alone. In a house full of roommates, those rare moments of peace felt like a small miracle. Just the two of us, no one else around. Relief washed over me. But then, Grey Knight—ever the wildcard—pulled out something I wasn't expecting. Heroin. Compressed into tiny, bright blue pills with a line right down the middle, like a perfectly divided secret.

I watched him with wide-eyed curiosity as he pulled out a credit card, using it with an almost practiced ease to split the pill and then crush it into a fine powder. There was no hesitance in his movements, no flinch of remorse, despite him once confessing to me that he was an addict. But in that moment, all I saw was the man I was still infatuated with, the man I'd always had these ridiculous goggle-eyes for. He was magnetic, and I was under his spell, like always.

"Do you want to try it?" he asked, his voice a seductive whisper that seemed to suspend time itself. He launched into a playful yet detailed tutorial on heroin—the art of the snort, the precise measure of a tiny line, complete with a crumpled dollar bill—and while my inner voice pleaded caution, my adventurous spirit, ever reckless and yearning, urged me to embrace the thrill.

Blinded by innocence, I was not fully aware of heroin's dark allure and the deadly danger lurking within its powdery embrace; yet, in that heady, vulnerable moment, buoyed by his comforting presence, I surrendered to curiosity and snorted my first hit—a decision as intoxicating as it was wildly unwise.

WAHBAM! WOWZERS! The sensation was immediate and overwhelming. A rush, electric and dizzying, shot through my body. Every inch of me sank into this blissful, euphoric state, a place where all my worries dissolved, and nothing but calm remained. Grey Knight and I collapsed onto the couch, our bodies melting into the cushions like butter on a hot skillet. It was a high that made time irrelevant.

I remember sitting there, eyes half-lidded, my mind floating somewhere far from reality. My body felt heavy, but in the best possible way, like a warm, weighted blanket had draped itself over my limbs. I was utterly and completely at peace, my heart beating in a slow, steady rhythm, my breath deep and relaxed. Even my sex drive—which was usually already on overdrive—flared up into something almost unbearable. I wanted him, needed him, and everything felt amplified, like I was seeing him through an entirely new lens.

We talked, too. Oh, did we talk. In that euphoric haze, the conversation flowed effortlessly, without filters or walls. It was like the drug opened up a portal to his heart, and for the first time in ages, we connected in a way I had longed for. He was vulnerable, open, and real—qualities that, in sober moments, he often kept hidden behind layers of defense. We felt like our most genuine selves, stripped of all pretense, and it was intoxicating in every sense of the word.

A few days later, we did it again. More blue pills, more highs, more heart-to-heart conversations that made me believe we were finally tapping into something deeper. We were like tourists in this strange, euphoric land, exploring its pleasures together. It became our thing—our secret, our shared escape. At first, it was just once in a while, on days off. But soon, it turned into a weekly ritual. Then, a few times a week. Every time, we dove deeper into this new world we had discovered, riding wave after wave of bliss. It brought us closer, or at least it felt that way.

Three or four months passed, and by then, we were doing it nearly every day. The orders for more pills became more frequent. We had fallen into a rhythm—place the order, pick up the pills, split them, get high. Rinse, repeat. We had our routine down to a science, and I was hooked. Baited by heroin, reeled in before I even realized what was happening.

And then, one day, as the high wore off, I felt something I hadn't before—sweat. Not just a little, but all over my body, like I was trapped in a sauna. Panic set in. Oh shit, I thought. This is withdrawal. The sweat was my body's way of screaming at me, telling me I was addicted, hooked. I wasn't a happy camper, to say the least. So, as addicts do, we ordered more. Fast pickups to keep the sweats at bay, to avoid the creeping anxiety that came with withdrawal.

We kept going, high after high, day after day. But here's the kicker—we still maintained our lives. We worked, went to the gym, took care of Mocha, and pursued our acting dreams. On the outside, everything looked fine. We were crushing auditions, I was working on film projects with my talented friend Isaiah—an ambitious, brilliant soul I'm grateful to call a friend. Together with our little gang, we created magic on set, collaborating on project after project, building our portfolios, and chasing that Hollywood dream.

But behind the scenes, heroin had become our lifestyle. It was no longer just an escape—it was the glue that held us together, the drug that made everything feel right, even when it was oh-so-wrong. And in the middle of it all, I wondered: Is this what it looks like, moving forward? Is this our version of love now—highs, withdrawals, and everything in between?

I cherished the closeness, the conversations, the way we opened up to each other when we were high. But deep down, I knew. This wasn't sustainable. This wasn't forever. This was a ticking time bomb, and we were sitting on top of it, waiting for it to blow.

We went on with our lives as if nothing had changed, as if the subtle, creeping dependence on heroin was nothing more than a background noise, just a hum beneath the surface. But truthfully, our world had become a dance with fire. We were tiptoeing around the disaster, balancing just enough heroin in our systems to stave off the hell of withdrawal but not quite enough to climb into that euphoric high we once gloried in. The balance was delicate, and the pursuit of it was relentless. It felt like a constant chase, a race we couldn't afford to lose, lest we tumble into the pits of withdrawal. And yet, no matter how much we consumed, it was never enough. We needed more. Always more.

Money disappeared faster than we could make it, vanishing from our wallets as if it had legs of its own. We found ourselves on car rides to the seediest parts of town, hunting down the "big dawg," our source. Grey Knight had befriended him in a twisted sort of way, chatting him up as if they were long-lost buddies, exchanging jokes and, of course, always talking drugs. One day, the big dawg casually mentioned the heroin we'd been buying was laced with rat poison. "Rat poison!" My mind screamed. My stomach turned. But did we stop? Nope. Not even a flinch. That's how deep we were.

The routine became clockwork. Splitting costs, splitting drugs, and sometimes even splitting hairs over how much each of us would get. Grey Knight, being twice my size, always needed more. Always. And sometimes, that tension would flare up like a matchstick, sparking little fights. We weren't much different than two dogs gnawing at the same bone. We always carried a credit card and a rolled-up dollar bill for those quick fixes, snorting lines in the most inappropriate places—bathrooms, alleyways, even the car, parked somewhere inconspicuous. It didn't matter. The urge to get high overpowered any sense of dignity.

No one knew. Our roommate, my close friend, was blissfully ignorant of the disaster unfolding under her own roof. None of my family or other friends had the faintest clue what I was entangled in. It was a double life. In some ways, I became a ghost of the person they once knew. I mastered the art of hiding in plain sight, slipping into this new identity, one marked by secrecy and shame, but, outwardly, everything looked just fine.

Then came the Hawaii trip. My mom and stepdad, Joey, wanted to treat us to a vacation—how generous, how loving, how utterly oblivious. They didn't know our wallets were strapped to heroin. They didn't know we were hanging on by a thread, our bodies craving the poison just to function. They offered to pay for everything, insisting we could pay them back for airfare later. I laughed—on the inside. How could I possibly explain where all my money had gone?

We were terrified. How were we going to maintain the charade around my family? They couldn't see us high, and worse, they couldn't witness us going through withdrawals. A double-edged sword if there ever was one. But Grey Knight and I thought we were clever, oh yes. We hid our little blue pills inside an Altoids tin, mixing them with wintergreen mints. Genius, right? The pills were nearly the same color and size, perfect camouflage. We stuffed them into our luggage and braced ourselves, hearts pounding as we passed through airport security.

I don't think I've ever been so scared in my life. My palms were sweating, my heart racing—if there was ever a moment when I might pass out from sheer panic, that was it. The thought of getting caught, of a drug-sniffing dog busting us wide open, made me tremble from head to toe. But somehow, by some stroke of luck or fate, we made it through. I could've kissed the ground in relief when we touched down in Hawaii.

Our plan was simple: stretch our supply, keep it quiet, and try to enjoy the vacation. But nothing ever goes as planned, right? Grey Knight, as always, plowed through his stash faster than I did. Of course, he did. And there we were, halfway through the trip, running out of heroin with no way to get more. My anxiety spiked. The thought of enduring withdrawals while trying to act normal around my family? Absolute hell.

I tried to ration my pills, taking tiny amounts, just enough to stay functional. But Grey Knight caught on, and, like always, I felt obligated to share. That irritated the hell out of me. I had paid for those pills, just like he had his. But in his moments of weakness, it was always about him. His need, his pain, his desperation. I was chained to him, just as much as I was chained to the heroin.

The withdrawals hit hard, and he claimed sickness, hiding away in the bedroom while I played the part of the dutiful daughter. I was shaking inside, my mind screaming at the injustice of it all, but outwardly, I was calm. Collected. A liar. Lying was what I had become best at.

The trip, despite everything, had some magical moments—whales and dolphins surrounding us during a sunset sail, a black sand beach where the ancient Hawaiian spirits supposedly roamed. We even swam with wild dolphins, tears of awe filling my goggles as I marveled at the beauty of it all. But those moments couldn't erase the reality that I was living a lie.

Back at home, things escalated. We needed more, always more. And then, one day, the big dawg stopped responding. Dead. Overdose. Just like that, our supplier was gone, and we were left scrambling. Grey Knight, in his desperation, found an even darker path—fentanyl. Stronger. Deadlier.

The memory is seared into my brain, as if it happened yesterday, not years ago. It's the kind of memory that plays on a loop, uninvited, in the quiet moments when you're trying to sleep. The details are still sharp, every second of it crystal clear. I remember when he brought it out—the small, sinister bag, casually placed on the closet shelf, like it was nothing more than an afterthought. He fixed up a few thin lines of fentanyl, just a couple of caterpillar tracks, one for him, one for me. He warned me, in that tone of his, as if we were about to embark on some grand adventure. "Little by little, okay?" His words were dripping with caution, but also excitement.

I barely took a sniff—just a hair—and waited. Nothing. No rush, no euphoria, nothing. So, like an idiot, I sniffed up a little more. Still, no immediate effect. I remember lying down in bed, though I couldn't tell you why. Maybe I was bored, or maybe my body already knew what my mind hadn't yet grasped. That's where the memory stops for me. Everything after that is a blank, a void where time and space disappear, swallowed whole.

According to Grey Knight, I didn't fall asleep. No, I fell into oblivion. He found me with my eyes rolled back into my head, completely unconscious, lifeless. And what did he do? He undressed me, threw me in the shower, and let the water rain down on me for six hours. Six *hours*. He told me later how he splashed water on my face, shook me, and begged me to wake up.

Anything to pull me back from the brink. It wasn't until those long, terrifying hours had passed that I finally came to. But waking up wasn't the peaceful, groggy transition from sleep. No, it was waking up into terror. I shot out of that unconscious state with pure panic coursing through me, screaming, trembling, crying so hard I could barely breathe. My mind was a mess of confusion. I had no idea what had just happened, no clue where I was, or why the hell I was soaking wet and naked in the shower.

Grey Knight was white with fear, pacing, shaking, muttering about how he thought I was gone. How, for six long hours, he didn't know if I was going to make it. He was terrified, apparently, watching what he thought might be my final moments. A near-death experience, though it wasn't him on the brink of death. It was me. He told me the whole story later, which is the only reason I can recount it to you now. My last clear memory was lying down in bed after trying fentanyl for the first time. The rest? That was history I never got to witness firsthand.

And you know what's even more twisted? At no point did Grey Knight think to take me to a hospital. Not once. He didn't even consider it. He decided that he was going to play the hero, that he could save me with water and willpower. No doctors. No medical attention. Just him, drenched in panic and drenched from the shower, waiting for me to come back to life. And by some fucking miracle, I did. I woke up from what could've easily been the end of me.

But as the fog cleared and the reality of it all sank in, something else dawned on me. This wasn't just about my survival. It was about his choice. He chose not to get me help. He chose not to call an ambulance, not to rush me to the emergency room where I desperately should have been. Why? Because of the fentanyl. Because we were high, and he was high, and getting help would've meant exposure. It would've meant consequences, and that scared him more than the thought of me dying right in front of him. He picked drugs over my life.

That's the part that still crushes my soul when I think about it. The weight of it, the sheer selfishness of that choice, it's like a blow to the chest every time I relive it. There's no way around it. Grey Knight failed me when it mattered most. The man who swore he loved me, who begged for second chances, who claimed he'd changed, chose to cover up his drug use instead of getting me the help I needed. He chose secrecy over my life.

And there it is—**Strike One**.

Our brains were wired for the chase—a cat-and-mouse game where the mouse was a fix, and the cat was our relentless pursuit. There wasn't space for anything else in our heads, not even after that near-death experience, which should have been a wake-up call. It should've rattled my bones and made me swear off that poison forever. But no, it was just a blip on the radar, a minor "oops" on the way to getting our next high. Like life had hit a pothole, and we just swerved, hitting the gas even harder. No breaks, only gas. Looking back, it was like we saw death flash in front of us, and instead of screaming, we shrugged. That's how deep we were.

I'd love to say I felt some deep shame, some burning desire to change, but honestly, I was more focused on the impending withdrawals than the fact that my boyfriend had just saved me from overdosing in our closet. The withdrawals were the only monster I couldn't outrun. That hollow, gnawing panic that set in when you realized your stash was low. You couldn't think about anything else. And man, the mental gymnastics I would perform to justify all of it—it was Olympic-level.

Here's the thing about heroin: It twists every aspect of your life, even the things that are supposed to feel good. Like sex. Yeah, I said it. When I was high, I craved it like some sort of primal beast. My body was practically screaming for attention. It was like my "cookie jar" (yes, my cookie jar) was sitting out on the counter, waiting for someone—*anyone*—to come raid it. But Grey Knight? He was the opposite. If heroin turned me into a sex-starved wild thing, it turned him into a statue. Nothing moved him. So, there I was, living in sexual purgatory, begging for attention, feeling like I was rotting away from the inside out. It was tragic, but in a way, almost comically so. My cookie jar? Growing stale. My pleas? Unheard. My frustration? Through the roof.

And as for the rest of my life? Heroin was busy eating away at me, gnawing at my soul like a termite infestation. My body was shrinking, my energy was fading, and I was becoming a shell of who I used to be. There was nothing left of the "me" I once knew. Every argument with Grey Knight felt like a high-stakes battle, and our communication? Nonexistent. The only thing we talked about with any passion was pills, and even those conversations were tinged with tension. We had drifted so far apart that I sometimes wondered if I even knew him anymore. Was he the man I once loved, or just the guy holding the key to my next high?

But it wasn't just Grey Knight I had problems with. I was angry at the world. I blamed him for everything, but deep down, I knew it wasn't all his fault. Still, I couldn't admit that. It was easier to paint him as the villain, the big bad wolf, while I played the innocent victim. To anyone who would listen—my friends, my mom—I spun this sob story about how Grey Knight was abusive, how he was the one hooked on drugs. I conveniently left out my own addiction. Why would I admit that? That would mean facing the truth, and I wasn't ready for that. I had no accountability. None.

It got to the point where I started borrowing money from my mom. At first, it was innocent enough. I told her I needed help with bills. But then the "small loans" turned into regular occurrences, and before I knew it, I was drowning in debt. Every time I asked for help, it felt like a piece of my soul crumbled away. My mom didn't know what was really going on, and I wasn't about to tell her. The guilt should have been overwhelming, but somehow, heroin numbed even that. The drug had stripped away my ability to care about anything other than my next hit.

Eventually, I couldn't take it anymore. The pressure, the lies, the bottled-up emotions—it all became too much. So, one night, I grabbed a journal and started writing. I poured out every raw, messy, heroin-hazed thought I had. I wrote as if I were screaming into a void, desperate for someone—*anyone*—to hear me. And yeah, I did it on purpose. I left the door open, knowing Grey Knight would see me. I wanted him to read it. I wanted him to see how broken I felt, how lost we both were.

Here's what I wrote, unfiltered, straight from my soul:

"So apparently I am unintelligent huh? Gosh I can't stand it sometimes like it makes me want to quit. You come up with all these assumptions of who I am based from the past but that

was when I was dying in my own little world of depression going through all that crap. You make me sound like the worst fucking human being but yet you say you'll "never stop loving me" I don't believe it. I just can't. Imagine don't trust you. You make me feel like I'm a piece of shit to you. Like why me now? Why me? I wish you could answer me truthfully why you truly love me? Because you don't exactly show it in every way I believe in. Am I really just a pretty girl to you and that's all? Because every single fucking man treats me that way. Every one of them. Yeah, fuck what's on the inside of haley, she's a trophy wife so I'll steal her away before any other bastard. Psst! Relationships suck yo. I could care less. What's most important to me is on the inside. Looks only last for so long. I'm so over playing that game. I need to be accepted for who I am before you even come near me. Ugh! Ugh Grey knight! You say I'm not smart! How fucking nice of you to say such a thing. Why do you even think it's acceptable to even use that word to me?

Think before you go spilling the beans because your words can be brutal. They hurt me like it'd hurt others. Also shows too that intelligence doesn't matter to you when dating me. Ugh Grey knight! I DO NOT KNOW! I DO NOT GET HOW YOUR MIND WORKS! Why would you want to be with someone if you can't have intellectual chats with. The funny part is YES, FUCK YES!!! There's so damn much that's a part of me that you don't see. I want to obviously show you but I can't convince you to do anything.

You are you. I don't want to and I sure can not do it even if I wanted to. I am just sick. I want to feel wanted. I want to feel worthy. I want to be able to talk without repeating myself. I want to know that you believe in me and ALL that I do. I want to get lost in chats with you. I want you to fucking trust me. I want you to listen. I want you to be my partner-in-crime for the rest of my life but fuck, we obviously have much to communicate on and issues to sort out. I want life to be easy with you as any relationship should be. But why all of this? I believe I do it to myself…right? I do. I know I'm hard on myself, but I have dealt with chaos in countless ways by too many people through it all it's all been so lonesome, pushes me to my corner with barely one person to talk to through everything. Not even one single person I can keep around in my life.

What's wrong with me? No. It's not me. It's the fact that im treated in a "special" way vs the world vs all women. Although I definitely believe that beautiful, down to earth women such as myself get that treatment as well. Boo you suck people who give me that treatment. The majority don't get it. Even men, even grey knight don't get what it's like. In conclusion all I can do is be miss independent miss Wonder Woman. Stay strong. But some moments I only want to curl up in your (grey knight) arms and LET IT GO! I am full of imperfections and I am learning about myself all the damn time. Even more so being with you Grey knight because I am at that life-changing time in my life. Even more with just your presence, you're such a positive influence to me. I want us to meet in the middle. I want it to happen now. I wish you would accept me for all that I am and do which its like you do. You're obviously still here and say you're not leaving but if you don't like something than you are so quick at all costs.

There are times that I ask myself what I truly mean to you. What is your answer? I'm not even big on being insecure as much as before, but I can say I am insecure with you and I don't know what you see in me that brings fireworks in your eyes. Are we at that stage again at spending too much time together? I know I need another job, maybe even a full separate job away from you to create some common space. I feel you don't appreciate me and I don't excite you or bring you a REAL FUCKING SMILE on that handsome face. FUCK! It's so pretty to see but I don't pleasure you simply like before now it's only being high. ONLY right now."

I was terrified, but at the same time, I hoped it would break him open. And it did. When he read it, something in him shifted. The walls came down, and for a moment, we were able to see each other again—not as addicts, not as enemies, but as the broken people we were.

That journal entry? It loosened the reins. For once, we found a way back to each other, even if only for a moment. It wasn't perfect, but in the chaos of our lives, it was enough.

Chapter 6

The Devil's Carousel

Writing about that time—about the heroin years—feels like ripping open a wound that should've healed long ago. It's as if I'm reaching back into a nightmare, into some twisted alternate universe where I can't quite believe I was the star of my own personal horror movie. It's surreal, like watching a film where you know every plot twist but still can't quite accept that it's *your* life. Digging into these memories is like stumbling through a dark maze, where every turn reveals a void, a blank, like someone went in and erased half my brain. The memories aren't just faded; they're gone. Wiped out. Like my mind's trying to protect me from the ugly truth of what I've lived through.

Even sitting down to write this out feels like trying to catch smoke. It's elusive, slippery. My mind just *doesn't want to go there.* The day I decided to finally face this head-on, I woke up the next morning feeling like I'd been suffocating in my sleep. I'd slept like a baby but woke up at the edge of a panic attack. My chest was heavy, tears burning my eyes, my nerves on fire. All day, I was trapped in this suffocating haze—couldn't even leave the house. I canceled every plan and couldn't even bring myself to drive. It felt like my body was revolting against the very idea of facing the past. I couldn't breathe, couldn't think. And for what? For memories that are more like puzzle pieces I can't find, let alone fit together? But here I am, trying anyway. Even if I don't have the full picture, I'll do my best to arrange the broken shards into something, even if it's messy, incomplete, and jagged.

Heroin didn't just pull us into hell—it dragged us down and locked the doors behind us. The closer we got to rock bottom, the more we lost our humanity. We weren't people anymore. We were two desperate creatures, clawing for our next fix. Nothing else mattered. It was always heroin, heroin, heroin. Grey Knight and I against the world. We thought we were in control, but we were just lost. So lost. We weren't living in the same world as everyone else—we'd crossed over into some twisted dimension where nothing made sense anymore. We were thieves in the night, hiding from the light of day, bound together by our shared obsession.

Bye-bye, Alice in Wonderland. We were no longer sipping tea at whimsical tea parties; we were falling down, down, *down* into a rabbit hole that had no end. Our lives crumbled around us, but we were too focused on the chase to care. Money? Gone. Stability? A distant memory. We couldn't even hold down a living situation. We moved from one place to another like vagabonds—crashing at friends' places or shacking up in a dingy bachelor pad just to scrape by. Each move was chaos personified, but we lived for the chaos.

Moving out of Hollywood was a mess. My "friend"—if I can even call her that—tried to pin the blame for a car scratch on me, even though I'd watched her do it with her own reckless driving. She was careless and petty, but it was all part of another nightmare. And then, there was the roommate situations—what a disaster. One guy, this party-loving snake, waited until we were out of town and *cleaned us out*. Like, literally everything. Every single thing I owned—gone. Clothes? Gone. Kitchen stuff? Gone. Even the smallest, most random items vanished, like a thief had wiped the place clean. I came back expecting to pack for our move, only to find the place picked bare. The worst part? My engagement ring. The one thing I thought I'd kept hidden, safe, tucked away in a watch box beneath layers of padding—gone. That ring meant everything to me. It wasn't just a shiny object; it was a symbol, a token of the life I thought I was building with Grey Knight. And now, it was just another casualty of our chaotic, drug-fueled life.

But, you know, material things can be replaced. The ring, the clothes—they were just stuff. What really stung was how low we'd fallen. We were even stealing food just to survive. Pocketing snacks like we were pulling off some high-stakes heist, when really, we were just a couple of addicts too broke to eat. We got good at it, though—dressed the part, looked the part, acted the part. No one suspected a thing. Because when you're as desperate as we were, you learn to survive by any means necessary. The only thing that mattered—*the only thing*—was making sure we had enough heroin to get through the day. That was it. Everything else was secondary. We needed it to stay alive, but we knew it was slowly killing us.

Sitting front row to your own destruction is bizarre. It's like watching a slow-motion train wreck, knowing you're the one driving the train but unable to stop it. Grey Knight? He seemed unfazed. He charged through it all like a ram, head down, focused only on the next hit. I don't know if he felt what I felt, or if he just buried it deeper. But I still had this tiny flicker inside me, this faint pulse that said, *This can't be your life. You're better than this.*

I started pushing back. I wanted out. I wanted to detox. I wanted to quit cold turkey, rip the Band-Aid off, and fight my way through the hell of withdrawals. I started demanding that we do it together, that we quit on our next few days off. It wasn't just a want anymore—it was a *need*. We had to claw our way out, or we'd be lost forever. I wanted us to fight together, to hold each other accountable, to survive this. Because deep down, I knew this wasn't me. This wasn't who I was supposed to be. I was better than this. I *had* to be.

I loved Grey Knight. I really did. But I couldn't be part of this world any longer. I couldn't keep spiraling down into this bottomless pit of addiction and chaos. I'd already transformed into someone I didn't recognize. Every day, I looked in the mirror and asked, *How did this happen?* How did I let myself become this stranger staring back at me?

The answer wasn't clear, but I knew one thing: I had to fight my way back. Because if I didn't, I was afraid I might never find my way out.

We attempted to quit cold turkey, a term that sounds so bold and definitive in theory, but the reality? It was chaos incarnate. We finished our last bits of heroin like it was some sacred ritual, an offering to the gods of withdrawal, and braced ourselves for what was to come. We were like babies attached to their pacifiers—always needing that tiny, familiar comfort within reach. But this time, the pacifier was gone, and the panic and anxiety set in immediately, rushing through us like a flood. It wasn't a gentle wave. No, it was panic in its rawest, most pathetic form. The anticipation of what we knew was coming was enough to make our skin crawl. Pathetic, isn't it? The way we searched the apartment like lost children hoping to stumble upon some forgotten stash. High and low, we scavenged, licking up whatever powder might be left behind, as though some miracle would keep the inevitable at bay. Looking back now, I can't help but laugh at the absurdity of it all. Like starved animals.

But when the sweats kicked in, that laugh caught in my throat. That's when it truly marked the beginning. It didn't matter how many times I'd been through it, the first drip of cold sweat made my heart race like I was running from some invisible predator. The creeping physical anxiety—a beast I had never encountered until heroin sunk its claws into me—became a suffocating fog. You hear the word "anxiety" thrown around a lot, but this was something else. I had lived a life relatively untouched by true anxiety, and yet here it was, consuming me whole. Not the sort of jittery feeling before a test or a job interview. This was something else. This was pure, physical pain woven into every muscle, every joint. It was as if every cell in my body was in revolt, rejecting me. Then came the spasms. Imagine feeling as though your body is at war with itself. Muscles twitch and spasm like they're in a cruel game of Simon Says, only no matter what you do, you can't make them stop.

My muscles jerked uncontrollably, turning my limbs into restless, fidgeting messes, unable to find a position that didn't make me feel like I was trapped in my own skin. It was like I had become a puppet of my own pain, flipping from bed to floor, standing, sitting, never still for more than a few seconds. Like a toddler throwing a tantrum—but this wasn't tantrum-level discomfort. This was survival. The sweat? It poured out of me like I was melting from the inside. Goosebumps rippled across my skin, making me shiver and shake despite the fact that I was wrapped in every blanket I owned, bundled up like a mummy. Cold sweats. That name is far too gentle for the reality of it. It felt like my body was being dunked repeatedly into ice water, but I was burning up from the inside. You can't win against it, no matter how many layers you throw on. My body rebelled against itself. The endless cycle of torment that escalated with every passing hour.

It was as though time had slowed down, ticking away like some sadistic clock, mocking us as our symptoms grew worse. My heart pounded wildly, erratically, like it was trying to escape my chest and leave me behind. I would gasp for air, each breath jagged, as my chest clenched tighter. And that runny nose? Tissues everywhere like confetti at a depressing party. No matter how much I tried to fight the chaos inside me, the agitation gnawed at every inch of my being. Sleep? Forget it. Food? Impossible. It was like trying to function in a world where nothing mattered except for the agony pulsing through every cell of my body. And all I could hate to think about, through the haze of pain, was heroin. Sweet, destructive heroin. It became the cruelest irony— Grey Knight wanting the very thing that had broken us to be the thing that could save us.

If you Google it, the experts will say heroin withdrawal takes anywhere from six to twenty-four hours to kick in, but that's just theory. The reality is, it hits differently for everyone, depending on how deep you are, how far gone. Grey Knight was bigger than me, and his intake was much higher, so his symptoms came fast and furious. Mine? It took about three or four hours before the storm truly began. And when it did—well, it was as though time stretched itself into some cruel parody. A minute felt like an hour, and each second dragged us further into the pits of withdrawal. We weren't just fighting withdrawal; we were fighting for our lives. The detox was like staring down death's barrel. I think we both believed, foolishly, that maybe, just maybe, we could get through it. We rode that storm together, trying to hold on to the last shreds of ourselves, but there was no denying it. We were in hell, and there was no roadmap out.

It's hard to convey what that kind of suffering feels like. Describing it now makes my skin crawl—breath caught in my throat, and anxiety that grips me just thinking about it. It's an all-encompassing horror show—it's a full-body assault—a biological, psychological, and spiritual battle wrapped up into one. I've heard it called the "Asian flu" before because it lasts about 72 hours. Seventy-two hours of pure, unfiltered suffering, but there's no flu that can prepare you for this kind of raw, unrelenting torment. And when we hit the twelve-hour mark, you get so stripped down to your bare bones that you wonder if you'll ever make it through alive. Abdominal cramps like knives twisting inside you, nausea that ripped through your gut until you were throwing up everything—even when there was nothing left. That's the kicker—there's nothing to throw up, but your body still tries. It's like your stomach is waging war on itself, trying to claw its way out through your throat. I'd sit there, crying on the bathroom floor, bile burning my insides, wishing for an end. But it never came.

And then there was Mocha Bear. Our sweet, goofy dog, the only innocent one in this spiraling mess. Grey Knight and I were dog lovers through and through—the kind of people who'd stop on the street just to pet a stranger's dog, who celebrated Mocha's birthdays with burgers and candles. We loved her like she was our child. But heroin? Heroin changed everything. We became neglectful, too absorbed in our own misery to give her the attention she deserved. I hated it—hated that we were failing her, hated that the detox made even the simplest things, like feeding her or taking her out to potty, feel like impossible tasks. Poor Mocha, she deserved so much better. We were monsters, not fit to be her parents, and that truth gutted me more than anything else.

I remember one time, during one of our countless detox phases, Mocha rammed her knee into the sliding glass door. She let out this pitiful little yelp, and it broke my heart. We couldn't afford to take her to the vet, so we did our best to nurse her at home, icing her leg and hoping it would heal. And it did—sort of. But it felt like a metaphor for everything that was happening. We were bandaging the wounds without ever really healing them, putting a temporary fix on a situation that was far too broken for quick solutions.

After endless hours of cramping, sweating, and tears, a deceptive calm would finally settle—if only we could survive that damned twelve-hour threshold, when nausea morphed into a demonic beast threatening to hurl our very guts into oblivion. Each cycle of withdrawal evolved into a living nightmare, twisting our torment into grotesque, ever-shifting forms. Grey Knight, ever the provocateur, would be the first to shatter our fragile resistance with his mocking, relentless demands for a fix, his voice a razor-sharp whisper slicing through the silence. And though every instinct screamed for me to resist, the moment he started heading out the door, his toxic pull dragged me along, leaving me powerless to escape the inevitable plunge back into heroin's deadly embrace.

After narrowly escaping the razor's edge of detox, we were drawn deeper into the abyss with an alluring new method: smoking heroin off foil—an offering of speed, a shortcut to the euphoric escape we both so desperately craved. The rush hit us instantly, an intoxicating wave that surged through our veins and made us believe that this, this was the answer to everything we had been running from. We pursued that elusive dragon, convinced it held the key to unlocking a life we'd never known—one filled with suppressed joy, menaced by the satisfaction of a fleeting high. It was seductive, yes, but the devil came closer in that smoke, wrapping its fingers tighter around our necks. Somewhere between the pleasure and the haze, I danced close to the flames, caught in the throes of a near-death experience *again*—**Strike Two**.

The details of that experience dissolve into myth, as if fate—wielding its twisted sense of mercy—deliberately blurred the memory to shield my fragile mind. What I have left to cling to are the fragmented pieces Grey Knight has shared—his raw, unfiltered version of events, for I was too far gone to be truly aware. So, alas, I can't share the story with you this time, but honestly, that's for the best. Leave it to the gods of forgetfulness to guard what remains of me.

Fuck! Quitting cold turkey? Yeah, that was a colossal fail. Looking back now, I can't even pretend to be surprised, but at the time, it felt like the biggest relief in the world when we'd clean up, shower, shove some food into our bodies, and chug as much water as we could stand. We'd do everything possible to feel even remotely alive again, as if pretending we had it together might make it true. But then, we'd find ourselves scraping by, financially drained, and hyper-focused on one thing: heroin.

I'll never forget how bizarre it was, the way my body felt after a fix. There was this disgusting, eerie sensation that came with "coming back to life" after being curled up in the agony of withdrawal. Even if we'd only gone twelve hours without using, it felt like an eternity. The initial high was blissful, sure, but there was this weird moment after, like I had to readjust to feeling *normal*—except normal now meant being on heroin, just in larger and larger doses. It's like your body tricks you, convincing you that this version of you is okay, is stable, when you're anything but.

It didn't take long for things to spiral even further—just a few days, maybe. We were already buried in a deeper financial hole, sinking fast. The only solution? Quit cold turkey again. Simple, right? The next week, Grey Knight and I, as if we were rehearsing for a twisted play, lined up three more consecutive days off together. And again, we knew we had to face the demon that was detox. The ongoing cycles of detox that followed, we were seasoned veterans—*we thought*. We had a clearer idea of what to expect, but that just made the panic rise quicker, stronger than the first time. We were staring down death again, and this time, we knew exactly how it would feel. The agony would wash back into our lives, crawling into our bones, our blood, our souls. We dreaded it, but we couldn't avoid it.

As much as we wanted to quit, the moment the symptoms hit, the terror overshadowed our resolve. It was like being trapped in the jaws of a dragon—knowing you had to fight to survive, but the fire was too hot, too painful. Desperation clawed at me. I even tried to be sneaky, hiding little stashes of heroin behind Grey Knight's back, thinking I could wean myself off. But he had eyes everywhere—there was no getting past him. The second he realized I had some left, I had to share it. And if I didn't, the rage would ignite in him like a ticking bomb.

And so, the pattern would repeat. He'd explode, and we'd be running out the door, chasing that next fix like it was oxygen. The fear of withdrawal—of the lightning-strike nausea, the horrific vomiting—was stronger than any desire to quit. It was terrifying, and that's not an exaggeration. It scared the living shit out of us, both of us.

There is nothing quite as soul-crushing as that gut-wrenching nausea—the kind that strips you of all desire to eat and leaves you battling an enemy within. In the throes of detox, food loses its allure completely. Even if our lives depended on it, we'd be the worst culinary connoisseurs ever, incapable of coaxing a morsel of pleasure from a meal during withdrawal.

Then comes the twelve-hour peak, when the horror truly begins. By this time, our stomachs have surrendered to nothing but bitter bile, and it doesn't take long before that toxic brew is violently expelled. What follows is a relentless, almost cinematic barrage of purging—a terror so intense it defies belief. I often marvel that my eyes didn't pop out or my veins burst from the sheer shock of it all.

In a desperate bid for relief, once we understood just how unbearable the nausea was, we did everything in our power to tame the chaos. We even attempted the unthinkable—shoving a measly yogurt cup down our throats—in a vain effort to soothe the violent purging. Did it work? Only for a fleeting moment, as the yogurt, or whatever feeble sustenance we managed, would promptly be cast out, as if mocking our futile efforts.

At our most vulnerable, one of us might be found clinging to the cold, unforgiving embrace of the toilet, immobilized by the overwhelming intensity. And on those rare, cruel occasions when the nausea struck us both simultaneously, it devolved into a desperate, almost absurd battle over that one sanctuary. In hindsight, however, the absurdity of our squabble over the bathroom became a source of dark humor—a moment we'd later laugh about, marveling at how even the most severe circumstances could spark a bout of ridiculous camaraderie.

The idea of enduring that kind of agony again was worse than anything we could imagine. So, what did we do? We failed. Over and over. Week after week, we'd prepare ourselves, determined to quit. But every time, the detox would win. The aches in our bones, the burning in every cell of our bodies— it was too much. Even though we knew exactly what was coming, we were weak. Exceptionally weak. But we tried, oh how we tried, like clockwork, fitting our attempts to quit into whatever slivers of time our schedules allowed.

And when we failed, we got creative. We'd try anything—anything to dull the withdrawal symptoms, to take the edge off. Living at the bachelor pad had its advantages in that sense. The roommates were always into cocaine, so we scavenged for as much powder as we could find, snorting it like it was some magical cure. Spoiler alert: it wasn't. We tried going outside, hoping nature would somehow make us feel human again, but being around people felt impossible. It just made us more paranoid. Then there were the edibles—*so many edibles*—hoping to overdose on THC and knock ourselves into oblivion. When that didn't work, we turned to heavy liquor. Anything to escape the pain. But nothing worked.

We'd heard about Suboxone, this miracle drug for opioid detox, and we thought that might be the answer. It was supposed to help manage cravings, reduce withdrawal symptoms, and generally stop us from spiraling. So, we asked around, discreetly, until we got our hands on some. But Suboxone came with strict rules: no heroin for 12–24 hours before taking it. *Twelve hours.* That might as well have been a lifetime. We knew we had to hit the peak of withdrawal first, and let me tell you, that was terrifying. The thought of making it through those twelve hours made my skin crawl. Every hour was a battle, and waiting for the twelfth hour felt like torture. But the alternative? Taking it too early and triggering even worse withdrawal symptoms. It was a razor's edge.

When we finally did take the Suboxone—these flimsy little film strips you had to tuck under your tongue and let dissolve—it sometimes worked. We'd feel the faint stirrings of normalcy creeping back in, but it wasn't a guarantee. Even on the best days, when the Suboxone did what it was supposed to, we'd still find ourselves back in heroin's grip eventually. Every time we came close to breaking free, we'd stumble right back into the cycle. We weren't strong enough, or maybe we just didn't want it badly enough?

Even worse was seeing Grey Knight go through it, knowing I couldn't really help him, and he couldn't help me. He tried to play it tough, but his pain tolerance was low—typical man, right? Women, we're built for this kind of thing, for pain. But I could see it in his eyes, the sheer desperation as he begged me to cave. He'd plead, convincing himself that just one fix would solve it all, make it stop. And every time, I tried to hold the line. "Think of Mocha," I'd tell him. "Do it for her." Mocha, our dog, was my emotional anchor in all of this madness, my motivation to keep fighting. But eventually, his begging wore me down, and like clockwork, we'd both cave. The chase for the fix began all over again.

It was exhausting, like sprinting through a never-ending marathon where the finish line kept shifting just out of reach. A brutal rollercoaster, one minute soaring high, the wind in our faces, and the next we were hurtling towards disaster, every twist and turn throwing us into terror. It remains the most fucked-up, traumatizing period of my life—the kind of chaos that no dictionary could ever do justice to, as if language itself breaks under the weight of something so raw and brutal. We tried quitting—what felt like a hundred times (at least a quarter)—each failure sinking us deeper into that pit, a black hole with no escape, no bottom. We threw everything at the pain—distractions, numbing agents, anything we could grasp—but nothing worked. It was hell, in all its unfiltered, raging glory—and still, somehow, we kept crawling back to it, as if this poison held the answer to everything we were searching for. And the two near-death experiences? Just the cherry on top of this godforsaken sundae. Twisted, right? A bit dark, yeah. But that's how I survived it—all that insanity, all that pain—by laughing in the face of it. Dark humor became my armor, my shield, my way to stay *sane* when everything threatened to swallow me whole.

If you were to ask what propelled me to summon every last ounce of willpower to break free from addiction and conquer the brutal detox, my answer would be unequivocal—it was all for Mocha. I never imagined I'd become the person stumbling through life ensnared by drugs. When I first moved to LA, I swore, "I'll never do drugs," yet gradually, I transformed into someone I hardly recognized and certainly didn't admire.

That harsh truth struck me like a bolt of lightning, and amid the chaos emerged my radiant beacon: my little Mocha bear. Witnessing her spark dim beneath the weight of my despair was the wake-up call I desperately needed. In the depths of my self-destruction, my baby girl became my inspiration—a tender reminder of the person I was meant to be, a fierce, protective mama bear.

In those tumultuous days, I came to understand that dogs are creatures whose unwavering love and loyalty are gifts we scarcely deserve. They offer a boundless, soul-healing affection even when our hearts are fractured. Despite not "having it all" with Grey Knight through those dark times, it was Mocha who shone like a burst of sunlight, keeping me afloat when everything else seemed to be collapsing.

There was an almost magical connection between us—a silent, telepathic understanding that transcended words. In those suffocating moments, her passionate kisses were like tiny rebellions of hope, each one a promise that together, we could rise above the chaos.

Looking back, I can now laugh at the absurdity of those desperate, chaotic days—a bittersweet reminder that even in our most harrowing struggles, humor and love can illuminate the path home. Mocha is my treasure, the reason I fought through the anguish, and the light that continues to guide me back to who I truly am.

Chapter 7

Grey Knight's Last Ride

Grey Knight planted his foot down with a determination that surprised even me. After an exhausting cycle of cold turkey detoxes that left him battered, he'd reached his breaking point. I could hardly believe it—yet a swell of pride surged through me as he sat down, eyes blazing with resolve. "I'm done," he declared, a quiet thunder rumbling in his voice. He wanted to get sober... and he wasn't fond of acting. But most importantly, he wanted to break free from his drug dealer's grip, which meant leaving Los Angeles behind. My heart sank at the thought. This was the city where dreams sparkled, right? The very heart of the film industry where my budding career was finally taking flight—despite the weight of heroin dragging me down. Each month brought a new project, a new glimmer of hope, and now he wanted to walk away? How could I possibly abandon the city where my ambitions were blooming?

Grey Knight's idea of "home" wasn't the glamorous glitz of Hollywood anymore; it was the rugged charm of Wisconsin. At least as a "reset" button. He believed that being around family would be the salvation we both desperately needed. But I had never stepped foot outside California—an adventurous spirit I might be, but Wisconsin felt like a foreign land, devoid of any sign of the film industry. The thought of leaving my friends, my lifeline, gnawed at me. Yet here I was, tethered to Grey Knight like we were both drowning, holding each other up with sheer willpower and love. It was Grey Knight and me against the world, and boy, was the world an unforgiving place.

At that point, we'd clawed our way through so much chaos—the spiraling depths of heroin addiction, the madness of withdrawal, and a year and a half of dancing dangerously close to death. It felt like the last shadows of humanity we had left were screaming to be saved. We both knew we needed to fight our way back. Heroin had us in its suffocating grip, and deep down, we recognized this wasn't who we were. We were young, alive, and full of unfulfilled dreams! How had we let this poison dictate our lives? Staring down the barrel of our mortality was terrifying. I'd had two near-death experiences that should have shaken me to my core, yet somehow, I kept injecting that venom into my veins. It was madness! What higher power had intervened to pull me back from the brink? Was it you, God? My guardian angel? My beloved Grandma Rita always promised to watch over me, and I felt her presence even now. She had to be the reason I was still breathing, still standing. It was time to armor up and embark on this quest for sobriety; there was no way I was going to become just another statistic.

In that pivotal moment, we resolved to vanish from Los Angeles, taking our first steps toward Wisconsin. The thought of disappearing from this vibrant city shattered me, triggering a retreat from social media and a painful severing of ties with friends. We had to detox in secret once we got to his hometown; his family could never know the depths of our addiction. Grey Knight had a long history of struggles that left scars on his family's hearts. He had been through rehab four times, each time half-heartedly, and the pain they had endured was a weight I couldn't bear to add to. They had tried everything, attending meetings and supporting him without enabling him, and the thought of them seeing him like this again was unbearable. They were the epitome of what parents should be, and I cherished their unwavering love.

As the countdown to our big move began, we faced the harsh reality of our situation—our finances and strength were dwindling, and the urge to leave behind our wreckage was palpable. We put in our notice at the bachelor pad, stripped our lives down to the bare essentials, and tossed most of our belongings into the trash. Our car was crammed to the roof with what little we had left. The days leading up to the move felt like a race against time, and with each passing day, we were living out of that cramped vehicle. It was humbling, to say the least. We'd find quiet neighborhoods to park in at night, curling up with our dog, Mocha, while the weight of our circumstances pressed heavily on our hearts. Our last desperate pick-up of heroin before leaving felt like a betrayal, but in our broken world, it was our twisted form of comfort. We loitered in parks, pilfering yogurt cups and snacks to fill our bellies, and once our final paychecks arrived, we slipped away from Los Angeles without a backward glance.

With limited funds and a plan that was more hope than reality, we set off on our road trip to Wisconsin, vowing to detox along the way. The idea was ludicrous, and soon we found ourselves battling anxiety in that cramped car. I draped my duvet over my lap, bracing for the inevitable chills that accompanied withdrawal, while Grey Knight, somehow composed, drove us onward. I remember sweating through that comforter, leaving it a smelly relic of my struggle. Halfway through Nebraska, we decided to stop for the night, even managing to sneak Mocha into our hotel room. But as the detox clawed at us, we succumbed to the desperate thought of scoring more heroin. Grey Knight, ever resourceful, instructed me on how to find a dealer while driving. I felt the weight of my conscience as I ventured out to meet a stranger for a fix, only to return with a bitter taste of betrayal—just a handful of worthless candies.

What should have been relief turned into devastation. Not only had we lost precious money we didn't have, but we had also lost the escape we so desperately sought. Acceptance washed over us like a cold wave; we had no choice but to focus on getting to Wisconsin safely and drug-free. Maybe it was a blessing in disguise, we thought so. It was the only way to face his parents, to show them we were better than this. Once there, we were offered a lifeline by Grey Knight's best friend, Tedd, who invited us to stay rent-free while helping him move. I was still grappling with withdrawal symptoms, but somehow, Grey Knight seemed to glide through it. He jumped at the chance to help Tedd, while I rested, trying my best to put on a brave face. Meeting his friends for the first time was surreal—I had never envisioned it happening like this.

Arriving in Wisconsin felt like pressing a giant, glowing reset button on my life. A fresh start, for sure—but not an easy one. Once I scraped through the agonizing grip of heroin detox, I could finally feel the faint stirrings of life inside me again. And when I say "slow," I mean molasses-in-a-wisconsin-winter kind of slow. We were broke—like, laughably broke. I can't remember if we even had two pennies to rub together. But hey, a new beginning is a new beginning, right? We had a new state, no jobs, and no one besides Grey Knight to call a friend. It was like life hit the restart, but forgot to give me a manual.

Grey Knight took on the role of tour guide, driving me through his childhood haunts with the excitement of a kid showing off a new bike. He introduced me to his family, his friends, the places that held echoes of his youth. And somehow, amidst the rolling hills and quaint little towns, I felt a surprising sense of belonging. The people were warm and funny—Midwestern hospitality, where everyone acts like they've known you forever. It was comforting, even if I had no idea what I was doing there. The humor, the warmth—it was all my style, and yet… deep down, I was still nursing wounds I hadn't quite acknowledged.

The heroin addiction lingered like a ghost, haunting me at every turn, even though we were trying so hard to put it behind us. Every day felt like I was crawling out of a hole, only to find another one waiting. But Wisconsin, with all its simplicity and small-town charm, gave me the environment I needed to heal—at least externally. Inside, I was a bit of a mess, wondering, *What the hell am I supposed to do here?* Wisconsin wasn't the dream destination. I didn't see a future for myself there, but at that moment, it was what I needed to survive.

Living with Ted and his boyfriend helped soften the edges. The four of us vibed, creating this cozy little bubble where I could slowly piece myself back together. Meanwhile, Grey Knight landed a job at one of the city's fanciest restaurants, which felt like a step in the right direction. I snagged a bartending gig at a popular downtown spot. We were finally getting back to what felt like a somewhat normal life. Normal-ish, anyway.

But bartending in Wisconsin came with its own set of challenges—and surprises. For one, you can *drink* while on the clock. Something I was totally unprepared for. My first shift? I ended up tallying 30 shots. Yes, *thirty*! Spaced over a twelve-hour shift, sure, but still—who was I kidding? I'm not built for that kind of chaos! That was where things started to go off the rails. It wasn't long before my shifts ran late into the night, sometimes until 3 or 4 a.m. My old soul wasn't cut out for that kind of grind.

So, to keep up? Well, let's just say I made a new friend—one who dealt in powdery white "solutions." Yes, I started buying cocaine to get through those marathon shifts. It was so unhealthy, so unlike me, but it seemed like the only way to survive. I was playing a dangerous game, and deep down, I knew it.

Meanwhile, Grey Knight would occasionally swing by the bar, hanging out, partying, and checking in on me. Or maybe "checking up on me" is more accurate. Bartending meant mingling, flirting, and making everyone feel like the king or queen of the night. That's just how the job worked, but it made Grey Knight insecure. I get it—I'm a natural flirt, but my heart? It's always been his. Still, it stirred something ugly in him, and before I knew it, we were back in that toxic loop—jealousy, mistrust, arguments. It was as if the Wisconsin air was heavy with ghosts from our past, dragging us back into the same rocky place we fought so hard to leave behind.

As if that weren't enough, Grey Knight started spiraling, too. As if my late night hours had to be his as well. Late nights, heavy drinking, and cocaine. Lots of cocaine. The same old demons we thought we'd buried were creeping back. There was one bar in particular that became his haunt, a place where the drinks flowed freely (thanks to a bartender friend), and the cocaine was always within reach. Double trouble. I joined him at first, trying to keep up, trying to convince myself that it was all just fun. But it wasn't long before the word "addiction" became a neon sign flashing in my mind. I knew it. He knew it. And yet, here we were again, standing at the edge of the abyss.

I found myself turning into that girlfriend—the one waiting outside the bar at 2 a.m., begging him to come home. Threats, arguments, tears—they didn't work. He was in too deep, and I was losing him to the very thing we had fought so hard to escape. I was losing myself, too. The late nights, the drugs, the empty promises—it was all too much. We'd make it until the sun came up, high as kites, and I'd wonder how long we could keep pretending this was sustainable.

I became the nag, sure. But was I wrong? Watching someone you love slip back into addiction is like standing on the shore, watching the tide take them out to sea. You can scream, cry, flail—but sometimes, it feels like all you can do is watch them disappear.

In the midst of all this chaos, I found solace in helping Grey Knight's sister, Meghan. She was a single mom, and I admired her resilience. Babysitting her daughter, Prudence, filled me with a joy I hadn't felt in a long time. Watching Mocha and Prudence bond was heartwarming; they were two peas in a pod, and their interactions melted my heart. It painted a vivid picture of what family could look like, and I found myself dreaming of a future with Grey Knight.

Just as I began to find my footing in Wisconsin, I landed an opportunity that reignited my passion. A modeling agency accepted me, and before I knew it, I was cast in a major campaign for US Cellular—Mocha and I, shining across downtown Milwaukee. It was a thrill that reminded me of my dreams, and I couldn't help but feel grateful for this twist of fate.

A few things have changed, and let me tell you, life has this strange way of throwing irony at you when you least expect it. After what felt like a lifetime of late nights and stale tips, I finally put a stop to working at the bar. I wasn't cut out for that world anymore—the chaos, the constant hum of intoxicated chatter, the hollow routine of it all. The fact that it flared up more drama between us—I definitely wanted out. But life, in its unpredictable wisdom, threw me a lifeline, and I grabbed it. I got hired at the best steakhouse in Milwaukee. Can you believe it? It's funny, isn't it? Back in Los Angeles, Grey Knight and I had worked at one of the most renowned steakhouses in the city. And now, somehow, we found ourselves in Wisconsin—of all places—both working at the best two steakhouses in the state.

There's something poetic about that, as if the universe kept nudging us toward these moments of strange symmetry. This job was a lifeboat—a rescue from the turbulent waters I had realized I was drowning in. Stepping into this place felt like slipping into a cozy kitchen where the air is heavy with the smell of sizzling steaks and garlic. It gave me the one thing I hadn't known I was craving: room to breathe. Space to reimagine, to reevaluate. Swapping my old gig for this new one wasn't just about changing restaurants. No, it was like someone hit a cosmic reset button on my sanity. I hadn't realized how deep I'd sunk into the chaotic bar scene until I clawed my way out, gasping for air. Maybe it's the steak fumes clouding my judgment, but my thoughts feel sharper, my body lighter—like my soul had been simmering in the wrong broth for far too long.

And let me tell you, I've found unexpected joy here in Wisconsin, of all places! I never thought I'd say this, but I've grown to love the quirky charm of this Midwestern lifestyle. Working at this restaurant, it's like I've uncovered a hidden gem—a supper club, of all things. It's different from anything I've known before, sure, and the work has its moments, but I've found myself actually *enjoying* it. Who knew?

Now, let's talk about the true revelation: the spirited ice cream drinks! Oh yes, you heard me right. Booze and ice cream, blended into what I can only describe as pure magic in a glass. I mean, c'mon, how could I not fall head over heels for that? These aren't your average cocktails—no, no. These are Midwestern wonders, like the Brandy Alexander and the Grasshopper, glorious concoctions that make your taste buds dance with delight. I loved them so much, I even started whipping them up at home! It's like every sip transports me to a happy place, where ice cream and alcohol swirl together in sweet, boozy perfection.

And speaking of transitions, it's wild how life shifts in ways you don't see coming. I don't even remember what enabled it, but somehow, Grey Knight and I found ourselves moving into the spare bedroom at his parents' house. The kind of move you never think you'll make until you're unpacking your boxes under someone else's roof. It wasn't glamorous, but it was necessary, and maybe in some strange way, it felt like the universe was telling us to slow down. Breathe. Recalibrate. It's funny how life does that sometimes, shoving you back into the arms of family when the ground beneath your feet starts to crack.

But while my mind might have been clearing up, my eyesight wasn't so lucky. I began to notice things, like the way streetlights at night started to blur around the edges, or the way menus at the restaurant became fuzzy in the dim light. It hit me like a punch to the gut—my vision was going downhill, fast. The kind of downhill that makes you question everything. Was it the heroin? The constant strain on my body? I have no idea, but I remember thinking, *This can't be good.* My eyes, my windows to the world, felt foggy, almost as if I was seeing life through a dirty lens. It's terrifying, that realization—that the one thing you depend on most is slipping away, and you're too messed up to know why.

So, I went in for an eye exam—no big deal, right? Well, fast forward to me walking out with a prescription for glasses. Glasses! For the first time in my life. Now, don't get me wrong, I wasn't exactly mad about it. But let me tell you, the second I slid those frames on, my mind went into overdrive. The wheels were turning, and not in a fun, "oh-look-how-smart-I-look" way, either.

Because here's the thing: My eyes didn't start going bad until *after* heroin became the leading actor in the tragic little drama that was my life. Coincidence? Maybe. But in my heart, I can't shake the feeling there's a connection. It's just a theory, mind you, but one that feels like it's been lingering, hiding in the shadows, waiting for the moment I'd finally start to see clearly—literally and metaphorically.

I mean, I guess it could be age. Could be genetics. But nah, something tells me it's deeper than that.

Meanwhile, Grey Knight had his own battles. One of his close friends from high school, Joe, had gotten himself into a mess that was more than just a brush with trouble. This wasn't a speeding ticket or a bad night out—Joe had six felonies hanging over him like a decapitator. Six. I mean, that's the kind of weight that doesn't just crush a person; it pulls the entire family into its orbit of despair. Grey Knight's parents, who had known Joe since he was a kid, were painfully aware of the trouble, the tension practically oozing through the walls of their home. Grey Knight, being who he is, couldn't just sit by and watch his friend spiral out of control. He made it his personal mission to check on Joe, to talk some sense into him—if that was even possible at this point. It was one of those moments where I saw the raw concern in him, the kind of loyalty that runs deep, the kind that makes you realize that no matter how far we fall, there's always someone who wants to pull us back up.

And then there was us. Our relationship, fragile as it was, seemed to be at a breaking point, riddled with insecurities flying in every direction like glass shattering. The weight of it all—the moves, the drugs, the chaos—pressed down on us, and Grey Knight, in all his earnestness, proposed a solution. *Marriage.* He believed, wholeheartedly, that getting married would be the ultimate fix. The thing that would make him feel secure, anchored, safe. It's funny, isn't it? The way we look for these grand gestures, these monumental changes, thinking they'll be the glue that holds everything together. But the truth is, I wasn't so sure.

Chapter 8

A Toast to Trouble

Grey Knight reached out to Joe, eager for a reunion and to finally introduce me as "my girlfriend." One evening, we drove to the modest apartment he shared with his great aunt, a sweet, elderly lady who moved like she was gliding through molasses. As we cruised through the streets, Grey Knight regaled me with tales of Joe, the class clown everyone adored. "He's hilarious!" … "I love someone who can make me laugh!" I chimed in, buoyed by the prospect of meeting such a vibrant personality. But then came the twist: Joe wasn't just funny; he was also a master manipulator with a high IQ, able to charm anyone into doing anything. "He's got a handful of felonies and a hefty addiction to heroin and crack," Grey Knight said, and my jaw nearly hit the floor. "And he lives here rent-free, thanks to his wealthy parents!" I felt a knot of unease tighten in my gut. Great, I thought, I was about to meet the world's most dangerous class clown.

The evening went surprisingly well, but as we left, my protective instincts kicked into overdrive. "I don't want you hanging out with Joe. He's bad news, and he'll drag you down with him!" My voice was surprisingly steady, filled with a crystal-clear urgency. I wasn't trying to be a nag; I was just trying to save Grey Knight from the very storm we had barely weathered together. My intuition was screaming, but it felt like I was talking to a brick wall. He continued to see Joe, and my frustration simmered beneath the surface. I didn't want to be the outsider, so I reluctantly joined their escapades. Before I knew it, we were back on the dark rollercoaster of heroin addiction. How could we resist? Grey Knight, a fellow addict, dove right in, snorting heroin and smoking crack before I even knew what hit us. The euphoric sensation wrapped around us like a long-lost lover, igniting our cravings and reigniting the chaos we thought we'd escaped.

Before I could blink, we found ourselves spiraling deeper into addiction. I watched Joe smoke crack with a mixture of revulsion and intrigue. It felt dirty, but addiction has a way of numbing moral judgments. Instinctively, I joined in, trying my hand at it as well. At first, I couldn't figure out how to smoke it properly, but when I finally did, it was as if the universe cracked open. Joe was certainly the instigator; he embodied that reckless spark we craved. In a sober moment, I can confidently say I've never liked cocaine or crack. But when you pair heroin with crack, it's like a twisted symphony of highs and lows, a dark dance on the edge of chaos. Joe warned me it was the worst combination, but who was I to resist? Each hit was a whirlwind of bliss, a dance on the razor's edge, as we sank into a haze of dependence. Snort, smoke, inhale, repeat. We were back in the throes of addiction, shackled even tighter than before.

Right before we plunged into this rotting hellfire, we decided to get married. Grey Knight had proposed years earlier, but when we rekindled our romance, I hesitated to pick up where we left off. I wanted a fresh proposal, a sign of commitment. But eventually, I agreed; getting married had always been a dream of mine. As soon as I said yes, we shared the news with our families, and excitement bubbled up around us. Most of his family lived nearby, while mine was hugging the west. My mom was the only one who could make it, which made my heart swell with gratitude. We opted for a small, intimate ceremony at Grey Knight's parents' beautiful home, their backyard adorned with the vibrant hues of fall—a perfect backdrop for our October wedding. Fall in Wisconsin was nothing short of breathtaking, with leaves transforming into a kaleidoscope of colors. I was enchanted by the beauty, a far cry from the palm trees of LA.

But as the wedding day approached, I became a nagging, controlling fiancée. I despised this version of myself, but the partying had spiraled out of control. Days before the wedding, I fired off a heartfelt letter to Grey Knight, expressing my frustration and fatigue over sleepless nights of revelry. "If this doesn't stop, I'm not going through with the wedding!" It felt like my breaking point. His loving devotion reassured me that we could work through it. My stepdad, Joey, called to congratulate me but added, "If you have any doubts at all, don't do it!" His words echoed in my mind, and I wrestled with my inner turmoil. Was I ignoring a crucial warning? I had been so swept away in the excitement that I overlooked the little voice whispering, *Grey Knight may not be your happy-ever-after*. But, despite my intuition's cries, I chose to believe in love. After all, I had given him my whole heart, and that's where I wanted to stay.

As if that wasn't enough, we were ring-less the day before the wedding. My mom, sensing the urgency, took us to the mall to replace the original wedding ring. With our funds slim, we ventured into Swarovski, where Grey Knight picked out a stunning crystal ring that sparkled with new beginnings. I beamed, feeling the weight of the moment. Now, we could dive headfirst into the wedding feels.

Yet, the memory of our wedding day is hazy. While we may have put the partying behind us, we immediately slid back into heroin addiction. I remember insisting on having no one in the room while I got ready; I woke up feeling like a fevered ghost, aches and chills radiating through my body. My mom brought me a magical medicine ball tea from Starbucks, hoping to ease my symptoms. As I drank, I felt the sweat of toxins leaving my body, but internally, I sensed it was a warning. Ignoring the signals, I slipped into my wedding dress, did my hair and makeup, and snorted a line of heroin to keep the buzz alive. As I walked down the aisle, I asked Joe, Grey Knight's dad, to escort me. I felt a surge of happiness knowing that Joe was becoming family.

As Ed Sheeran's "Thinking Out Loud" played, I was flooded with emotion. There he stood—my husband-to-be—looking dashing with tears of joy in his eyes. This moment was everything I'd dreamed of. The ceremony unfolded like a scene from a fairytale, filled with laughter and heartfelt vows. Grey Knight began with humor before transitioning into the most touching words I'd ever heard. I thought I was going to cry and shed the happiest tears being overwhelmed by love, but I struggled against the sickness, and potential warning signs coursing through me.

When it was my turn, I handed him my bouquet and read my vows:

You are like nothing else in the world. My Grey Knight, my dream come true. When I'm with you, it's like I'm split in two. Part of me is going crazy because you ignited a fire in my soul that I never knew existed. My other half is peaceful and calm, just perfectly content knowing I found the one who completes me. With you, I found a once-in-a-lifetime love. You are the finest, most courageous, most beautiful person I've ever met, and even that is an understatement. I love the shit out of you, and that is only the beginning... I vow to fiercely love you, now and forever. To always laugh with you & sometimes at you. To have and to plug my nose when you stink. I will give you all the love and support we give our dog, Mocha. I vow to still grab your butt, even when we're old and crusty. To trust you even when we wander off from GPS navigation. No matter what challenges come our way, I'll be Robin, *and you'll be my Batman. I promise to not spend all our money on new clothes. To agree to disagree on football teams and always share my ice cream. I choose you for life. You are my favorite person, my hero, the place I will always call home."*

I was proud of my vows, a mix of humor and heartfelt devotion. The nickname "Grey Knight" fit him perfectly—his favorite color was grey, and I saw him as my knight in shining armor, and Batman being our favorite superhero. The rest of the day was filled with laughter, a long table of loved ones at a local restaurant, and plenty of photos in the stunning fall landscape. We were goofy and loving, capturing memories that would last a lifetime.

Yet, a few things felt missing. For one, we skipped the traditional bride-and-groom dance—a staple at weddings! Secondly, there was absolutely no intimacy that night. Yes, I'll say it: no sex. With heroin coursing through our veins, our physical connection felt like a distant memory. Still, strolling through the autumn scenery for photos was blissful. We were a photogenic pair, capturing both silliness and stunning moments.

Later, we hit the bars with Ted and his boyfriend, celebrating our "Just Married" status with strangers who showered us with free shots. For me, it was less about the booze and more about the excitement of being newlyweds. We danced and laughed, the chaos of the night wrapping around us like a warm embrace. All in all, October 17, 2018, was the most simple, yet best day of my life. Sure, there were uneasy emotions lurking beneath the surface, but the joy of marrying my Grey Knight was everything I had ever wanted.

Chapter 9

Till Jail Do Us Part

Two weeks after the wedding, I found myself in a situation I never imagined. Picture this: I'd be at the gym with Grey Knight, pretending everything was fine, but secretly sneaking off to the bathroom, phone in hand, to call my mom. My voice would crack, tears streaming down my face as I'd sob, "Mom, I made a big mistake!" The reality of my rushed decision to get married was suffocating me. It felt like the universe, or whatever higher power governs this chaos we call life, was screaming through me, asking why I'd ignored my intuition. Why had I shut down that little voice inside me that had been whispering, then shouting, *Don't do this*?

I'd find every excuse to call my mom, whenever I could carve out a moment of solitude, crying into the phone about the overwhelming sense that something bad—something catastrophic—was looming over me. I couldn't bring myself to explain the details to her then. I was trapped in this swirling mess of nerves and fear, knowing deep down that Grey Knight's increasingly frequent interactions with Joe were setting the stage for something dangerous. Joe, a figure who at first seemed peripheral, was suddenly always around. And then, out of nowhere, Grey Knight lost his high-paying job at the steakhouse. The excuse was flimsy, but the real problem, hidden from his manager, was that he was spiraling deeper into drug use. With no job, no income, and a growing addiction, the pressure mounted.

We weren't paying rent because we were staying at his parents' house, but that just meant more money for drugs. It wasn't just my mom who got to hear me unravel over the phone—there was also Isaiah, my friend from college. Occasionally, I'd secretly redownload Instagram just to send him a desperate message. One night, when the frustration in my relationship boiled over, I packed my things and moved out. That night, I called Isaiah, begging him for help, but even though he offered—he was even ready to buy me a plane ticket home—I couldn't bring myself to accept it. I wanted to escape, but I couldn't. I felt relief hearing his voice, but also guilt. How could I leave when I was part of this mess? I couldn't even tell him the full truth, not that I was using heroin myself.

Then there was Joe's "solution." Grey Knight fell under his mentorship, and it wasn't the kind of guidance anyone would want. Joe had this system—a way to fund their habit. They'd steal expensive tools from places like Home Depot and Fleet Farm, then turn around and sell them on Facebook Marketplace for quick cash. That cash would go straight to the dealer, and the toxic cycle would start again. It was dizzying how quickly this became our new routine. And that gut feeling I'd had, the one telling me that something terrible was coming? It was right. I could feel the weight of it pressing down on me as we sunk deeper into this criminal lifestyle.

At first, Grey Knight tried to hide it from me, sneaking around with Joe, as if I wouldn't notice. But I wasn't blind. I have sharp instincts—I knew what was going on. Besides, when your husband's not in bed at 3 a.m., it's not hard to put two and two together. The thing is, I wasn't just mad because he was out stealing. I was mad because he was out getting high without me. It's twisted, I know. But when addiction has its claws in you, rational thought goes out the window. When he disappeared, I'd be left at his parents' house, scrambling to come up with excuses when they asked where he was. Lying to his parents, who were nothing but kind to me, made me feel like the lowest form of human. Eventually, with enough of me complaining, Grey Knight started bringing me along on their "missions."

And so, sleepless nights became our new normal. I'd sit in the car while Grey Knight and Joe were inside, lifting tools from shelves. We'd bounce from one store to the next, trying not to look suspicious, posting items online, meeting buyers, and then racing off to meet dealers. We drove to some of the sketchiest neighborhoods imaginable, where I'd sit alone in the car, my nerves frayed, wondering if we'd make it out alive. Occasionally, we'd hit a dry spell—money running low, tolerance through the roof—and the detox would begin. The cravings gnawed at us, leaving us edgy and frantic. I hated Joe at first. But after a while, I just accepted it. This was my life now.

My dog, Mocha—my intended beacon in the unyielding darkness—often found sanctuary at her parents' house. The pang of guilt for leaving her behind was a constant, throbbing ache in my chest, yet I remained profoundly grateful that she had a haven untouched by our toxic energy. To Grey Knight's mom and dad, my eternal thanks for cradling our little firefly during those tempestuous days. When she wasn't embraced by their gentle care, she was with us, and in our chaotic realm, she was never truly alone.

Mocha was much more than a pet; she was our steadfast accomplice on every madcap adventure. Whether we were meandering through shadowy back alleys in search of dubious dealers, cruising through neighborhoods that whispered of danger, or daringly tagging along on impulsive store heists, she was there—her bright eyes absorbing the riot of our world, where even the air reeked of drugs and desperation. Every memory of those toxic days pricks at my heart, yet amidst the chaos, her angelic spirit was the spark that ignited my will to rise. It was as if she whispered, without words, that life—despite its brutality—was still worth fighting for.

In the midst of our spiraling madness, Mocha's unwavering love was a bittersweet elixir, a silent promise that even in our darkest moments, joy and love could still be found. With her by my side, I learned to laugh at the absurdity of it all, and in those stolen, tender moments, her very presence transformed despair into a wild, fierce determination to *WAKE THE HELL UP* and reclaim the person I once was.

There were nights when we'd sleep in the car, afraid to go home. One of those nights stands out to me like a bruise that never fades. Grey Knight and I sat in the dark, and for once, we talked—not just the surface-level stuff, but the raw, painful truth. We were exhausted, emotionally wrung out from the nightmare we'd been living. We had reached the lowest point, far lower than I'd ever thought possible. We hadn't just hit rock bottom—we'd built a home there.

Through tears, Grey Knight confessed how much he hated what we'd become, and how sorry he was for dragging me into it. I cried, too, but not just from sorrow. I told him how, somehow, despite everything, I'd fallen even more in love with him. And he had, too. It didn't make sense. How could I feel that way in the middle of this madness? But it was true. We had sunk to the lowest of lows, but it had also shown me how unbreakable we were. No matter how bad things got—no matter how much we hurt ourselves and each other—we stayed. We clung to each other like survivors of a shipwreck, our love the only thing keeping us from drowning completely.

But I was drowning in other ways. I didn't recognize myself anymore. Heroin had turned me into someone else. I'd lost myself somewhere in the haze, and it scared me. Yet somehow, even through the chaos, our love survived. It was wild, wasn't it? How could something so destructive also bring us closer? We barely made love anymore, but it didn't matter. The bond we had, twisted as it was, ran deeper than anything I'd ever felt. We even dared to dream of a future together, one where we'd pull ourselves out of this mess and make something better. But deep down, I wasn't sure I believed it.

Inside me, a war raged—a tempest of conflicting emotions. On one side, my angelic self still saw beauty in the world, clinging to the belief in love, in Grey Knight, and in the notion that together we could conquer anything. *"Us against the world"* became our rallying cry throughout the dark days of addiction. Despite the perils that lurked in every shadow, Grey Knight always stepped forward with unwavering courage, protecting me as I, in turn, became his steadfast rock. We were each other's anchor in a storm that threatened to swallow us whole.

Yet, beneath that fragile bastion of hope festered a newly birthed darkness—a bitter, smoldering anger that had taken root within me. I loathed everything that had led us to this point: the shattered dreams, the abandoned career, the life that seemed like a distant memory. I despised being ensnared in addiction and complicit in a lifestyle that spiraled into criminal chaos. What began as a quiet seed of resentment had exploded into a raging inferno, fed by heroin and crack, cigarettes, and a relentless despair, transforming us into gaunt, hollow figures, teetering on the brink of our own undoing.

And yet, I never let that fury find its voice. I swallowed it whole, tucking it away in the darkest corners of my soul, and warriored on. In that silent struggle lay a defiant, bittersweet melody—a reminder that even amidst the chaos, hope could still flicker.

In the end, I always chose love. But at what cost?

It had been over a month since my expected payday for the US Cellular print ad, and I was caught in a whirlwind of excitement and fear. If you don't know, in the world of acting and print work, it's standard to be paid within 30 days after a shoot. That paycheck felt like a beacon of hope—until we plunged back into hell with drugs. Suddenly, the excitement was gone, replaced by a gnawing dread. I was scared out of my mind. Unlike the boys who had embraced petty theft as their means to fuel their habits, I was, by some cruel twist of fate, the only one holding down a legitimate job. Every hard-earned dollar I made was funneled straight into the insatiable vortex of our addiction—a self-imposed irony I could neither escape nor deny.

If I didn't willingly lend out my cash for our next fix, it wasn't long before Grey Knight, ever the mischievous partner in crime, would swipe my card and pull a withdrawal without my permission. My paycheck from that humble print job? Gone in the blink of an eye, devoured by the whirlwind of our self-destruction before I could even savor its arrival.

I had always prided myself on being the responsible one—meticulously managing my money, my phone, my every resource—yet fate had a wicked sense of humor, leaving me utterly powerless. Imagine thinking you're the master of your own universe, only to have the rug pulled out from under you in one savage moment.

Enter Grey Knight, my charming bandit, whose relentless habit of filching my hard-earned cash made my days feel like a perpetual con. Somewhere along our misadventures in Wisconsin, he lost his phone for good, a bizarre twist that rendered him completely dependent on my device. Every secret drug deal, every sneaky meeting, every call to family or friend had to go through me, like I was the unwitting gatekeeper of his chaotic world.

Now, despite being officially bound together—he and I, a duo stitched so tightly that our lives were inextricably intertwined—the irony was almost laughable. Our forced intimacy felt like an absurd, claustrophobic dance, where every step was haunted by a creeping fear. Each day, dread gnawed at my mind until I found myself swallowing my guilt, my terror, and that inescapable sense of being trapped, bottling it all up like a ticking time bomb waiting to shatter.

And yet, amid the relentless chaos, I couldn't help but find a perverse, dark humor in our predicament—a twisted comedy where responsibility and rebellion waltzed hand in hand. It was as if I'd become the unwilling ringmaster in a circus of misfortune, where every act was a maddening blend of passion, absurdity, and heartache.

This chaotic lifestyle carried on for a solid two months until that one unforgettable night. Joe had convinced Grey Knight to take things to the next level in their criminal ventures. A hotel under construction was ripe for the picking—tools, copper, all sorts of valuables. I was sick of being left out, so I tagged along, bringing Mocha with me for company, my little slice of sanity. We parked near the site, and I stayed in the car with Mocha while the boys disappeared into the trees. I distracted myself with my phone, wondering how long they'd be gone. After what felt like ages, they returned. Nothing major happened that night, but the gears were already turning in their heads. They planned to go back the next day.

When the night rolled around, they waited until the early hours—around 3 a.m.—to make their move. I stayed at Joe's place with Mocha, trying to keep my mind occupied with TV while they executed their plan. Grey Knight, as always, borrowed my phone since he didn't have his own. I had my iPad to stay in touch with him, but as the hours dragged on, I fell asleep. When I woke up, it was to Grey Knight standing over me, his face a mix of exhaustion and pain. He'd hurt himself—possibly broken something—but, in true Grey Knight fashion, he toughed it out. No doctors, no insurance, no help. Just pure grit.

The sun was rising as they rushed to the car, hauling bags filled with stolen goods. Joe barked at me to help unload, and in a panic, I grabbed whatever I could—heavy bags, coils of wire—barely comprehending what I was involved in. Everything was stashed in Joe's garage, their little treasure trove of stolen items. But Joe's paranoia kicked in hard. He started freaking out, convinced the cops were on their way, all because of some security cameras at his parents' place. Did they see us unloading the car? Did they rat us out? The tension in the room was suffocating. Grey Knight pulled me aside and told me to get Mocha and go to the car. As I walked outside, my heart skipped a beat.

A black car pulled up in front of me, and men in bulletproof vests stepped out. My stomach dropped. "Are you Haley?" one of them asked. I nodded, my heart pounding in my chest. I had a stash of heroin hidden in my wallet. I was terrified. The detective explained that they had been watching Joe for a while and assured me I was just a witness. Relief washed over me—until they found the heroin in my wallet. *Fuck.* I was screwed. They took it, of course, but let me go with them to the station. I watched as Grey Knight and Joe were arrested, my heart breaking, knowing things would never be the same.

Walking into the police station was terrifying. The fear of the unknown hung over me like a dark cloud, but part of me felt "okay" with it, if that makes any sense. I was a witness, like they said. At least, that's what I told myself as I sat there waiting to be interviewed, my stomach doing somersaults. The cops were friendly enough, even let me charge my phone, while the guys? Well, they were already behind bars, waiting their turn for questioning. Thank God for small mercies. I wasn't behind bars—yet. I felt oddly relieved, despite getting caught with possession.

Then, my in-laws showed up. I had to hand Mocha, my baby, over to them, and that's when it really hit me. The cops were still being kind, letting me release her to his parents, but the look on their faces… broke me. Heavy tears streamed down my cheeks. I couldn't hold back, not for one more second. It was that sinking, gut-wrenching feeling—*Is this it? Is my life over?*

Eventually, I got called into the interrogation room. Detective Jeffrey Griffin, that's the guy who would be interviewing me, introduced himself, and when he heard my name, his entire vibe shifted. Turns out, he's got a daughter named Haley, too. I saw it in his eyes—instantly, he had a soft spot for me. It was a weird comfort in the most uncomfortable moment of my life.

I had never been in a room like that before. Not even close. Just moments earlier, all of us had done heroin together. My mind was spinning.

I didn't know what to say, or even what not to say. I was totally drained and weak in every sense of the word. So, I just answered his questions. One by one. Slowly. I could feel him digging deeper, each question cutting closer to the mess that had unraveled over the last two chaotic months—dates, situations, specifics.

Then, out of nowhere, Grey Knight stormed by the room, handcuffed and furious. He shouted at me with this wild, protective aggression. He wanted to protect me, I know that. But he scared the hell out of me, too, and watching him get aggressive with the cops? It was horrifying.

I admit it—I didn't know better. I didn't know what I was doing. But with Officer Griffin, I didn't hold anything back. I was an open book, spilling every detail he asked for. And after that terrifying episode with Grey, the detective's energy shifted again. He started playing this weird father-figure role. When I broke down, sobbing about how I wanted to leave Grey Knight, it was like the floodgates had opened. Tears poured out of me like a dam had burst, releasing every bit of pain and fear that had been bottled up for months.

And there he was—this tough, no-nonsense detective—suddenly turning soft. Stern, but soft. He saw right through me, past the mess, into whatever innocence was still clinging to me. Every time we talked about Grey, he became protective, almost gentle, urging me to leave him. But the questions? The interrogation was still brutal and relentless. He wanted every detail—dates, events, the whole sordid timeline.

That's when I learned something that knocked the wind out of me. Apparently, sitting in the car while they were out stealing tools made me a party to the crime. My head nearly exploded. I mean, *fuck*! Why had I done that?! All because I didn't want to be alone? Because I thought I needed Grey and Joe around to feel safe while getting heroin? I confessed to a crime I didn't even know I had committed. The look on my face must have said it all because Officer Griffin could see I was clueless. But still, ignorance didn't make it okay.

I gave him everything. Every single, agonizing detail. I poured out the last few months of my life, the tangled web of lies, addiction, and desperation.

When it was all over, Griffin thanked me and said I had been a huge help to their investigation—mostly about Joe, but also a bit about Grey Knight.

Once the questioning was done, they shipped us off to another county's station. This time, though, they put handcuffs on *me*. I thought my world had already fallen apart, but this? This was the final blow. The weight of those cuffs felt like my soul had been ripped out of my body. It was unbearable. I couldn't breathe. And again, they put us in separate cop cars. Grey Knight and I locked eyes through the windows, unable to speak, trying to communicate with nothing but our gazes. He was trying to console me, but it was heart-wrenching. Sweet, yes, but gut-wrenching all the same.

The sky was already bruised with darkness, and the air felt heavy, almost like it was pressing down on us, reminding me that this was real. No way to escape it. We all got booked in, and the process felt surreal, like I was watching someone else live my nightmare. Fingerprints and mugshots, the removal of jewelry, all the tedious documentation—the whole humiliating process. But this time, there was no interrogation. None of those glaring lights or detectives with their rehearsed intimidation tactics. It was eerily quiet, and maybe that's what made it worse—like the calm before the storm.

One moment, though, hit me like a punch to the gut. They asked me to take off my wedding ring. I can still feel that sharp twist in my heart when I handed it over. It was just a piece of metal to them, but to me, it was everything. That ring symbolizes devotion, love, a bond I couldn't even begin to describe. Now, it was gone—separated from me like I'd been separated from everything else in my life. A reminder of everything we had been through. Now it was gone, and so was I. And in that cold police station, my soul felt sucked dry. Would I ever get it back? Or had I just lost another part of myself in this downward spiral?

Hours dragged on, and after what felt like an eternity, we were released as it was creeping into the early hours of the next day. I was physically and emotionally drained. My phone clung to life at a measly 10%, barely hanging on as I dialed Ted for a rescue. We were homeless—Grey Knight's parents had made it painfully clear we weren't welcome back. No place to go. And to top it all off, the heroin had burned through my system, and the withdrawals were gnawing at me from the inside. I could feel the detox slamming into me like a freight train, and the anxiety of finding a way home was suffocating.

And here we are—just me and my phone, clinging desperately to its dwindling battery as if it were the last vestige of hope in a world gone mad. If this wasn't the very definition of living on the edge, then I don't know what is.

The withdrawals were an unrelenting beast, growing fiercer as the night deepened, wrapping me in a cloak of despair that made every second stretch into an eternity. In that midnight hour of torment, I reached out to Ted—a name that, in that moment, sounded like salvation incarnate. When he answered, thank God, his voice cut through the chaos like a lighthouse beam, offering refuge for the night. A sliver of hope, fragile yet vital, in a storm that seemed determined never to end.

But just when I thought I had things under control, my phone betrayed me. I was mid-Uber request when the screen went black. Dead. Gone. We had no way of leaving the station. Panic surged. We begged the front desk to use their phone to call a cab, which they reluctantly allowed. For a while, though, we were stuck there, freaking out over whether we'd be able to leave this godforsaken place and, worse, what would happen if the detox took us down before we found a way out.

When the cab finally came, we slid into the backseat, but the anxiety didn't end. Watching that taxi meter climb felt like watching my life unravel in real time. I had $35 to my name—literally all I had left in the world. The tension was unbearable. *What if we couldn't pay? What if we ended up stranded with nothing?* Every second felt like a gamble. Somehow, by some miracle, we made it to Ted's, and I just about died of relief when I realized we had barely enough to cover the fare. No tip, but at least we weren't going to be thrown out onto the street.

As I handed over the cash, the realization hit me like a ton of bricks. I had officially hit zero. Actually, scratch that—I was a few hundred dollars in the negative thanks to Grey Knight draining my account. It was insane, truly. How had we managed to keep ourselves afloat this long, balancing on the thin edge between total financial ruin and fueling our addiction? It boggles the mind how we scraped by, living in and out of bankruptcy like it was some twisted game we couldn't quit. But being convicted… that was the final blow. The cherry on top of the wreckage.

When we pulled up to Ted's house, it was early morning—one of those eerie, quiet times when the world is barely waking up, and you feel like you're the only person alive. We didn't even speak as we walked inside, just dragged ourselves to the spare bedroom and collapsed into the bed. There was nothing left in us but exhaustion, desperation, and the looming shadow of detox. No money. No home. No car. No Mocha. Absolutely nothing, except for Ted's kindness, giving us a place to crash. And I mean it when I say *thank heavens for that*, because without him, we'd be lost. Homeless again.

The moment we sank into that bed, it was like the weight of the world crashed down on us. For three days, we didn't leave that room. Not once. Well, except for the occasional stumble to the bathroom. The pain was unbearable, but the worst part was the emptiness, the nothingness that consumed me. Ted brought us water every now and then, but other than that, it was just us—sweating, shaking, groaning through the detox. Every pore in my body was screaming, leaking out the poison we'd willingly put in, and all we could think was, *This is what rock bottom feels like.*

We twisted and turned, soaked the sheets with our misery, and battled insomnia like it was the devil himself. There's nothing romantic about detox. It's ugly. It's raw. And it's real. Every second felt like a slow death. My heart, my soul, my everything was empty. What was next? How do you even begin to recover from this kind of devastation?

Then, a pivotal moment arrived. My mother-in-law, Michelle, called me. She told me she was coming to get me, just me. Not Grey Knight. Confused but too exhausted to ask, I cleaned myself up as best as I could and waited. When she arrived, I assumed I'd be seeing Grey Knight soon, so I didn't say goodbye. Little did I know, my life was about to change forever.

Michelle dropped the bomb. My parents had worked with Officer Griffin. If I left Wisconsin and went back to California, all charges against me would be dropped. My world spun. My two suitcases were packed, and there was a flight waiting for me in two hours. I was leaving. Tears streamed down my face as the reality set in. I never said goodbye to Grey Knight. I just left. It felt like I was abandoning him, but deep down, I knew it was the right thing to do.

At the airport, they brought out a wheelchair for me. At first, I was shocked. I didn't need a wheelchair, did I? But as soon as I sat down, I realized how weak I was. Detoxing had drained every ounce of strength from me. Mocha, thank God, was allowed to fly with me, her service dog card saving the day. My in-laws walked me all the way to the plane, and as I sat there, waiting for takeoff, I felt a mixture of relief and devastation. I was going home—but I was leaving everything behind.

Landing in Sacramento, my heart felt like it had been swapped for a brick—heavy, unmovable, sinking lower with every breath. Five years. *Five long, messy, beautiful, heartbreaking years.* Gone in the blink of an eye, like someone had hit fast-forward on a movie I wasn't ready to stop watching. The love of my life had slipped through my fingers, and now, here I was, touching down in a city that felt both familiar and foreign, carrying nothing but my luggage and the weight of everything I'd just lost.

My mom and stepdad, Joey, were waiting for me. Despite everything, I felt a sense of comfort in seeing them. Joey, always the jokester, cracked a line that made me laugh for the first time in months. "Smeagol!" he called out, comparing my gaunt, pale appearance to the twisted creature from *Lord of the Rings*. It was a silly, lighthearted joke, but in that moment, it felt like a lifeline. It was the first real laugh I'd had in so long, and it reminded me that maybe—just maybe—I wasn't entirely lost.

But as we drove away from the airport, Mocha in my lap, I couldn't help but wonder what was next. How would I recover from this? How would I move on from the chaos I left behind? The answers were unclear, but for the first time in what felt like forever, I had a glimmer of hope. I was with family. I was going home.

ACT III

The Bloom She Built

✦ ✦ ✦

They mistook her softness for weakness.
They didn't see the steel in her petals.
She rose from ruin with grace sharp enough to cut.
Every scar became a color.
Every heartbreak, a layer of gold.
She didn't stumble into power.
She designed it, petal by petal,
until the bloom became the crown

Chapter 10

Cold Turkey in the Foothills

They moved me into their home, and it was strange—a sort of reset button I didn't ask for but desperately needed. You see, I had never actually lived with my mom and stepdad before. Only visited on weekends when I could tolerate the slow, sleepy town of Foresthill, a place that seemed so distant from the world I knew. My mom had moved here for peace of mind, a healthier life tucked away in the foothills, but me? I craved the pulse of civilization, the noise, the rush. Still, despite all that, this was a different kind of move. One I had to make, for my own good, for survival. It broke my heart to be thousands of miles away from my husband, but it was necessary. No more drugs, no more dangerous situations.

But man, was I weak. *Weak* doesn't even cover it. I felt like I was collapsing inward, a shell of a person. Sweating bullets one second, freezing like I was stuck on some Arctic ice floe the next. There wasn't a smile left in me, no matter how hard I tried to force one. That first shower back? Jaw-dropping, and not in a good way. Joey had been right—I was white as a ghost, skin and bones, barely a person. Thirty pounds gone in three days of detoxing in that Wisconsin apartment, just me, the bed, and the struggle to stay alive. When I stepped on that scale, one hundred and ten pounds stared back at me. For someone standing at five-seven, that's not just thin—it's unhealthy. I didn't fit in any of my clothes, and I had to face the cold reality of what I'd done to myself.

First order of business, though, was proving I was back, alive, and kicking. My mom snapped a photo to send to the detective as proof I was home safe in California. You should see that picture—I looked like a ghost, a shadow of myself, with eyes that had sunken into my skull and a forced grin that didn't fool anyone. But I was there, I was alive, and I made sure to call Officer Griffin myself. I thanked him for his help, and with that formality done, the real work could begin.

My parents were gentle with me but direct. They had every right to ask the tough questions and to give me a full-on earful of lectures. After all, my personal hurricane had just wreaked havoc on their peaceful life. The biggest question they had, though? "Are you going back to Grey Knight?" And that's where the inner battle began. I loved him. God, I loved him more than anything. But I had to face the hard truth. "No," I told them, though it killed me inside. I had to put myself first for once, and saying that out loud felt like ripping my heart out. But there was no going back—not to him, not to the life we had. It hurt like hell, but I knew it was the right thing to do.

There's no better way to put it—I was dead inside. It might sound dramatic, even impossible to imagine, but I had *no idea* who I was anymore. Zero. My identity had been wiped clean, like a chalkboard, after years of scribbling nonsense. Sure, I was still grappling with detox, and those three days in bed with my husband? Absolute hell. But I had no clue what was coming after that. I felt soulless, just a body existing in the world, as if something essential had been scraped out of me and replaced with nothing.

Withdrawal depression wasn't a choice—I never purposely leaned into those crushing, inevitable feelings that came with detox. It was as if my body and mind, in a silent rebellion, forced me to face a raw, unfiltered emptiness. I found myself grappling with a new breed of sorrow, one that wasn't about reliving past regrets but simply the unavoidable cost of breaking free from a hellfire I'd long endured.

In a desperate bid for solace, I clung to the belief that I was finally far removed from the chaos—a sanctuary among family where I should feel safe. Yet, this depression was unlike anything I'd known before: a deep, relentless numbness that left me questioning everything, even in the comfort of familiar arms. The irony was palpable—a secure haven on the outside, while inside, an uncharted void threatened to swallow me whole.

Amid the silence of that inner storm, faint whispers rose like a murmur against the void, urging me to "warrior up" and grant myself grace. They were a subtle rebuttal to the harsh realities of detox, a reminder that there was a damn good reason I was still here instead of dead. Even as I struggled with this profound, heart-wrenching melancholy, those whispered urgings lingered, leaving me to wonder: What does it truly mean to rediscover who I am?

I'd lost a lot of weight, but that didn't seem to matter. I was always freezing, like I was trapped in some Arctic wasteland where no amount of clothing and body fat could warm me up. And my energy? Nonexistent. I was drained beyond empty, barely able to move. My days were spent huddled on the couch, wrapped in a blanket, only getting up to go to the bathroom. I couldn't even summon the joy I usually felt for Mocha, my sweet, loving dog. And that, for me, was the final, gut-wrenching validation of how far I'd fallen. I mean, dogs are magical, aren't they? Four-legged bundles of unconditional love, and Mocha? She's been my baby for four years. She fills me with happiness just by existing. But I couldn't lift a finger for her. I couldn't give her a single scrap of affection, and it *destroyed* me.

I needed her love more than anything in those moments, but I couldn't even take care of her, much less myself. I could barely *move*, let alone speak or function. Still, Mocha knew. She could sense it, the pain radiating off me. She'd snuggle up close, lick my face, trying to comfort me in the way only dogs know how. And it broke my heart even more to see her trying when I had nothing to give back.

Thankfully, my parents picked up the slack and took care of her, which—if you really think about it—tells you just how *gone* I was. Every day, though, the symptoms started to ease, bit by bit. But sleep? That was the cruelest part. I barely slept at all. Those first few days, I didn't get a wink of it. The next two weeks were pure torture—maybe an hour or two of sleep here and there, but I'd spend most nights tossing and turning in my bed, a bed that should've been the epitome of comfort, and yet… nothing. My mind was spinning, racing through every painful memory, every mistake. Grey Knight was still a phantom in my thoughts, his absence gnawing at me, making me cry into my pillow, missing him so much it hurt.

I cried *constantly*, worrying about him, about us. I felt like I was falling apart in slow motion. And the strangest part? Despite the insomnia, I didn't feel tired in the traditional sense. My body was weak, yes, but I wasn't sleepy. I was stuck in this limbo of exhaustion without rest. And eating? Forget about it. I had to force myself to even look at food, let alone eat it. Slowly, painfully, I worked my way up to a meal again. By the two-week mark, I finally managed to shovel down something halfway decent. I even tried smoking a cigarette, thinking it might help with the recovery, but Joey—my stepdad—wasn't having it. And guess what? He was right. It tasted revolting, instantly transporting me back to the days of chain-smoking with heroin and crack. So, I tossed them out. Good riddance. It was all part of the slow, painful process of recovery. Another reminder of how far I'd fallen, and how far I still had to climb.

During those early weeks back in California, living with my parents, my whole world felt like it had been shattered. Trying to rebuild my soul from the ground up? That was the weirdest, most surreal experience of my life. But the simple truth? I'd been given a second chance. That's what I kept telling myself—*This is your second chance at life.* First, I had to let the detox symptoms run their course, and only then could I start rediscovering who Haley really was.

One little blessing? That payday I had been waiting on? It came through, and suddenly, I wasn't in the red anymore. My account had more money than I'd seen in months, and it felt like a sign, like I had a second chance. I was incredibly grateful, like the stars were aligning just for me. My guardian angels, watching over me.

But then came the bad news. I checked in with my mother-in-law, Michelle, and Grey Knight's best friend, Ted. Apparently, the moment I got picked up from Ted's place? That was also the moment Grey Knight stole money from him and fled. Just ran off. My heart stopped. I could barely breathe. The thought of my husband, the man I loved, out there on the streets, was too much to bear. Where did he go? How was he even finding heroin without a phone? He'd been using mine for months.

It was obvious—he was back at the trap house, living on the streets, relapsing. The thought of my husband out there, homeless, wrecked me. Michelle and Joe eventually found him and gave him a blanket and some clothes. But the damage was done. My tears fell like bullets, and I wailed like a child. My husband, living on the streets? How had it come to this?

A few days later, Michelle told me Grey Knight had been arrested. Again, I broke down, sobbing as my heart shattered all over again. He'd been caught stealing a woman's purse, another felony to add to the list. Michelle, bless her, tried to calm me down with her gentle, loving voice. She told me this was for the best—he'd be safe, off the streets, forced to get sober. And you know what? She wasn't wrong. Grey Knight spent a week in jail, and when he got out, he called me.

Hearing his voice, seeing his face on FaceTime? My soul soared with relief. He looked more like the man I fell in love with, the sober version of Grey Knight. He told me he was checking into rehab, and I could finally breathe again. But even then, hearing all of this from thousands of miles away, with no way of reaching him—it tore me apart. I wanted nothing more than to be there for him, to help the love of my life through this. But all I could do was trust that he'd find his way.

Joey, bless him, agreed with me—I didn't need rehab. Not for addiction, anyway. I wasn't an addict, not in the traditional sense. I was a person who had lost herself and been influenced by someone else's demons. Rehab wasn't the answer, not for me. What I needed was time to figure out who I was without the drugs, without the chaos, without Grey Knight. No, this was my battle, and I was going to face it my way.

Still, I had to keep moving forward. I had to keep trying to find myself again. So, I made a decision: I needed to get away. Los Angeles was calling, and I had the means to answer. My parents weren't thrilled with the idea of me flying off to LA so soon after coming home, but they understood. I needed this. They even took me shopping, since none of my clothes fit anymore, and off I went, two weeks back in California and already on a plane.

The weekend in LA was everything I needed to rediscover parts of myself I thought I'd lost, a perfect cocktail of energy, excitement, and a dash of magic. Just touching down in that sprawling, sun-kissed city felt like my soul exhaling for the first time in months. Los Angeles—where the air itself is electrified with ambition—pulled me back to life. The buzz of the city, the familiar faces, the industry hustle… it all began to stir something deep inside me.

My time was blissfully full—reconnecting with friends, whether we were chilling, hitting the town, or grabbing a bite. It felt like a reunion with parts of myself that had been dormant, waiting for this moment to stretch out and breathe again. And then, of course, there was *the* photoshoot. Ah, modeling, my first love. I had arranged it with Kevin, my favorite photographer. I hadn't stepped in front of the camera in what felt like a lifetime, and let me tell you, I was rusty. A little jittery even. You know that feeling when you step back into something that used to feel like second nature but now feels a bit foreign? That was me. But once we got started, oh man, the fire reignited in ways I hadn't expected.

There was something magical happening behind that lens. The nervousness melted away, replaced by pure adrenaline and joy. I mean, I knew it would be fun—getting back in front of the camera always is—but this was deeper. This was *important*. It was like something inside me whispered, *This is where you belong.* The photoshoot was art. Pure art. We created something beautiful that reignited not just my passion for modeling, but my whole spirit. And if that wasn't enough, Isaiah had a spec commercial idea brewing, so we shot that, too. Another layer of creativity sparked within me. Modeling, acting— it was everything my soul had been starving for without me even realizing it.

But the most poignant moment wasn't even in front of the camera. It was that first night, sitting across from Isaiah over dinner. There's something about those late-night conversations, the ones that happen after long stretches of absence, where you feel safe enough to peel back your layers. And peel back, I did. I told him everything. The past five months. The hiding out in Wisconsin. The MIA status. All of it. He listened, really listened, and then offered something that hit me like a lightning bolt. "Date yourself." Those two words. They stuck. Because, honestly, the thought of letting someone new in felt impossible, like rebuilding a house after a hurricane had swept through. I wasn't ready for that—not even close. I needed time, space, and healing.

The weekend came and went in a whirlwind of creativity, connection, and self-discovery, and before I knew it, I was back in the foothills of Northern California. As I stepped back into my quiet life, I reached out to a few close friends, downloaded my social media apps again, and reconnected with the "world" at large. But, something inside me had shifted. That trip to LA wasn't just fun—it was a wake-up call. It was a reminder of who I am and what I'm passionate about. I fell back in love with LA. I knew, without a doubt, I had to return. LA wasn't finished with me, and I wasn't finished with it.

Of course, my parents had their questions. "What's next? What's the plan?" I didn't have answers for them. No car, no job, just the sensation that I had been spiritually and literally reborn. The future was this vast, open field, and I had no map. Yet, I wasn't scared. Not this time. And just like that, the universe threw me another lifeline. A friend from San Diego—Arianna—offered to drive up and help me move down there. San Diego! Only one stop away from LA, which was perfect. It was like the universe was orchestrating my journey back to where I needed to be.

Here comes the kicker—before I was set to jet off to San Diego, a letter arrived that turned my world upside down. Out of the blue, I received a court summons, a notice to appear in just a few weeks. WHAT?! I was stunned. I'd always believed that Officer Griffin had practically saved me from this mess—after all, I was convinced he'd dropped the charges thanks to some secret deal struck with my mom.

Fueled by a cocktail of disbelief and desperate curiosity, I chased him down, peppering him with questions about that bizarre court order. Yet his words were nothing more than elusive whispers—vague hints that deepened the mystery rather than cleared it. My young, fragile soul was left spinning in a whirlwind of uncertainty, trapped in a web of unanswered questions. I couldn't afford to bolt at the last minute, so with a heavy heart and a mind adrift in enigmas, I set the whole matter aside—clinging to the absurd hope that, somehow, fate would step in and untangle this knot.

Two weeks later, Arianna arrived. We packed up my things, loaded her car, and with my dog, Mocha, by my side, I said goodbye to my parents' house. It was time. Time to leave the nest and fly again.

So, here I am, wings spread wide, catching the wind, moving forward into whatever comes next. San Diego is just the next stop on this wild ride. But LA? It's waiting for me. And I'll be back, stronger and more alive than ever.

Chapter 11

Confessions at a Speakeasy

New city, new me—or at least that's what I kept telling myself. As much as I loved my family and appreciated their support, there was a sense of restriction that clung to me whenever I was home. Moving away again felt like the first deep breath I'd taken in what seemed like forever. The detox symptoms had finally subsided, thank God, and my body was inching its way back to some kind of normal. I felt like a warrior, battle-scarred but ready to reclaim my power, to rediscover myself in this new chapter of life. Southern California may not have been Los Angeles—my ultimate dream—but hey, a few skips away felt close enough. I saw it as more of a retreat than anything, a brief pause before I threw myself back into the hustle. But more than that, it was a chance to confront my demons head-on.

After everything I had been through, burying my trauma under layers of numbness wasn't going to work anymore. Suppressing my pain had always been my forte—I could probably write a manual on it—but this time was different. The nightmare I had just crawled out of? It still felt too raw, too surreal. It was like waking up from a bad dream and finding the monsters still lurking in the corners of my mind. But I was standing. Barely, maybe, but standing nonetheless. No one else knew the hell I had just walked through, and that's how I wanted it for now.

San Diego felt like a soft landing—at least at first. There was one friend, Arianna, who helped me ease into things. We weren't the closest, so spilling my story to her wasn't on the table yet, but her presence was comforting. She welcomed me into her cozy, one-bedroom apartment that she shared with her boyfriend. Mocha, my loyal companion, and I snuggled up on their couch, which, honestly, felt more like a throne of fresh possibilities. I didn't care about the size of the space—it was a fresh start, a breath of cool Pacific air I hadn't realized I was craving.

The honeymoon phase with San Diego was intoxicating. New job, new life, and the high of knowing I was free from the drugs and far, far away from that circus I'd left behind. I got a gig at Greystone, the top steakhouse in town. The relief that came with having a job—any job—was pure, unadulterated bliss. It gave me a sense of purpose, however temporary, and that was enough to keep the smile on my face. Even if I was barely holding it together on the inside, I was glowing.

One night after a particularly long shift, I stumbled upon a speakeasy— Vin de Syrah. I'd never been to a speakeasy before, so I figured, *Why not?* With the wine I'd tasted earlier still tingling on my tongue, I descended into this Alice in Wonderland-inspired haven. The place was mostly empty, a handful of people scattered about like props in some secret play. I wasn't here for the crowd, though; I was here for the wine. Sitting at the bar, I struck up a conversation with the bartender until the guy sitting nearest to me chimed in—his name was Anthony.

You know those rare moments where the conversation just flows like you've known each other for years? That was us. Hours passed like minutes. By closing time, he asked if I wanted to grab some food. Now, here's the kicker—I thought he was gay, so naturally, I said yes. His energy was pure, no weird vibes, and I was living in the moment, enjoying. We found a diner nearby and kept talking, diving deeper into one of those rare, effortless conversations that nourish your soul. The kind that makes you think, *I just made a real friend today.*

But as life would have it, nothing was ever that simple. The stress of a potential warrant hanging over my head gnawed at me like a persistent itch.

After a tense back-and-forth and endless waiting for the DA's word, he finally let slip—just two days before the court date—that I was facing a burglary charge in another county. Double-booked in two jails in one night? Quite the resume-builder, if you ask me. My young, fragile soul nearly shattered at the news—a swirling cocktail of frustration, fear, and disbelief that left me reeling. I couldn't possibly be expected in court tomorrow when I was already across the country! The specter of being dragged back to Wisconsin loomed large, like a bad punchline in a cruel joke.

In that absurd, heart-pounding moment, I made a vow to myself: stay as far from the cops as humanly possible—even if it meant not jaywalking on a sunny day. With a heavy heart and my mind swirling in uncertainty, I set it all aside, clinging to a desperate hope that somehow, against all odds, things would work out.

Meanwhile, Grey Knight was tucked away in rehab somewhere in Wisconsin, doing his thing. He was finally allowed phone calls, and we reconnected. Every time we talked, it felt like a balm to the open wounds, even though deep down, I knew we were heading toward different futures. He talked about getting back together, about us figuring things out in person, and while a part of me desperately wanted to say yes—to run back into his arms—the other part of me knew better.

The heartbreak came in waves, though. There were moments when I felt elated, riding the high of my newfound freedom and sobriety, but those moments never lasted long. Eventually, I'd crash. Hard. The depression that followed was like being trapped in a dark, soundless void. I'd spend days crying, chain-smoking cigarettes even though I hated the taste, the smell—everything about them. Maybe it was because smoking reminded me of him, of us. Mocha, bless her heart, became my emotional crutch, offering me unconditional love while I sank deeper into my own misery. She would pull me toward men who looked like him, desperate to sniff out her dad in strangers. Every time, my heart broke a little more.

Anthony became my anchor in those days. We kept exploring the city, grabbing drinks at his favorite spots, talking about everything and nothing. I quickly realized that he wasn't gay—turns out, he was just a genuinely good guy, the kind of guy I hadn't encountered in a long time. One night, after several glasses of wine and the safety of his easygoing energy, I found the courage to share my story. I let it all spill out—tears, heartache, trauma. It felt like choking on shards of glass, but I pushed through. And he listened. Really listened. I could see the shock in his eyes, but he didn't flinch, didn't pull away. Instead, he shared his own story—one that mirrored mine in ways that blew my mind. He had been the addict in his relationship, the Grey Knight in my story. We were two souls who had lived parallel lives, somehow crashing into each other at the exact right moment.

That connection, that understanding—it was everything. From that point on, we conquered the city together. Laughter, new adventures, countless memories—it was a whirlwind. We drank more than I ever had in my life, but I didn't care. I was living in the moment, reveling in the recklessness of it all. We'd hop from bar to bar, meeting people, making friends, and for the first time in forever, I allowed myself to just exist without pressure. But beneath the surface, I knew. I wasn't the same. This wasn't me.

Eventually, Anthony suggested I try Nar-Anon meetings, and for some reason, I listened. Maybe it was the way he talked about them, how they had helped him in his own recovery. We bounced from meeting to meeting until I found one that fit. I wasn't sure if it would help, but I was willing to try anything at that point. I needed to figure out what to do about my life, my trauma, and my husband. Loving Grey Knight felt inevitable, but I had to start putting myself first, even if that meant walking away from him.

It was around that time that I felt a pull to seek something bigger— something divine. I found a nearby church and started attending services. Sitting in those pews, tears streaming down my face, I felt something shift. It was like a small piece of me was being put back together, week by week. And then, on Easter Sunday, it happened. The pastor called for anyone who wanted to be baptized, and without even thinking, I stood up. This was my rebirth, my second chance. I should've been dead after everything I'd been through, but here I was, alive and standing in the light. I took the plunge, feeling the water wash away the weight of the past, and for the first time in a long time, I felt clean. Whole, even.

It was far from the end of the journey, but it was a new beginning—a beacon of hope in what had been a dark, twisted tale. I knew the road ahead would still be rocky, but I was ready to walk it, step by painful step.

Chapter 12

Drama Ditch

Life in San Diego took a sharp left when Arianna asked me to move out. I mean, sure, I'd been living on her couch for months, which wasn't ideal, but I figured we were friends—or at least housemates who could tolerate each other. It wasn't long before things started to unravel, like a sweater tugged on one thread too many. The moment Arianna told me to leave was less a blow and more a blessing in disguise—a beacon of freedom, shining through the thick fog of her toxicity. I mean, how could I not see it coming? Living with her and her boyfriend was like being trapped in a B-list soap opera on a bad cable channel. The kind where you don't want to watch but somehow, you can't look away. She treated him like garbage, but let's be real, I wasn't exactly getting the royal treatment, either.

I could go on about the details of her madness, but why waste breath on someone so determined to be the villain of their own story? Arianna was the kind of girl you steer clear of in high school—the Regina George of her own making. She was sharp-edged, passive-aggressive, and had a talent for making you feel unwelcome even in your own space. It was like every day she woke up and asked, *How can I make things worse for everyone around me?*

And then there was the Ouija board incident. If you've never had the pleasure of dealing with someone dragging a Ouija board into your living room unannounced, let me tell you—run. Fast. Imagine this: She plops the thing down in front of a 14-year-old, like it's no big deal, and I just about lose it. I mean, who thought bringing spooky spirits into the mix was a good idea? "Not today, Satan!" I suggested, in the politest way possible, that she kindly chuck it into the nearest dumpster, and from that moment, the countdown to my exit began. The energy in that place? Dark, negative, suffocating. It didn't take a spirit board to see that.

When Arianna told me to move out, I didn't feel hurt—I felt free. You know that feeling when someone finally says the thing you've been waiting to hear? That was me. Sleeping on that lumpy couch had been murder on my back, but the real damage was done to my soul, enduring her constant pettiness and venom. You don't realize how much someone can suck the life out of you until you're not around them anymore. So, when she kicked me out, I smiled and thought, *Thank God.*

But let's be real—moving out wasn't all sunshine and rainbows. I didn't have a backup plan. I had no idea where I was going or how I'd swing the rent, but life, in its weird way, always seems to toss you a lifeline right when you're about to go under. Enter Eric.

I found an ad for a roommate online, and I'm telling you, it was like fate had stepped in. Eric was everything Arianna wasn't: kind, chill, and completely drama-free. When I went to check out the house with Mocha in tow, I braced myself for the worst. After all, my luck hadn't exactly been stellar so far. But the moment I stepped inside, I could *breathe*. It was a five-bedroom house, a veritable palace compared to the hellhole I'd just escaped, and it was full of light, good vibes, and—get this—*friendly roommates*. I moved in faster than you can say "U-Haul."

Arianna, of course, had the audacity to act shocked. As if I was supposed to grovel at her feet for another night on her grimy couch. She made a big fuss about a piece of furniture she had originally told me to keep but suddenly wanted back. It was classic Arianna—trying to control the narrative even after I was long gone.

Life in the new house was a total 180. The owners were laid-back, the other roommates respectful, and the dogs? They were living their best lives. Mocha and Leya, a goofy pitbull, became best friends in minutes, running around like they were auditioning for a buddy comedy. And me? I had my own room again—four walls, a door, and space to just *be*. No passive-aggressive notes on the fridge. No toxic energy. Just peace.

But the real surprise? Eric. You ever met someone and felt like you've known them forever? That was Eric and me, like two puzzle pieces finally clicking into place. We were both Geminis, which might explain the immediate connection—goofy, chatty, and always down for a good laugh. We spent hours binge-watching TV shows, trading bad jokes, and getting lost in conversations about life, the universe, and whatever else popped into our heads. Eric became my rock, the stability I didn't realize I was desperately craving.

Not long after, one of the other roommates moved out, and I knew exactly who to call. Sara, Arianna's *former* best friend. We'd hit it off the moment we met—bonding over our shared horror at Arianna's antics—and I knew she'd be a perfect fit in the new house. When she moved in, it was like the final piece of the puzzle slid into place. Finally, I had a support system, a little found family in a city that had once felt so isolating.

But all the while, in the background of this newfound joy, there was the shadow of my marriage to Grey Knight. He had pleaded guilty to his charges—something I still couldn't fully wrap my head around. The courage it took for him to admit to his wrongs, to stand there and own up to everything, was admirable, sure, but where did that leave me? He was stuck in Wisconsin, tethered by probation, while I was thousands of miles away, trying to make sense of the rubble left behind. Five years of probation. Five years where we'd be worlds apart.

Grey Knight had found God, was working through the twelve steps, and had completed rehab, which I was genuinely proud of. But the question hung in the air—what about us? How do you rebuild a marriage when the pieces are scattered across two different states, two different lives? I didn't have the answer. What I did know was that I needed to focus on healing myself. I was broken in ways I didn't fully understand yet, and dating, or even thinking about the future, seemed impossible.

Anthony only came to the first few meetings with me, but those early days were everything I needed. Not just for me, but for both of us. His presence was like an anchor, grounding me when the storm inside was too overwhelming to face alone. I'll never forget how I stayed silent in those initial meetings, the words trapped somewhere deep, as if opening my mouth would unravel the tenuous grip I had on my emotions. It took a few sessions for me to finally muster the courage to speak out, a little at a time, like a dam breaking, one crack at a time.

Each meeting had its own rhythm—a topic of the night that acted like a conversation starter. Someone would share, then another, and another, until every voice that needed to be heard had spoken. At first, I just listened, absorbing the stories like they were my own, feeling the weight of the collective experience. And then, when I felt brave enough, I joined in. It was terrifying at first, but also, in a strange way, liberating. The very first motto I took to heart was this: "Don't stress over the things you can't control." Simple, yet profound. It hit me right in the core, a truth that I desperately needed to live by. To this day, that piece of wisdom still guides me. It was my life raft when I felt like I was drowning.

Listening to everyone's stories was like opening a door I had bolted shut. Things I had buried deep, memories I didn't want to confront, slowly resurfaced. The nightmare I had tried so hard to forget crept back in. But instead of running from it, I faced it in that room. Surrounded by people who understood—really understood—I felt safe. Safe to cry, to feel weak, to be vulnerable. And boy, did I cry. Most meetings had me in tears, breaking down walls I didn't even know I had built. But it was the best place for it. There, in that circle, among people who had walked through the same fire, I found a strange sort of peace. They got it. They got me.

After each meeting, Anthony and I had a tradition. He'd drive me home, but before I got out, we'd sit in his car for what felt like hours, just talking. We'd dissect everything that had been said in the meeting, everything we had kept quiet about, everything on our hearts. We unraveled it all—our frustrations, our grief, our hopes. It was raw, unfiltered, and somehow, it helped. Those post-meeting chats became just as therapeutic as the meetings themselves. We started to see our situations through new eyes, like we were slowly peeling away layers of hurt and misunderstanding, one conversation at a time. And in that shared vulnerability, we found healing.

Eventually, Anthony stopped coming. I kept going alone, but I didn't mind. By then, those meetings felt like home. The more I spoke up, the more the people in the group—especially the older ones—started coming up to me with advice, stories, and support. It was like having a room full of surrogate parents, each one offering something different. One woman, I'll never forget her, gave me hope like I hadn't felt in ages. She and her husband, both addicts, had fought through the darkness together and come out the other side, stronger and still in love. Their story was like a light at the end of a tunnel I wasn't sure even existed. But then there were the other stories, like the woman who lost the love of her life when he relapsed. Addiction was a dangerous game, I learned that quickly. It didn't care about love, about promises, about anything. It took and took until there was nothing left.

My head was a mess most days, scrambling to make sense of everything. How was I supposed to move on when I didn't *want* to move on? The truth gnawed at me daily: I had to let go, but part of me just couldn't. It was an inner battle that wore me down. Would I ever get over him? Probably not. And that realization tore me apart. But week after week, I returned to the meetings. Speaking my truth became the only thing that kept me from falling apart completely. Anthony and I stayed in touch, even when we weren't attending together. Those check-ins were our lifeline.

In between meetings, life in San Diego started to take on a different energy. Anthony and I began going out more, making nights out feel like mini-adventures. It was like I was reliving my twenties but with a reckless twist. At 21, I hadn't even gone out once a week. But now? Three or four nights a week, I was out, soaking up the nightlife like it was the only way to numb the chaos inside me. There was this wild freedom in it, but also a sense of impending disaster, like I was teetering on the edge of something I couldn't control. San Diego saw me more drunk than I'd ever been back home, but I didn't care. It was how I coped. I told myself it wouldn't last forever, that I was just blowing off steam. And I *was* having fun, but deep down, I knew I was also running from my emotions.

As the nights out became more frequent, so did my vices. Vaping became part of the routine, and after a few drinks, the urge to smoke would hit me like a freight train. I'd been on and off with cigarettes for months now, always hating the habit but indulging in it when life got hard. The moment I'd finish one, I'd go into full-on recovery mode—hand sanitizer, lotion, perfume— anything to erase the evidence. Because as much as I wanted the escape, I couldn't stand the lingering smell of the thing I was using to numb myself.

Looking back, those nights were a wild mix of fun and self-destruction, but they were part of the process. A messy, chaotic process that, for better or worse, got me through.

Aside from all the drinking, which admittedly became a bit of a crutch, I found just as much joy—and maybe even more adventure—in exploring the city itself. San Diego was like this treasure chest of new experiences, and I was diving into it headfirst. My new roommates and I spent countless hours outdoors, taking the dogs on hiking trails that seemed to stretch into the clouds. Every time we returned, the dogs were exhausted but happy. Mocha, my faithful little Aussie, wasn't the best swimmer at first. She'd splash around a bit, never venturing past her belly, and I had to laugh at her hesitance.

Aussies, I learned, aren't big on swimming. But Eric and I were determined to teach her. Slowly but surely, she learned to paddle with a bit more confidence, though I'm pretty sure she did it more to please us than for her own amusement. The beach became a second home, and those afternoons spent with sand between my toes and the sound of waves crashing nearby were some of the most peaceful moments I'd had in years.

Of course, it wasn't just beaches and hikes. There was a rhythm to life in San Diego that felt electric, like the city itself was alive and calling me to experience everything it had to offer. My friend Sara and I found ourselves at the beach multiple times a week, laughing at our failed attempts at surfing—until, that is, we started to actually get the hang of it. Then there was the Bachata. Sara was a pro, and me? I was a complete novice, but oh, how I loved it. There was something about the way the music filled my veins, made my body move almost without thinking. We'd hit the dance floor once a week, and I lived for those nights. Sara would be off flirting and drinking, embracing the nightlife in her own way, while I? I just wanted to dance. To move. To sweat out all the pent-up emotions and let the music carry me somewhere else, somewhere lighter.

Concerts became a regular part of our routine, too. One of the best nights was when a shy, quiet guy—one of my friend's friend—invited me to see Luke Combs. He worked for a country radio station and had an extra ticket. Naturally, I was all in, especially when I found out there'd be a meet-and-greet. I mean, Luke Combs *and* Morgan Wallen? Sign me up! Meeting them was surreal. I stood there, beaming from ear to ear, and when I finally got to shake Luke's hand, I thanked him. I told him, probably way too seriously for a fan encounter, how his music had pulled me through some of the darkest times. And it was true. On the nights when anger boiled under my skin, when sadness felt like it might drown me, his songs were a lifeline. That concert, that entire night, was a highlight of my time in San Diego. Fun wasn't just something I chased anymore; it was part of the very air I breathed.

And Isaiah? We stayed connected, even managed to see each other a few more times. The second time we met up, I was more settled, less emotionally chaotic, or at least I thought I was. Out of nowhere, as we sat catching up, I blurted, "I should write a book about everything that's happened! I mean, can you even believe this is my life?" He looked at me, and with that same supportive smile he always had, cheered me on. "Do it," he said. "You should absolutely do it." The words hung in the air, and I sat there, feeling both thrilled and terrified. What had I just said? Writing had never been my strong suit. Hell, I wasn't even someone who wrote in a journal. But now, the idea wouldn't leave me. It lingered, buzzing in the back of my mind, like some challenge I didn't feel equipped to tackle but couldn't ignore.

And then, life threw in one of its little cosmic coincidences. I had been planning a trip for training for a new job, and of all places, it was going to be in Wisconsin. Funny, right? Well, that didn't pan out, but it stirred something in me. If I was going to go back to Wisconsin, maybe I should visit my husband. We hadn't seen each other since everything fell apart, and the idea of reuniting, sober and hopeful, felt like a chance for a fresh start. My parents? Oh, they weren't thrilled. I had sworn up and down that I wouldn't go back to him. But I had to do what felt right for *me*. And here's the kicker: My visit would fall on our one-year anniversary—serendipitous! How's that for timing?

My husband was excited. So was I—at least, at first. Reuniting felt like the right move, like the kind of story where love triumphs over adversity. A fresh start. Eric took care of Mocha while I flew off to Wisconsin, where I was greeted with open arms. That first embrace felt like home—warm, safe. But the moment we started moving through the city, driving past familiar places, it hit me. *Hard.* The memories came rushing back, and they weren't kind. Every corner we turned brought back a ghost from the past, a reminder of the pain we had shared, and I struggled to keep my tears in check. I wasn't ready for how intense it would feel. Even lying in bed beside him, wrapped up in the comfort of his arms, I found myself crying quietly into the night. It was overwhelming. Maybe this wasn't the best idea, or maybe it was exactly what I needed. I couldn't tell anymore.

Being with his family again was bittersweet. They had been nothing but kind to me, and I felt like I owed them so much. I needed to apologize—to show them in person just how sorry I was for everything that had happened. Seeing them again, I felt embarrassed, ashamed most definitely. No apology could undo the damage, but I had to try. I had to express myself, to own up to my mistakes, because otherwise, the weight of it all would crush me.

We celebrated our one-year anniversary with a beautiful dinner, and for a moment, it felt like maybe, just maybe, there was hope for us. Grey Knight, sober and more clear-headed, gave me a glimpse of what our future could look like. But could I trust it? Could we really rebuild, knowing how fragile we both were? I wasn't sure of anything, and that uncertainty gnawed at me the entire trip. Leaving him and saying goodbye at the airport felt like ripping my heart out all over again. It was like experiencing the breakup on repeat, only this time, I didn't know when—or if—I'd see him again.

Coming back to San Diego after that visit wasn't the homecoming I expected. It felt like my heart had been ripped out, twisted, and shoved back into my chest in all the wrong ways. I spiraled—like, seriously spiraled. The depression was relentless, wrapping me in a haze so thick I couldn't see past my own pain. Healing wasn't this neat, linear process everyone talks about; it was like being strapped to a rollercoaster with no seatbelt, flipping upside down and spinning in all directions. It was one hell of a ride—one I didn't ask for, but there I was, holding on for dear life.

Thank God for Mocha. That sweet ball of fur was my rock. She had been my saving grace through the darkest days, back when heroin had me in a chokehold, and I fought tooth and nail to get free—for her and, eventually, for myself. Mocha had seen too much for a dog. She'd been there for the sleepless nights, the shady drug deals, and the moments of sheer chaos that no pet should ever witness. And now, it was like she carried the weight of all that with her. She had this anxiety around people that broke my heart. Every time someone new approached us, she'd let out this soft but determined muffle, as if to say, "Don't mess with my mom." She never hurt anyone, but man, she was protective. My little Mocha—the sweetest angel who could flip into full-on guard dog mode if needed. It was like she was always on high alert, always looking for her dad. Watching her pull on the leash, sniffing the air as if she might catch his scent, tore me apart. Every time, without fail, I'd find myself blinking back tears.

And men? Forget it. Mocha didn't trust men anymore. Not after everything. It took her *three months* to warm up to Eric when I first moved in, and now, after everything, that distrust was back in full force. With women, she was fine, but men? She'd shy away, her little body tense, her eyes full of uncertainty. I think she took after me in that sense—afraid of what might come next, bracing herself for the worst. She had every right to feel that way. She'd been through hell, just like I had. But she was still my angel, and I made it my mission to give her the best life possible. After all, she'd been there for me when I could barely be there for myself.

Leaving my husband for the second time felt like ripping open a wound that had barely started to heal. It hurt more than I expected, more than I was prepared for. And here's the thing—when I got back to California, I couldn't shake the feeling that he was still with me. Not in some romantic, love-will-conquer-all way. No. It was like his spirit was following me around, haunting my every move. But not in a creepy, ghostly way. More like a presence that I couldn't escape. It was the weirdest thing, and I'm not even embarrassed to say it because, well, it's the truth. I'd never felt anything like that before. Normally, with breakups, I'd cry for a few weeks, maybe eat a pint of ice cream, and then bounce back. No big deal. But this? This was something entirely different. It was as if he was with me every single step, even though I knew he wasn't.

At first, I thought maybe I was losing it. I didn't tell anyone because, seriously, how do you even begin to explain that kind of thing? But I wasn't going to sugarcoat it either—this breakup had rocked me to my core. Maybe it was a consequence of spending so much time together, of being so deeply intertwined in each other's lives. Whatever it was, it felt real. And it wasn't going away.

As the year crept toward its end, I found myself reflecting on everything that had happened. It had been a year since the explosion of chaos that started just after New Year's Day 2019, and I was trying to make sense of it all. I thought about my phone calls with Grey Knight, and something about them felt off. It was like we were slipping back into old patterns, the ones that used to drive me crazy. I could feel the selfishness creeping in again, but I tried to give him the benefit of the doubt. Sobriety had to be his number one priority, I knew that. But I was fragile. I needed more from him, and it hurt that he didn't seem to notice.

So, I did what I always do when I'm hurt—I pulled back. Not to play games, but to see if he'd notice. To see if he'd fight for me. But he didn't. If anything, he seemed fine with less communication, and that stung more than I could admit. So, I made the hard decision to let go. If he wasn't going to try, why should I?

On New Year's Eve, I found myself in bed with Mocha, a glass of champagne in one hand and tears streaming down my face. I wasn't celebrating; I was praying. Praying that I could finally let Grey Knight go. I needed to move on, even though I didn't want to. I wrote down my resolutions, but the most important one was letting go. It was the hardest thing I'd ever done.

Funny thing is, as the clock struck midnight and 2020 began, the only part of him I managed to release was his spirit. That strange, lingering presence that had followed me all year—it was gone. I finally felt a sense of freedom, like I could breathe again. But getting over the heartbreak? That was another story. I had no idea when, or if, that would happen. I wasn't being pessimistic; I was just being honest with myself. I truly believed that I'd never find love like that again. I wasn't even interested in looking. After everything I'd been through, I knew I needed to focus on myself. To find myself again. To rebuild, piece by shattered piece.

And that's exactly what I did. I poured all my energy into healing, into learning how to love myself again. It wasn't easy, but it was necessary. My life had to be about me now. Me and, of course, my Mocha.

Chapter 13

King's Cup Karma

Even though the new year arrived with a lot less of Grey Knight, my focus was still squarely on rehabilitation. Weekly Nar-Anon meetings were my anchor, while I filled the rest of my days with fun activities, trying to smile through the cracks, trying to heal. Life had become a steady rhythm—small joys, small steps. But then, just as I felt like I was finding my feet again, the world came to a screeching halt. The global pandemic hit, and suddenly everything shifted. You all know how that went. It was like someone pressed pause on life. Stay home. Stay safe. Don't work. Everyone racing to apply for unemployment as if it were some grim lottery.

Luckily, I was ahead of the curve, already receiving those government checks before most people even had a chance to figure out the paperwork. There was a sense of fortune in that—a small island of stability in a storm. And I'll be honest, I lucked out with my living situation. Six people in one house meant that boredom wasn't even on the table. With that many personalities, there was always something going on. It was like living in a sitcom—complete with Netflix marathons and impromptu debates about which show to binge next.

Eric and I led the charge on that front. We'd stay up for hours, talking about anything and everything. There was something so comforting in our conversations—no awkward pauses, no forced small talk, just two souls trying to figure out the world from the safety of the couch. Of course, others took the lockdown as a sign to party, and we all got swept up in that lifestyle, too. Weekends became a blur of drinking games, cornhole tournaments, and backyard bonfires. For a while, it felt like a never-ending holiday.

Conversations with Grey Knight? Yeah, they continued, but they became fewer and farther between. Looking back, I can see that it was inevitable. The distance between us was growing, not just physically but emotionally. It was like watching a sandcastle erode slowly with the tide—no

143

matter how much you try to hold onto it, it slips away. I couldn't force it. I couldn't chase him, no matter how much I wanted to. There were days when I blamed him for everything. When I let myself wallow in the fantasy that maybe, just maybe, he'd come back and make it all right again. He even encouraged it at one point, sending me the song "All on Me" by Devin Dawson, practically giving me permission to dump all the blame on him. And believe me, I did.

Music has always been my refuge. There's something about the way a song can wrap around you, pull you out of the darkest corners of your mind, or sometimes sink you deeper into them. The country songs of heartbreak, of love lost and found, were the soundtrack to my healing. I played that song, and others like it, on repeat, letting the lyrics do the crying for me when I couldn't muster the strength. There's something so cathartic about singing along with a song that knows your pain better than you do. It felt like I had found a way to release the emotions that had been bottling up inside, like steam escaping a pressure cooker.

Talking wasn't my thing. I'd barely told anyone the full story of what I'd been through, and even with my new friends, I still felt like I was carrying the weight alone. Anthony knew, and eventually, I told Eric. But the more I tried to share, the more I realized how isolating it could be. I remember opening up to a girlfriend, Sara, expecting some sort of relief in the confession, but instead, I got a comparison—her story of dealing with alcoholism in a relationship. I appreciated her attempt to relate, but it wasn't the same. Addiction is a monster with many faces, and the one I dealt with felt incomparable. I found solace in my meetings with others who *did* understand, who knew the specific pain of loving someone drowning in their own demons.

So, I stopped trying to explain, stopped sharing. Words had never come easily to me, and after everything I'd been through, they seemed to dry up altogether. Instead, I leaned on distractions—happy moments, small victories—and let time work its magic, hoping that someday, the wounds would fully heal.

The pandemic was a wild, unexpected chapter in all of our lives—one filled with an unholy mix of dread, boredom, and the kind of surreal tedium that makes you wonder if you're living in some sort of bizarre alternate universe. For me, it was a carousel of mixed emotions, made all the more unpredictable by the fact that I was stuck at home with the same small circle of people, day in and day out. And trust me, when the walls close in like that, you find out just how creative (and slightly insane) you can get when it comes to killing time.

Now, I'd like to say I handled the pandemic with grace and calm, but if I'm being honest, it was the nightmare I had already crawled out of that really tested me. In fact, the first month was less of a mental health check and more of a full-blown rage. My roommates and I, well, we threw ourselves into a party mode so intense, you'd think we were living in the last days of the Roman Empire. And let me tell you, when you're stuck with a group of people 24/7, you either learn to love them or go absolutely nuts. Thankfully, we leaned into the former. Our biggest talent? Going hardcore with a little game we liked to call "Ice." Picture this: hiding a beer somewhere in the house, and the poor soul who finds it has to get down on one knee and chug it like a champ. We had a blast sabotaging each other in the most creative ways, and the absurdity of it all never failed to make us laugh until our sides hurt.

But the crown jewel of our shenanigans was undoubtedly "King's Cup." A game that should come with a disclaimer, because it's as dangerous as it is fun. For the uninitiated, King's Cup involves pouring a bit of your drink into a communal cup—the "King's Cup"—as you play, and whoever pulls the fourth King card has to down the entire concoction. I can't even begin to describe the hideous cocktail that usually resulted. Spoiler alert: I almost always pulled that fourth King. It was like some cosmic joke. I swear, the gods of drinking games had it out for me. The result? My roommates got to know the drunk version of me far more intimately than anyone else ever has. Let's just say, by the end of that first month, my liver had logged more miles than a seasoned marathoner.

By the second month, a curious transformation began to unfurl within me—a reluctant return to sanity, if only in small, halting doses. The incessant drinking, once our reckless anthem, gradually ebbed away (thankfully), replaced by an obsession: fitness. I found solace in twice-a-day workouts, each drop of sweat a silent rebuke to the absurdity of the chaos that had become my life. It was as if I was trying to literally sweat out every last ounce of the madness.

When I wasn't pounding the pavement or lifting weights in our makeshift garage gym, I surrendered to the comforting glow of Netflix marathons. My friends and I embarked on wild binges through one series after another, our laughter echoing in between the increasingly quirky shows we discovered. And believe it or not, in the midst of a global pandemic, we even managed to keep the spirit of Bachata dancing alive. A handful of friends would drop by—just enough to preserve that intimate yet raucous vibe that made us feel alive, a subtle rebellion against isolation.

Of course, the drinking had its perks—until my jeans began sending me silent, yet unmistakable, messages of discontent. That was my tipping point. I made a resolute decision: enough was enough. I couldn't allow the quarantine fifteen—or, as it soon turned out, the quarantine thirty—to stealthily claim my body. So, I quit drinking cold turkey and threw myself wholeheartedly into the world of fitness.

Our garage was morphed into a sanctum of self-reclamation. It wasn't much—a jumble of kettlebells, various dumbbells, Beachbody DVDs, and a stubborn workout bench—but I was going to take advantage. Fitness became my saving grace, a beacon of hope in the relentless gloom. Yet, lurking beneath the surface of my newfound regimen was an old, irresistible passion: boxing. I'd once dabbled in it during a brief stint in LA for a spec commercial, and the raw, primal thrill of landing a punch had ignited something deep within me. Determined to reignite that spark, I set up a heavy bag in the garage—though not in any conventional way. Lacking the means to hang it properly, I ingeniously propped it up on our sturdy workout bench.

In true DIY quarantine fashion, I ordered an empty punching bag online and filled it with sand and shredded old clothes. It was a janky, makeshift contraption, more patchwork determination than professional equipment, but it worked wonders. The weight I'd been carrying—both literal and metaphorical—began to drop away. Energy surged through me as I rediscovered a semblance of myself.

Boxing swiftly became my therapy—a silent, cathartic dialogue between my fists and the burdens I could no longer bear. Whenever life's weight grew too oppressive, I retreated to my garage, laced up my gloves, and went to war with that unreliable punching bag. I'd squat down, meeting the bag's awkward height with every furious punch. Each strike was a release—a chance to pour out the anger, the sadness, the bitter resentment that had been festering deep inside. When I finally collapsed in a sweaty, tear-streaked heap, I felt inexplicably lighter, as though I'd managed to offload a fragment of my inner turmoil.

In those bruised, vulnerable moments, I discovered a bittersweet truth: even in the midst of chaos, passion and humor can emerge. Every jab, every thunderous hit, was a defiant act of reclamation—proof that I was still here, still fighting, and still capable of laughing in the face of absurdity.

Now, the big highlight of it all? My birthday. And let me tell you, we were a household that didn't mess around when it came to birthdays. Pandemic or not, we were going all-out. It was a smaller gathering, sure—because, you know, global crisis and all that—but still packed with enough fun to keep us on our toes. My roommates pulled out all the stops: a piñata, an ice cream cake (the only kind of cake I'll even touch because, yes, I am the self-proclaimed Ice Cream Queen), and my absolute favorite—ribs. The only thing that could top all that was another round of King's Cup, because why not tempt fate? And surprise, surprise—I lost again. Some things never change.

What did change was the sudden cake fight that broke out later that night. Drunk, full of ice cream and ribs, I found myself hurling cake like a five-year-old at a sugar-fueled birthday party. In my infinite wisdom (or lack thereof), I decided it would be a fantastic idea to leap onto my friend's back, fully believing in that moment that I was some kind of ninja. Except...he ducked, and instead of gracefully landing, I flipped right over him and landed headfirst onto the kitchen tile. And just like that, the party screeched to a halt. My friend Sara was freaked out, and rightfully so, because I was knocked out cold. When I finally came to, I tried to play it off like a champ—"It's fine! I'm fine!"—but even I couldn't ignore the fact that I had just eaten tile for dinner. They were all too worried to let me off the hook, though. No more booze for me that night. Everyone kept me awake, constantly checking in, like I was their new high-maintenance pet. Honestly, I was grateful— especially when the headache the next morning made it feel like my skull had split in two.

Turns out, I had a concussion. A trip to the ER confirmed that, along with a hilarious conversation with the doctor who laughed when I explained how I'd gone full cake-ninja the night before. "You thought you were a ninja, didn't you?" he teased. Yeah...cake-fighting and front flips were apparently not covered by any ninja training I'd skipped.

The real kicker? No insurance. But, thanks to the wonder of Medi-Cal and the fact that no one had any income to claim, I managed to snag free coverage. So, in the end, it wasn't all bad. A concussion, a free ride on the health insurance train, and some unforgettable memories to add to the chaotic ride that was 2020. What a time to be alive, right?

Eric's birthday was coming up just two weeks after mine, and I knew from the start it was going to be one for the books—something unforgettable and hilarious, just like him. Eric was the kind of guy you could always count on to bring the laughter. Laid-back, goofy, and armed with that quintessential Canadian charm, he was the jokester of the house, never missing a chance to crack us up. We had an effortless connection, the kind of friendship that felt like we'd known each other forever. So naturally, I had big plans for his birthday—plans that would make him laugh until he cried, or at least question why he lived with a bunch of maniacs.

The idea hit me like a flash of inspiration: We'd prank him in the most ridiculous way possible. Eric had this notorious, unapologetic love for boobs—yeah, we all knew it, and we were going to lean all the way into it. I spent an entire afternoon baking him a cake shaped like, well, you guessed it—boobs. And that was just the beginning. We blew up a blow-up sex doll and taped it to his bedroom door, like a gift from some twisted fairy godmother. Then, we added the finishing touch: a sea of balloons, all carefully adorned with nipple drawings, surrounding his door like some absurd balloon forest. To top it off, we decided the only fitting way to wake him up was to blast the Canadian national anthem at full volume. Because, you know, when in doubt, play the anthem.

When Eric finally stumbled out of his room, bleary-eyed and confused, and saw the scene we had set up, his face was priceless. We all doubled over with laughter, barely able to catch our breath. Another birthday prank, another victory! Eric took it like a champ, laughing just as hard as the rest of us. The truth is, he deserved it—all of it. Underneath all the jokes and the goofy exterior was a guy with a big heart.

Over time, living with Eric meant getting to know the person beneath the laughs. He had been through a lot, more than most people realized. I learned he had a past as heavy as mine—heaviness that is daunting to oneself. He had once been married and had three kids, but the relationship had been toxic and abusive. His wife had been violent toward him, but when he sought justice in court, they sided with her. Just because he was a man. The injustice of it burned, but the real heartbreak came from the fact that he had to leave his kids behind to save himself. He fled from Canada, hoping for a fresh start, but the scars were deep. His ex painted him as the villain, and while he tried to reconnect with his children, the distance—both emotional and physical—made it nearly impossible.

Hearing his story broke my heart. There was a loneliness in Eric that he rarely showed anyone, but once he shared it with me, I could see it clearly as day. I made it my mission to pull him out of his shell, to be the friend he needed. We started doing more together, inside the house and out, and it was beautiful to watch him slowly come back to life.

For his birthday request, Eric had something a little wild in mind: acid. I'd never done it before, and being in the middle of a pandemic, we figured, why not? If we were going to be stuck at home, we might as well make it memorable, and safe. So, we gathered up the roommates, built a bonfire in the backyard, and embarked on a psychedelic adventure together. I'll admit, I was nervous at first, but with these people around me, I felt safe enough to let go. We laughed, we bonded, and the world seemed to melt away as we sat under the stars, giggling our way through the trip.

Afterward, I lay low for a while, letting my body recover from the whirlwind that was life. But soon enough, reality hit hard again. A few months prior, my mom had texted me with devastating news—my aunt Kay had passed away. I flew up to Northern California for the funeral. Aunt Kay had always been someone special to me. Growing up, I spent a lot of time with her and her son, my cousin Cody. She lived nearby, and I was drawn to her in a way that I wasn't with the rest of my family. I always felt like the black sheep, standing out in a sea of redheads and freckles. But Aunt Kay? Shared more familiarity with me. And every time she showed me pictures of her younger days as a model, it was like seeing a glimpse of myself. It made me feel like I belonged, at least to someone.

Losing her hurt more than I could express, but I was grateful for the chance to reconnect with Cody and my uncle. At the funeral, I spent time catching up with Cody, someone I hadn't seen in far too long. We were always close—just a couple of goofy kids who found joy in being around each other. But when I went looking for him during the funeral party, I found him holed up in a bedroom, looking like a shell of himself.

"What's wrong?" I asked, my voice low with concern.

He started to vent, unraveling everything that had happened in my absence. His health had taken a nosedive—he had a rare heart condition that required constant hospital visits, costing hundreds of thousands of dollars. And on top of that, he had spiraled into addiction, hooked on painkillers and, worse, heroin. My heart dropped. I tried to stay calm, but inside I was screaming. As tears welled up in my eyes, I shared my own experiences, desperate to make him see how deadly the path he was on could be. I begged him to get help, to try again, even though he had already been to rehab and run away each time.

He made me promise to keep it a secret, and I did. But I also couldn't just walk away. I kept checking in, praying each time that he'd tell me he was done with the drugs. Hoping that, somehow, he'd find a way to save himself before it was too late.

Somewhere along the line, I got this call from my husband—a random Tuesday afternoon kind of call, the sort where you answer expecting him to talk about missing each other, but instead, he says something wild like, "Hey, how about you dive into your case? The time is now!" Just like that. As if I had a cape hanging in my closet and I was meant to swoop in, conquering the legal system with a wave of my hand. His reasoning? Oh, just a small matter of the entire world flipping upside down and court cases now being held on Zoom. Apparently, this was my golden opportunity. You know, since the virtual world had suddenly become our new reality.

And in his attempt to be supportive—because that's what husbands are supposed to do, right?—he offered to help me by covering a public defender. Not exactly a glamorous solution, but I mean, they're cheap, and help is help… right? That phone call was the catalyst. It jolted me into action. The wheels of my brain, once rusty with procrastination, started to churn. I fired up my laptop, fingers trembling with that first brush of motivation, and sent off a request for a public defender. Simple enough. Except—cue the plot twist—my request was denied. Why, you ask? I wish I could tell you. To this day, I can't remember the exact reason, only that I wasn't allowed one. Just my luck. Now, suddenly, I was in the market for a real attorney. And, yes, the next question on my mind was: *Is my husband still footing the bill?*

Let's just say hope springs eternal, but I wasn't about to count on anyone but myself. Anxiety gnawed at me like an unwelcome guest, but I pressed forward, channeling whatever courage I could muster. I scoured the depths of the internet, and after what felt like a speed-dating session with the legal system, I landed on an attorney in Wisconsin. First one I spoke to—sure, but he had this air of authority, this vibe that said, "I've been doing this for 30, maybe 40 years. Trust me." So, naturally, I latched on. I mean, a track record like that? You cling to it like a life preserver when you're drowning in uncertainty. And let me tell you, I was practically gasping for air.

Meanwhile, back in San Diego, life stumbled along in its pandemic daze. Things moved forward, if you could call it that. It was more like trying to dance in quicksand. But then, out of the blue, an old friend texted. This guy from LA, one of my many Bumble flings, was in town and wanted to catch up. Seemed like a nice break from the chaos, a chance to breathe and reconnect. His name was Jeff, and we agreed to meet at this cute little spot in Gaslamp, the kind of restaurant where you can barely hear yourself over the trendy buzz of people trying to pretend the world isn't falling apart.

We chatted, laughed, and lost ourselves in a comfortable haze of reminiscing—until he casually lobbed a curveball that left me reeling. "Remember when we went on those dates?" he asked, as if the word "dates" carried some sacred weight. Dates? As in… plural? I was stumped, my mind sifting through hazy recollections, desperately trying to summon any memory beyond that first coffee outing—where I'd brought my trusty dog, Mocha, along as a not-so-subtle emotional buffer. Yes, that date was etched in my memory, but the rest? They had seemingly vanished into thin air.

My stomach clenched—not from heartbreak or regret, but from the stark realization that I had never truly invested. I approached those dates purely for fun and entertainment, a lighthearted distraction from life's relentless complexities. I'd always kept the romance firmly at an arm's distance, purposely guarding my heart so it wouldn't bear the weight of deeper connection. It wasn't that I was heartless; I was simply protecting myself, building a fortress of playful detachment around my fragile core. And yet, deep down, I knew it wasn't entirely fair to the men who dared to hope, who brought their own dreams and vulnerabilities to our fleeting encounters.

Jeff, blissfully unaware of the calculated distance I maintained, began recounting the second and third times we went out. He painted vivid pictures of quirky restaurants, offbeat conversations, and spontaneous bursts of laughter that had filled those evenings. As he spoke, a thin veil lifted from my foggy recollections, allowing tiny fragments of those memories to surface— each one a bittersweet blend of lighthearted flirtation and deliberate aloofness. How had I managed to forget such significant pieces of my own life? It was as if I had meticulously erased the chapters that might have revealed too much of the truth: that I was dancing on the edge of intimacy, keeping everyone at arm's length to safeguard my soul.

In retrospect, I see the irony in my choices. These dates, intended as mere diversions, were also my way of shielding myself from potential hurt— a humorous, self-imposed exile from deep connection. I chuckle at the absurdity now, the way humor served as both my shield and my silent prison. Every so often, a stray memory resurfaces, a reminder of a path not fully taken, and I feel a tender pang of vulnerability. Even as I laugh at my own detachment, I know that somewhere in that bittersweet paradox lies a part of me still yearning for a love that dares to cross those carefully drawn boundaries.

That conversation was like a punch to the gut. I was already on the emotional equivalent of a rollercoaster—hurtling through the ups and downs of healing, grappling with things I'd buried so deep, I didn't even know they existed anymore. But this? This was an unexpected drop, the kind that leaves your heart in your throat. Those lost memories, they were from the time right before heroin came crashing into my life. Was that it? Was that the line where my memories started slipping away? How much had I truly lost?

I realized then and there that this wasn't just about forgetting a couple of dates. It was about everything I hadn't let myself deal with, all the internal work I'd been too scared—or maybe too numb—to face. I'd been drowning it out with booze and fleeting good times, telling myself I was just living in the moment. But there was so much more beneath the surface, waiting to be dredged up.

Still, not all was lost that day. In his unintentional wisdom, Jeff sparked something in me. Sure, he was a director in the film industry, and the sheer energy of his creative world was inspiring in its own right. But then he dropped the bombshell that changed everything: "Why not use your unemployment money to move back to LA?" Boom. Fireworks. My heart practically exploded. That was it. That was the sign I didn't know I'd been waiting for. Game. Over. LA was calling, and suddenly, it wasn't just a dream—it was the next chapter.

But before I packed up my life and headed for the City of Angels, I had one more thing to do. I'd made it through my first hearing with the attorney. Step one, complete.

Chapter 14

Secrets in the Sun

I dove headfirst into the apartment hunt, my mind completely focused on one thing—moving back to Los Angeles. San Diego had been good to me, sure, but the energy there didn't quite match my ambition. It was like wearing a dress that fit well but wasn't my style. I needed more. The city was fun, full of sun-drenched beaches and endless parties, but I didn't feel fulfilled. I felt like a piece of me—the most important part, my drive—was missing. Friends? I made plenty. Some, like Anthony, were solid gold. He was the kind of guy you could rely on, the kind who would pick you up from the airport at 2 a.m. without grumbling. And Eric? He was like a brother to me, our bond was effortless and easy.

But then, there were the others. The party animals. They were a good fit for the phase I was in at the time, and I loved them for it—Sara and Michelle, especially. We had a blast together, living in the moment and creating memories that would last a lifetime. But if I'm being honest, I knew they weren't the kind of friends I wanted to keep around for the long haul. We had fun, but something was missing. Depth, maybe? Or just a sense that we were growing in different directions.

Career-wise, San Diego left me cold. I was like a puzzle with a giant piece missing, and that piece was film. I managed to squeeze in a few photoshoots, one short film, and a commercial here and there, but the industry wasn't thriving down there. It was frustrating, like being in the wrong place at the wrong time. My jobs, if you could even call them that, felt wrong—unfulfilling, like I was playing someone else's game. Nothing clicked, and eventually, I took it as a sign. I didn't belong there, not long-term.

That's not to say I didn't have a blast. Oh, I did! San Diego was a city of adventure for me. I lived life to the fullest, explored every event and corner of the city, and felt more active than I ever had in LA. The gorgeous beaches, the endless fun—it was all unforgettable. But at the end of the day, it wasn't my cup of tea. I realized that what I really craved was the hustle, the grind, and the creative pulse of LA. My career always held my focus like a laser beam, and I was ready to get back to it.

Now, let me tell you—finding a roommate when you've got a dog in tow is a special kind of hell. I mean, does anyone enjoy that process? Ha! I sure don't, and I'm pretty sure most people agree. Just thinking about it makes me want to drink a glass of wine. Or two. But I was determined, and eventually, I struck gold with a duplex. Three women lived there, along with their cat, and somehow, they didn't mind adding me and my dog into the mix. After the interview, I got the green light. That was it—I was packing up and ready for my grand return to LA.

Before I left, of course, there had to be one last hurrah. My friends threw me a going-away party, and true to form, it was full of love, laughter, and drunken debauchery. They decked out the house with the most hilariously savage decorations—balloons that said things like "GTFO," "Hope You Fail," and "We Were Just Starting to Like You." It was perfectly on-brand for our humor. Priceless.

Once I packed up the truck, Eric was kind enough to help me with the move. He was a great driver, and honestly, I think he was looking for a distraction. As we hit the road, my excitement bubbled over. I was ready. Ready for LA. Ready for the film industry. Ready to tackle it all with this new version of myself. But Eric? He was feeling something entirely different.

As we drove, we did our usual thing—joking around, laughing, talking about everything and nothing. But after a while, his mood shifted. I could see it in his face. He got quiet, and then the tears came. He told me how much my presence had meant to him, how I had cracked open his shell and showed him what true friendship felt like. He had been struggling for so long with loneliness and suicidal thoughts, and having me in his life, even for a little while, had made him feel more alive. He thanked me—really thanked me— and it broke my heart in the best way.

We promised we'd stay close, and I meant it. Anthony and Eric were my people, and I wished I could have packed them both up and taken them to LA with me. That moment in the car, with Eric opening up like that, was one

I'll never forget. It was raw, it was real, and it was everything. It reminded me that no matter where I was headed, the people who mattered would always be there, no matter the miles between us.

Moving into my Hollywood apartment felt like stepping into a new chapter—one where I'd be surrounded by all-female energy, which, if I'm being honest, wasn't exactly my comfort zone. I'd spent most of my life around male friends, where things were less complicated, more direct. But deep down, I secretly craved female friendships. Real ones. I'd longed for that sisterly connection, even though the thought of navigating all that estrogen made me a little nervous.

The girls I moved in with were already a tight-knit trio. They had their inside jokes, their routines, their little quirks, but they were warm enough, welcoming me and my little bundle of fluff, Mocha, into their home. As usual, Mocha stole the show—her wagging tail and big puppy eyes were an instant hit. She's got this magical way of drawing people in, a little like a walking teddy bear on four legs. Before I knew it, we were settling in nicely, and I was jumping back into my LA circle with ease.

The timing couldn't have been better. My return to LA kicked off with a mix of reuniting with old friends and diving back into the industry. It was like slipping into a familiar, yet upgraded version of my life. The first big event? A weekend getaway to Joshua Tree for Isaiah's birthday. The desert air, the sprawling skies, and the laughter of friends filled me with a sense of belonging I hadn't felt in a while. Being back with my tribe was like coming home. LA can be overwhelming—trust me, I've been through the rinse and repeat of needing to escape its madness before. But this time? I felt different. More grounded. Ready to take it on with fresh eyes. Grey Knight and I were in a good place, which made everything else feel that much more manageable.

To top it all off, I scheduled a photoshoot for new headshots—because let's be real, you've got to stay on top of that game in LA! I booked a print job, did a few other shoots to update my portfolio, and threw myself right back into the bustling energy of the city. And it felt incredible! LA has this way of lighting a fire under you, and I was ready to burn bright.

One of the brightest moments of my return was reuniting with Carlos—an irreplaceable friend whose presence always turned ordinary days into something magical. He invited me to a Friendsgiving dinner at his home, and stepping into that space filled with fabulous, joyful souls felt like a burst of sunlight breaking through a long, gray winter. The warmth of that gathering, the laughter, and the shared stories ignited a spark of happiness I hadn't realized I was missing.

Carlos and I had clicked from the very first moment we met back in Venice—when I'd just moved into that quirky apartment with Grey Knight and Jason. It was love at first sight between us, a connection that defied explanation. He's the kind of friend you'd half-jokingly promise to marry if life were a fairy tale, though the reality is that he's gay—and we laugh about how our paths might have taken a wildly different turn under other circumstances.

What makes our bond even more delightfully ironic is our mutual taste in men—a quirky, unspoken language between us. I still chuckle when I recall him remarking, with genuine admiration, that Grey Knight possessed a striking handsomeness that I felt as well.

Carlos's home was a haven of energy, where every corner buzzed with laughter and the promise of new memories. Surrounded by his wonderfully welcoming friends, I couldn't help but feel that life, in all its unpredictable twists, had led me exactly where I needed to be. In those moments, I was reminded that sometimes, the best parts of life are found in unexpected reunions and the subtle magic of genuine connection.

Now, here's the part where I get real with you—let's just say I've had my fill of wild nights. But that night, I was introduced to ketamine. I was cautious, of course, but curious. And once most of the party cleared out, a few of us hopped on what we called the "K Train." And let me tell you, it was *the* ride of a lifetime. Physically, I was planted on the couch, but mentally? I was jumping from one dimension to another. My creative juices were flowing like never before. I felt like an astronaut, moving in slow motion, every step like a giant leap. It was a little ridiculous how spazzy I became, dancing around and being absurdly goofy. By the time the effects wore off, it was as if my soul had landed back in my body. I couldn't deny the fun I'd had—it was wickedly unforgettable—but it was also validating. I knew in my heart that I wasn't chasing the high. It was just a wild night to savor, nothing more.

The holidays rolled by, and I continued deepening my connections. Isaiah and his girlfriend Nicole invited me to the beach one random Saturday, where I met someone who would change my life—Natasha. It's rare for me to click with another woman so quickly, but Natasha and I? Instant chemistry. She had this thing for Australian Shepherds, which of course, magnetized her right to Mocha. We started hanging out more, our energy bouncing off each other in the best way. She was goofy, laid-back, and full of light—the kind of female friendship I had always wanted but rarely found.

Natasha lived in downtown with her recent ex, Julius, which was… interesting. Before meeting him, she had painted him out to be a real jerk, so I was ready to be on high alert. But when I met him face-to-face, it shook me. I've always trusted my gut when it comes to people—I can read someone within minutes and decide if I want to continue the conversation. And Julius? He was one of those once-in-a-lifetime souls. Warm, genuine, the kind of person whose presence instantly puts you at ease. He told me he worked as a therapist with people in the throes of addiction, abuse, and trauma—people like me, people with stories.

And that's when something crazy happened. I found myself spilling my own story to him. It wasn't something I shared lightly—at that point, very few people knew the depths of my past. But there was something about Julius that made me feel alarmingly comfortable, and before I knew it, I was crying through my story with him. He was an excellent listener, offering advice that took my breath away. The way he spoke, the wisdom he shared—it was magnetic. By the end of the conversation, I found myself more connected to him than I was to Natasha, which, let's be honest, was a bit awkward. But truth be told, Julius and I had both fought battles to get to where we were. That kind of resilience bonds you to people in ways that nothing else can.

A few months later, Natasha asked me to move into an apartment with her. She was on the verge of getting her own Aussie, and we thought it would be the perfect little family setup. We had only known each other for about four months, but I thought, "Why not?" I had been burned by roommates in the past, but something about this felt different. Maybe this time, it would work. Maybe this time, I'd finally find the balance I had been searching for.

Here we go again—one more leap into the unknown.

We found ourselves the perfect apartment—brand new, spacious, and everything we could've dreamed of. The ceilings were so tall they felt like they could touch the sky, and with two bedrooms, a rooftop lounge, an in-unit washer and dryer, and even a dog bathing station, it was just what we'd hoped for. It felt like a dream we were just waking up to, and trust me, Natasha and I were *thrilled*. The living room and kitchen were one big open space, perfect for Natasha to work her magic. With a desk for editing and an at-home studio, it quickly became a hub for creativity.

We filled every corner of that apartment with our energy, making it feel like home. It wasn't just a place to live; it was our sanctuary. We'd host friends, chill out, or spend hours chatting away with each other. Our laughter seemed to echo off the high ceilings, filling the space with joy. It was easy— *so* easy—with Natasha. There was no drama, none of that girly nonsense I can't stand. Instead, it was just us, being silly and weird, fully embracing every goofy moment like kids at recess. We'd take turns cooking for each other, sharing meals like a little family, and talking late into the night, still getting to know each other better. It was effortless, the kind of connection I'd been craving for years.

But, of course, nothing is perfect forever. It didn't take long for us to realize that our dream apartment came with a side of chaos. We were the very first tenants in that 1,100-square-foot slice of heaven, and yet, we had the maintenance guy, Ezekiel, on speed dial. Week after week, something would break down—plumbing issues, appliances on the fritz, you name it. But every time we called, it was Ezekiel who showed up, and over time, we got to know him pretty well. He was a few years older than Natasha, and she was a few years older than me, so we all vibed like we were this quirky little trio.

One day, while Ezekiel was fixing yet another problem, I quietly asked him if he'd help me hang up my punching bag. It was a secret mission, I told him, in exchange for coffee and breakfast. He agreed, so I fed him. Not long after, Natasha worked up the courage to ask him for a favor with her studio setup, and of course, she fed him too. Before we knew it, Ezekiel wasn't just the guy we called for maintenance issues—he was a friend. He had this intimidating look about him, but in reality, he was just a big, gentle teddy bear, the kind of person who makes you feel safe without even trying.

Everything was fun and games until we threw our first party together. It was still mid-pandemic, with COVID-19 hovering like a dark cloud over society, but we were careful with our guest list. Natasha was far more cautious than I was, and for good reason. She worked from home, barely left the apartment, so her exposure was minimal. Meanwhile, I was out and about—going to the gym, working, living life a little more freely. I'd just landed a new serving gig at a steakhouse in Santa Monica, which was a huge relief after a long stretch without steady income.

Easter was around the corner, and we decided to host a Sunday brunch on our rooftop. It was a small gathering, just a few close friends, and we cooked up a feast. It felt like the perfect start to our new chapter—until one of Natasha's best friends showed up late to the party. From the moment she arrived, something felt... off. I couldn't quite put my finger on it. She was sweet, don't get me wrong, and her energy was lovely, but my gut was telling me something wasn't right. Still, I brushed it off, thinking I was being overly sensitive.

The next morning, Natasha began shouting from the living room, eyes wide with panic. Her friend—the one who set off my intuition alarms—had tested positive for COVID-19. My stomach dropped. *Oh, shit.* We immediately masked up and rushed out to get tested. Natasha came back positive. I, miraculously, did not. Relief washed over me, but it was mixed with frustration. I had only been two weeks into my new job, and now I had to call in and explain that I'd been exposed. Thankfully, they were understanding and paid me for the two weeks I had to quarantine at home.

Natasha, bless her heart, offered to vacate the apartment, so I wouldn't get sick. She packed up and left for a while, giving me the space to ride out the exposure period. As soon as I could, I booked my appointment to get vaccinated. I didn't want to take any more chances. The film industry was demanding of it as well. Natasha, on the other hand, was strongly against it. She had her opinions—strong ones—and while I respected her right to feel that way, it definitely caused some tension. I didn't push it, though. I've never been one for heated debates, especially about something as personal as health decisions.

So, I let her be. She had her way, I had mine, and we coexisted just fine. But that whole experience made me realize how differently we viewed the world. It wasn't a dealbreaker, but it definitely added a layer of complexity to our otherwise carefree living situation.

Despite the hiccups, that apartment was a whirlwind of good times, creative energy, and moments of pure connection. Natasha and I might've had our differences, but in the grand scheme of things, we were in sync where it mattered most. We created a home, a space filled with laughter, friendship, and the occasional maintenance emergency. And even though life wasn't perfect, it was perfectly ours.

An Australian Shepherd puppy was coming into our lives, and the excitement was palpable. It felt like a whirlwind as Natasha and I plunged headfirst into puppy research. And really, who doesn't get swept up in the magic of a new pet? The smell of puppy breath, the velvety softness of fur that's impossibly silky, and that adorable chaos when they just won't stay calm in your arms? Natasha was all in. I was all in. We were giddy like kids waiting for Christmas morning. After weeks of scouring breeder websites, Natasha finally found the one—a reputable breeder in Kansas with an expansive Aussie farm. AKC registered and all the credentials lined up, which eased any of her worries.

The breeder flew to Denver to deliver the puppies to their new families, and Natasha could barely contain herself. She had her heart set on a blue merle male, which was the best setup we could've asked for—one female dog, one male. No fighting for dominance, no alpha struggles. Mocha, my own little queen bee, was already six years old and well into her stride as the regal matriarch of the house. So, introducing a wild ball of energy into her domain? Yeah, it was going to be interesting.

When Natasha finally returned with Howie—this ridiculously handsome ball of fur with two piercing blue eyes—I knew we were in for a ride. Howie's energy was off the charts. He was a tornado with fur, zipping around the apartment like he had rockets strapped to his tiny paws. Mocha, who had long since retired from the hyperactivity of her younger days, was less than thrilled. She watched him with this disdainful look, like, "Who let *that* into my house?" Her alpha energy was full-blown, and I could see her mentally reclaiming her throne. Mocha had always been a bit of a diva, and frankly, she wasn't impressed with Howie's boundless enthusiasm.

Adjusting to life with two dogs in the house? It took some practice. It wasn't just the logistical side of things, like feeding and walking them; it was navigating their personalities. Mocha had long ago decided she was over the whole "dog park social scene," so having a puppy bouncing around in her space was not her idea of a good time. Natasha and I quickly realized that we had our work cut out for us. There were moments when I wasn't sure they'd ever get along. But slowly—*so* slowly—they warmed up to each other. Howie, despite his youthful exuberance, learned to respect Mocha's boundaries, and she, in turn, softened. After a few months, the tension eased, and I could see this beautiful, tentative bond forming between them. They were becoming family, and in turn, so were we.

Living with Natasha felt like living with the sister I never had. We started calling ourselves "soul sisters," and it didn't feel like an exaggeration. I had long craved a deep, meaningful female friendship—someone who felt like more than just a casual friend. And here she was, right under my roof. We didn't just live together; we *lived* together, if that makes sense. We shared our space, our lives, our secrets, and even our closets. We'd swap clothes without asking, and laugh about how our styles were blending together.

There was something incredibly intimate about it. We'd spend hours talking, sharing stories from our pasts, our hopes for the future, and the little details of our day-to-day lives. We'd cook for each other, a comforting rhythm that made the apartment feel like a true home. Whenever we had the chance, we'd be silly and playful—dancing around the living room, making up ridiculous inside jokes, and embracing the kind of lighthearted fun that you can only have with someone who feels like family.

Inside, my heart was bursting with love and joy. It was like finding a piece of myself that had been missing for so long. I had always been independent, always prided myself on going at it alone, but with Natasha, I realized how much I'd craved this—this sense of sisterhood.

And then there were the dogs—our Aussies, Mocha and Howie, were like the beating hearts of the place. Having two of them in the house was pure, chaotic joy. Every day was a whirlwind of wagging tails, toy-strewn floors, and the pitter-patter of paws racing down the hallway. Natasha and I spoiled them in the best ways—bins of tennis balls, tug-of-war ropes, plush toys that barely lasted a day before being shredded in a frenzy of excitement. One time, we dropped an entire box of tennis balls in the living room just to watch them go nuts, darting in every direction like little furry rockets. It was madness, but the kind of madness that made you laugh until your stomach hurt.

We bought those trendy talking buttons for dogs, fully intending to train them to "speak," but let's be honest—our real goal was comedy gold. The moment we realized we could record anything, it was game on. Forget basic words like "treat" or "potty." Our buttons shouted gems of our own.

The dogs, of course, were unimpressed at first, staring at the buttons like we'd finally lost it. But soon, with some curious paw presses, they started catching on. Sort of.

Mocha, of course, had to adjust to the invasion of her domain. As the reigning queen of the apartment, she wasn't exactly thrilled with Howie's boundless energy. But after a few weeks of snippy exchanges and side-eye glares, they began to settle into a rhythm. It was like watching a mismatched dance—awkward at first, but eventually, their steps aligned. They became family, and in a way, so did we. Natasha and I took turns with walks, potty breaks, and all the joys that come with being dog moms. We laughed and played, but we also built a routine, a rhythm that felt like something deeper than friendship. I couldn't help but feel like, for the first time in a long time, I had found my home in LA.

But as the warmth and ease of our home life grew, the storm clouds of my court case loomed overhead. Zoom meetings with my attorney became a regular part of my life, each one more frustrating than the last. My attorney—kind-hearted as he was—felt like a ship that had lost its sails. The man was in his 60s, battling health scares like they were on his to-do list. First, it was a bee sting that nearly killed him, and then, twice, he was hit with COVID—both times landing him in the hospital—in a coma. I couldn't help but feel for him, but at the same time, my case hung in the balance.

I wasn't just going to sit by and watch my future slip away. I took matters into my own hands. That's how I've always operated—if you want something done right, you do it yourself. I even reached out to Joe's parents, trying to get a copy of the security footage that would clear my name. But they shut me down. It felt like banging my head against a brick wall. I wasn't at the crime scene—I knew it, and they knew it—but proving it felt impossible. And through all of it, my attorney, my lifeline, was barely hanging on himself. I couldn't tell him I didn't think he was doing enough. How could I? The man was fighting for his life, but so was I, in a different way.

Insert another heart-throbbing component into my life's chaotic narrative: One morning, I awoke to the shrill ring of my phone and a call from my mom—a call that carried the same searing pain as the day she told me Aunt Kay had passed. Her voice, trembling with sorrow and inevitability, delivered a message that shattered the fragile peace of my sleep: "Cody's gone." I was still drifting between dreams and wakefulness when her words hit me like a freight train, jolting me into a state of high alert.

My heart clenched as I processed the news. "Cody—my cousin, my kindred soul—five years younger, with a lifetime still waiting for him, was gone. In that instant, grief erupted within me like a volcano. I couldn't hold back the torrent of emotions; I broke down in loud, desperate sobs that shook the very walls of my room. Natasha, ever attuned to my unspoken pain, burst through the door in a flurry of worry and disbelief. I had completely lost it—lost the fragile control I'd managed to cling to after so many battles.

I recalled the last time I saw Cody, at his mother's bittersweet celebration of life. I had poured every ounce of energy into trying to lift him from the abyss, urging him to fight for sobriety, to rise above the seductive pull of his demons. I remember his eyes, once full of promise, now shadowed by the ghosts of his struggles with heroin—a vicious dance with darkness that I knew all too well. The memory of him teetering on the edge, caught between fleeting moments of hope and the crushing weight of despair, ignited a fresh wave of pain that I wasn't prepared to bear.

The loss of Cody was a brutal, unyielding reminder of how fragile life can be. It wasn't just the loss of a cousin—it was the loss of a bright, vibrant soul who had once dared to dream of a better tomorrow.

I vowed then, through the haze of tears, to keep Cody close in my heart—to miss him fiercely and love him unconditionally, despite the pain of his absence. His loss was a wound that might never fully heal, a scar etched deep within my soul. But as I clutched that memory close, I found a bittersweet strength in the pain, a solemn reminder that every soul lost leaves behind a legacy of love and lessons learned.

RIP, Cody. Your struggle is over, but your spirit will forever echo in the chambers of my heart, a haunting melody of what might have been and what we all must one day face.

Grey Knight was still in the picture, but only just. We'd talk occasionally, the conversations light and surface-level. But there was a growing distance between us, a space that seemed to stretch wider with every passing day. I could feel him slipping away, and it broke my heart in ways I wasn't ready to confront. He'd say things like, "I'd move mountains for you, Haley," and I knew he meant it, but it didn't change the fact that he wasn't *here*.

Seeing him sober, living a life that I had always wanted him to live, felt like someone twisting a knife in my chest. This was the version of him I had dreamed of—the healthy, happy, present man I had once imagined a future with. But now? Now he was a ghost, a lingering presence in my mind, and I was left to figure out how to build a life without him. It was like he had cast a spell on me, and no matter how much I tried to move on, he was always there. And now, he was living a better life for himself, but not with me.

And me? I couldn't let him go. Grey Knight still had my heart, and I couldn't seem to get it back. It was like I was suffocating without him, trapped in this endless loop of missing someone I couldn't have, someone I shouldn't want. Dating wasn't even an option for me. I couldn't imagine letting someone else into my life when every fiber of my being still belonged to him. He was always in my thoughts, always on my mind. No one else felt right. It was like a spell—one I couldn't break, no matter how much I tried to move on.

Still, in the midst of all that heartache, life was slowly coming together. I landed a job at a steakhouse in Santa Monica that helped me get back on my feet financially. I started seeing LA with fresh eyes, feeling like I was rebuilding, piece by piece. I tried reconnecting with Nar-Anon meetings, but they didn't resonate with me like they used to. Instead, I decided to find a therapist. There was this undeniable pull inside me, this deep sensation in my gut that I had unfinished business. Something buried so deep within that I knew I needed help unearthing it and healing it. Therapy felt like the right path.

In the midst of all this personal growth and recovery, one bright, thrilling milestone lit up the horizon—I finally got a car! Seven long years in Los Angeles without a set of wheels was no joke. I'd become the queen of Uber, the hitchhiker in designer sunglasses, endlessly reliant on friends and Grey Knight to get me from point A to point B. My Uber receipts were a horror story of their own, and every time I had to ask for a ride, a little bit of my independence chipped away. But now, at long last, I was about to have my own ride.

And the best part? Natasha, with her flawless credit score, graciously offered to co-sign on the lease for my new Honda. I couldn't believe it—she was a part of this milestone, helping me take this huge step toward real freedom, and I was endlessly grateful. Sure, there was a tiny catch. For the first year, I'd have to breathe into a breathalyzer every time I started the car—a humbling little routine, but hey, small price to pay for independence, right? A few puffs into a machine seemed like a manageable hurdle for the freedom of having my own set of wheels.

But, of course, there was a twist. Just as I was diving into car shopping, finally savoring the thrill of picking out a vehicle, Natasha—out of nowhere—decided she needed a new car, too. She already had one, a perfectly good one, but suddenly, she was brimming with excitement about upgrading. "I'm getting a new car, too!" she announced, her eyes sparkling with this newfound enthusiasm. I was blindsided. My moment of joy and independence seemed to inspire her to go all out, and within a blink, she'd arranged for her dad to lease her a brand new BMW. Insurance and all.

It was like she had to one-up me, to make my huge milestone feel like just another Tuesday. I hate to admit it, but her little "upgrade" stole a piece of the joy from my own experience. My humble Honda, with its breathalyzer and all, was my hard-won ticket to freedom. But there she was, rolling out with a luxury BMW, like it was a casual accessory she could just switch up at will. The whole thing felt like a classic Hollywood plot twist, the supporting character swooping in to outshine the star, and for a moment, I felt the sting of it.

Mom started visiting more often, too. She'd come every couple of months, and while our relationship had its challenges, those visits were mostly good. I'd take her around the city, show her the places I loved, and occasionally, I'd invite friends along to ease the intensity. My mom? She's a clean freak, and every time she visited, she'd rearrange and reorganize some corner of the apartment—anything to keep busy. Don't get me wrong, she's great at it, but it drove me crazy sometimes. "Relax, Mom! You're supposed to be on vacation!" But that's who she was, always mothering, even when I just wanted to feel like an adult. I'm a grown woman, and this constant fussing over my space felt like a subtle reminder of the mother I needed in childhood but didn't quite have. Now that I was an adult, I just needed her to *be*—not clean.

Career-wise, things were on the up. I was working on a web series with Isaiah and the gang, and I was picking up modeling jobs and commercials. Mom and I even planned a special trip to get matching tattoos—little chocolate chip cookies to honor Cookie Grandma Rita, our way of keeping her memory alive.

It felt like coming home—but with a twist. Stepping back into the city I loved, the city that had once been my everything, was exhilarating. This time, though, it was *Los Angeles without Grey Knight*. My previous chapters in LA were written with him as the main character. Every street corner, every cafe, every sun-drenched moment seemed haunted by memories of us—memories that ranged from heartwarming to heart-wrenching.

Detaching from those ghosts and reclaiming the city as my own was no small feat. It was like taking a paintbrush to a canvas already crowded with someone else's story and slowly, painstakingly, creating something new. Rewriting my LA life without him wasn't just a process—it was an art form. Every step I took down familiar streets, every sunset I watched from a different perspective, was a stroke of independence on a masterpiece I was finally painting for myself.

It was bittersweet, of course. The memories lingered like faint pencil sketches beneath my new colors, but they didn't define me anymore. With each passing day, I felt the city shifting, reshaping itself in my mind. LA wasn't just a place we shared; it was becoming *mine*.

But there was one thing swirling around in the background of all this— a secret that Natasha thought she could keep from me. Ezekiel, our maintenance guy-turned-friend, had been hanging out more and more, and it didn't take long for me to see what was going on. At first, it was subtle, almost like they were trying to keep it hidden from me. They tried to be sneaky— sneaking him over when I was at work, thinking they could fly under the radar. But I'm no fool. I could see the way they looked at each other, the way he'd stay over when I'd leave. They thought they were sneaky, but I saw right through them. One day, I called them out, and their blushing faces told me everything. They were "secretly" seeing each other, and Ezekiel was even staying over some nights. It didn't bother me at all, but it did start to feel like I was the third wheel in my own home. Natasha would deny it, play it off like nothing was happening, but the truth was as clear as day.

Life was complicated, messy, and beautiful all at once. Through it all, I kept moving forward—slowly but surely, rebuilding the pieces of my life, one step at a time.

Chapter 15

A Lotus in the Mud

At the beginning of the year, second year into marriage, Grey Knight dropped the words I had been dreading but somehow knew were coming—"We need to get a divorce." It was like a knife to the heart, sharp and slow, twisting in deeper with every syllable. It wasn't sudden; this was a long, slow burn, a process we had been circling for what felt like forever. But knowing it was coming didn't make it any easier. In some ways, it was the right thing to do—necessary, even—but that didn't change the fact that it shattered me in ways I wasn't prepared for.

I always imagined I'd marry once and only once, the "forever" kind of marriage. That was the dream, the fairy tale I had clung to so tightly. And for a while, I thought Grey Knight was my forever. But now, I had to face the cold, hard reality of saying goodbye, officially and legally. He apologized deeply, knowing this was my dream, knowing how much I had wanted this to last. He told me he was sorry for breaking my heart again, for being the reason my fairy tale was ending. And though I had been trying to move on, to build a life without him, there was still a part of me clinging to the hope that we could somehow make it work. But we couldn't. I knew that, and so did he.

The divorce process was surprisingly quick, almost anticlimactic. We filed the papers, and before I knew it, we were staring at a Zoom screen, waiting for the judge to make it official. My nerves were screaming. I wasn't just saying goodbye to a man I had loved—I was saying goodbye to the life I had imagined with him. It felt like each heartbreak I had endured with Grey Knight was hitting me all over again, like waves crashing against the shore, pulling me under.

The judge, with his endearing Midwestern charm, tossed out a Mumford & Sons reference, and somehow, it hit like a bullseye. *Our band.* Grey Knight and I erupted into an unexpected, soul-saving laugh, the kind that chases tears back where they came from. How did he know? Their concert was one of our best memories—music so alive it felt like it could carry us. For a fleeting moment, in that sterile meeting, the weight lifted, and laughter became its own kind of grace.

For a moment, I was grateful—his humor softened the edges of an otherwise devastating moment. But the flood of emotions was too strong. I fought to hold back the tears, but it was a losing battle. Even though this was something that needed to happen, it didn't make it any less heartbreaking. For something as monumental as a divorce, it felt strange that the process itself was so... easy. It was the emotional aftermath that was anything but.

While navigating the emotional wreckage of my divorce, I was also knee-deep in my burglary case—a frustration all its own. My attorney, bless his accident-prone heart, seemed to be battling death at every turn. Three times, I kid you not, he had near-death experiences while representing me. Bee stings, COVID, you name it. Half the time, I couldn't even reach him, and when I did, it was always, "Hey, sorry for the radio silence—I almost died, but I'm recovering now. Let's get back to your case!" Talk about whiplash. One minute, I'd be anxious, wondering if my case was moving forward at all, and the next, I'd be feeling guilty for being mad at a man who was literally fighting for his life.

It became this exasperating cycle—every time I thought we were getting somewhere, he'd drop off the map again. And there I was, stuck in limbo, wondering if he was even going to make it to sentencing day. To add fuel to the fire, my case was being handled in a courthouse notorious for being "by the book"—very Republican, very strict. My attorney kept stressing that this was going to be a tough battle, but that wasn't going to stop me. I was fighting for my life, for my record, and I wasn't about to let some outdated ideology stand in my way.

I did everything I could to gather proof of my innocence. The text messages that could've cleared me had mysteriously disappeared, and when I reached out to Joe's family for security footage, they slammed the door in my face. That rejection was like a punch to the gut. Joe's mother, the one who had ratted him and Grey Knight out to the cops, wouldn't even consider helping me. It felt like betrayal on top of betrayal. But I kept fighting.

Finally, sentencing day was scheduled for October. And it had to be in person, which meant I had to go back to Wisconsin—the land of nightmares. Just thinking about returning to that place made my skin crawl. But this was it. This was the moment of truth. What was going to happen to my record? I booked my trip with a sense of dread and nervous anticipation, coordinating with Grey Knight, who—despite everything—was still offering to help. He was in recovery, working through the Twelve Steps, and saw this as an opportunity to make amends. "You need a ride to the courthouse? I've got you," he'd say. "You need anything at all? I'm here."

Part of me was grateful, and part of me was terrified. Seeing him again in person was something I wasn't emotionally ready for. I didn't want to drown in my own tears the way I had the last time we'd been together. This trip wasn't just about my case—it was about facing the place that had broken me in more ways than one. I was heading back into the storm, praying that I wouldn't be swallowed whole.

The anticipation of the sentencing was like a heavy weight on my chest. The trip itself felt surreal, like I was walking back into a past life, haunted by memories of heartbreak, betrayal, and fear. I didn't know what would happen in that courthouse, and I didn't know how I would feel seeing Grey Knight again. But I knew one thing—I had to face it all head-on. No more running. No more hiding. It was time to confront the mess my life had become and hope, somehow, to come out the other side intact.

As the days leading up to sentencing crept closer, I couldn't help but feel the tightness in my chest, the overwhelming sense of dread mixed with the faintest glimmer of hope. Would I walk away with my head held high, or would I crumble under the weight of it all? Only time would tell.

On my flight to Wisconsin, my anxiety was like a second passenger— quietly growing, tightening its grip the closer we got. I reached out to my attorney multiple times before the flight, hoping for some kind of reassurance, a plan, *anything*. Silence. By the time I touched down and my phone came back to life, there it was—a voicemail from him. Relief washed over me for half a second, but then I listened. Once again, he was too sick to show up. COVID had gotten him again, like some relentless plague with a vendetta against my life. He sounded frail and apologetic, promising to figure out some way for me to still be represented in court.

I could feel my nerves rising into a full-on panic, the kind where your mind starts racing with worst-case scenarios. Of all the times for this to happen, it had to be now. The eve of my court date. My future literally hanging in the balance, and I didn't even know who—if anyone—would be there to fight for me. In a moment of desperation, I did what felt natural—I called Grey Knight. Despite everything, he had always been my source of comfort. He picked up immediately, and before I knew it, he was offering to scoop me up from the airport. The second I saw him, everything inside me softened. It was like seeing a piece of home, the part of me that I could never let go. In his presence, all the noise and panic in my head just… quieted.

I couldn't help it—seeing him again, hearing his voice, looking into his eyes—it was like coming undone in the best way. For all the distance between us, both literal and emotional, I was still hopelessly, stupidly in love with him. The kind of love that swallows you whole, no matter how hard you try to climb out. Grey Knight was, and always had been, my home. And seeing him in person only confirmed what I already knew—I would never stop loving him.

He took me to the restaurant where he was working now, and I watched him behind the bar, the picture of calm and control. It hit me all at once— how far he'd come. From the chaos of our past to this moment, where he was not just surviving, but thriving. Sober, working as a bartender in the middle of his recovery journey. I was so proud of him. We had a lot to catch up on, and the conversation flowed easily, but something was different this time. I wasn't just catching up with the man I used to know; I was getting to know this new version of him. And I was mesmerized by it all. It was like I was seeing him with fresh eyes—sober, centered, and somehow even more magnetic than before. I couldn't stop staring at him, my heart spilling over with feelings I'd tried so hard to bury.

But then, out of nowhere, he dropped the bomb. He had a new girlfriend. The words landed like a punch in the gut, knocking the wind right out of me. I did my best to keep it together, to smile, to congratulate him. He told me how wonderful she was, how supportive she had been of his journey, how much she meant to him. And all I could do was nod and say all the right things, even though my heart was sinking into a dark, hollow place. He even suggested that I meet her, as if that would somehow make everything okay. But I couldn't. I just couldn't. The thought of seeing him with someone else was too much to bear.

I wanted to be happy for him—really, I did. I wanted to be that kind of person. But how could I be happy when my heart was still so completely his? How could I look him in the eyes and not feel that familiar ache of wanting him, even though I knew I shouldn't?

Despite the heartbreak, something incredible happened that day. We finally talked—*really* talked—about the mess of our past. We aired it all out, the pain, the mistakes, the broken pieces of ourselves that had collided and left scars on each other. For the first time, I heard his apologies, and they felt real. Being face-to-face, I could see the sincerity in his eyes, and the way his voice wavered with emotion. And for the first time, I let myself accept his apologies. All the hurt, the anger, the resentment—I let it go, if only for that moment. I saw his pain, his tears, and it made a difference. It was a breakthrough, not just for him, but for both of us.

And I had my own apologies to offer, too. I was sorry for taking Mocha without compromise. I was sorry for never fully taking accountability for my role in our downfall. I was sorry for the ways I had hurt him, even if I hadn't fully understood them at the time. That day, something shifted. It was raw, emotional, and cathartic in a way I didn't expect.

Seeing him healthy, sober, and owning up to his past was bittersweet. I was proud of him—so incredibly proud—but it didn't erase the hurt. I knew he had found someone new, and as much as it tore me apart, I respected him for finding love again, for moving on when I couldn't. It's a hard place to be, loving someone who's no longer yours but still wishing them the best. I hated it, but I also knew it was the right thing to do.

During that trip, I had the chance to reconnect with Ted—someone from our tangled past who, if I was being honest, deserved an apology. It wasn't one of those casual, "Hey, sorry about that" throwaway apologies. No, this was years overdue, a knot in my chest that had needed undoing for far too long. So there we were, face to face, clearing the air in a way that only real conversations can. There's something about speaking your regrets out loud, looking someone in the eyes, and finally releasing the weight of old mistakes—it makes the apology *real*, something you can almost touch.

Between apologies and nostalgia, I couldn't help myself—I had to ask. "How is he?"

Ted didn't hesitate. Grey Knight seemed happy, moving forward, doing well—all the things you want to hear about someone you once built an entire world with. But then Ted hit me with something I wasn't expecting. He told me that, in his heart, he believed *I* was the reason Grey Knight finally went to rehab. That the moment his mom whisked me away from our miserable, sweat-soaked detox, when I vanished to California without so much as a kiss goodbye, something inside him shifted. That my absence forced him to face himself in a way that nothing else had.

Whether that was true or just Ted's perspective, I felt the words settle deep in my bones. A mix of emotions surged through me—pride for the man I once loved, sadness for the boy I had to leave behind, and an ache for the story we never got to rewrite.

The happy tears came before I could stop them—because at the end of the day, all I've ever wanted was for him to find his way, with or without me. But knowing that my presence, and even more so, my absence, had pushed him toward healing? That was a feeling I didn't know how to carry.

But the thing with Grey Knight lingered. No matter how much we talked, no matter how many apologies were exchanged, the truth was undeniable—I was still in love with him. And I had no idea how to let that go.

In the whirlwind of emotions that followed, I knew one thing for certain: This trip was a turning point. It wasn't just about court dates and apologies. It was about facing the past, confronting the things that had been left unsaid, and finding some kind of closure. Even if it wasn't the kind of closure I had hoped for, it was something. And for that, I was grateful.

A backup had been called in. Thank God. At this point, *someone* was better than *no one*. Grey Knight was the one to take me to court, and just minutes before walking into that sterile, soul-crushing courtroom, I met my new attorney—my "replacement" attorney. I couldn't believe it. There he was, shaking my hand like this wasn't the most anxiety-inducing moment of my life. The man had been briefed on my case, sure, but *fifteen minutes* before we were due in front of the judge? I was doing everything in my power to remain calm, but inside, my nerves were on fire. This was my life on the line—my record, my future—and I had to put my trust in someone who had just read the CliffsNotes version of the mess I'd been tangled in for months.

How did I even end up here? The anxiety of dealing with my original attorney—bless him and his health issues—had nearly driven me insane, and now I was staring at this stranger, hoping he could deliver a miracle. I kept thinking, *This is crazy. This can't be happening.* But it was. I was about to stand in front of a judge who held the power to decide my fate. I had to stay calm, composed, and collected. Easier said than done when your heart is racing, and your brain is screaming, *I'm innocent! I swear!*

The courtroom felt cold, clinical, like stepping into a void where everything personal is stripped away. Just the facts. Just the law. My new attorney stood beside me, armed with whatever knowledge he had been able to gather, and the judge laid out my options like cards on the table. I braced myself, every muscle tensed for the worst. But then, something shifted. The judge saw it—my innocence, my desperation, my truth. The original burglary charge? Dropped. Reduced to two misdemeanors: theft and trespassing on a construction lot.

A weight I hadn't realized I was carrying lifted off my shoulders. My entire future flashed before my eyes, and for the first time in months, it didn't look like a prison sentence or a lifelong mark on my record. The only fine I had to pay was for the court. No massive penalties. No additional fines. *I lucked out.* There had been a real chance I was going to be paying a much steeper price, and I couldn't help but feel like I had just dodged a bullet.

As I walked out of the courtroom, feeling the air hit me like a breath I hadn't taken in months. Grey Knight appeared around the corner, his eyes lighting up with that familiar warmth, his smile wide like sunshine breaking through clouds. He congratulated me, and we both felt the relief of the moment. No more burglary charge hanging over my head. No more legal chaos. It was over. *Finally.* I could fly back to Los Angeles with far less baggage than I'd come with, though I knew in my heart that seeing him again was going to stir up emotions I hadn't fully buried.

The time to say goodbye loomed over me like a dark cloud. It was coming, and I could feel the sting of it settling in my chest long before it happened. The moment I had been dreading since the minute I saw him was now just seconds away, and I was fighting to play it cool, even though inside, I was crumbling. How do you say goodbye to the person who still owns your heart, even after all this time? How do you let go when every fiber of your being wants to hold on for just a little longer?

We stood there, the world feeling like it had shrunk down to just the two of us. I wrapped my arms around him, pulling him in for one last hug, trying to memorize every second, every sensation. His warmth, the way his arms felt around me, the familiar scent that brought back a thousand memories. My senses were on overload, and my heart… my heart felt like it was being ripped apart. That hug? I'll cherish it forever, like a goodbye I never wanted to say, but had to.

And with that, it was over. I let him go, knowing it was the end of something that had defined so much of my life. The door closed, and I felt it in every inch of my being. I had to move forward now. But as I walked away, my heart still clung to him, breaking all over again.

That trip to Wisconsin threw me back into the depths of heartbreak, a wave of pain crashing over me as soon as I landed back in LA. I wept, sobbed, like I was right back where it all began—standing at the edge of that emotional cliff where I first realized I had lost him. The fresh wound of walking away from him felt just as sharp as it did the first time. My heart ached with the weight of it all. Every moment spent with him had stirred up memories of our love, like reliving the highlight reel of our relationship, and now, having to say goodbye all over again broke me in ways I didn't think were still possible.

I didn't want to let him go. I *never* wanted to say goodbye to him. But I had to. That was the cruel truth of it—our chapter had ended, and I wasn't sure if we'd ever cross paths again. I wondered, *Will I ever see him again?* And the answer I didn't want to admit to myself was probably not.

Thanksgiving came just a month after I returned home, but the emotional baggage took its time to unload. I had spent weeks untangling myself from the heartbreak, but when Natasha and I decided to host a Friendsgiving at our apartment, I threw myself into the planning. It was exactly the distraction I needed. We wanted it to be big, but not reckless, especially with the shadow of COVID still looming over society. So, we agreed to be cautious, handpicking our invites with care. Natasha invited her friends, I invited mine, and we blended the two lists into what turned out to be the perfect group—a mix of people who, by some miracle, all clicked.

Our home buzzed with life that night. About thirty people showed up, just enough to give it that warm, crowded feeling but not so much that it felt overwhelming. The energy was *perfect*—a seamless blend of personalities, everyone vibing, laughing, drinking, and eating together as if we were all lifelong friends. We went for a potluck style, asking everyone to bring a dish to share, and soon, our kitchen counters were packed with platters, bowls, and trays of every kind of Thanksgiving dish imaginable. The centerpiece of it all? The turkey. That was my domain. I had been perfecting the art of roasting a turkey over the years, and I took it upon myself to handle the bird. No one else really jumped at the opportunity, which was fine by me—I had fallen in love with the ritual of prepping and cooking the turkey.

I went all out, prepping this massive 30-pound turkey like it was a culinary masterpiece. Stuffed, seasoned, and yes, bathed in butter and beer— because if you're going to roast a turkey, why not get it a little drunk? Thanks to Joey and his BBQ skills! When that bird came out of the oven, golden and sizzling, it was like I had just delivered a newborn into the world. The crowd devoured it within minutes, tearing into it like they hadn't eaten in weeks. The kicker? I didn't even get to try my turkey! Every bite was savored, and the table practically groaned under the weight of all the side dishes—mac and cheese, charcuterie platters, mashed potatoes, and all the fixings you could dream of. People were scattered all over the house, balancing plates on their laps, perched on the couch, even sitting on the floor, but no one cared. It was all part of the charm.

The night was electric. It also happened to be one of my friend's birthdays, and of course, we took full advantage of that fact. At the height of the evening, we broke out into song, then I smashed his cake right into his face, to the delight of everyone watching. The party had officially crossed into legendary status. We played drinking games, cranked up the music until the walls vibrated, and laughed so loud I'm honestly surprised the neighbors didn't call the cops. But that's how you know it was good, right? The kind of night that people talk about for months, even years later, as if it were some mythical event.

Friendsgiving wasn't just a party—it was an escape. A night where, for a few hours, I could forget about the heartbreak, the uncertainty, the lingering feelings for Grey Knight. It was a reminder that despite the pain, life moves on, and sometimes, in the middle of it all, you can still create something beautiful—something unforgettable.

It didn't take long before the drama hit full force, shaking up what had once been a harmonious circle of friends. I won't bore you with every ugly detail, but let's just say it started with the intention to smooth things over between Natasha and Isaiah's girlfriend, Nicole. That was the *plan*, at least. But, as things tend to go, the situation quickly spiraled out of control, Natasha dragging me, Isaiah, and even Ezekiel into the mess. It felt like someone had thrown all the wrong ingredients into a boiling pot of drama, and what emerged was something toxic.

Suddenly, Natasha was trying to wedge herself between Isaiah and me, hoping to pull me closer after she lost their friendship. This was heartbreaking because Isaiah and his girlfriend had been the ones to introduce me to

Natasha in the first place. We had all gotten along so well, and now here I was, still living with the person who had sparked the fire that tore us all apart.

And where was Ezekiel in all of this? Well, poor Ezekiel was like a moth to Natasha's flame. He was smitten, totally captivated by her, so when the drama escalated, he naturally sided with her. Of course, that put a wedge between him and me. *Why does it always have to go this way?* It felt like I was the rope in a tug-of-war between Natasha and everyone else, being pulled in two different directions. I had never seen this side of Natasha before—the drama, the manipulation, the way her true colors began to show, and let's just say, I wasn't a fan of the hue.

Ezekiel, bless his heart, fell hard for her. He went above and beyond to show his love, doing anything she asked of him, only to be shut down in the coldest, most heartless way. It was like watching another episode of drama unfold in real time. I had a front-row seat to the emotional wreckage of their "relationship," if you could even call it that. Natasha kept denying everything, insisting there was nothing going on between them, but the more I saw, the more I realized how deep the manipulation ran. She tugged at Ezekiel's heartstrings, stringing him along with promises of something more, leading him to believe they were on their way to becoming a couple. He confided in me, sharing the intimate details of their conversations, and anyone who heard what I did would think they were on the brink of something real. I supported it! She didn't just reject him, though—she completely denied that anything had ever happened between them. She kept up the charade, lying through her teeth, even as I stood there watching it all unfold. I was living with her—I saw the whole thing play out firsthand, and still, she lied to my face.

It was painful to watch. I saw Ezekiel go through the emotional ringer—this sweet, kind soul who just wanted to be loved, left questioning everything. Living through that time in our apartment was *rough*. The tension was high, and the atmosphere suffocating. I felt stuck in the middle, torn between people I cared about who couldn't even look at each other without seething. Natasha was hurting after losing two friends, but instead of taking responsibility, she doubled down, filling the air with negativity and trying to make me feel like I was somehow to blame.

The bomb that truly wrecked Ezekiel's heart? He confided in me one night, his voice shaky, his eyes full of pain. He told me that he had been waiting—waiting for marriage to give up his virginity, something deeply meaningful to him. But Natasha had taken that from him. She had led him on, made him fall in love with her, and then took something he had been saving for the person he thought he'd spend his life with, only to turn around and act like it never happened. *How could I not believe him?* Ezekiel was one of the kindest, most genuine people I'd ever known. He wouldn't lie about something like that.

That wasn't all, though. He shared other incidents that painted an even uglier picture. Pictures of them together, looking very much like a couple, proof that their relationship had been far more than what Natasha was claiming. It was infuriating. I don't do well with liars, and this was too much. I confronted Natasha, but she didn't flinch. She kept lying, even with the truth staring her in the face. It was exhausting, living in the middle of this emotional minefield, trying to navigate my friendships while feeling the weight of their crumbling relationships bearing down on me.

But before the year ended, amidst all the chaos, I found something that brought me happiness. Something that felt like reclaiming a part of myself. I scheduled a tattoo appointment, something that I had been dreaming of for a while—a lotus flower on my shoulder. The symbolism of the lotus had resonated with me for some time, and I felt an unshakable connection to its beauty and meaning. In many cultures, the lotus represents purity, rebirth, and strength. Rising from the mud, unstained and untouched, the lotus is a symbol of resilience, blooming out of murky water into the light. For me, it represented *me*. My past, my struggles, my rebirth. It was like the universe had handed me this metaphor for everything I had been through—the darkness, the pain, and my journey to rise above it all.

The lotus also symbolized transcendence, a blossoming from the depths of struggle into something whole and pure. That was my story. That was my journey—emerging from the mud of my past, no longer burdened by the weight of my mistakes or the pain others had caused me. It was an epiphany, a moment of clarity that I knew I had to honor. I wanted this tattoo to be a badge of honor, a permanent marker of my growth, my resilience, and the strength it took to get here. I wasn't just surviving—I was thriving. And I was *proud* of that.

When I met with the artist, I had a specific design in mind, but as we collaborated, we transformed it into something even more extraordinary. It became a realism piece, with several variations of the lotus flower at different stages of bloom, intricately intertwined across the front of my shoulder. We added a quarter moon, symbolizing the time to release negativity, to let go of everything that no longer served me—including Grey Knight, the past, and the heartbreak I had carried for far too long.

The tattoo session lasted six hours, and by the end of it, I was overwhelmed with emotion. When I looked in the mirror and saw the finished piece—those delicate, blooming flowers, the moon, the story etched into my skin—I couldn't hold back the tears. But this time, they were tears of joy, of release. I was glowing, inside and out, with a sense of pride I had never felt before. This was more than just art—it was a testament to everything I had been through, everything I had overcome. It was me, reborn, with a new sense of strength and purpose.

The tattoo wasn't just about the ink—it was about ownership. Of my story, my scars, my survival. And in that moment, I fell in love with it, and with myself, on a level I hadn't expected.

Chapter 16

Red Flags Wrapped in Glitter

Sliding into the new year came with a new resolve—a willpower stronger than ever to finally let go of Grey Knight. I kept reminding myself how *desperately* I needed to move on. I mean, it's been three years of trying to heal my broken heart. *Three years!* And that's just the heartbreak. The trauma? Well, that's a whole other mountain I've been climbing. Last year, I survived the divorce, made it through the court case, and tackled two huge life changes head-on. Now, here I am, stepping into another year, and I can't shake the thought: *This has to be the year I finally get over him.* Right?

But here's the thing—*why can't I?* Why, after all this time, does he still have such a hold on me? I feel like I've been possessed, bound to him in a way I've never experienced before. I've never, *never,* struggled this hard or this long to move on from someone. I keep telling myself I should be happy for him. He's moved on and found someone else, so why can't I? I gave him my heart, but somehow, I never got it back.

I've spent these three years clawing my way back to life, trying to rebuild myself from the ground up without him in it. But it's been scattered and hectic, like trying to piece together a shattered vase that will never quite look the same. I got so used to him—so deeply intertwined with him—that now I'm fighting like hell to feel whole again. I look happy on the outside, but inside? I feel hollow. I feel like I've been living in this constant state of longing, like I'm not quite *right* without him by my side.

But something shifted recently. After all this time, I can finally feel him starting to drift from my everyday thoughts. It's like the fog is lifting. There are moments, real moments, where I feel... free.

Part of this shift came from getting serious about my mental health. Thanks to Medi-Cal, I had access to therapy, and the best part? It was completely free. I found a therapist and told her about this rotting pit of feeling sitting deep in my gut. This heaviness that told me I needed to heal, but I had no idea *how* to release it. Nar-Anon meetings had helped me a lot when it came to working through the addiction side of things, talking it all out. So, I thought maybe if I dug deep into my relationship with Grey Knight—the abuse, the addiction, the heartbreak—I could unravel the knots that were keeping this nasty, buried feeling inside me.

But when I told my therapist all of this, she simply said, "I don't really know much about that." *Great. Now what?* Do I just keep going anyway? I wasn't sure, but I decided to give her a chance. She suggested we keep talking, keep working together, so I gave it a try. We spent the first few months just getting to know me—untangling my story bit by bit. It wasn't immediate, but there was something about sharing all of it, even the stuff that felt too heavy to say out loud, that started to help.

Before I landed the steakhouse job, I was working at another restaurant. It wasn't terrible, but it wasn't enough to keep me afloat either. I needed more, so I started searching for other opportunities. Sales had always intrigued me—it felt like a natural transition from serving, and the best part? There's no cap on what you can earn. So, I threw myself into the search and ended up interviewing for a sales agent position with Aflac. The hiring process was unlike anything I'd experienced before—it was almost backward. First, they hired me, then I had to study for my health and life insurance license, pass the exam, and only *then* could I start the actual application process to become an agent.

When I got hired, I was ecstatic! They were so impressed with me that they even sponsored my license, covering the cost so I wouldn't have to. The average person takes about a month to study and pass the exam, but I'm not the type to take my time when I set my sights on something. I crammed like my life depended on it—six to eight hours a day, nose in the books, grinding through the online schooling. Even when I was working nights at the restaurant, I studied until my eyes were sore, practically bleeding onto the pages.

And guess what? I passed the exam in two weeks. Both the online one and the state exam. I hustled harder than I ever had before, and it paid off. I was waiting for my license to arrive, eager to finally get started. In the meantime, I kept up with the Aflac training, moving through the process at a steady pace. My mentor at Aflac was thrilled—he couldn't wait for me to officially come on board and start selling. I felt like I was on the brink of something big, something that could finally give me the financial stability and independence I'd been fighting for.

Life was moving forward. Slowly, but surely. And as each piece fell into place, I felt like I was getting closer to the version of myself I wanted to be—stronger, more resilient, more free. I wasn't fully healed, not yet, but for the first time in a long time, I could see the light at the end of the tunnel. And that? That was something worth holding on to.

The steakhouse job was turning out to be more than just a financial win—it was becoming a source of unexpected joy. I started to form real friendships, something I hadn't had in a long time, especially with women. Two of the girls I worked with quickly became like fresh air in my life, and it wasn't just the typical workplace banter; we actually began spending time together outside of work. We'd grab dinner, have deep conversations over drinks, and laugh until our stomachs hurt over the most ridiculous things. These weren't just casual work friendships; they were starting to feel like real connections, the kind I hadn't realized I was missing.

After years of being guarded, of keeping women at arm's length, it felt incredible to open up and invest in these relationships. It was like I was rediscovering the joy of female friendships, and I was intentional about nurturing these bonds. I can't even describe how freeing it was to find that sense of belonging with them. I poured my energy into watering these friendships, letting them grow into something beautiful. It was like watching flowers bloom after a long, harsh winter.

But there was someone else at work who caught my attention, too—Billy. A newer employee with this air of mystery around him that I found myself drawn to. There was something about the way he looked at me, something in his eyes that made me want to know more. We started chatting at work, slowly at first, testing the waters, and before long, we were spending time together outside of work. I could feel that attraction building, but I kept telling myself, *No! Don't mix business with pleasure!* Not after everything I'd been through with Grey Knight.

Of course, that resolve didn't last long. We started going to the gym together, which was the perfect excuse to get to know each other without crossing any lines. It was innocent enough—just a couple of coworkers working out, being productive. But the more we hung out, the more I realized I was drawn to him in a way I couldn't ignore. We'd go bowling with other coworkers, hit up karaoke nights, and it was in those moments, outside of work, that I really started to see him differently. There was this ease between us, a natural chemistry that I couldn't resist.

Before I knew it, without intention, Billy and I were a couple. It happened so organically, one thing leading to another until I was breaking my own rule—*he was the exception.* Maybe I told myself that to ease my own guilt, but honestly? It felt right. For the first time since Grey Knight, I felt like I could actually *see* myself with someone new, and that in itself was healing.

Billy and I would spend hours talking on the couch, asking each other deep questions, and peeling back the layers of our pasts. There was something cathartic about those conversations. They weren't just surface-level chit-chat; we dove deep, working through our emotional baggage together, understanding each other's triggers, and healing old wounds. It was like we were helping each other unravel the past, learning how to be better, healthier, and more open.

I'm a sucker for intellectual conversation, and Billy matched me in that. Coming from a relationship with Grey Knight, where communication was practically non-existent, it felt like a revelation to be with someone who was so willing to talk—about everything. It felt fucking *good.* We were creating a space where we could both be vulnerable, something I hadn't had in so long. And for Billy, this was huge, too. He had been married for ten years, a whole decade of his life spent with someone who ended up in divorce. That's a massive chapter to close, and it had taken him four years of therapy just to start feeling like himself again.

We made a pact not to repeat the same mistakes we'd made in past relationships. We wanted to build something healthier, something grounded in trust and communication. And, honestly, it felt like we were succeeding. Billy was different from me in so many ways—where I was a social butterfly, he dealt with social anxiety in public settings. He was quieter, more reserved, but that balance was exactly what I needed.

Astrologically, Billy was a Libra, which intrigued me. Libras are all about balance and harmony, and that's exactly what he brought into my life. I'm someone who is constantly on the go, always chasing the next thing, restless in my energy. Billy, on the other hand, had a way of grounding me, of reminding me to slow down and take a breath. He taught me how to find moments of stillness, how to balance the high energy that had always driven me. It wasn't something that came naturally to me, but being with him felt like the perfect counterbalance.

He even encouraged me to stick with therapy when I was considering giving it up. "Give it three months," he said. So I did. And slowly, as the sessions continued, I felt parts of myself softening. Billy wasn't just a romantic interest—he was becoming a catalyst for my personal growth.

Together, we hiked up and down trails with Mocha, spent quiet nights in talking through life's complexities, and found a rhythm that felt effortless. For the first time in years, I wasn't just surviving—I was starting to thrive. And it felt damn good.

My thirtieth birthday was coming up, and I didn't want a party or some typical celebration. I wanted to do something unusual, something that would shake me out of the funk I had been living in. I wanted to travel. Really *travel*—not just a weekend getaway, but somewhere far, somewhere international. The only places I had been outside the U.S. were Mexico and Canada, and that felt like a lifetime ago. I wanted to see the world, or at least a part of it.

So, I did something bold—I asked Billy if he wanted to come with me. I knew it might be too soon, given everything that had happened, but I needed a change, and traveling alone didn't appeal to me. To my surprise, he said yes. We started tossing around ideas, different countries, and destinations, but one kept coming back to us: Costa Rica. It wasn't outrageously expensive for the first big international trip, and I had heard nothing but great things about it. So, we pulled the trigger.

We fell down the rabbit hole of planning, researching the best spots, mapping out a trip that would take us through different regions, blending adventure with relaxation. I had never felt more excited about something in a long time. It felt like the escape I so desperately needed, a chance to reset, to shed the weight of the last few years and start fresh.

As we dove into the planning, the thought of turning thirty no longer felt daunting. It felt like a turning point, a moment to step into a new chapter, leaving behind the drama, the heartbreak, and all the complicated entanglements of my past. Costa Rica was going to be more than a vacation— it was going to be the beginning of something new.

As the final weeks before our trip approached, something hit me that threw my entire world off balance. One morning, I woke up to a pain so sharp and unbearable that it had me screaming through tears. My right leg felt like it was on fire, from my lower butt cheek all the way down to my ankle. The muscle was so tight it felt like it might snap, and no matter what I did—whether I tried standing, sitting, or even lying down—there was no relief. I was in pure agony, freaking out because nothing seemed to help. I couldn't even get comfortable for a second.

Naturally, the nerd in me went into panic mode, googling every possible symptom. Sciatica kept coming up, but I wasn't ready to diagnose myself. After a frantic trip to the doctor, I learned that I had irritated my sciatic nerve—not quite sciatica, but close enough. One of the largest nerves in the body, it turns out, and now I had to deal with the consequences. Apparently, I had "sparked" the nerve, which sounded less terrifying than a full-on diagnosis, but still, it was serious enough to make me rethink a few things. The solution? Stretching. A lot of it.

And, of course, it all made sense—I never stretched. I was the type to strut into the gym like it was my adult playground, going hard with strength training, and throwing myself into intense workouts without ever giving my muscles a chance to properly warm up or cool down. It was my pride and joy, my stress reliever, my happy place. But apparently, the day before this excruciating pain set in, I had gone a little *too* hard on leg day, and my body was making sure I knew it. So, I caved. I bought one of those Theragun massagers and committed to daily stretching, working on my body like it was my job. I couldn't imagine how I was supposed to explore Costa Rica if I couldn't even walk.

I laughed at myself through the pain, recognizing that as I crept closer to my thirtieth birthday, I was literally feeling the aches of aging. It was like a cosmic joke. I had already experienced my first twinge of back pain at twenty-five, which kicked off my quarter-life crisis, but that had faded quickly enough. This? This felt like my body's way of reminding me that time waits for no one. But after weeks of massages, stretches, and forcing my body to heal, I managed to beat the pain out of my system just in time. By the time we boarded that plane, I was nearly back to normal—thank God.

During those weeks of recovery, something else happened that shook things up in a completely different way. I ended up visiting a psychic—twice. The first time was totally random. My friend Kyle and I were hanging out, trying to figure out what to do with our day, when I blurted out, "Why don't we go see a psychic?" It was a joke at first, but Kyle latched onto the idea, and suddenly, we were booking a session. It was hilarious—neither of us had ever done anything like this, but we were open to it, though we both agreed to take whatever she said with a grain of salt.

We found a psychic on Melrose Ave, and within minutes of sitting down with her, she was connecting to the spirit world, delivering messages that hit us like a ton of bricks. We sat there, laughing like school kids at how eerily accurate she was, her words cutting through us in ways we hadn't expected. How did she *know* this? It was surreal, to say the least. We sat with her for two hours, letting her go deep into both of our pasts, pulling up memories and emotions we had buried. The session felt less like a psychic reading and more like therapy as she exposed old wounds and lingering pain.

By the end of it, Kyle and I were both shaken. We walked out, our minds blown, talking about how freakishly spot-on she was about everything. Even though I stayed cautious, not wanting to believe everything I heard, there was no denying that something had clicked. It was an experience I wouldn't forget anytime soon.

A couple of weeks later, I found myself craving more guidance. One random day, I impulsively decided to go back and see her again. This time, I was still dealing with the sciatica pain, though it was manageable enough for me to walk. The second session felt different—more subdued. She wasn't rattling off messages left and right like the first time, but I stayed open, willing to see where the reading would take me.

She pulled out her Tarot cards, placing a crystal on top of one, just like before. I couldn't see the cards, but I watched her eyes widen as she flipped them over. The card under the crystal? The Death card. My stomach dropped as she delivered the message: "The sickness may lead to death if not attended to." She went on, telling me to take care of my health, to reexamine what I was doing wrong. She warned of serious illnesses—heart disease, cancer, you name it—that could take root if I wasn't careful. The energy in the room grew heavier with every word, and I could feel her growing more intense, almost as if she was trying to scare me into taking action. And it worked.

By the end of the session, I felt worse than when I walked in. The dark cloud of negativity she had placed over me was suffocating. I couldn't shake it, even though I knew I had a doctor's appointment already scheduled for the following week. It was as if her words had dug into my psyche, planting seeds of fear I couldn't uproot. I left the psychic that day with a weird sense of dread hanging over me, replaying her warnings in my head. *Calm down*, I told myself. But still, the fear had settled in. The messages lingered, and I couldn't help but wonder—what if she was right?

Bear with me as I jump around a bit—there's so much going on in different areas of my life right now that it feels like I'm spinning plates in every direction. A week after the whole psychic situation, I finally had my doctor's appointment. It was supposed to be a follow-up for the sciatic nerve pain I'd been battling, making sure I was on the right track to recovery. It had been at least five years since I'd seen a doctor—besides that one trip to the ER for my birthday concussion back in San Diego. So, here I was, meeting my new assigned doctor, and suddenly, it felt like I was trying to condense the last five chaotic years into a single conversation.

"Doctor, not only am I dealing with this nerve pain, but I was an addict for two years—on heroin, of all things." The words tumbled out faster than I could catch them, like they'd been sitting at the edge of my tongue, waiting for the right moment to escape. "I need to make sure I'm healthy—*really* healthy. That drug wrecked my body in ways I don't even want to think about, and now that I've fought my way back, my health isn't just a priority—it's non-negotiable. And as if that wasn't enough, let's not forget my mother's side of the family is basically cursed with cancers, past and present. So, yeah… I'd love to know if there's something lurking beneath the surface, just waiting to strike."

Once I started, I couldn't stop. It was as if the floodgates had finally burst—trauma, battles, exhaustion, all of it pouring out in one breathless confession. My body had been whispering to me for months, nudging me, warning me that something was off. And now, standing on the edge of this new chapter in my life, I wasn't about to ignore it any longer. I had survived too much, lost too much, to leave my fate to chance.

But it wasn't just the nerve pain or the scars from addiction. There had been something else, a slow and steady buildup, like a ticking clock in the back of my mind. I'd noticed that my body had started reacting—violently— to certain foods. I've always been incredibly in tune with my body, like it's my best friend. I can feel when something's off. Hell, I could always tell the exact moment my period was about to start, which is no small feat! You know when shark week is creeping up, and you just know? That's the kind of connection I've always had with my body, so when things started to go wrong, I couldn't ignore it.

It started with the usual culprits—foods that always gave me trouble, like marinara sauce, which has been my sworn enemy for years. The acidity would leave my stomach in knots, and don't even get me started on dairy and gluten. A slice of pizza or a bowl of ice cream would guarantee an all-out war in my gut. I knew the drill: eat those foods, expect the aftermath. But then it started happening with *everything*. For months leading up to this doctor's visit, *every single meal* wrecked me. My stomach would revolt after anything I ate. My close friends knew me as the queen of farting—it became this running joke. I was always gassy, always tooting, but I never thought much of it beyond the humor. If farting gave me relief, why not embrace it? Better out than in, right? I was basically Shrek at this point.

But as funny as it was, my body wasn't laughing. The gas was relentless, and my friends started to notice more than usual. "Your stomach is always hurting," even acquaintances would comment. I tried to figure it out myself. I bought an at-home food sensitivity test, hoping for answers, and the results came back saying I was on the brink of being lactose intolerant and celiac. Well, that wasn't exactly shocking, but it didn't explain why *everything* was messing me up. Desperate for relief, I even bought a colon cleanse, thinking it might reset my system. The cleanse itself? Fantastic. But did it solve my problem? Not even close. Every meal still left me in pain, zapping my energy and making my days unbearable.

The discomfort had gotten so bad that even my intuition was screaming at me. It was like my body was saying, *Something is really wrong here.* So, when I sat down with my doctor, I didn't hold back. I laid it all out there—heroin addiction, my constant stomach issues, and the kicker: my family history. Everyone on my mom's side had either had cancer or been taken by it. That grim legacy loomed over me like a shadow, and I wasn't about to let it slip by without a fight. Seeing Cookie Grandma Rita's process was enough for me.

"I need to be fully checked out," I told the doctor, my voice more demanding than I'd intended. But I had to be bold. I wasn't willing to mess around with this. When I mentioned the family history of cancer and the years I spent lost in addiction, I could see the concern flash across her face. She immediately scheduled me for an ultrasound. "Let's take a look at what's going on in your stomach," she said, trying to keep her tone calm, but I could sense the urgency behind her words.

The truth was, I needed answers. I needed to know why my body was screaming at me every time I ate, why I felt so out of sync with myself. As much as I joked about being super gassy, I reached a point I knew deep down that something was wrong. And now, I was finally on the path to figuring it out—hopefully before it was too late.

It's time. The long-awaited adventure to Costa Rica was finally here, and my excitement was off the charts. My 30th birthday, June 4th, was right in the middle of all the activities we had lined up, making it feel even more special. We were both ecstatic to be exploring new territory outside the U.S. and, in a way, it was also a chance to see how well Billy and I worked together as travel companions. Travel is the ultimate test for any relationship, right? We had spent months researching, planning, and stacking up one activity after another, practically filling every minute of our eight-day trip with adventure. I mean, we were going to shuffle from one fun experience to the next like pros.

Living with Natasha and knowing how much she adored dogs, I asked her if she could take care of Mocha while we were away. She graciously said yes, which was one less thing to worry about—*we were ready to go.* We rented a car so we could explore the country at our own pace, starting with Manuel Antonio, where the jungle teems with exotic wildlife, then moving to Tamarindo, a laid-back beach town on the west coast, and finally to Monteverde, where the famous cloud forest awaited. It was the perfect mix of beach, jungle, and mountains, but it also meant a few road trips along the way.

Our first night in Costa Rica, we hit the ground running. We made a beeline for the nearest bar, eager to toast our first night with celebratory drinks. The bartender, as luck would have it, was not only fantastic at his craft but also generous with advice. He introduced us to the local signature shot called *chiliguaro*—kind of like a Bloody Mary, but with a spicy, exotic kick. One sip and I was hooked.

The next day, our first big excursion was white water rafting, and let me tell you, it was a wild ride! There was a moment I nearly got flung off the raft, but the thrill of the roaring waves had me in a state of pure adrenaline-fueled joy. And then there was Tamarindo, where we hopped onto a boozy boat ride—enjoyable but not quite as wild as some of the other passengers, who were getting seasick from too much sun and booze. We kept our cool, though, soaking in the vibe, and jumping off the boat.

The night before my birthday, we found ourselves at a lively bar downtown. Billy mentioned that my 30th birthday was just hours away, and the bartender took it as his cue to get me *properly* drunk. I requested a flaming shot, and whatever he gave me sent me flying straight into the fastest drunk I'd ever experienced. I woke up on the morning of my big 3-0 with the worst hangover of my life. There's something about turning 30 that makes your body remind you—you're not 21 anymore. *Thanks, aging.*

But we rallied! The first thing on my birthday agenda? Ice cream, obviously. We went to the best-rated spot in town, and I savored every bite like it was a sacred ritual. Then came the surprise—my mom had secretly arranged a horseback riding session on the beach. It was a dream come true, galloping along the shoreline, the wind in my hair, and the ocean beside us. We rode up into the mountains, where we spotted monkeys swinging and howling in the trees. It was magic.

For dinner, I had to have steak—it's my favorite, and we found the best restaurant in town to celebrate. But, I have to admit, there was one thing that got under my skin: Billy didn't arrange any special birthday surprise at dinner. No candle in the dessert, no celebratory song—nothing. I'm not the kind of person who craves big shows of attention, but still, it stung. I couldn't help but compare it to how Grey Knight and I used to celebrate each other's birthdays, always making it special. I confessed to Billy later how much it bothered me. It wasn't about the candle, really—it was about wanting to feel seen, appreciated. It spoke volumes, you know?

But I wasn't about to let that be the defining moment of my birthday. The real highlight? I had booked a bungee jump to kick off my 30s with a bang. *Literally.* It was something I'd always wanted to do, and now I was in Monteverde, Costa Rica, staring down at one of the world's most stunning bungee locations. Billy, terrified of heights and death (understandable), bailed last minute. But I wasn't backing out. This was *my* moment.

We arrived in Monteverde, known as the cloud forest because the clouds settle low to the ground, creating an eerie, almost mystical atmosphere. I was strapped in and taken out on a trolley cart suspended between mountains. The clouds were thick, and from my vantage point, it looked like people were plunging into a soft abyss—a scene straight out of Jurassic Park. And then it was my turn.

They adjusted the resistance band, sparking a flash of fear in me. I was standing 167 meters high, staring down into the vast, foggy drop, and let me tell you, the ground looked *very* far away. I psyched myself up to dive, but just as I was about to go for it, something under my toes shifted, and my fear shot through the roof. For a moment, I hesitated, but then I heard the crew ask, "Want me to push you?"

"No." I wanted to dive. *I needed* to dive. So, I did. I threw myself off the edge, screaming my head off, and felt a rush of adrenaline like nothing I'd ever experienced. I laughed and screamed all the way down, tears streaming from my eyes—though, I didn't even realize it until they pulled me back up, snapping a photo. I had the biggest grin, eyes practically glued shut from all the tears. It was a funny photo, to say the least, but it was one of pure bliss.

Bungee jumping—*check*. It was a freaky, nerve-wracking, soul-shaking experience, and I was absolutely on a high for the rest of the day. Sure, I was still a little shaken, but I was also flipping *elated*. We spent the rest of the day exploring the actual cloud forest, soaking in the beauty of the wildlife. The weather turned rainy and chilly, but it only added to the atmosphere. And, of course, we made sure to grab more chiliguaros along the way.

By the time we headed back, it was clear that Billy and I worked well together as travel companions. We navigated every twist and turn of the trip with ease, and it ended up being one of the most memorable adventures of my life.

A few months passed in limbo, waiting for my license to come through. In the meantime, I was given the green light to start the application process with Aflac. It seemed simple enough at first—a standard form asking for the usual personal details, recent employment history, nothing too complicated. But then I hit *that* section, the one that asked if I'd ever been charged or convicted of any crimes. I froze. It was the first time I'd been confronted with this question since the whole ordeal, and the toxic wave of memory flooded back.

I hesitated, my mind racing. *Charged? Convicted?* Technically, I had been convicted of a crime, even though I hadn't been charged at the scene. I checked "no" for charged and "yes" for convicted, trying to stay as honest as I could while submitting the application. But deep down, I felt uneasy, like the past was about to rear its ugly head once again.

Sure enough, not long after I submitted it, I got a call. The woman on the other end was kind but direct. She asked about my answers in the crime section. *Fuck.* I had answered it wrong. I felt the heat rise in my chest as she gently said, "I understand, but I'm going to need more information."

It felt like getting busted all over again. But I wasn't guilty! I was innocent—I swear! So, I took a deep breath and laid it all out for her. I told her the entire story about being wrongfully charged, about not being anywhere near the scene of the burglary. She listened, and to my surprise, she believed me. But then came the hammer: "I still have to submit a claim to the board." That's when the real weight hit me. The board. Those sticklers who followed the book to the letter, who weren't exactly known for showing sympathy toward anyone with a criminal record—whether wrongfully convicted or not.

I was stuck in limbo once again, waiting for their decision. Would they let me move forward with Aflac? I kept hearing mixed reviews. Some said they were lenient, others said they were strict, but none of it gave me any peace. I just had to wait it out, one agonizing day at a time.

Coming home to Mocha after all that was like hitting the reset button. Her little wiggle-butt greeting me at the door, tail wagging so fast it was practically a blur, her goofy smile lighting up the room as if she'd just seen her favorite person in the world. And maybe she had. It was the best feeling, like a balm for all the stress I'd been carrying. Natasha had taken great care of her while I was away, sending me cute photos throughout the week to keep me from missing her too much.

Returning home felt great—at first. But as soon as I settled back in, Natasha turned my homecoming into a bit of an issue. She felt like I should've paid her for watching Mocha while I was gone. It caught me off guard. We'd been living together for a while now, and I'd always thought of us as close, like sisters. Watching each other's pets should've been a given, right? I would've been more than happy to help her with her dog if the roles were reversed. I love dogs, and I thought that's just what friends do for each other.

I tried to smooth it over by offering to return the favor the next time she went away, and she eventually took me up on that. I watched her dog without a second thought, thinking that would settle things. But deep down, it left a bad taste in my mouth. Friendships shouldn't feel transactional. We were supposed to be close—*really* close—so why was she making this into a thing? It felt like she was only complaining because she was struggling financially, barely scraping by each month, and saw this as an opportunity to get some extra cash.

It was a brief complaint, but it bothered me. The recent drama with our friends had finally calmed down, and I thought we were back on steady ground. But moments like this made me see things differently. Little cracks in our relationship started to show. They weren't big enough to cause a rift, but they were there, nagging at me. I couldn't help but notice the subtle shifts in her behavior, the small things that started to unfold in ways I hadn't seen before.

It was like, in the aftermath of all the chaos with Isaiah, Nicole, and Ezekiel, I was beginning to see Natasha in a new light—one that wasn't as rosy as I'd once thought.

Subconsciously, I had started to notice how much Natasha's true colors were beginning to shine through. It wasn't something I acknowledged right away—it crept up on me, like the slow unraveling of a sweater, thread by thread. The more time I spent around her, the more I saw her for who she really was. I've always been easygoing, willing to compromise over the little things. If she didn't like the brand of oatmeal, fine—we'd buy her favorite. If she didn't like how something was arranged, sure—she could rearrange it however she wanted. Why argue over something so small, right? So again and again, I let her have her way. It didn't seem like a big deal, but over time, I realized I was giving more ground than I wanted to.

Her working from home only intensified this. She was *always* there, always in the space we shared. The pandemic had her scared to venture out, so she stayed holed up, creating this constant presence that became suffocating. I found myself silently wishing she would just leave the house, even for a few hours, so I could have some peace to myself. Even when I retreated to my room, closing the door for some much-needed alone time, she'd come in without knocking, chatting away as if the boundary didn't exist. At first, I didn't mind—it was just Natasha being Natasha—but as time went on, especially during moments when I craved solitude, it became too much.

She was an extrovert to the extreme, constantly needing someone to talk to in order to feel fulfilled. She couldn't be alone, and as much as I supported her photography career, helping her set up for shoots and making our space look "professional," it irked me that she often pushed me out of the way. "It's easier if you're not here," she'd say, or she'd give me a vibe that said, "Just get out of my way." I'd find myself shuffled off, watching as she struggled to get by without taking any responsibility for her financial instability.

She didn't want to work another job to keep herself afloat. Instead, she called her wealthy father, asking for money whenever things got tight. It was easy for her; she had grown up accustomed to that kind of privilege. Meanwhile, I was out here grinding for everything I had—shopping for a car for the first time in seven years, something I was beyond excited about. But when I told her about my plans, her response wasn't excitement for me. No. Instead, she decided *she* wanted a new car, too. And just like that, her dad leased her a brand-new BMW, fully covered, insurance and all.

It kind of stole the fun out of it for me. It wasn't about the car itself—it was the realization of how starkly different we were. She had everything handed to her, and I had to work extra hard for every single thing I owned. The separation between us became more obvious with each passing day. I don't begrudge anyone for their privilege, but it became clear that I couldn't fully connect with someone who didn't understand the grind, the sacrifice, the struggle. Most people in LA have to juggle multiple jobs just to survive, but Natasha? She spent each month barely scraping by, praying for one or two paid photoshoots so she could make rent, and when that didn't work out, Daddy's wallet was her safety net.

I started to notice how unhappy she was, though she never admitted it. The constant negativity that poured from her mouth was draining. Every day, it was something—complaints about money, about work, about life. And for a while, I was the supportive friend, offering what help I could. But the flood of negative talk became overwhelming. There was no self-awareness on her part. She was always the main character, always center stage in every scenario. When even your closest friends feel compelled to speak out about her character—voicing their lack of admiration—it speaks volumes louder than silence ever could.

Our home, which had once felt like a sanctuary, became her platform. We had both started new relationships around the same time—me with Billy, and her with someone exceptionally sweet. Whenever Billy came over, she'd find a way to insert herself into our time together, demanding attention, making herself the focal point of every interaction. It was subtle at first, but as it became more frequent, it started to grate on me. Meanwhile, when her boyfriend was over, I'd give them space, no questions asked. But she couldn't seem to do the same for me.

By the time we'd been living together for a year and a half, I couldn't ignore it anymore. My senses became clearer, my patience thinner. I had seen how she handled drama, tearing up friendships, and I realized that burning bridges was a recurring theme in her life. Her falling out with Isaiah and the rest of our group wasn't the first time this had happened—it was a pattern, one that people whispered about long before I got caught up in it. I was starting to feel like the last friend standing, and I knew, deep down, that our friendship wouldn't survive once our lease was up.

I even told Billy, "I think the moment we move out, this friendship will evaporate." He reassured me, told me that maybe things would get better once we had some space from each other. But I wasn't so sure. I had already seen the cracks in her character, and the longer we lived together, the more obvious they became. She was the best roommate I'd ever had, sure, but as a person? I didn't want to tolerate her toxicity any longer.

I saw how controlling she was, how the constant negativity weighed on me, sucking the life out of the room. I witnessed her use people—like Julius and Ezekiel, two men she painted as villains, but who, in reality, were absolute sweethearts. She used them for their resources, their kindness, and discarded them when they no longer served her. She wore a mask, one that had fooled me for a while, but I could see through it now.

And the way she treated her new boyfriend? This angelic guy who didn't deserve half of what she dished out. It hurt me to see it, to know that the person I once thought of as a sister was someone I no longer recognized. I hate to speak badly of anyone, especially someone who had been such a big part of my life, but there comes a time when you have to be honest with yourself about the people you allow into your world. And I was starting to realize that maybe it was time to let Natasha go.

Chapter 17

Meet Meatball

It didn't take long after my birthday for life to throw me one hell of a curveball. I'd been feeling off—my appetite had vanished like a magic trick gone wrong, and my mood was sinking faster than the Titanic. So, there I was, lying on an exam table, covered in that icy gel they use for ultrasounds, staring at a screen that looked far too calm for the chaos brewing inside me. The technician, though? She wasn't calm at all. Her face gave it away almost immediately. She squinted at the screen, moved the wand around a few more times, and then—cue the ominous music—she called for backup.

I felt the panic bubble up inside me like a soda can about to explode. "What did you find?" I asked, trying to keep my voice steady. But their faces said it all—shock, confusion, fear. It was like watching a bad horror movie where the actors didn't even have to say a word for you to know something was seriously wrong. They muttered about needing more tests, which is never what you want to hear. I wanted to scream, "Just tell me already!" but instead, I was stuck there, swimming in the deafening silence between their glances.

And then, the word I'd dreaded my entire life tumbled out of their mouths: tumor. They could see something lurking in there, something that wasn't supposed to be. The ultrasound wasn't clear enough to paint the full picture, so they ordered more tests—MRIs, CAT scans, bloodwork—you name it. At this point, I was practically living in that hospital, going in and out like a frequent flyer collecting unwanted miles. Meanwhile, they kept whispering "tumor" like it was a dirty little secret, and all I could think was: *Oh my God, it's happening. My worst nightmare is happening.*

You see, cancer had always been my biggest fear. It was the shadow lurking in the corner of every "what if" scenario that ran through my brain at 3 a.m. Watching my Grandma Rita fight and lose that battle left a scar on my heart, and with my mom's side of the family riddled with cancer, it felt like an inevitability. And now, here it was, knocking on my door.

But, hey, life's nothing if not a little ironic, right? While the fear was gnawing at me like a rabid dog, at least I didn't have to worry about the financial side of things. Thanks to Medi-Cal, all these tests, these appointments, and all this bad news weren't costing me a dime. I was practically a VIP patient at this point, with the app to prove it. After every visit, I'd get my test results pinged straight to my phone, and there I'd be, curled up on the couch like a detective in a Netflix thriller, Googling every single term I didn't understand.

Turns out, my tumor was about two inches big and round, like some alien lifeform that had taken up residence in my body. And as I kept peeling back the layers of this medical mystery, the fear grew, but so did a strange sense of determination. I wanted answers, and I wanted them now.

After what felt like an eternity—*three long months* of poking, prodding, scanning, and waiting—I finally sat down for the appointment I knew would change everything. I brought Billy with me because, honestly, I wasn't sure I could handle whatever was coming alone. My gut had been screaming at me for weeks, a quiet but persistent whisper: *Brace yourself.*

The doctor pulled up my CAT scan, and there it was, staring back at me like a cosmic joke—my stomach, lit up like a damn Christmas tree. And not the soft, twinkling lights kind—the full-blown, Vegas-strip, blinding beacon-of-doom kind. He went full professor mode, flipping through images like it was a slideshow from hell—head to toe, toe to head, every possible angle of my body dissected in grainy, medical-grade black and white. But one image stole my breath. A head-on view of my stomach, where I could see everything—the delicate framework of my organs, veins twisting like roots in the earth, my body laid out in shades of ghostly grey. And right there, dead center, a searing white tumor beamed at me, bold, unapologetic, *impossible* to ignore.

I felt my stomach drop, as if my body already knew before my mind could catch up.

Then came the words.

"You've got cancer."

Everything after that blurred, like sound suddenly stopped existing. Something about it being extremely rare, malignant, and oh yeah—sitting right at the head of my pancreas, lounging there like it paid rent.

For a moment, I just sat there, letting the words wash over me. You'd think I'd be screaming inside, but weirdly enough, I felt… prepared. All that obsessive late-night research had set me up for this moment. It was like I'd been bracing for impact, and now that it had arrived, I wasn't crumbling. Not yet, anyway. The doctor didn't sugarcoat it either. Surgery had to happen, and it had to happen *now*. The word "urgent" was practically blinking in neon above my head.

But me being me, I wasn't about to let cancer throw a wrench in my plans just yet. Billy and I had already made plans to visit my mom and Joey up north, and damned if I was going to let a ticking time bomb in my pancreas ruin that trip. So, I pushed the surgery back. Just a little. One last visit with my family before the rollercoaster really started. The surgery was officially scheduled for September 8, 2022—the day after we got back to Los Angeles.

It was like I was buying myself one more moment of normalcy before plunging into the unknown.

The moment I stepped out of that sterile, chilly hospital, it all came crashing down. Tears poured out of me like a dam breaking. It was as though I was finally, finally releasing every bit of terror I'd been hoarding for months—years, even. The darkness of my past was following me in ghostly whispers: heroin addiction, a monstrous ex-husband who nearly erased my sense of self, endless cycles of heartbreak and the brutal, dizzying rounds of rehabilitation. I'd survived one storm only to find myself on the edge of another. And now? Now, I was told I'd need to rush into surgery for cancer. Cancer. Could the universe be serious?

My emotions were running at an all-time high—higher than I'd ever known possible. A cocktail of fear, fury, exhaustion, and, yes, even a pinch of humor, swirled in me, growing stronger by the minute. As the shock sank in, I felt my tears start to morph, like I had to laugh or else I'd crumble. So, in my twisted way of lightening the darkness, I decided to give my tumor a name. Meet "Meatball." Yes, it had to be named something as absurd as

"Meatball," because what else would you call a round, two-inch menace sitting there inside you like a bad joke? It might as well be a meatball, right? The whole thing was absurd. Laughable, if only it didn't hurt so damn much.

And believe me, I was obsessed—I researched this cancer like my life depended on it, which, frankly, it did. I Googled late into the night, scrolling through pages and articles, learning everything I could about this strange, unwelcome visitor. It was rare—oh, not just rare, but one of the rarest of the rare. Neuroendocrine cancer, medically speaking. "One percent of all pancreatic cancers," they said. It's a cancer you'd expect to find in someone over 60, but here I was in my 30s, defying odds I never signed up to defy. And as if to add insult to injury, the ribbon color for this cancer? Zebra stripes. I kid you not. Zebra stripes. Apparently, even the universe agreed that this was rare enough to deserve a pattern, something chaotic and unexpected, like the experience itself.

As much as I tried to keep my head high, my emotions were rattling around inside me, wild and untamed. Outside, I did my best to look composed, to walk around as if I was holding it all together, but inside? Inside, I was a mess. Yet, oddly enough, calling it "Meatball" helped. It was like a twisted badge of courage, this little laugh I could share with myself when the terror crept in too close.

The strange thing was, once I knew where the tumor was, I could feel it, lurking like a dark, silent guest. My mind played tricks, convincing me I could feel every millimeter of it. And, as if it had a personality of its own, "Meatball" would flare up with pain whenever I was alone in my thoughts, especially as the surgery date loomed closer. Sometimes, the pain would even steal my breath, like it was trying to squeeze the life out of me, a silent reminder of its power. But I held on to my laugh and my will to fight. I was facing my fear with a smirk, however shaky because that's what I did. That's what I'd always done.

And there, beneath the absurdity, beneath the tears, I found a strange strength. It was small and fragile, like the first green sprout after winter, but it was mine. "Meatball" and I were in for one hell of a fight, and I was ready to give it everything I had.

In what I'd decided would be my last hurrah before surgery, we packed our bags and made the trek up north to my mom's side of the family, a place that had always been my little oasis from the world. Northern California in late summer is a contradiction—a blend of golden fields and smoky skies, always under the uneasy threat of fire. But right then, I wasn't thinking of any of that. I was simply relishing the warmth of family, the kind you can only get from a house full of voices talking over each other, us kids splashing in the pool, and from Joey and his brother's magic touch at the grill. Joey, my mom's husband, is something of a BBQ wizard—his ribs could make a grown man cry, and his burgers were the kind of juicy that could ruin your shirt if you weren't careful. I leaned back, letting the laughter and food wash over me like a warm blanket, the thought of surgery lurking quietly at the back of my mind.

Still, the reality of what was coming snuck in here and there. I'd done my research, every terrifying Google search, every clinical study on the prognosis of rare pancreatic tumors, watched videos, convinced that this knowledge would somehow armor me for the procedure. I was as prepared as anyone could be—or so I told myself. It was my way of pretending I had a handle on it, that I was in control. But even with all the facts and figures I'd armed myself with, the reality was impossible to grasp. I couldn't shake the disbelief that *this* was my reality. Surgery. The word hung over me like a black cloud, something I couldn't quite believe was about to descend. It felt surreal, like something that happened to someone else.

On our last day there, I was trying to soak up the poolside tranquility with extended family, savoring, knowing soon, I'd be exchanging it for the sterile lights and unfamiliar faces of a hospital. It was all going as well as it could—sun, laughter, shared moments that felt almost like an antidote. When the time came to start packing up for the drive back to LA, I felt a pang of sadness. My whole family had rallied to come along, eager to be there for me through the procedure. My mom, Joey, my dad, my stepmom—all of them putting their differences aside to surround me with love. I couldn't deny how much I needed them. Their unity felt like a rare gift, a strange harmony in the middle of chaos.

Just as we were about to leave, the day took a dramatic, straight-out-of-a-movie twist—one of those wild, left-field turns that would almost be funny if it weren't so terrifying. Mom and Joey's house sits high in the foothills—beautiful, peaceful, and a prime target for wildfire season. Every summer, the threat looms, but for Joey, it's never just a passing concern. The man listens to fire reports like they're gospel, his ears permanently tuned for the next ember waiting to turn their home into kindling.

And today? That ember had arrived.

The fire had sparked, and it wasn't just creeping—it was *ripping* through the forest, devouring acres at a speed that made even the newscasters sound rattled. Joey was glued to the reports, his posture shifting from tense to borderline volcanic. His brow furrowed deeper by the second, his jaw clenched so tight it could crack a walnut, the lines on his face etching in real-time as the reality set in. The fire was close—*too close*. I could practically hear the battle playing out in his mind, torn between staying to support me and doing what his gut was screaming at him to do: protect everything they had built.

But in the end, there was no choice. The fire was coming, and Joey knew better than anyone—you don't wait to outrun a wildfire.

Joey grew visibly tense, his eyes darting toward the horizon as if he could see the flames himself. In a split-second decision, he realized he couldn't come with us to LA. The fire was too close, the risk too great. He had to stay back and protect the home they'd built, the place he'd poured so much of his heart into. He was practically out the door with a quick, anxious goodbye, rushing back to take whatever action he could.

In a way, it felt like a punch. Joey had been a rock for me, especially in moments when my own world felt like it was falling apart. He'd been a steady, comforting presence—a kind of second father, someone I'd come to rely on. Knowing he wouldn't be by my side during the surgery was a bittersweet loss. But I understood. This was his life, his sanctuary, and it was now in real danger. My mother, meanwhile, was torn in two, her eyes darting between Joey and me as she grappled with the impossible choice of staying to protect her home or coming with me to face one of the biggest battles of my life.

The emotions in those last few minutes were like something out of a movie—raw, tangled, vibrating with fear and love. When life decides to test you all at once. My mom and Joey shared a tense, hurried goodbye that seemed to say everything they couldn't out loud, and then, a quick kiss and her eyes lingering on him as if memorizing his face before departure. And so, with a heavy heart, my mother chose to be by my side while Joey stayed behind to guard their home from the roaring flames creeping ever closer.

Driving away, watching their house shrink in the rearview mirror, a strange sadness settled over me. I couldn't ignore the irony: We were all in battles of our own, each one unique and terrifying in its own right. For Joey, it was flames licking at the edges of his world; for me, it was the disease inside me, something equally relentless and consuming. I was fighting for my life, he was fighting for his home, and somehow, we were each holding on in our own ways, connected by the things we loved enough to risk everything for. As we drove further away, I couldn't shake the feeling that we were all—each of us—on the edge of something vast and wild, clinging to love even as everything seemed ready to go up in smoke.

To add even more heat to the situation—pun fully intended—Joey was in. The second he got home, he went into full survival mode, preparing for the absolute worst. Fire season is always a threat in the foothills, but this? This was different. He moved through the house like a man on a mission, securing what he could, mentally calculating what mattered most, and weighing impossible decisions against an unpredictable force of nature.

Then came the evacuation order—the final gut punch. No more stalling, no more second-guessing. The fire was coming, and when fire comes, you don't negotiate. So, Joey and my brother packed up and left, not knowing if there'd be anything to return to.

For two long, smoke-choked weeks, his home stood on the frontlines of an inferno while hundreds of firefighters fought tooth and nail to keep the wildfire from devouring everything in its path. What a terrifying, surreal time. As long as they've lived up there, I can't recall a fire season ever getting this bad—bad enough to force Joey to walk away, even when every instinct told him to stay and fight.

It's the kind of chaos you pray you never have to experience, but when you do, it changes you. Because if there's one thing you learn when staring down a wildfire, it's this: when fire decides it's coming for you, you don't get to argue.

My dad and stepmom, Lois, made the long journey down to Los Angeles, determined to be by my side for what would be, without question, one of the biggest days of my life. The morning after they arrived, it was time—*surgery day*. There's a strange, disorienting feeling when you're forced to wake up before dawn for something so monumental, as if the world isn't quite real yet, like you're walking through some hazy dream. We made our way to the hospital, each of us silent, lost in our own thoughts as the city slept around us. Once we arrived, the fluorescent lights flickered on, sharp and unforgiving, dragging me into reality. I was surrounded by my parents—all of them, minus Joey, who was back up north holding down the fort against a wildfire. Their love was like a shield around me, yet the weight of what was coming loomed larger than ever.

I felt oddly calm. Awake. Maybe it was denial or self-preservation, but it was like I'd become an outsider looking in, watching the scene unfold like it was someone else's life. And yet, somehow, I hadn't really *registered* the intensity of what was about to happen. It was like I was a spectator at my own event, only half aware that it was my life, my body, about to go under the knife. My dad, who was always the rock, looked at me with a face I'd never seen before—etched with fear, vulnerability, love, and something that resembled helplessness. I'd only ever seen him cry once, years ago, when our family dog passed away. But today, as he held my hand, a few tears slipped down his cheeks. It was a sacred kind of moment, one I wanted to pocket and protect forever, as if somehow, through his tears, I could understand the magnitude of what lay ahead.

And even with all that, I'd kept myself from calling this thing by its name: *cancer*. I'd spent months calling it "Meatball," letting myself laugh at this little intruder as if it were nothing more than a stubborn nuisance. I'd avoided the word like the plague, clinging to anything that felt a little less brutal, a little easier to swallow. But standing there, hearing the doctor's solemn description, there was no room for jokes. It was time to face reality.

He began explaining the Whipple procedure, and a surgery so intense it sounded like something out of a medical textbook rather than something happening to me. "The Whipple procedure," he said, his voice almost too calm, "is a complex operation designed to remove tumors in the pancreas. We'll be removing the head of the pancreas, gallbladder, duodenum, a portion of the stomach, and surrounding lymph nodes." My eyes widen. I blinked, trying to keep up with the list of parts they'd be taking from me. "Then, we'll reconnect the remaining organs to ensure the digestive system functions properly." In other words, they were planning a complete architectural redesign of my insides.

Seven hours under anesthesia. My body rearranged, my insides reconstructed, like they were building a whole new house inside me. I could feel a ripple of fear that I'd been holding back finally creep in, touching every corner of my mind. My dad's tears, Lois's worried smile, my mom's soft touch on my shoulder—they were all bringing me back to the reality I'd been trying to ignore. I felt so small, so incredibly vulnerable, yet so surrounded by love. But their love, their presence, made this surreal experience feel just a little more real and somehow bearable.

Billy, on the other hand, was noticeably absent. He didn't want to wake up early, didn't see the point in coming along for what he shrugged off as "you got your family." It stung, sharp and deep, a kind of emptiness that sat heavy in my chest. His version of "support" had been, at best, a series of dismissive jokes and casual indifference. The absence of his concern was loud—deafening, even. It gnawed at me, making me wonder if I'd been fooling myself all along. It was as if he refused to accept the gravity of it all, choosing instead to skate around the edges, making light of a situation that was anything but. And as strange as it felt to admit it, his apathy made me wonder if he ever really cared at all. Because if the tables were turned, if he were the one facing a fight like this, I'd be there beside him in a heartbeat, bending over backward, doing whatever I could to make it easier for him. And yet here I was, the one about to go through hell, and he was MIA. I had to let it go, to shake it off.

I couldn't carry his indifference along with everything else. Instead, I looked around at my parents, my beautiful, worried, *present* parents, each one there to hold me up, to give me their strength. My dad, Lois, my mom—all of them together in this surreal moment. A rare, bittersweet harmony. It was like I was surrounded by pillars, each one standing steady, each one brimming with love. It was such a rare sight to see them all working as a team for me. And as they wheeled me away, their faces lingered in my mind, filling me with a kind of courage I didn't know I had. This was real. This was happening. And no matter what lay on the other side, I had the gift of their love holding me together, right here, right now.

Mom was glued to my side for the entire two-hour prep, her hand like a lifeline I didn't know I needed. She's an empath through and through, the kind of person who feels everything with her whole heart—so much so that I sometimes wonder if I got all my sensitivity from her by osmosis. She was doing her best to keep smiling, putting on this brave face, but I could see the truth in her eyes: She was holding back tears, her shoulders drawn tight with the silent weight of worry. She stayed strong for me, though, each squeeze of her hand reminding me that no matter what happened, she was right here.

Then, the doctor made his grand entrance and kicked things off with a couple of shots that hit like tequila, given the sudden "loosey-goosey" effect that washed over me. Suddenly, the hospital room felt less like the prelude to an intense operation and more like the start of a very strange party. I was just easing into the fuzzy comfort of those shots when the doctor hit me with a choice I didn't see coming: "Would you like hardcore pain meds, or we could do an epidural?"

An *epidural?* I shot her a look, then glanced at Mom, like, *Did he just offer me the same thing they use for childbirth?* The thought flashed through my mind, leaving me both amused and slightly horrified. So, the pain was going to be *that* intense? Without hesitating, I gave the hardcore drugs a hard pass—no way I was going back down that road. So, an epidural it was. I looked at my mom, and she looked back at me, both of us letting out a quick, nervous laugh that said, *What the hell are we getting ourselves into?* Humor was our shield, our little rebellion against the crushing weight of reality that neither of us was ready to fully face.

Honestly, I'd never been afraid of needles, but as I sat there with both arms already hooked up to IVs, I wondered just how many more they were planning to sneak into me. Finally, they wheeled me down the cold, sterile corridor to the final prep room, a place that felt like an operating theater straight out of a sci-fi movie—flooded with bright white lights that made everything feel a little too real. I was still riding the wave of those "tequila shots," feeling a bit like the life of the party (even if it was a hospital party), and decided it was my moment to rally the troops. With all the bravery of a slightly tipsy cheerleader, I thrust my fist in the air, looking at the nurses as if they were my squad, and shouted, "Let's get this 'Meatball' out!" I swear I heard a chuckle or two, though I was so high on the meds by then that it could've been my imagination running wild. Either way, I felt like a leader going into battle.

Then came the epidural. They had me sit up, spine straight, and warned, "You're going to feel a little pinch—that's the worst part." *A little pinch.* Ha! Understatement of the century. It was less of a pinch and more of a sharp jolt, but I bit down and stayed still. Then I felt it—a sensation so odd, so uncomfortable, that it became its own kind of pain. And just when I thought it was over, I felt it—a slow, deliberate push as the needle tunneled deeper, its path a strange and unsettling sensation that seemed to travel from my back all the way to my stomach. Every second felt like a test of patience, an excruciating countdown, as if I could feel each millimeter of metal burrowing into me. I gritted my teeth, glad I hadn't seen the size of that needle beforehand, or I might have made a run for it.

The epidural would be my armor against what was coming. A saving grace, numbing the aftermath of the surgical trauma, especially where the tumor clung to the head of my pancreas—a place where I'd been told pain would be inevitable. The doctors had told me this, and now, it was all feeling a bit too real. This was going to hurt, but at least the epidural would provide a buffer against the worst of it.

As the final preparations were underway, I looked up at the surgeon with one last, bizarre request. "When this is over, I want the 'Meatball'—the tumor—back," I said. "I want to dispose of it myself." Call it crazy, call it morbid, but something in me needed to hold that thing, to confront the physical piece of cancer that had hijacked my body and my life. I wanted to look it in the eye—so to speak—and tell it goodbye on my terms. I'm not sure what reaction I was expecting, but the nurses shared a look that was half-curious, half-disbelieving, like they couldn't quite believe what they were hearing. But I didn't care how strange it sounded. This was my battle, and I was taking it personally. I needed that closure, that final act of defiance.

And with that, I was ready. Or as ready as anyone could be. As they wheeled me into the operating room, my body wrapped in sterile sheets and my mind a curious mix of fear and adrenaline, I took one last look at my mom, her worried smile giving me courage. Here I was, about to face down this invisible enemy, but I had love and a defiant spark of humor on my side. I might be scared, yes, but I was also ready—ready to reclaim my life, one small step at a time, starting with the removal of a tumor, the "Meatball" that had overstayed its welcome.

"Ten… nine… eight…" and then—*lights out*. The anesthesia swept over me like a wave, pulling me under with a heavy, comforting finality. Somewhere beyond my consciousness, I knew the surgeons were ready, tools poised, about to split me wide open. And oddly enough, in those last moments before oblivion, I felt a strange relief, knowing I was exactly where I was supposed to be for this complicated, rare surgery. I'd done my research, of course, and discovered that this wasn't just any hospital—this was the top place in Los Angeles for the Whipple procedures. USC+LAC, the pride of Medi-Cal insurance, held the best success rates for this surgery, even with its reputation as the "bottom tier" of insurance plans. The irony was almost laughable, really, that this hospital—a place so many looked down on—was about to save my life.

I did my homework—meticulously. I combed through credentials, scoured patient reviews like a detective, and even dug up the occasional obscure article because if someone was going to be slicing into me, I wasn't leaving anything to chance. I didn't just want the best—I *needed* the best. Someone sharp, precise, and damn near flawless, because this wasn't just a routine procedure. This was life or death.

And according to my research, this particular surgery had a history—a messy one. A complication-riddled, anxiety-inducing, let's-not-think-too-hard-about-it kind of history. Of course, medical advancements have made the process far more refined, but that didn't change the fact that what I was facing wasn't just any surgery—it was a monster of a procedure. One that demanded perfection.

But after all my obsessive research and panic-readings, the surgeon passed my test with flying colors—doctor approved; my life was officially in their hands.

Seven hours later, I blinked my way back into existence, though the anesthesia had wiped away any memory of those hours. I must have said some pretty ridiculous things as I came to because my parents were laughing, their faces lit with amusement and relief as I finally woke up, fully coherent. They each took turns greeting me, holding my hand, their love and support washing over me as the reality of it all slowly returned. There was something deeply comforting in waking up to their faces, like an anchor in a sea of unfamiliar sensations.

And oh, there were *sensations*. I reached instinctively to touch my neck, feeling the prickly discomfort of IV needles in place, and the tubes running through my nose. I was some Frankenstein's monster of tubes and medical gear, with wires and lines sprouting from every angle. I felt weak, so weak I could barely move, and then there was my stomach. *My stomach.* I glanced down and was met with the sight of a grotesque swelling—a massive, ballooned, painful mess that looked like I'd swallowed a boulder. Lifting the hospital gown cautiously, I discovered an impressive line of stitches running from the bottom of my breasts straight down the middle, curving neatly around my belly button. It was like a roadmap, tracing where they'd cracked me open to rebuild me. And just above my hip, two additional tubes had been inserted, draining the residual fluid from the operation. They must have sliced me wide, wide open, but I had to admit, the stitching was clean and precise—my surgeon had done a beautiful job.

When she came by to check on me, the surgeon's face beamed with a satisfied smile. "Textbook," she announced. "We got it all." She walked me through everything they'd done: half my pancreas was gone, my gallbladder removed, my stomach reduced to half its size. They'd taken out what they needed and built a new path inside me to keep everything flowing smoothly. And best of all? Zero complications. *Cancer-free.* It was like an exhale after holding my breath for months.

And then, in a moment of pure delight, she pulled out her phone and showed me the image of my tumor—my "Meatball"—in all its grotesque glory. I'd asked, probably sounding a bit insane at the time, if I could keep it. "Hospital policy," she'd said, shaking her head, "no personal keepsakes from inside the body." But she hadn't forgotten my request. She'd snapped a picture and now handed it to me as a sort of victory token. I know, I know, call me a freak, but curiosity had gotten the best of me. I needed to see the thing that had caused so much turmoil, so much pain, and so much uncertainty. Now I had it, captured in pixels, a dark souvenir of a battle won.

And as if that weren't enough, she had more news. While I was out cold, they'd also run a genetic test—a full panel to check if any faulty genes might explain this rare cancer. "Dun dun dun…" I muttered, half-joking, half-bracing for the worst. But her answer shocked me: *none.* Not a single defective gene. It was a mystery, one with no clear answers. "So why me?" I whispered, letting out a sigh that felt like the final release of every last ounce of tension. She shrugged gently, explaining that, for now, the cause of this particular cancer remains unknown. A part of me felt strangely victorious—I wasn't at fault, wasn't cursed with some doomed gene. This was just an unlucky roll of the dice, a brutal twist of fate.

But the news didn't end there. Speculation had been swirling around me for weeks, like a storm I couldn't outrun. The whispers, the what-ifs, the terrifying possibility that cancer and the brutal surgery I had just endured might have taken more from me than I realized—that I might never be able to have children. It was another layer to an already impossible reality, one more thing cancer threatened to steal.

And then, finally, clarity. The verdict? My body was still capable of bringing life into this world if that chapter ever came for me. No radiation. No chemotherapy. No irreversible damage.

"You got out scot-free," the doctor said, grinning.

I was too stunned to laugh, too exhausted to cry, but the relief filled me like the warmest light, thawing a fear I hadn't even realized had settled deep inside me. Somehow, after all of it—the surgeries, the sleepless nights, the moments I wasn't sure I'd make it through—I did it. I was walking away from the fight of my life with my head held high, scarred but stronger, standing on the other side—*cancer-free.*

The cause of my cancer? Still a mystery. The research had told me the same thing over and over: no clear answers. But you know what? I was alive. And in that moment, that was all that mattered.

I didn't fully grasp the enormity of this "cancer journey" until I was laid out in recovery, every nerve and muscle screaming the truth I'd been avoiding. Before surgery, I was under some blissful delusion that I'd be back on my feet in two weeks. A quick reset, a bump in the road, right? The surgeon's warning of "two months minimum" had slid off me with a smirk. The warrior in me doesn't exactly back down; I thought, *I'll be the exception. Just watch.*

But reality hit hard, and with it, the cold understanding that I'd signed up for a battle of a whole different breed. The days before surgery, I'd mustered up every bit of courage to have "the talk" with my manager, that vulnerable, teary confession where I laid it all out: cancer, surgery, and a need for disability relief. She listened, nodding and offering support, her empathy almost making me crumble. The relief of her acceptance was real, but I held onto my warrior act, convinced I'd blaze through this.

Recovery, though, had other ideas. It catapulted me into a journey of complete surrender. Stuck in bed, barely able to shift without wincing, brought me face-to-face with a helplessness I'd never known. I was too weak to even stand, let alone make some miraculous "bounce back." The aftermath of the Whipple procedure was like a storm rolling through every fiber of my body, leaving me flattened. The doctors had remodeled my insides like they were designing a new house, re-routing everything to function without half my pancreas and stomach, and no more gallbladder. They warned me that my return to solid foods would be a slow crawl, but I hadn't anticipated it being this slow. Eating was out of the question; all I could stomach were ice chips and sips of water. And if I ever craved a burger, it was purely theoretical—I didn't have the energy to even think about real food. This "diet" was humbling, to say the least.

Then, there was the pain. Constant, throbbing, sharp pain, like a thousand tiny needles prodding at my insides. In my hand, my only relief—a tiny button, my lifeline to the epidural. I pressed that button as often as it allowed, clutching it like a magic wand that dulled the throb in my core. Every push of that button brought a brief reprieve, a numbing wave that dulled the agony, if only briefly. But sleep was a rarity. The painkillers knocked me out here and there for a precious hour or so, maybe two if I was lucky, but as the pain, gnawing and unrelenting, crept back, I'd lie there, counting the seconds, wondering how much more I could take. Each night stretched into eternity and was replaced by a sleepless haze of discomfort and exhaustion.

My family, bless them, rotated visits, filling the sterile space with a little warmth and familiarity. Even Billy showed up daily, doing his best to seem supportive, though the pain kept me from fully engaging. But it wasn't until a few days in, when they finally propped me up in a chair, that I felt the full impact of what my body had been through. Sitting up for the first time was a humbling experience; I was a stranger in my own body, weak and helpless.

The next day, I was given the green light to start walking, though "walking" was generous. My first attempt at standing was a monumental effort. My belly, swollen and heavy, felt like a boulder strapped to my torso, pulling me downward with each shaky step. For a moment, I thought, *Is this what pregnancy feels like?* I clung to the nearest person, my makeshift crutch, each step more painful than the last. I shuffled forward like a snail, tracing a tiny circle around the hallway, barely making it halfway before I was ready to collapse. But each day, I forced myself to go a little further, my own silent rebellion against the pain that tried to hold me back.

By day six, I was practically clawing at the walls, desperate to escape the hospital. I was still on a liquid diet, still painfully bloated, and the pain wasn't going anywhere, but cabin fever had set in. I wanted out, even if I had to crawl out. As a parting gesture, the nurses brought me my first solid meal—

a bowl of spaghetti and meatballs. My mom and I locked eyes, and then we both burst out laughing, a deep, belly-aching laugh that hurt so much but felt so good. They didn't know, of course, that I'd spent months calling my tumor "Meatball." But here it was, a plate of irony served right as I was about to leave.

It was like the universe had pulled a cosmic prank, a nod to the battle I'd just fought. I couldn't help but appreciate the absurdity, the perfect, twisted poetry of it all. As I sat there with my mom, tears of laughter mixing with the sheer exhaustion of it all, I felt something shift. I had survived this ridiculous, grueling journey, and with a laugh and a plate of spaghetti I could barely look at—I was ready to reclaim my life, one bite at a time.

The doctors walked me through the meticulous map of my recovery as if they were preparing me for an expedition to a far-off land. "Start with small meals—forever," they said, each word landing like a stamp in my newly altered passport of life. "Don't lift anything over fifteen pounds for the next few months. No work for two months, and you'll be on surveillance watch for the next five years with regular testing." Just like that, my life had a whole new set of rules. Then, as if they were passing out candy, they handed me a prescription list—nausea meds, painkillers, and finally, a bottle of OxyContin. I felt a chill just holding it. The last thing I wanted was opioids, given my past. Yet, ironically, those tiny white pills were the only things that cut through the unrelenting pain.

The first thing I needed to do—no, *craved* to do—was throw myself into the shower, though my body felt too weak to even walk there. I didn't have the strength, and I barely had the will, but I had to feel the rush of warm water wash over me, to cleanse away the stale stickiness of days spent glued to hospital sheets. The scent of antiseptic, the sterile chill clinging to my skin—I couldn't escape them fast enough. Six days of immobility had left me feeling trapped in my own body, as if my own skin was foreign. I made my way slowly to the bathroom, every step a small rebellion against the pain tethering me to the bed.

When I reached the bathroom mirror, I froze, blinking, unable to believe the image staring back at me. It was like meeting a ghost in the mirror—a shadow of myself. Who was this person? A stranger—frail, like a faded echo of who I once was. My face was sallow and hollow, my eyes sunken, and my hip bones jutted out, stark and sharp, like ridges on a skeleton. Where there had once been curves and muscle, was now a frame that had been whittled down to nearly nothing—skin and bones.

Then I looked down, and my stomach—the sight hit me like a punch. Bloated and painfully swollen, it stood out like a twisted caricature against my thin frame. It was a cruel contrast, this heavy, distended belly on a body so starved and frail. I placed a tentative hand on it, feeling the strange fullness that was anything but natural. The numbers on the scale felt just as surreal: 110 pounds. I'd lost twenty pounds, but the sight in the mirror made it feel like I'd lost so much more. My body had become something unfamiliar, a strange, fragile casing, like the remnant of a life interrupted.

I stood there, numb, grappling with this new reality. I barely recognized myself; I was a stranger in my own reflection, someone I'd never met before. In that moment, the enormity of it all—the surgery, the pain, the journey still ahead—pressed down on me. I don't know how long I stood there, staring, caught between horror and disbelief, feeling like the ground had shifted beneath me. This was me now, stripped down, raw, my stomach bloated painfully against the rest of my tiny frame, a stranger in my own skin.

The silver lining in all of this? My sweet Mocha Bear. Seeing her when I got home felt like a miracle, an instant balm for my worn-out soul. She greeted me with all the love she could muster, her whole body wiggling in that special, Aussie way, her tail swishing back and forth, eyes sparkling with joy. But I had to be cautious—extra cautious. I couldn't let her jump on me or curl up against my stomach where the incision was still fresh and tender. Playtime was out of the question; our usual long walks were on indefinite hold.

Mocha is a clever girl, though, an Aussie through and through. I knew she'd understand if I could just *show* her. So, in our first quiet moment together, I carefully lifted my shirt, revealing the long, angry scar running across my stomach, still raw and healing. I leaned down and let her sniff it, thinking her sharp senses would tell her all she needed to know. She leaned in close, her nose working as she took it in, sniffing cautiously as if piecing together a mystery. And then, as if a switch had flipped, her eyes softened, and her mood sank.

Without a word, she scurried away and hid, her ears drooping, wearing the saddest expression I'd ever seen on her sweet face. She looked... heartbroken, like the weight of my pain had somehow seeped into her. Everyone around us gasped, feeling the rawness of her reaction. My heart clenched seeing her response. It was a look that spoke volumes, a dog's way of saying, *I know you're hurting, and I won't make it worse.* She understood, in that wordless, instinctive way animals do. It was like she instantly grasped that her usual exuberance could hurt me. And though her reaction broke my heart, her sensitivity was nothing short of amazing.

From that moment on, Mocha became my gentle companion, my quiet protector. She stayed by my side, nestled close without ever pressing too hard, her warm, fluffy body curled up against me like a soft shield. She'd nudge me with her nose, pressing gentle kisses onto my face, her eyes filled with understanding. Her extra kisses, her tender nudges—each one felt like a tiny, unspoken spell, sending comfort straight to my core. I'd hold her tight, letting her warmth ease the pain, both physical and emotional, as we melted into each other, her soft breaths steadying mine. In those weeks of recovery, she was my shadow, my constant, her quiet strength becoming the elixir I didn't know I needed.

Nausea was now my new constant companion, an unwelcome guest I couldn't shake. The nausea came on like a cruel prank from my newly rewired digestive system, a sick reminder that half my pancreas was gone. Hospital sleep had been a rare, fractured mess of one- or two-hour stretches, interrupted by nurses, machines, and that ever-present dull ache. But home offered little reprieve; the pain followed me, coiled and throbbing in the pit of my stomach, keeping me awake through the early hours. It felt like the pain had ratcheted up a notch.

The Oxy would knock me out for a blissful three hours, a brief retreat from the burning in my stomach. But when those three hours were over, I'd be wide awake, gritting my teeth, counting the seconds until I could take my next dose. I hated that waiting game, the countdown that stretched each minute into an eternity. Plus, the memory of addiction would spark up. No, thank you.

Pain took on a new meaning. It wasn't just the kind that makes you wince; it was bone-deep, raw, relentless. Unforgiving. Imagine lying down and realizing you can't just… sit up. I had to clutch the bed sheets, using them as leverage to roll onto my side, then grab hold of something else to haul myself upright. Every motion was a negotiation with my body, a surrender to weakness I didn't want to acknowledge.

And then, a flash of inspiration hit—Isaiah, bless his soul and blunt wisdom, gave me a game-changing suggestion: "Try an edible," he said. And oh, was he right! I didn't hesitate. I ordered a stash that very day, and let me tell you, the game changed completely. I tossed the Oxy and leaned into my edible routine, overdosing myself on at least 25 mg each night, sinking in a haze of calm. For the first time in days, I managed a solid six hours of sleep. Wish it was more than, but that'll do for now. Those little gummies became my nightly saviors, and I clung to them until the pain finally began to loosen its grip.

Eating was its own odyssey. My beautiful, angelic mother, bless her tenacity, moved in with me and took on the role of caregiver. Miss Independent? Not so much anymore. I was humbled in a way I'd never known. Every last ounce of my strength was gone, leaving me so weak I could barely shower myself, let alone cook or take care of myself. Mom took over everything—she cooked, cleaned, looked after my sweet Mocha, who seemed to sense the chaos in her own way. Each time Mom brought me a meal, it looked like a feast, though it was barely enough to fill a cereal bowl. I could only manage a few bites. It was frustrating, demoralizing, but she was patient, coaxing me through each bite as if she were feeding a child. I was too weak, too nauseated, my stomach too shrunken and foreign. She handled everything—caring for Mocha, tidying up, supporting me in ways I hadn't known I needed and answered every small cry for help I had. I lay in bed, binge-watching movies, existing in this strange, liminal space of survival, tethered by my mother's patience and kindness. Her quiet strength held me together through the blur of days.

The weeks stretched into a haze of recovery, one hour bleeding into the next. For the first few weeks, I was mostly bedridden, only beginning to shuffle around after that.

Coming out of surgery also brought on a storm of love and support that felt overwhelming in the best possible way. Flowers, gifts, and plants poured in from friends and family—a true *downpour* of affection that turned our apartment into a riot of color. Bouquets filled every corner, spilling over tables, counters, even windowsills, until it looked like we were hosting the world's most vibrant indoor garden—or maybe a very cheerful funeral. The scent of fresh blooms hung in the air, mingling with the quiet hum of my recovery. It was impossible to feel alone, surrounded by so much love, by so many thoughtful gestures from people who cared.

My closest friends kept calling and took turns visiting, each one bringing their own energy and warmth, their presence lifting my spirits as I stayed parked on the couch, too weak to do much else. They'd chat with me, filling the air with laughter and stories, moments of normalcy that felt like gold. I was blown away by their kindness, the sheer consistency of their care. I'd always known I had good friends, but this was different—it was love that showed up when things were hard, love that refused to look away. It was a beautiful and humbling reminder of who my true friends were, and it filled my heart to bursting.

Of course, the real MVP was my mom. I'll admit, I was a bit nervous about spending such a long stretch of time with her. We hadn't been under the same roof like this for ages, and there's always that hint of uncertainty about how things will go. But having her there turned out to be the greatest blessing, one that went far beyond what I could have imagined. She was my rock, my lifeline, there for every small struggle, every request, every whispered, "Mom, could you...?" She took care of everything: cooking, cleaning, running errands, even tending to both our dogs. She poured herself into my recovery, giving without a second thought—her time, her patience, her warmth. I truly don't know how I would've made it without her by my side.

Meanwhile, Natasha was… present but removed. She did her own thing, understandably, while I was cooped up in recovery mode. She let me use her room, as it had a TV, since mine didn't, which was a small mercy for which I was grateful. But beyond that, she stayed on the sidelines, a spectator rather than an active supporter. And then, in a twist that floored me, she complained to my mom about not sharing the meals my mother had been cooking.

Imagine—my mother, who had already given everything to support me, being nagged for not grocery-shopping for someone else. It was laughable, except that it wasn't. Mom had been sharing meals freely for as long as I could remember, but this was different; this was a long haul, an unending stream of giving. Natasha hadn't pitched in for groceries, hadn't lifted a finger to help, yet here she was, voicing her entitlement. It hurt, not just for me but for my mom, who didn't deserve even a whisper of that complaint. I couldn't let it stand, but I also chose to focus on gratitude and recovery rather than frustration.

My heart swelled with thankfulness for my mother's endless support, her unbreakable patience. She gave me more than help; she gave me love in every form, through every act. And to her, I owe everything—my strength, my healing, my sanity through those rough weeks. Mom, thank you, from the bottom of my heart. I came out on the other side because of you.

Oh, this recovery, this war with my own body, was nothing like I'd imagined. A lesson in humility, in surrender, in accepting help when I didn't want to admit I needed it. I had gone into it, thinking I was invincible, convinced I'd be the one to bounce back. Instead, I was cracked open, vulnerable in a way I'd never been before. My mom, my friends and family, my dog—each one of them propped me up, carried me through the darkest days. And now, looking back, I see that while the surgery may have taken out the cancer, it was this endless, painful process of healing that truly transformed me. It was a trial by fire, a wild experience, one I'll never forget—a journey I never would've chosen, but that, in some strange way, reshaped me from the inside out.

Chapter 18

Diagnosis: WTF

I beat cancer. I still have to say it to myself sometimes, just to let it sink in. I faced down my biggest, most paralyzing fear and came out on the other side. And it wasn't just any cancer—I took on the rarest of the rare, the 1% of all pancreatic cancers, the elusive kind that hides in shadows, waiting. And somehow, I caught it in time. No genetic markers, no family legacy of illness, just a one-in-a-million fluke that landed in my lap. It's nearly impossible to believe, and yet, here I am, breathing and grateful. The statistics alone would've told me I didn't stand a chance—pancreatic cancer, the silent killer, the one that people rarely catch in time. But for reasons I'll never fully understand, I knew. I *knew*, and I spoke up. I caught it. I did the impossible. I'm still here, breathing, and that reality humbles me every day.

Thank you, universe, God, Grandma Rita, guardian angels—whatever miraculous power pulled me through. Because I know, as surely as I know anything, that if I hadn't listened to my intuition, hadn't voiced that whispering fear, I might not be here. I'd have let the "Meatball" simmer and grow, hidden and deadly. As much as I shudder to think it, the end would've come without warning, the silent passage of something dark and deadly inside me. I was a whisper away from a different ending, from never knowing what was happening until it was irreversible. I believe that in my bones. But instead, I get to tell this story—**Strike Three**.

There was one moment in particular, one that will stay with me forever. I was bedridden, weak as a leaf, when my mom came over, her eyes misty, brimming with tears. She touched my hand softly and said, "Cookie Grandma Rita was watching over you." Her words went straight to my heart, unlocking every tear I'd been holding back, my vision blurring as the floodgates opened. I lost it right there; she was right. Grandma Rita had always said she'd watch over me, that she'd be my guardian angel. And in that fragile moment, I felt her presence so clearly, as if she were right there beside me. And then, as if from a distant echo, I remembered my last session with the psychic—her cryptic warning about a health scare, the insistence that a health scare would be in my future. Back then, I'd brushed it off. And yet, here I was, saved by that uncanny intuition. It was like a surreal, cosmic puzzle had fallen into place, and I was left reeling, blown away by the mystery of it all.

This entire journey shook me to the core, dismantling everything I thought I knew about myself, about my strength, about my limits. My body was a battlefield, reduced to skin and bones, fragile and unsteady. Eating became a delicate negotiation, a small battle in its own right. And then, there was the embarrassing, humbling reality of not being able to go to the bathroom for weeks post-surgery. It was as if my own body had declared a strike. My stomach, once my anchor, now felt foreign and fragile, unable to do even the simplest things without effort. And then, the embarrassing, frustrating reality of going *weeks* without a single bowel movement after surgery. It was beyond uncomfortable; it was a physical betrayal. I had no appetite, couldn't get through more than a few bites, and even when I did eat, my body barely cooperated. It was like a cruel, ironic twist, and all I could was endure it, one uncomfortable day at a time. Pushing, straining, forcing my weakened muscles to do the simplest things—it felt impossible.

And then there was the scar, a badge of survival if ever there was one. It stretched across my abdomen, stitched and sealed with a glue designed to dissolve slowly over time. Each day, tiny flakes of the stitching would fall away, revealing a raw, pink line that marked me, permanently. I wasn't just me anymore; I was someone with a history, with a story etched into my skin. I couldn't even lift fifteen pounds, couldn't do the simplest things without feeling the incision pull, every slight movement reminding me of the fragility of my healing core. But this scar, this careful stitching—they were a testament to the skill and dedication of the surgeons and nurses who'd guided me through, patching me up and helping me cross back into life. They'd given me a second chance—I owe them a debt I can never repay, a gratitude so deep it reaches my bones.

This journey cracked me wide open, leaving me exposed, broken, and then reshaping me, piece by fragile piece. I emerged scarred and changed, grateful and deeply humbled. I've lived through something rare, something miraculous. And now, with every breath, I know that I'm more alive than I've ever been.

Did I actually recover? Did I really process and digest this whole surreal journey? Absolutely not. Even now, two years later, I'm still trying to catch up to it all, still unpacking the weight of what happened. Those two months on medical leave weren't just about physical healing; they became a masterclass in surrender, a forced lesson in what it means to slow down and give myself grace—a word I had to learn to embody. This wasn't like being stuck during the pandemic; this was a whole different beast, a confinement of body and mind. My world narrowed to a single focus: letting myself heal, learning to live in the in-between spaces.

For someone as hardwired as I am to push, to strive, to be the relentless go-getter, this journey was as much about restraint as it was about recovery. Giving myself grace became an act of survival—grace as a verb, an ongoing, active choice. I had to wrap myself in patience, to whisper to my inner warrior that it was time to rest. This was one battle I couldn't muscle my way through, one journey where the best thing I could do was nothing. And nothing, for me, felt like a foreign language. It played tricks on my mind, coaxing me to believe I could handle it all alone. But there was my mom's voice, always a beat ahead, reminding me to take it easy: "Put it down! Don't touch, don't lift!" She was right there, my ever-vigilant sentinel, making sure I didn't sabotage my own recovery. And for the first time, I had to let her be right.

This wasn't a case of just resting my body; this was about respecting the depths of what I'd endured. The "Meatball" had been carved out of me, and now every inch of my body was a reminder of the fragile, tentative new start I'd been given. I had just turned thirty, young enough to heal, but old enough to understand the gravity of it. This temple of mine would mend, but only if I learned to stop and let it.

In those moments of forced stillness, gratitude became my anchor. Yes, there were moments of frustration and pain, but there was also this bone-deep thankfulness that I'd come out on the other side without needing chemo or radiation. And I was wrapped in love, the kind that didn't just show up—it stayed. My friends called, sent messages, and took turns visiting, bringing laughter and light when I needed it most. They brought picnics to the beach, little escapes that reminded me there was life outside of my pain. And in those moments, I saw my truest friends rise to the surface, proving their love wasn't just words.

Family, of course, was there, unbreakable as always. Joey couldn't be there in person, caught up in the raging fire near their home, but I knew his heart was with me. And then, there was my mom. My incredible, relentless mom. Healing with her by my side was like facing a mirror, a deeply personal journey wrapped within the physical one. I've said before how I sometimes found her *too* motherly, how her fierce love could feel overbearing now, maybe because it hadn't always been there when I was younger. And yet, here I was, laid bare, reduced to needing her as I never had before. My body was fragile, my spirit vulnerable, and she was my full-time caregiver, the one handling every small detail, every delicate task I couldn't manage.

But this time, I had no choice but to let her in, to let her take care of me in ways that I once resisted. So, I surrendered again, allowing myself to ease into her care, silencing the independent fighter in me, letting go of the need to prove I could do it alone. I watched myself soften, letting my mindset shift, allowing myself to enjoy the quiet moments, the time off, the simple *being*. For the first time in ages, I let myself be her daughter, unguarded and open. I wasn't Miss Independent; I was simply Haley, letting myself receive the love I'd held at a distance for so long.

And in this strange, twisted way, I realized I needed this journey. As much as it hurt to admit it, I needed this humbling experience to break down the walls I'd built around my mom, to let her see me as vulnerable and to let myself feel the closeness I'd been craving. This experience had shaken me, cracked me wide open, but it had also carved a path to her that I hadn't been able to walk before. I don't know if I would have allowed myself to let her in so deeply, to feel the gravity of her love, without this struggle.

By the last two weeks of medical leave, I could feel life slowly returning to me, inch by inch, breath by breath. I was finally able to step back into the world, carrying a little extra grace, a little more patience, and a closeness with my mom that was as tender and unbreakable as a scar. And I knew, without a doubt, that I'd come out of this not just as a survivor but as someone profoundly changed, and infinitely grateful.

Now that I had a taste of normalcy again, I was beyond ready to seize it—time to jump headfirst into a new acting class! The moment I felt even the slightest hint of energy return, I didn't take a breath; I went straight to the search bar, hunting for the next chapter of my acting journey. LA is a haven for every acting style and technique under the sun, like a giant marketplace for the artist's soul.

My resume would prove that I've been around, trying everything from improv to method, "shopping" my way through classes, hoping to find the one that would stick. But this time, it wasn't about "trying" something. I was ready for commitment, determined to stay in a class every single month, no excuses.

After an exhaustive search, I landed on the Baron Brown Studio in Santa Monica, a place that felt like a perfect match. I sent in my inquiry, secured an interview, and, without a second thought, got accepted into their program. Was it impulsive? Oh, absolutely. But after everything, I was fired up, ready to move forward, and I couldn't bear the thought of waiting. The program itself was intense: a two-year commitment, complete with a strict attendance policy—no lateness, no absences, unless you were sick or facing a legitimate family emergency. The only other acceptable excuse? A speaking role. No background work—this was serious.

The best part? The program was all about the Meisner technique, one I hadn't tackled yet, though I knew it was beloved by actors everywhere. And here's the kicker: right before the interview, I'd randomly bought *Sanford Meisner on Acting*. Talk about cosmic timing! It was like the universe itself nudged me toward this program. I felt the pull, undeniable and electric. So, with every ounce of excitement I could muster, I paid my deposit, locked in my spot, and prepared for class. The wait began, and I felt ready, ready to throw myself into this, to stretch, to grow, and to immerse myself in the art I loved. This was a new beginning.

How was therapy going? Well, I kept at it, week after week, working through layers I didn't even know I had. To be honest, it stung that the specific mission I'd walked in with—the one goal I'd wanted to tackle head-on—wasn't my therapist's cup of tea. But as things unfolded, she ended up guiding me through some of the most pivotal and unexpected moments of my life: cancer, the ups and downs of a new relationship with Billy, and my tangled history with relationships in general. With Billy, I decided to approach things differently. Vulnerability had always been my Achilles heel, my voice buried deep, thanks to years of swallowing words and stuffing down feelings, conditioned by past emotional and verbal wounds. This time, I committed to using my voice, to *being seen*, to expressing my needs and my emotions, openly and honestly. No numbing, no hiding, no pretending to be "fine."

After three years of blissful solitude, I hadn't exactly been hunting for a relationship. And neither had Billy. Yet, here we were, and I was determined to do it right. Fortunately, Billy had already put in his own hours on the therapist's couch, which meant our conversations could go places—raw, deep, uncomfortable places where growth happens. With the support of therapy, I began showing up fully, stretching into parts of myself I hadn't accessed in years. And then there was cancer—a mountain I hadn't expected to climb. My therapist walked with me through the surreal, terrifying terrain, gently challenging me to confront it head-on. "Stop calling it a 'Meatball.' Call it cancer." That word landed like a punch. But I realized she was right; hiding behind my humor, behind nicknames, was a shield I couldn't afford to keep up if I wanted to heal. To truly process it, I had to name it: cancer, tumor, the dark thing that had invaded my body. Each time I spoke the words, they tasted bitter, but each one chipped away at my fear, leaving room for something deeper—acceptance, maybe even strength.

The most earth-shattering insight she gave me, though, was a simple but profound truth that stopped me cold. "Addiction was in your control; cancer wasn't." I felt like the floor had dropped out from under me. That statement sank into me with a force I hadn't expected, setting off a wave of thoughts and emotions that spun through me like a tornado. *Whoa.* That single sentence unraveled years of tightly held beliefs. Addiction, my battle with willpower and self-destruction, had always been my fight, something I could wrestle with and, eventually, overcome. But cancer? It had arrived uninvited, unstoppable. And I realized, in a new way, that sometimes life throws battles at us that have nothing to do with strength or resilience, but everything to do with fate and surrender.

Then, there was Billy. We'd been together for nine months, but just as the year was drawing to a close, things started to get a little stormy. I'll spare the messy details, but let's just say that Billy was carrying his own set of scars, and some of them started bleeding into our relationship. He was like a lost puppy, still reeling from the wreckage of a decade-long marriage and a divorce that had left him a shadow of himself. He'd always lived by that old saying, "happy wife, happy life," and he'd gotten so lost in that identity that he didn't quite know who he was outside of it. I could relate, having once buried myself in my relationship with Grey Knight, sacrificing pieces of myself to make it work. But Billy was going down some strange, murky roads that I hadn't seen before, making choices that left me staring, questioning who this man really was.

It was like he'd emerged from the shadows, and suddenly, I was seeing a different side of him—a side tangled up in unresolved pain and slow-brewing drama. It felt like I was living in the middle of a smoldering fire, watching it build, wondering when it would ignite. Every day, the tension simmered a little stronger, and I couldn't shake the feeling that something was going to give. And trust me, the explosion was on its way—just wait.

On the brighter side of things, those women I'd been bonding with at work were quickly becoming some of the closest friends I'd had in years. It all changed when they surprised me by picking me up from my mom's house after my surgery and whisking me away for a ride. That day, something shifted. We knew each other from the steakhouse, sure, but suddenly, we were more than just coworkers—we were friends, real friends, the kind you can lean on and laugh with. It felt like something I hadn't had since middle school, a true group of girlfriends where everyone just *clicked*.

I was thriving, surrounded by these wonderful, genuine women, all of us vibing effortlessly, sharing deep, meaningful conversations one minute, then roaring with laughter the next. The memories were stacking up, and so were the bonds—growing deeper with every shared moment, every story, every ride out together. It felt rare. You can bond with coworkers, but when you start investing in friendships beyond the work walls, that connection takes on a different depth. We'd crossed that line from coworkers to confidantes, and I suddenly had four phenomenal women who felt like a sisterhood.

Life shifted, and two of these ladies left the steakhouse, which, oddly enough, only strengthened our friendships. It was like the universe had sealed our bond. The three of us left behind became a trio, our little "Powerpuff Girls" crew—a name we'd given ourselves that felt hilariously fitting. We spent days together, falling into this easy rhythm of sharing everything and anything, creating a three-way group chat that stayed buzzing with messages. Whether it was venting, celebrating, or just sharing the everyday weirdness of life, that group chat became a safe haven. It was a thread of connection that kept us close, even on our craziest days.

The magic was in our differences. Each of us had a unique personality, a different perspective that blended perfectly into a friendship that was rich with insight and warmth. We always had each other's backs. Advice flowed freely, colored by our distinct personalities, each perspective offering a fresh angle. It was special—exceptionally special. And, in a way, it was exactly the support I didn't even realize I'd need for what was looming on the horizon with Billy. But that's a story for later…

The first day of acting class kicked off in mid-November, and I could hardly keep still, buzzing with excitement. This was my fresh start, my two-year journey into something real and raw, and I was all in. When I walked into the room, it felt like stepping into another world—half theater, half classroom, with a small stage on one end and rows of chairs set up like an audience. The room practically pulsed with possibility. I found a seat next to this radiant girl with a megawatt smile, Halle. She had this magnetic energy, instantly warm and welcoming, and within seconds, she was saying hello to everyone, introducing herself like we were old friends reuniting instead of strangers. And just like that, everyone else joined in, each of us offering our names and bits about ourselves, no awkwardness, no forced politeness, just an immediate sense of ease. It was one of those rare, magic 'first days' where every trace of nervousness melts away, and you just *are*, present and open.

Then, Anne Dremann, our teacher, took her place at the front. She launched into a sweeping introduction, laying out the terrain of the journey we were about to embark on, describing the next two years as both a transformation and a challenge. And as she spoke, I felt this strange, comforting familiarity wash over me. I was hooked, I saw her—*Cookie Grandma Rita.* It hit me like a flash of déjà vu, as if my grandmother's spirit had reincarnated in this woman standing before me, guiding me into the next chapter of my life. I couldn't explain it, but I felt drawn to her, feeling that unmistakable warmth, like she was a piece of home in this new world. I didn't know Anne at all yet, hadn't exchanged more than a polite greeting, but I felt an immediate connection to her that was almost electric, in my bones. There she was, my new teacher and —maybe—an aspiring mentor. I could barely believe it, but I knew I was in the right place.

Anne's words cut straight through, and her explanation of the Meisner technique grabbed hold of me, heart and soul. "This training is going to break you down, layer by layer, peeling back the onion layers until you're like a six-year-old again—unfiltered, no walls." That sentence hung in the air, daring us to imagine what it would feel like to be so exposed, so real. I knew then that this wasn't going to be just another class or a skill to pick up. This was a journey into my own depths, a reckoning with every part of me I'd built walls around, and I was captivated by it, almost intimidated—but in the best way. And that feeling of kinship with Anne, the way she felt like my grandmother's spirit reborn, only deepened my commitment to the path I was stepping onto.

For those who don't know, the Meisner Technique is an approach built on three core elements: emotional preparation, repetition, and improvisation. The philosophy behind it is simple yet profound: These elements are designed to strip away the rehearsed, the predictable, allowing actors to stay fully engaged in the moment with their scene partners. It's about authenticity, about reacting truthfully to the stimuli around you instead of relying on lines or memory alone. Anne explained that the first year would be all about the basics—repetition exercises, independent activities, and, most importantly, emotional preparation. Our focus was vulnerability, the kind that reaches down to the bones. And I was ready. I'd already been working on opening up, shedding my own defenses, but this? This was like permission to dive all the way in, to pull back the layers until only the rawest version of me remained.

I didn't realize it then, but signing up for this class was like taking on a second job. It wasn't just an acting program—it was a commitment to excavating the parts of myself I'd buried, a vow to keep digging, to uncover, to expose, to *become*. And I couldn't wait to see who I'd find beneath it all.

As December rolled around, so did that inevitable thirty-day notice for our lease renewal. Decisions loomed like clouds, heavy with the promise of change. We'd been warned: rent was about to jump a few hundred dollars, and this time, there'd be no room for negotiation. I could almost feel the finality of it; the sweet little deal we'd scored last year as new tenants was long gone. And, honestly, as much as I loved our space, I'd been feeling that undeniable itch for something different, something that was *mine*.

After a decade of roommate roulette, filled with some gems but far too many nightmares, I was finally ready to live alone. Don't get me wrong—living with Natasha had been surprisingly wonderful. She'd been one of my best roommates, someone I could laugh with and share life with. But as we edged closer to that two-year mark, I could feel a pull in a different direction. Living with her had been like a window into her world, a close-up view of her habits, her spirit, her quirks, and as much as I loved her, I needed space. I craved a home that was just mine, a place where I could unwind, where there wouldn't be the soft hum of another person's life overlapping with mine. I was ready to end the era of roommates—at least until the day might come when I move in with a partner.

Natasha, though, was still dreaming of our next steps together. She'd even hinted at the idea of finding a new place, moving our little "family" somewhere else. And I couldn't help but feel a pang of guilt. As much as I'd enjoyed our time together, I knew deep down that it was time for a change, a leap into independence. So, in the spirit of this newfound commitment to honesty, I took a deep breath, summoned my courage, and told her gently but firmly that I thought it would be healthiest for both of us if we went our separate ways. She took it in, her face softening, but I could see the hurt flicker in her eyes. She didn't say much, and in that moment, I felt the weight of my decision settle in. But I knew I had to honor it. This was something I needed to do for me.

It was bittersweet, no doubt about it. Our friendship had always felt solid, but lately, there had been a growing sense that I needed more distance. This close-up friendship, this "roommate bubble" we'd built, had been wonderful, but I needed to see what life looked like outside of it. Would our bond survive the separation, or would it quietly fade? I had no idea. But in that moment, I knew I had to put myself first. I was done with the roommate life, with compromising in my own space. It was time to claim a place where I could come home to quiet, to peace, to a space that was all mine.

So, the hunt began. This time, though, there was a thrill to it, a feeling of possibility around every listing I clicked. I was stepping into a new chapter, the promise of a space where every inch was a reflection of me, where I could finally breathe fully, laugh loudly, and unwind completely. I couldn't wait to turn that key, walk through the door, and know that for the first time in a long time, I was truly, blissfully, home.

Chapter 19

Breadcrumbs & Bullsh*t

This whole moving process became an adventure of its own. It wasn't just your typical apartment search—it was the kind that turned into a journey, with my dog Mocha as my faithful (and furry) co-pilot. We combed through listings, scoured neighborhoods, and toured way too many places far too early. But of course, as anyone who's ever moved in a city knows, the magic really happens in those final two nail-biting weeks before move-out. It's a race, an art of tactical procrastination, where finding the "perfect place" feels like a myth, but settling for "good enough" feels like a win. Throw a dog into the mix, and suddenly, your choices shrink down to a postage stamp.

So, I made an executive decision: Mocha was getting an upgrade. No more of this landlord-imposed dog fee nonsense. Mocha was officially promoted to Emotional Support Animal, complete with papers to guarantee she could accompany me wherever I set up camp—no pet deposits, no extra monthly fees. It was a stroke of genius, honestly, though that didn't help with our last place, where I paid a cool five hundred for the privilege of Mocha's company, plus fifty dollars a month. Meanwhile, my roommate Natasha, clever as ever, snuck her dog Howie in under the radar after we moved. She'd moved him in after the lease was signed, managing to sidestep every extra fee. The apartment gods had favored her once again. I get it—apartment managers can be particular about pets, but the unfairness of it all made me want to howl right alongside Mocha.

While I was proactively searching and lining up options, Natasha, the ever-free spirit and freelance photographer, was… shall we say, blissfully unburdened by the logistics of life? She didn't have steady paystubs, and two weeks before our lease ended, she hadn't even glanced at other apartments. It drove me up the wall! I mean, here I was, lining up paperwork, readying applications, and she was—well, in no rush. I'd watch her casually apply to jobs here and there to get some income verification, but otherwise, nothing. I kept thinking, "Girl, this is insane!" In a city like LA, you can't just wing it and hope for the best, especially when you're inches away from the deadline. Natasha, though, seemed to be testing the boundaries of exactly that.

Finally, as we hit those last crucial days, she sprang into action. She set up a "nomad plan" to bounce between places since she couldn't afford a security deposit or even split a place with a roommate. I'd be lying if I said her approach didn't make my palms sweat, but all I cared about at that point was her having a plan so we wouldn't get charged for overstaying. And, miraculously, she pulled it off! Talk about cutting it close.

As for me, I had my sights set on two promising apartments in Culver City, practically neighbors, just a street apart. One of them was a perfect fit— spacious, bright, exactly the vibe I wanted. But, in classic LA fashion, the leasing office botched my application. Thankfully, the backup option—a small studio I hadn't even toured—came through, and I was officially approved. Smaller? Yes. But that was fine. I was ready for a change, ready for my own space. I rallied a few friends, and we got to work, beating the rain to haul boxes and bags in and out, keeping things fun and low-stress while Natasha tackled her last-minute move.

Natasha, though—oh, Natasha—she kept her big move to the eleventh hour, dragging out furniture and bag after bag even as the clock ticked down. She really kept the leasing office on edge, practically daring them to charge us extra. But somehow, she skated by without a scratch, and finally, she was out. Where to? Her boyfriend's place, of course. He was already living with and financially supporting his family—part of their culture, as she explained—so why not add one more? Rent-free, just like she planned.

As I waved her off, I couldn't help but marvel at her style. Her "nomadic lifestyle," as she called it, seemed less like free-spirited adventure and more like sidestepping responsibility. Still, there was an odd admiration in me for her audacity. Would I have gone to such lengths? Probably not. But as I settled into my new place with Mocha, I realized that, as different as Natasha and I were, we each made it work in our own ways. She had her path, I had mine, and maybe, just maybe, that's what kept our friendship—though unconventional—still intact.

Moving into my new apartment was a little like stepping into the final chapter of a long, exhausting novel. After weeks of chaos and cramped spaces, I had finally arrived at the beginning of something that was mine and mine alone. The whole place was an open invitation to breathe, to unfurl, to just be—and I intended to savor every square inch of my newfound solitude. In that first quiet moment, I stretched out, arms wide, spinning slowly in my tiny studio as if testing the walls to see how they held my dreams, my fears, and, yes, even my joy. For the first time, I didn't have to share the air with anyone else's energy, anyone else's clutter. It was a fresh, delicious slice of peace.

But alongside the peace came a sense of purpose. I wanted to build up my finances, to live with a cushion, a sense of grace—and a second job felt like the ticket to making that happen. Within days, the stars aligned, and I landed a serving gig at a brand-new Persian fine-dining spot just five minutes from my door. It was a hidden gem, draped in rich fabrics and dimly lit by amber-colored chandeliers that made every meal feel like a work of art. It felt like fate, the perfect counterpart to the steakhouse where I already worked. I was doubling up, building the foundation for the life I envisioned, one plate at a time. A small victory, but one I celebrated with a fist pump and a small dance in my new space.

Setting up my studio was like orchestrating a puzzle, each piece of furniture a calculated move. Living in a tiny space meant every single item had to earn its keep—multi-purpose or bust. I invested in a few statement pieces, items that gave me joy and served a purpose, transforming the space from a blank slate into something that whispered, *home*. By the time I was done, it was cozy, functional, and, best of all, mine. All that was left was to hang up my vision board, my sacred space for scribbling goals, dreams, and wild ideas that would one day unfold. But to get that board on the wall, I needed a little help.

Naturally, the first person who came to mind was Ezekiel, our trusty maintenance guy from my last apartment. He was talented with a drill and, more importantly, a friend—though a complicated one, thanks to the Natasha saga. I had distanced myself after he'd sided with her during the drama, and while it stung, enough time had passed for old wounds to soften.

I reached out, more out of a desire to rekindle our friendship than to use him for his skills, and he didn't hesitate to show up. He brought his tools and, with steady hands, helped me mount the board exactly where I wanted it. We shared a few laughs, catching up on life's updates, and by the end of the day, it felt like old times. Little by little, Ezekiel was becoming part of my world again, each conversation bridging the gap that had once seemed so vast.

And then there was Billy. Our one-year anniversary was approaching, and to celebrate, we booked a trip to Mexico—a promise of white sand beaches, endless sun, and a welcome escape from the everyday grind. It felt like a dream waiting to happen. But my acting studio had other plans. I'd bought the tickets before classes began, but when my teacher, Anne, heard about it, she practically went to war for me, lobbying for an excused absence. Then, out of nowhere, the big boss herself—Joanne Baron, queen of the acting studio—called me directly. She didn't mince words. Joanne insisted I cancel, her tone so intense I felt the ground shift under my feet. I could practically hear her mantra echoing through the phone: "The craft first, always the craft."

For a moment, I felt torn—sunny beaches with Billy or dedicating myself fully to my career. In the end, I caved, telling myself that commitment to acting meant sacrifice. The sting was real, but I had to shake it off. Joanne had put her foot down with such force that it felt almost like fate redirecting me. Little did I know, that stern call would save me from so much more than just a missed vacation.

February arrived, but instead of Mexico and margaritas, I found myself in the center of a relationship wildfire. Billy and I hit a wall—hard. The small rifts and unresolved issues that we'd kept pushing aside finally burst through the surface in one gigantic, unstoppable fight. Every piece of our relationship seemed to unravel, threads flying in every direction, and there was no sewing it back together. My heart cracked wide open, and as I sat with the grief and the shock, I couldn't help but feel a strange gratitude for Joanne's call. That canceled trip saved me from what would have been a disastrous getaway, a tainted memory that I now thankfully didn't have to carry.

There, in my little studio, I pieced myself back together, one day at a time. With every note I tacked to my vision board, every small goal I wrote, I felt myself healing, reshaping my heart and my life. My tiny space became a sanctuary, a fresh canvas where I could rebuild. And somewhere along the way, I started to see it all as a gift—the broken plans, the unexpected turns, even the heartbreak. It all added up to something that, in its own strange way, felt like hope. In that studio, just me and my dreams, I finally felt like I was exactly where I was meant to be.

Just before everything with Billy went up in flames, there was this one unforgettable, shining moment. My mom—triple threat that she is—had scored us some unbelievable, pinch-me-I-must-be-dreaming seats to a Lakers game. And not just any game, but the game of games. Fifth row, close enough to feel the energy of the court pulsing beneath our feet, the air alive with the hum of anticipation. It wasn't until we were actually on our way that I realized the significance of the night: LeBron James was about to attempt to break Kareem Abdul-Jabbar's record to become the NBA's all-time leading scorer. Legendary. My heart skipped a beat when I realized that this game wasn't just a game—it was history in the making, and I was about to be part of it.

The arena was electric, the lights brighter, the fans in a frenzy. We could practically feel the sweat as LeBron powered down the court, each basket bringing him one point closer to the record. And then, like a movie climax, it happened—he broke the record. The crowd erupted, and I was on my feet, caught up in the energy, screaming alongside everyone else. A piece of sports history had unfolded right before me, and I was swept up in the magic of it all, a high that would stick with me for days. Little did I know that just after that incredible night, my world with Billy would finally crack wide open.

The signs had been there, lingering like storm clouds on the horizon. Our relationship had been a slow burn, simmering with quiet frustrations and tiny fractures I kept hoping would heal. Billy was often lost, wandering in his own world, and I tried my best to be patient, to be the one who grounded him. We'd have these heavy talks where I'd sit there, doing my best to reach him, to understand his struggles. But lately, there was a shift—a subtle change I couldn't ignore. The openness that had once defined us started to feel one-sided.

He developed this maddening habit of breadcrumbing me with half-truths, offering just enough to keep me guessing, but never giving the full picture. Every conversation turned into a puzzle, me pulling answers from him piece by piece, as if he enjoyed keeping me in suspense.

I started feeling like an audience to his monologues. The back-and-forth we once had, that mutual curiosity, was gone. He'd unload, and I'd listen, but he never seemed to return the favor. It was as if my thoughts, my dreams, my ambitions were only background noise to his own journey. Selfishness was creeping in like a ghost, haunting our conversations until I couldn't unsee it. Every story, every complaint, every minor revelation revolved around his world, with no room left for mine. I felt like I'd become his sounding board, his silent audience, while my own voice got lost in the noise. It was exhausting, like he was pulling me into a whirlpool and expecting me to swim for both of us. And slowly, I began to realize how familiar it all felt. This was Grey Knight all over again—just wrapped in a different package.

But Billy's lack of ambition gnawed at me in a way I couldn't ignore. Here I was, chasing my dream with everything I had, and he was floating, making half-hearted jokes about being a "stay-at-home dad" even though he claimed he never wanted kids. There were cracks everywhere, and I couldn't pretend not to notice. He seemed content to ride along with me, expecting I'd carry us both while he coasted. And in the back of my mind, a voice kept whispering that I was settling, that I was watching the very standards I'd built for myself with Grey Knight erode. It was a startling realization, one that reminded me of every painful lesson I'd learned with Grey Knight.

Then, one night, the final blow landed. It was like he'd been setting the stage, carefully constructing his words to push me to my breaking point. He revealed his so-called "big dream"—a life goal so far from what I expected, so utterly ungrounded, that it left me stunned. It wasn't a career move, nor was it something I could relate to on any level; in fact, it was so offbeat, so deeply out of sync with my values and my own aspirations, it was something that didn't resemble any life I wanted. I felt a rush of betrayal, realizing that he'd kept this hidden, that he'd been stringing me along without ever revealing his cards. This wasn't a conversation; it was a setup, a carefully orchestrated script designed to put me in a corner.

The way he delivered it, too—oh, he was strategic. Every word seemed chosen to manipulate, to make me feel like there was only one path forward. I could practically see the chess pieces on his mental board, each move calculated to make me believe my only choice was to walk away. My heart was breaking even as I sat there, trying to wrap my mind around what was happening. I was furious, not just with him but with myself for not seeing it sooner. And as the reality sank in, my heart cracked wide open. I realized that the person I thought I'd been building a future with was nothing more than an illusion I'd bought into. I wanted to scream, to make him understand that he'd led me on, but it was clear he was already somewhere else, somewhere I didn't belong.

And the worst part? I didn't want to. Despite everything, despite the countless red flags, I still held onto a sliver of hope that maybe we could find common ground. But that night, as he spoke, I could feel the walls closing in, could sense that he'd written me out of his future without my knowing. I had been an afterthought in his grand plan of self-discovery.

As our conversation spiraled, I felt the weight of everything I'd been holding back. I was left with no choice but to accept it: the chapter with Billy was over, even if the words "breakup" never left our lips. The grief hit me like a tidal wave, all-encompassing and relentless, leaving me shattered in a way I hadn't expected. My chest ached, hollow and raw, as I let go of the illusion I'd built in my mind. The truth hurt, but I knew it was time to face it. This wasn't the partnership I'd wanted, and his selfishness, his indifference to my dreams, was more than I could bear. The end wasn't spoken; it was felt, a fracture that went all the way through my heart. The days that followed were surreal, a haze of grief and confusion, but also a strange, bitter clarity. I'd been holding on to someone who was never holding on to me.

The days that followed felt empty, a strange hollow feeling that echoed through my little studio. I mourned the future I thought we'd share, the dreams I'd let myself believe in, the version of him I'd clung to. But in the quiet that remained, I began to see things clearly, maybe for the first time. This wasn't the life I wanted; I deserved more than being a footnote in someone else's story. And as the tears dried, a new determination took root. My goals, my ambitions, my dreams—they were worth fighting for. And maybe, just maybe, this heartbreak was the spark I needed to chase them with everything I had.

Something else was happening besides the grief of what felt like a breakup. It was like an emotional thunderstorm gathering, a dark, swirling cloud inside me—something I'd only heard about in the abstract. I was sobbing, of course, sinking into that familiar weight of sadness, but then, suddenly, there was a shift, a visceral click. I didn't know what it was at first; I just knew that something different was unfolding.

"What do you mean, a switch?" I can almost imagine someone asking. Well, yes, exactly that—a switch, a literal flick inside of me. Like someone had come along and said, "Enough of this," and flipped some long-forgotten lever, sparking a fresh, wild emotion I'd never fully embraced: *anger*. Real, pulsing, raw anger.

It's strange how an emotion can feel so foreign, like meeting a relative you've only ever seen in pictures. I'd been acquainted with sadness, disappointment, and heartbreak in all their shades and depths, but anger? That was new. I'd always viewed it as a dangerous thing, a rogue emotion that other people felt. It had always been something I'd witnessed in others—a hot blaze that burned, sometimes too bright and too fast, and often leaving wreckage in its path. For me, anger had always seemed an almost mythical creature, something to be avoided or contained, something other people felt with ease but not me. But here it was, clawing its way up from inside me, demanding to be acknowledged, felt, even *owned*.

The sensation was intense and unnerving, like holding a firecracker with the fuse lit, and I felt a rush that was both terrifying and exhilarating. I wasn't just sad or hurt; I was angry. Truly, palpably, viscerally angry. And I could feel it—if and when it decided to surface—coming naturally, uninvited but present. It wasn't an unwelcome guest, exactly, but one that brought an edge, a little chaos, maybe even a sense of danger. Suddenly, my heart wasn't just aching; it was burning.

Navigating this new, fierce emotion was a delicate dance. I felt frantic at times, like a toddler with scissors, holding onto something sharp without knowing how to wield it. I'd never been taught how to express anger; it was a taboo emotion, something I'd always associated with fear. Growing up, anger was this volatile, unpredictable force—like touching a live wire. And yet here I was, touching it, feeling it ripple through my bloodstream, trying to understand it without letting it consume me.

Now, anger and I are like uneasy allies. It's not a part of me I ever expected to feel so intimately, but maybe that's what healing and growing are—making friends with parts of yourself you've never fully met. This journey, as uncomfortable and messy as it sometimes feels, is teaching me that even the "scary" emotions are part of who I am. Maybe that switch didn't just turn on anger; maybe it's showing me how to be more wholly, messily, and unapologetically… me.

Life seemed to be moving forward, with Billy and I both trying to grow closer while working through our own layers of hurt, hope, and healing. I threw myself into bonding with my girlfriends, finally letting loose and rediscovering the joy in shared laughter and late-night talks.

Underneath the surface, though, I juggled two restaurant jobs along with my third "job," acting class—a true labor of love where the emotional demands pushed me to explore the parts of myself I'd long kept hidden; a full-on excavation of my hidden fears, insecurities, and joys, peeling back the carefully layered onion of my defenses. And there, in the rawness of rehearsals and critique, I could finally see myself, a little more vulnerable, a little more real every day. I welcomed it, even if it sometimes felt like standing emotionally naked in a room full of mirrors. Vulnerability was my new best friend, and honesty was right there beside it, pushing me to speak up, to be real with myself in a way I'd never dared before.

As I bared my soul on stage, the fight for my health continued offstage. I was on a first-name basis with the hospital staff by now, making my quarterly pilgrimage for CT scans and routine check-ups. So far, the news had been good—each scan a small victory—but my body wasn't one to be tamed easily. My new constant companions? Nausea and, more often than I'd like, the unwelcome visits from vomit. Getting used to eating again was a trial by fire—or more accurately, a trial by bile. Every meal felt like a cautious gamble; too much, or sometimes even just the wrong bite, and my stomach would revolt. Post-surgery, my body was still adjusting, sometimes angrily reminding me that it wasn't quite back to its old self. The doctors, bless them, handed me nausea meds that helped but also came with the delightful instruction to avoid both driving and drinking while under their influence—a luxury I couldn't often afford with my packed schedule.

But then, they offered me a better solution: a special enzyme tailored just for me, designed for a body now missing half a pancreas. This wasn't just another prescription; it was my forever companion. this enzyme changed the game; it was like I'd been handed a golden ticket to the kingdom of small, manageable meals. With it, my meals became friendlier, less fraught with potential regret. Though, let's be honest, the occasional surprise vomit still made an appearance—just to keep things interesting.

Then, there was the scar—a fierce, raised line across my skin, an emblem of survival. When the glue finally dissolved, I almost celebrated. Applying scar cream became a nightly ritual, a way of tending to both my body and spirit, watching the darkened line lighten as if to whisper, *You're healing.*

But the gym? That was a whole other humbling beast of its own. Returning after surgery felt like being thrust back into a body I barely recognized; every lift, every squat reminded me of the muscle I'd lost. Instead of frustration, I chose grace as my mantra, letting myself savor the slow journey of rebuilding strength rather than fixating on the loss. My abs? Oh, those had gone into early retirement. For months, they stayed untouched, a necessary sacrifice in the name of healing. I was embracing patience, knowing my comeback would be slow, but I'd savor each step, each lift, each rep— one sweat bead at a time.

To shake things up, Billy and I traded our canceled Mexico trip for the snow-dusted slopes of Big Bear and, later, a trip to the mystical sands of Joshua Tree with Mocha in tow. The Big Bear getaway was sweet, like the calm before the storm, but Joshua Tree… Joshua Tree had other plans. Billy's passive-aggressiveness emerged, subtle but sharp, like the edge of a paper cut. I spotted it instantly, the remnants of my past with Grey Knight acting as my internal alarm system. I spoke up, hoping he'd recognize the pattern and stop. Yet, he shrugged it off, brushing my words aside like desert dust on his jacket.

The signs became harder to ignore, inching me back to those darker memories and filling me with a familiar unease.

The tension started to rise, slithering into our dynamic like an old, unwelcome friend. I hadn't clawed my way back to myself just to repeat history. Toxicity is a sneaky thing; it doesn't storm in—it trickles, drip by drip, until you're suddenly swimming in it. And here it was again, the ghosts of relationships past staring me down. Every red flag unfolded in slow motion, each one shouting a warning. I realized that I'd been here before—watching someone slip into habits that I'd once ignored, excused, even tolerated, hoping things would get better. But I wasn't that woman anymore. I was a survivor, someone who had tasted heartbreak and learned from it. And here I was, staring another version of it in the face. I had to ask myself: *had I really healed, or was I just testing the same broken waters, hoping somehow they'd changed?*

As the trip wound down, so did my tolerance for pretending. Life, I was realizing, wasn't about repeating patterns but recognizing them, honoring them, and then—finally—walking away from them. My journey was a messy, gloriously imperfect spiral, not a straight line. It was full of love and laughter, of brokenness and healing. And there I was, with a scar on my stomach, an enzyme in my purse, and a voice that finally knew how to say, "Enough." Life doesn't always give second chances, but I was learning how to give myself one, rewriting my story, one chapter at a time, still daring to face my own truth.

As summer tiptoed closer, teasing me with longer days and warmer nights, my birthday loomed, too, like a glittering promise. That's when my acting studio dropped an email bombshell into my inbox—a routine announcement, or so I thought, until one word caught my eye: *Italy.* I read on, my heart speeding up. They were offering a six-day intensive in the Alexander Technique in Italy, complete with discounted fees for the class, room, and board. Italy, discounted? My mind was spinning with images of cobblestone streets, endless pasta, and sunsets that felt like they were just for you. Italy was calling my name!

The idea of studying abroad, combining my love for travel and acting, was irresistible. Before I'd even fully considered the logistics, I was already dreaming and envisioning myself soaking in the wisdom of this revered technique. As my heart rate slowed down, I was already researching the technique, wondering what made it so special. Could it help me sharpen my craft? This was not just any acting method; the Alexander Technique was legendary for actors, helping them connect with their bodies in a way that transformed their performances. Anne, my acting teacher and mentor, whom I absolutely adored, reassured me that this opportunity would be a golden ticket. She told me with a wink, "Not only will it help your acting, it'll help your life. It's like magic for body awareness." Say no more—sign me up!

In a flurry of impulsive emails, I reached out to the class coordinator and mapped out a plan with Anne to balance the trip with my regular classes. Anne was more than supportive; when I sweetly asked if I could stay a bit longer to soak up every inch of Italy, she agreed without a second thought. *I love this woman.* Her trust in me felt like a gentle nudge toward everything I'd been working for. I promised myself I'd repay that faith tenfold, not just by showing up for my classes but by living boldly. This trip was going to be the adventure of a lifetime.

Anne's kindness and encouragement felt like a warm hug, and every week we grew a little closer, our connection deepening. I was so grateful to have a mentor who believed in me and cared enough to help me reach this dream. *Thank you, Anne, from the bottom of my heart*, I thought.

Anne, my dear, big-hearted mother hen. She's the sort of person who doesn't just say "be safe" but gets actively involved in orchestrating your safety from a thousand miles away. Her kindness has an energy all its own— warm and effusive, always hovering around me like a cozy blanket. So, naturally, when she heard I was planning a solo trip to Italy, her worries kicked into overdrive. She immediately set her sights on finding me a personal Italian guide, someone who could not only help me with the local lingo but also ensure I wouldn't fall prey to my own questionable sense of direction.

Her plan was as sweet as it was ambitious: Anne remembered a former student of hers living in Italy and decided he'd be the perfect travel companion for me. "You'll have a friend," she declared, hands clasped like she'd just revealed the plot twist of a movie. "Someone to keep an eye on you and show you around."

Within days, she'd tracked down his contact information, set up an introduction, and informed me she'd already "broken the ice" with him, which I imagine included the ultimate motherly interrogation about the circumstance. Soon, I found myself exchanging messages with this mystery guide, trading enthusiastic ideas about day trips, charming alleyways, and all the gelato I'd likely consume.

But, as fate would have it, the timing was off. My would-be Italian escort soon informed me that he was heading to a different, coastal part of Italy to escape the sticky, sweltering heat of the city, leaving me, for all intents and purposes, on my own again. So, alas, our rendezvous wasn't meant to be. But I couldn't help but smile at Anne's sweet, motherly persistence. Even if it didn't work out, the effort she put into crafting a sense of home for me halfway around the world was deeply appreciated.

It's not often someone goes to such lengths to make sure you're taken care of, especially when it's a trip they won't even be on. And I realized that, to Anne, my safety wasn't just a box to be checked; it was a mission. She wasn't trying to micromanage my adventure—she was simply stitching a little piece of herself into it, creating a safety net from afar, just in case.

There was a subtle beauty in the gesture, a warmth that I could carry with me, like a passport stamped with love. She couldn't physically be there with me, but she'd done her best to send a little slice of home along for the ride. In the end, knowing Anne had reached out, extended her arm across an ocean to bridge the distance, meant more than any tour guide ever could. It was a reminder that love isn't bound by borders or geography. And in a way, her act of kindness was the most precious souvenir of the journey before I'd even set foot on Italian soil.

So, with less than two months until the trip, I was thrust into a frantic race to get my passport renewed on time. I needed a way to speed up the process, and this teacher was a fountain of ideas. She suggested some tricks for expediting my renewal, and I, with all the determination of an overachiever, dove into "Mission: Passport Renewal," ready to pull every trick in the book. Between work, class, and the confusing limbo of figuring out my relationship with Billy, my days were already packed, but this trip was my North Star, keeping me buoyed and excited through the chaos.

I spent hours scouring the internet for every tip and trick to fast-track my passport renewal. I learned about the "emergency passport appointment" hack, which allows for expedited processing if you have proof of an upcoming international trip. But to prove my urgency, I'd need a plane ticket for a trip in the near future. Enter Delta Airlines, with its glorious 24-hour free cancellation policy. I booked a cheap flight to Mexico, scheduled for a couple of weeks out, and printed my reservation as "evidence" for my emergency passport appointment.

On the day of the appointment, I arrived at the passport office with my Delta ticket, nerves humming with excitement and a touch of ridiculousness. The line was monumental, full of other frantic travelers, but when it was finally my turn, I slid my ticket across the counter with a calm confidence that almost felt like acting. Within minutes, my passport renewal was officially in motion. Mission accomplished. I left the office grinning ear to ear, already plotting my next move—immediately canceling the Delta reservation from the safety of my couch. Feeling like I'd pulled off the ultimate travel heist— take that, expired passport. That wink I gave myself in the mirror was well-earned.

Planning this Italian adventure, setting everything in motion, and dreaming of an escape to a world of art and exploration filled me with a joy I hadn't felt in ages. It was like a spark lighting up a corner of my soul that had been dimmed by the murky waters of my relationship with Billy. Italy was the dream I'd needed, a promise of something magical waiting just beyond the horizon, a reminder that the world was vast, beautiful, and full of possibilities I hadn't yet tasted. Life was ready to whisk me away on a romantic (and business) adventure, and all I had to do was say yes.

With my birthday and my long-awaited passport in sight, the days were ripe with anticipation. The thrill of heading to Italy was as intoxicating as the promise of summer itself, and I could feel the countdown in every fiber of my being. But life, in its twisted wisdom, decided to add a layer of chaos, especially with Billy. The precarious dance of trying to fix things with Billy teetered between hopeful and hopeless. There were glimmers, yes, of the man he used to be, but under those flickers of familiarity, toxic behaviors had been clawing their way to the surface, making it clearer by the day that this wasn't the love we once knew. The cracks were becoming impossible to ignore, exposing toxic behaviors I had somehow missed—or maybe just ignored—in the past. There was a time we felt effortless, natural. Now, he was a bundle of confusion, admitting he was a lost puppy but making no move to change. If anything, his behavior only sharpened my view, like staring at a painting that you finally understand after standing back, watching it take shape in the clarity of hindsight.

Then, just three days before my birthday, he tossed a grenade. We were sitting in my studio, the usual banter circling around us, when he nonchalantly mentioned that he wanted to reconnect with an old coworker. But not just any coworker—the mistress he'd once cheated on his wife with. The impact was instant, a hot rush of fury radiating through my veins. I was a dragon with smoke in my lungs, seconds from bursting into flame. But I reeled myself back, determined to keep my composure, to avoid making a scene, even though I was trembling with rage. Instead, I masked my anger with a careful calm and started probing him, asking questions to see if he was truly serious. Perhaps, I thought, it was a fleeting thought, nothing more. But still, the damage was done. My insides were a tangled mess of instincts and red flags, and every instinct screamed, *Run!*

Why didn't I? Some part of me wanted to believe it was a slip-up, just a careless comment he'd forget. But that didn't stop the gnawing suspicion taking root in my mind, the voice that whispered, *Leave.*

Then June 4th arrived—my birthday. I kept things intimate, gathering a small circle of close friends for a wine-tasting day in Malibu. It was the perfect celebration, filled with easy laughter, sunlit vineyards, and the kind of carefree joy I'd been craving. I laughed until my cheeks hurt, swirled wine until I lost count of the glasses, and soaked in every moment with the people who truly cared. And yet, there was a weight pulling at me, a thread of resentment tied to Billy's casual betrayal, tugging at me throughout the day. Even with the laughter and love surrounding me, I could feel a slow simmer of resentment pushing him further away.

Then, just two days later, my true birthday gift arrived: my passport was finally ready. Holding that smooth, brand-new booklet in my hands felt like holding a golden ticket to freedom. It was official—I was going to Italy! The thrill of my first transatlantic adventure sent my heart soaring. The world had opened up, and it felt like a direct invitation to shed every ounce of worry and go reclaim a part of myself I hadn't seen in ages. I could practically feel the cobblestone streets of Florence beneath my feet, smell the espresso, hear the melodic murmur of Italian voices.

With my passport in hand, I threw myself into trip planning with reckless joy—my happy obsession. Thanks to my trusty travel credit card, I had enough miles to cover most of the ticket, leaving me with only a fraction to pay out of pocket. This six-day intensive had turned into a full twelve-day adventure, and I was loving every second of preparation. I planned it like an art, each city a deliberate brushstroke: I'd start with Florence, soaking in art and history, then move on to Tuscany for the Alexander Technique retreat, and finally, I'd end in Rome, where ancient ruins met modern life. The sheer magic of it all consumed me, keeping a smile plastered on my face through the chaos. Every detail—every café, every museum, every sunset spot I mapped out—was a piece of my own personal treasure hunt.

But with each passing day, Billy's discomfort became as obvious as the sun rising. Although he tried to hide it, I could see the insecurity oozing out of him, the way he squirmed every time I talked about Italy. He didn't need to say it; the jealousy, the possessiveness, was practically written in neon across his face.

And as if to twist the knife further, he had the audacity to bring up the mistress again. There it was—the raw audacity, like a slap in the face. *How dare he!* I thought, as my disbelief morphed into bitter clarity. The phrase echoed through my mind, looping like a furious mantra. Here was a man who'd shattered his own marriage by cheating with this very woman, and now he was hinting at doing the same with me.

A bitter truth clicked into place, a truth I'd been avoiding: he hadn't changed. Maybe cheaters never did. I'd let myself believe he could, that he would be different, that somehow we'd be the exception. But the rose-colored glasses were off, shattered on the floor, and in their place was a blinding clarity. He was a broken record, spinning the same toxic tune. And here I was, caught in its discord, wondering when it would be right to break free.

I kept my calm, though every fiber of my being wanted to shout. Instead, I played it cool, probing him with questions, feeling like I was peeling back layers to reveal his truth while hiding my own heartbreak. Inside, my mind spun with one question: *When was the right time to end this?* With my departure for Italy at the end of June, should I cut things off before I leave, or wait until after?

Breaking up right now, when I was floating on pre-Italy bliss, felt like robbing myself of this joy. But did I want to return from the trip, my spirit renewed, only to come back to the sinking weight of a relationship built on lies and betrayal? It felt wrong, yet somehow right, to hold onto that joy a little longer, savoring it without the weight of a breakup lingering over me.

The Italy jitters were thrilling, filling me with a sense of possibility I hadn't felt in years. I was about to embark on an adventure across the ocean, ready to embrace every ounce of passion, history, and art that awaited me. Yet the shadow of my relationship with Billy loomed, threatening to dim the excitement. But this trip, I knew, was mine—it was my gift to myself, a way to reclaim my independence, my courage, my happiness. And somehow, amid the countdown to Italy, I knew the answer was already clear. It was just a matter of time before I'd find the courage to say it out loud.

Chapter 20

How to Lose 10 Pounds in Two Weeks

I was a flurry of emotions, caught in this strange whirlwind of excitement and dread. Here I was, high on Italy jitters, counting down the days until I'd step into this dreamlike escape, ready to drown myself in pasta, gelato, and all things Mediterranean. But then, there was the other matter—the shadow on the edge of my excitement, like an uninvited guest at a celebration: Billy. I knew I had to break up with him before I left, yet I couldn't find the "right" time to do it. If I'm being honest, I wasn't exactly the type to be the heartbreaker; I never wanted to be the one who made someone feel small or unwanted. But that changed the day Billy casually mentioned he was, in essence, interested in cheating on me—floating the idea like it was the most natural, forgivable thing.

That was the moment I mentally laced up my track shoes, ready to sprint far, far away. And yet, somehow, I was still here, wondering when I'd finally have the courage to do it. My friends, of course, had their advice ready: "There's no 'perfect' time. Just rip off the Band-Aid." I knew they were right. The toxic behaviors I'd been tolerating were like stones in my pocket, weighing me down one by one. The buildup started in February, when he pushed me to the absolute edge, past any place I could reasonably return to. In that month, he crossed a line I didn't even know I'd drawn for him. My heart shattered, and my subconscious went on strike, rejecting him completely.

But my conscious mind was slow to catch up, still clinging to the shreds of what we had, offering him one last chance. I tried—really tried—to make it work, to salvage something from the ruins. But those red flags? They kept popping up like weeds I couldn't ignore. And my own body was sending signals, too, ones I'd stubbornly ignored. Every time I was near him, I felt this urge to leave, like my instincts were screaming at me to run. I wanted to avoid him, to bolt, to get as far away as possible. I was starting to realize that my behavior had changed, too—I'd begun treating him just as poorly as he treated me. And that wasn't who I wanted to be.

So, there we were, floating down a poisoned stream together, locked in this toxic loop we couldn't seem to break. All because, back in February, he'd wrecked something in me that couldn't be fixed, and I'd been grieving that loss ever since. I'd lost the boy I thought I loved and was left with someone I could barely stand. But this time, as I felt myself reach yet another breaking point, something clicked. My mind and body were finally aligned, and for the first time, I felt no sadness, no lingering doubt. There was a quiet, steely resolve inside me, a certainty that I didn't have to carry this weight any longer.

I was ready to break it off. No tears, no second-guessing. Just a clean, final ending before I stepped onto that plane, free and unburdened, ready to immerse myself fully in the adventure waiting for me. And with that decision, I felt lighter, like I'd finally put down the weight I'd been carrying. There was something beautifully empowering in realizing that I could choose my own happiness, that I could walk away without a backward glance. Italy, here I come. And this time, I'm leaving all the baggage behind.

Not long after my birthday, I pulled the trigger. *Why wait?* I thought. *Better to do this now than carry him with me to Italy.* I was tired of pretending that this relationship was anything but shattered. Billy had broken my heart back in February, leaving a trail of red flags like breadcrumbs, each one a reminder that he wasn't willing to protect what we had. And then, as if he thought I hadn't had enough, he dropped another bomb. I knew then that I couldn't keep dragging this out, that it was time to let go. So we had "the talk," and I ended it.

He cried. He begged. He clawed at the seams, trying to stitch us back together with every ounce of energy he had. But I was done. And when I told him so, it was like that reality only fueled him further. Day after day, he was relentless, coming back at me, ambushing me with pleas, trying desperately to turn my "no" into something he could work with. It was as if he thought he could wear me down, change my mind by sheer force. But the more he fought, the more he stoked a fire in me that I hadn't even known was there.

Do you remember when I mentioned that burning sensation, the one that made me start therapy? I could never quite place it—it was like a fiery knot lodged deep within, something I sensed was key to my healing but couldn't fully grasp. Billy, without even knowing it, struck the match that ignited it. His desperation, his pushiness, his refusal to let go—it all triggered something in me that had been lying dormant for too long. And once that flame was lit, there was no going back. It wasn't a slow burn, either. It was an explosion, like a bomb detonating in my core, expanding in strength, intensity, and purpose every time he showed up, every time he begged or pleaded or promised to change.

Suddenly, my body began reacting as if it were under siege. Within two weeks, I'd lost ten pounds, my frame thinning until I looked like a shadow of myself. The pounds just melted off without warning. I didn't even realize what was happening until I saw myself in the mirror—gaunt, almost brittle. His words were all-consuming, an exhausting onslaught of apologies, pleas, promises. And while he was selling me on this vision of a changed future, my subconscious mind was outright rejecting him, casting up all the warning signs I'd missed or ignored before. It was like my body and my mind had joined forces in a rebellion against him, against any version of us.

My two minds—the conscious and the unconscious—were locked in a brutal war. Consciously, I hated hurting him, hated being the "bad guy" in a breakup, something I'd never really had to do. Part of me wanted to believe in the words he was throwing at me, in the possibility that things could be fixed. After all, I'd wanted that in February, when I first felt him slip away. But my subconscious, the part of me that could see clearly, was immune to his stories, his pleas. It saw his words as empty promises, sirens luring me back into something toxic. Every time he pushed, my resistance grew, like an allergic reaction I couldn't stop. My body was literally revolting.

Imagine it: Billy attacking me from all sides with words meant to convince, meant to sway, meant to make me doubt myself. And yet, no matter how much he tried, my body fought back, clinging to this newfound clarity with an almost violent resolve. The weight loss was just the beginning. My body was turning itself inside out, like it was ridding itself of every part of him. Each pound I shed felt like a piece of his hold on me slipping away, a physical manifestation of the distance I needed to put between us.

In the end, his words no longer held power. The explosion he'd unwittingly triggered inside me had left nothing to return to—no scraps, no tenderness, just a quiet, relentless certainty that I was done. The burning sensation, the one I'd tried so hard to understand, had morphed into something transformative. It wasn't about him anymore; it was about my own freedom, my own power, and the healing I hadn't even known I needed.

Yes, I eventually started fighting back. Ever since February, when my "anger switch" turned on for the first time, I could actually feel it—anger, real and raw. A new emotion, one that I wasn't comfortable with yet but also couldn't ignore. As the drama with Billy kept piling up, anger trickled more and more into my reactions, especially with all the hurt he'd caused. I'd had enough of being the quiet one, the peacekeeper. But then, the moment I finally stood my ground, Billy did something unexpected. He told me I sounded just like Grey Knight. That I was treating him the way Grey Knight had once treated me, using the same words, the same tone, the same cutting force.

Hearing that hit me like a punch to the gut. At first, I brushed it off, but when he brought it up again and again, I found myself stopping cold, actually questioning my behavior. I took a hard look at myself, and, sure enough, I saw it. Maybe it was a milder version, but it was still there. He was right. Somehow, I was acting like the very person who'd broken me. How had I let that happen? Why was I letting myself go there, to that place, with someone who was hurting me now, in his own way?

But Billy didn't stop. Not with the breakup, not with the pleas, not with his relentless attempts to undo it all. Every single day, he'd come back with some new "proof" of his devotion, some elaborate gesture, a text, a call, an act of service, a promise. In a twisted way, it was almost sweet—almost. He was putting in more effort now than he ever had when we were together, and it was exhausting. There was this little part of me that appreciated it, but a much larger part kept thinking, *Where was this the first time you shattered my heart?*

I tried to make sense of it, to resist, but it wasn't until I leaned on my "Powerpuff Girls"—my trusted friends—that it finally hit me. They were the ones who called it out: "He's love bombing you." And suddenly, everything clicked. Every desperate gesture, every affectionate word, every act of "devotion"—all it was doing was pushing me further, making my body feel as if it were on the verge of collapse. Every argument we had, every time he showed up with a new line, it triggered something much darker, something I hadn't expected: flashbacks.

And they weren't just memories; they were haunting, visceral, almost alive. Moments from the ugly days with Grey Knight surged forward, the painful ones I'd tried so hard to erase. One after another, these memories flooded back—the anger, the abuse, the twisted memories from those dark days of addiction, buried traumas I'd kept locked away. It was terrifying, like someone had reached inside and torn open wounds I thought had healed. My body responded with this uncontrollable reaction, as though the memories were too much to hold.

Eating became a struggle. Not just the act of eating, but the entire experience: hunger became this foreign concept, easily forgotten or outright absent. When I did try to eat, my jaw would clench up, a remnant of an old issue I'd struggled with called TMJ. Only now, it was back with a vengeance. My jaw would lock, my body would tense, and I'd have to consciously force each bite, as if my entire body was resisting the simple act of nourishment. Sometimes, I'd get food down, only for my stomach to turn against me, rejecting it violently.

But the physical toll was just the beginning. My body was trembling constantly, like I was a live wire about to snap. My stomach churned, twisting itself into knots, like it was consuming itself from the inside. It was a frantic, relentless kind of stress, like the Tasmanian devil spinning wildly, unable to stop or catch a breath. I felt my weight plummet, losing ten pounds in what felt like mere days. The reflection in the mirror looked brittle, fragile—a version of me I barely recognized.

Each word out of Billy's mouth, each attempt to pull me back, made the flashbacks stronger, like he was unknowingly feeding this beast inside me.

And when I started Googling my symptoms, trying to make sense of the mess I'd become, there it was, staring me in the face: PTSD. That realization hit like a second bomb, the weight of it almost too much to hold. This wasn't just heartbreak. This wasn't just Billy. This was something bigger, something darker, and it had been lurking in me, waiting for a trigger to unleash its full force.

One night, in the middle of another one of his relentless arguments, I even called him Grey Knight. The words just slipped out, like my mind had blurred the lines between them. I caught myself, horrified, but I knew then what was happening. This wasn't about Billy anymore. This was about healing wounds so deep, they'd become a part of me, wounds that Grey Knight had left open long ago. And Billy, without realizing it, had pulled me back into that trauma, reawakening it in ways I couldn't ignore.

It became painfully clear that this was no ordinary breakup. This was a reckoning, a chance to finally face the buried trauma I'd been carrying for years. All the petty arguments, the hurt, the anger—it all faded, dissolved like dust, because this was about something much bigger. That old, rotting bomb inside me had finally gone off, and I couldn't ignore it anymore. It was time to dig deep, to heal in ways I'd never allowed myself to before. Billy, for all his hurt and confusion, had unwittingly brought me to this breaking point, but I knew now that I had to turn my focus inward. This battle wasn't with him anymore—it was with myself, and the work that lay ahead was long overdue.

Every time I tried to push Billy away, he pushed back harder. It was like he'd found a gear I didn't even know existed, and he was pressing it to its breaking point. The more he pressured me, the more this bomb inside me grew, swelling with intensity and force until it felt ready to burst.

And just like that, the lock on my trauma was broken. Memories came rushing in, dark and jagged, tearing through me like shards of glass. Scenes I had buried deep—locked away in the furthest vaults of my mind—came surging back with terrifying force.

The flashbacks didn't just haunt me; they hijacked me, dragging me backward into a version of myself I swore I'd left behind. I wasn't just remembering—I was reliving. Spiraling. Helplessly sliding down that same merciless hill, the one I'd hit rock bottom on before. And the worst part? I wasn't even given a choice.

I wanted to fight it, to claw my way out, to shake myself free—but this wasn't a battle I could win. The force of it was absolute, like an invisible current pulling me under, thrashing me against a past that refused to stay buried. I had no control. No exit. No escape. Just the weight of it, pressing down, drowning me in the ghosts of what once was.

But Amplified.

My excitement about Italy transformed, almost overnight, into something else entirely. Those jitters of anticipation dissolved into a violent storm of panic and anxiety. My body responded like it was under siege: a constant, pounding heartbeat, hands that wouldn't stop trembling, sweat pouring down my back. I tried to explain this to Billy—tried to get him to see that this had nothing to do with him anymore. "It's not about you, Billy," I kept telling him. "This is all about Grey Knight." But he didn't understand, and maybe he didn't want to. Frankly, I didn't have the energy to care. Whatever my body was going through was beyond him, beyond even me, and I had to throw every ounce of myself into dealing with it.

I was locked in a constant state of fear, tension woven into every inch of me. I couldn't focus, couldn't relax, couldn't even get comfortable inside my own skin. My body trembled like it was possessed, a frantic, vibrating mess of nerves and restless energy. *What is happening to me?* It was like I'd been hijacked, like someone else had taken control. There wasn't a name I knew for it—I'd never heard of anyone feeling like this before. So, here I am, doing my best to put it into words. Bear with me.

Imagine bottling up every ounce of negativity, every emotion linked to anger, frustration, hurt, and resentment. Imagine packing it all tightly into a small box and stuffing it so far down inside you that you almost forget it's there. Talk about major suppression skills! That's exactly what I'd done, piling all the pain and fury and trauma into this dark, hidden corner of my mind, thinking it would just stay put. But it didn't. That box was rupturing, spilling out all over my life, suffocating any last glimmer of peace.

Normalcy, that old friend of mine, was a memory I could hardly reach. I didn't even feel like myself anymore. Instead, I was this skinny, shivering shell, ten pounds lighter than I'd been just weeks before. PTSD had become my newest, most unwelcome companion, and now I was staring down a beast I didn't know how to tame. Everything seemed connected to that old, festering wound from Grey Knight, that trauma I'd thought I'd maybe healed from. But it wasn't healed; it was festering, growing. And now, with this new wave of symptoms, I realized just how deeply the roots ran.

The only thing I could do was try to understand this self-diagnosis I'd stumbled upon—PTSD. So, I tried explaining it to Billy. I broke it down as best I could, hoping he'd finally get it. And surprisingly, after a few days, he did a complete turnaround. He seemed to understand, or at least he wanted to help. Suddenly, he was trying to be supportive, even offering to "be there" for me. But it felt all wrong, twisted. I knew deep down that the very nature of our relationship was the last thing I needed.

The idea of a boyfriend—a male figure that close to me—felt like poison. I'd just started to realize that any intimate connection with a man might be fueling my PTSD, feeding the monster inside me. So I tried, desperately, to explain this theory to him. "Billy, I can't be in this dynamic right now. I need space, no men in my life this close. No triggers." It felt like I'd found a piece of the puzzle, something that could bring me peace. But, like clockwork, Billy pushed back again, inching closer, trying to find a way to stay in my life despite every boundary I tried to set.

The harder I tried to keep him at a distance, the harder he fought to close the gap. It was like he didn't realize he was fanning the flames, or maybe he did and just didn't care. Every time he crept closer, the beast inside me stirred, untamable and angry. It felt as if I were handling a bomb that could go off any second, a volatile, thrumming thing inside me that I'd spent years ignoring but could ignore no more. My energy was drained just by trying to hold myself together, to stay above water, to keep my sanity in check while he kept trying to pull me back under.

This was no longer a breakup; this was survival. Billy's inability to step back, to let me heal on my terms, was making things worse, far worse than he could understand. He couldn't see that he was the very thing I needed to escape. And as each day passed, it became clearer: I was going to have to save myself, even if it meant pushing him out for good.

Before leaving for Italy, I decided it was time to say goodbye to my therapist. We'd had a solid year together, a year of support, of unraveling some knots and tangles in my life, but ultimately, I felt it was time to move on. She wasn't able to help me with my true "mission," but she'd certainly been there for other chapters—she helped me navigate my relationship with Billy, and she walked beside me through my cancer journey, a heavy and defining experience. It was good, a positive endeavor overall, but I'd kept it up longer than I probably should have.

I'm not claiming to know it all, far from it! But through some tough life lessons and a pile of self-help books, I've gathered a good amount of wisdom on my own. Therapy, for me, was meant to be an intense, transformative experience. I didn't just want someone to pat my back and nod along. I wanted my mind cracked open, my viewpoints challenged. I wanted someone to pull apart my fixed ideas, to ask me the kind of questions that shift your whole perspective. Therapy wasn't just about tackling my demons with heroin, addiction, and my monstrous ex's abuse—it was about being stretched, pushed out of my comfort zone, given tools to look at my life from new, hard-hitting angles.

And while my therapist did offer some insights that jolted me—those little one-liners that made me sit up straighter—most of the time, I felt like she was just validating my feelings and summarizing them back to me. It was like drinking watered-down juice: not unpleasant, but not enough to keep me truly hydrated. Still, it was comforting to have someone I could confide in. And, looking back, the single best part of my time with her was how she helped me fix my relationship with my dad.

Ah, *the talk* with my dad—just thinking about it now makes my heart race a little. I finally mustered the courage to sit down, call him, and lay everything out. I asked him to just listen, to let me speak without interruption, as I poured out everything I'd felt. It was tough. Telling your dad how much his anger had hurt, explaining that feeling of being shut down and feeling like a punching bag…that's not easy. I was scared he'd turn it around, that he'd deflect and redirect my pain right back at me. But he didn't. He listened, truly listened, with a surprising openness, and he took everything to heart. That call changed us. With those words, we started rebuilding, and for the first time in a long time, I felt us growing closer again.

That moment alone made therapy worth it. But still, I felt it was time to end my sessions with her. It was clear I needed someone who could dive deeper into the world of opioid addiction and unpack the weight of my past with my ex—a therapist who could go to those depths with me, without flinching, and guide me through the pain I still carry. So, I left, feeling grateful but also ready for a new phase of healing, one that could finally bring me to confront the darkest parts of my story and perhaps, just maybe, bring me a little closer to peace.

A brilliant, almost daring idea crossed my mind—*I should make amends with Grey Knight.* It was actually Billy's suggestion—the one good takeaway from him lingering around when I told him to give me space. But the more I thought about it, the more it made sense. Every time I felt that boiling rage, every time that beast clawed its way to the surface, it all traced back to Grey Knight. I realized this chaos, this angry, burning monster inside of me, was rooted in the things I'd swallowed down and bottled up from our relationship. And now, years later, those feelings were exploding like firecrackers in my soul. Maybe this was my answer. Maybe amends could be my first leap toward real healing.

I knew the concept of the twelve steps from Nar-Anon meetings and from listening to Grey Knight's own journey through recovery. Maybe, just maybe, if I reached out and took that step, it would finally help me find peace with this beast living inside me. I felt the desperation coursing through me, the desperate need to make peace. It was a theory, yes, but it was a theory I was clinging to, and with only a few days left before my trip to Italy, I decided to act on it.

I reached out to him, my ex-husband, my heartbreak, and my weakness. I knew, deep down, he'd be open and receptive. When I told him I was ready to make amends, that I wanted to start with him, he welcomed the idea with surprising grace. It didn't matter that I hadn't done the other eleven steps—I was in the thick of my own pain, searching for a way out, and he was there, willing to meet me in this space. He even offered to help guide me through it, giving me a series of questions to work through, tools to complete the step.

I sat with his questions. Each one felt like a key, unlocking places I'd been afraid to go: "Who am I resentful at? What's the cause? How does this affect my self-esteem, my pride, my ambition?" And then came the tough ones: "Where were my mistakes? Where was I to blame? What did I do? Do I see any harm I caused?" I spent hours with these questions, digging deeper than I thought I could. I wanted to give him my truest, most honest answers. I warned him that this meeting would be raw, that it would be me opening the floodgates, dishing out every ounce of anger and pain I'd locked up for so long. He agreed, assured me he was ready for it.

As I prepared, I wrote it all down, everything I resented him for. Line after line, I laid out my anger: I resent you for this... I resent you for that. I didn't hold back. I couldn't. Not if I wanted to face this beast and finally free myself.

And so, just a few days before my flight to Italy, we scheduled a FaceTime call. This was it. The final act before I boarded that plane, my last piece of unfinished business. I had this wild hope, a dream even, that this conversation would unlock something, would give me the release I needed so I could finally close that chapter, breathe in some much-needed freedom, and leave it all behind on American soil.

I felt every nerve, every raw edge, as the moment approached. My heart was tangled with nerves—seeing Grey Knight's face again, the face that could still, somehow, make me weak. I was excited but also terrified, because this wasn't just some casual call. It was a delicate, loaded encounter, a meeting with the man who'd made me a hopeless romantic once upon a time but who'd also hurt me in ways I still couldn't put into words. My TMJ was acting up again, my jaw chattering like a ticking bomb, and I knew that if I let myself, I'd spiral. But I forced myself to stay calm, to be present. This was my one chance, my one chance to dump every ounce of pent-up anger on him in the hopes that it would, finally, lead to something greater than rage.

When the call started, I felt that mix of vulnerability and power. This was my chance. My chance to unburden myself, to lay it all out there and somehow make peace with it. In my heart, I had a small, flickering hope that this conversation would evaporate the soul-sucking PTSD symptoms, that I'd finally feel like myself again. But even if it didn't cure me, even if it didn't lift every ounce of pain, maybe it would be enough to help me walk onto that plane feeling a little lighter, a little more free, and ready for whatever lay ahead.

As the minutes crept closer to our FaceTime call, anxiety rushed over me like a tidal wave. I was so sure I was ready for this. I'd built myself up, repeated my reasons, and given myself every pep talk possible to muster the courage to finally unload all the resentment I'd bottled up over the years. But not with rage or malice—I was determined to let it go with grace, to cleanse my heart rather than wound his. This was about release, not revenge. I wanted to believe I was strong enough to do it. I believed I had the guts now, where in the past, I'd never dared to voice these things to him.

And then—"Hello, hello." We connected, and the moment his face appeared on my screen, my composure unraveled. His face, that familiar, once-beloved face, triggered something deep and raw in me. My heart softened, breaking the resolve I'd so carefully built up. *Are you kidding me?* This was supposed to be my moment to face him with strength, and here I was, turning to mush, nerves buzzing.

Still, I plunged forward, one question at a time. These are the resentments I've held toward him, each line a wound I've carried for years. I'd prepared my words, written down the list of everything I resented him for. But as I tried to speak, as I looked into those eyes I'd once fallen for, something in me twisted. Tears wanted to stream down my face as I choked out my list. It was so much harder than I'd imagined. I feel like I'm back in the past, swallowed by the same old, awful urge to protect him, to hold back. It's ridiculous! I'd built myself up, steeled myself for this moment, and yet, here I am, crumbling at the sight of him. The words, my feelings—they're lodged somewhere deep, refusing to come out, no matter how desperately I try to push them forward.

And he was… patient. So painfully patient. He watched me struggle, let me stumble through my words, and gently guided me, trying to help me through. But for some reason, the words wouldn't come. They were lodged somewhere deep, tangled with every unresolved feeling I'd buried. But I couldn't believe it—I still couldn't get it out.

My heart is pounding with words, with anger, with memories and grief, but it's like my voice and my body refuse to cooperate. Here I am, face-to-face with him, feeling both love and rage collide, but unable to release a single coherent sentence. That beast inside me, the one that had screamed for release, was suddenly quiet, leaving me to stumble in silence.

Finally, we reached the breaking point—the question about the harm I'd caused him. This was my chance to confront my own flaws, to take responsibility for the role I'd played. But that's when Grey Knight turned everything upside down.

"Haley, you didn't hurt me," he said, almost imploring. "You didn't cause any harm. *I* did." His voice was unwavering, almost kind, as if he were trying to absolve me of all the guilt I'd harbored. He's saying this with such clarity, such certainty, that I feel my words evaporate on my tongue. He kept insisting I wasn't the one who needed to make amends, that he'd been the one to break, to bruise, to wound. I was stunned, my carefully prepared words crumbling in my throat. He was right. I didn't hurt him. I never held the knife. I'd always known it somewhere deep down. But then… where does that leave me? I felt my hope falter, slipping through my fingers. If I hadn't caused harm, what did this moment even mean?

With his words, the hope I'd carried so carefully into this moment starts to slip away, slipping like sand through my fingers. He doesn't see a need for my apology. He believes the blame belongs to him alone. And yet, we continue, swapping apologies, acknowledging our past mistakes, wrapping our regrets in words as best we can. Somewhere in the flow of this strange, tender conversation, he says something that strikes me to my core, in both beautiful and painful ways, gently, with love in his voice.

"Haley, this is my final goodbye." The words landed like a punch to the gut.

I wasn't prepared for the finality of it. He explained, with that same gentle honesty, that it was time for him to truly close this chapter. His girlfriend—who had once been so supportive, so understanding of our history—had now stepped into a more serious role in his life. And with that shift came a decision I had no say in. He told me, in the most matter-of-factly way, that now felt like the right time to officially cut ties. No lingering connections. No unfinished business.

It was nothing personal, just logistics—a clean break for the sake of moving forward. A practical decision wrapped in careful words, but I felt the weight of it settle deep in my chest. I had been erased, not out of malice, but out of necessity.

"It's time," he said softly, gently, with love in his voice, offering me his best wishes, his hopes for my happiness. He said he was sorry and wished me every beautiful thing in the world. His sincerity was piercing. There was nothing left for me to do but return the sentiments, to offer him my own well-wishes.

It lingered in the air, heavy and unmistakable. I hadn't expected this, hadn't realized how much that finality would hurt. It's like heartbreak layered over heartbreak, an ache that's reopened despite all the years, all the healing, all the moving on I thought I'd done. Somewhere deep inside, I guess I hadn't truly let go, hadn't fully believed this would be the last goodbye. After everything we'd been through, I suppose I'd carried this secret hope that, someday, we'd come back to each other, that a love like ours couldn't ever truly end.

But this was different. This was real. This was the full stop, the closing line of our story. My greatest love, my treasured memory, my deepest heartbreak, the man who'd both wrecked me and taught me what it was to love… was finally saying goodbye. And in that moment, something within me shattered again, one last fracture, as if to say, *Yes, it's really over.*

Part of me felt like I'd found the closure I'd been seeking, that weight of years lifted ever so slightly. But there was another part of me—a soft, aching part—that knew I'd lost something irreplaceable. This goodbye, as tender as it was final, was the real ending. And with that, I could finally step forward, knowing I'd been given the release I needed, however bittersweet it was, to make peace with my past and find a way to heal.

What was I left with? Not the rush of relief I'd been hoping for, not the cathartic flood of closure I'd imagined would wash away the years of pain and confusion. No, what I felt was something quieter, more bittersweet. Saying goodbye to Grey Knight felt final in a way that was both strangely beautiful and sharply painful. I could sense the chapter closing, but did it bring the kind of lightness I'd craved? Not exactly.

I hadn't said everything I wanted to say. I hadn't been able to unleash my anger or pour out my pain onto him, despite all the preparation, all the speeches I'd practiced in my head. But as the silence settled, I began to realize that maybe that wasn't who I am anyway. No matter the ghosts I'd carried, the anger I'd buried, I wasn't the person who could lay blame at someone's feet without hesitation. It wasn't in me to tear him down, even if he might have deserved it. And maybe that was my unexpected victory: a quiet, graceful end rather than the storm I'd once imagined.

But there's still that beast inside, rattling its cage, waiting to be acknowledged. It didn't vanish with a simple goodbye, didn't evaporate with a few sentimental words. It's still there, lurking, a monster stitched together from pieces of the past few weeks—the heartbreak, the trauma bomb that went off in my chest, the constant anxiety and panic that's crept into every corner of my life. The nightmares, the physical reactions, the way it's seeped into everything, even my plans for Italy. This beast is demanding my attention, insisting I face it head-on.

But Italy—Italy calls to me louder. I can feel it, the magnetic pull toward those old-world streets, the sunlight that promises to warm me from the inside out, the rolling landscapes I know will remind me that beauty and possibility are still out there, waiting. All I can do is breathe, pack my bags, and take each day as it comes. I've done my best. I've given it all I had. Now it's time to shift my focus to what's next. Billy's lingering presence can stay in the background for now. I have only one goal ahead of me: Italy, and the chance to reclaim myself.

And this time, I'm doing it alone. No baggage, no men, no lingering shadows. I'm leaving with a free heart, a clean slate, and the strength of someone who's been broken and building themselves back up again. Grey Knight is officially in the past, closed, locked up, and stored away in a chapter that no longer belongs to me. Italy, on the other hand, is about to be the best thing I've done for myself in years. Yes, I'm still wrestling with an inner beast, a turmoil that feels like it's simmering just beneath my skin. But there's a warrior inside me, one that's ready for whatever comes next.

I keep repeating a mantra in my head, a little gift to myself, a promise for this journey ahead: *Italy will be my Eat, Pray, Love adventure.* The timing couldn't be more perfect, and I cling to the thought like a lifeline. It's my chance to rediscover who I am, to meet myself in a place filled with art and history and endless skies. I'll taste freedom in every bite of pasta, every lick of gelato, every sip of wine, every sunrise that lights up the Tuscan hills. I'll let the Italian air fill me up with something new, something I can hold onto. I'll find the parts of myself that I thought I'd lost.

So, here I go—heart open, warrior spirit intact, suitcase packed with only what I truly need. Italy is waiting for me, and whatever waits on the other side, I'm ready to embrace it with everything I have.

Chapter 21

Italy, Interrupted

Mom flew down from Northern California to stay at my place and take care of Mocha while I embarked on my Italian adventure. Now, Mocha isn't just your average pet; she's a diva in fur, a queen ruling her small kingdom with a mix of sass and stubbornness. She's also notoriously picky about who gets to care for her. But for reasons only Mocha knows, she's absolutely smitten with my mom. It's like they've formed some secret pact against me, an alliance of affection that leaves me as little more than the background character in their love story. Not that I'm complaining—knowing my mom had Mocha under her spell made the whole arrangement a lot less nerve-wracking. That part of the plan? Solid. The rest? Not so much.

Somewhere between packing and panicking, I completely dropped the ball on booking train rides between my destinations. Call it a side effect of what I've dubbed "the trauma box explosion," where planning and practicality go out the window in the wake of overwhelming chaos. When I realized my oversight, I teetered on the edge of a minor meltdown before convincing myself, *Meh, there are always trains in Italy, right? What's the worst that could happen?* I decided to channel the spirit of adventure—okay, maybe a little laziness, too—and just figure it out as I went. Rolling with the punches seemed like the perfect vibe for this trip.

I had one goal in mind: to fully surrender to Italy. To soak up the culture like the spongy tiramisu I intended to eat my weight in. The trip itself wasn't meant to be a rigid itinerary anyway. I had only one pre-planned day trip to the Amalfi Coast and a commitment to attend the intensive classes. Every other day? Completely unstructured. I imagined myself wandering cobblestone streets, getting gloriously lost in vibrant pasta, and eating gelato whenever the mood struck—which, let's be honest, would be at least once a day (non-negotiable). This trip wasn't just about sightseeing; it was a personal pilgrimage to rediscover parts of myself I'd buried or forgotten. My own "Eat, Pray, Love," with slightly more profanity and significantly more carbs.

I intended to devour life with the same passion as I intended to devour Italy's finest pasta.

There were deeper reasons, too, of course. This trip marked the cusp of my one-year anniversary of being cancer-free. My "Meatball," as I'd affectionately dubbed the cancer that tried to ruin me, no longer had the power to dictate my life. I'd decided that Italy would be the setting where I rewrite that narrative. And to commemorate the occasion, I'd set a lofty but meaningful goal: getting a tattoo. It had to be in Italy, it had to be special, and it had to happen on my final day, like a mic-drop moment to an unforgettable journey.

But before all that could happen, there was one thing standing in my way: my mom. Specifically, her compulsive need to "tidy" my apartment whenever she visits. Now, to outsiders, this might sound sweet. But I know better. Now, don't get me wrong—I love my mom, and I appreciate her intentions. But in her mind, "helpful tidying" often translates to a full-blown HGTV makeover. And while I usually bite my tongue, the last few visits to my studio had pushed me to the brink. I mean, it's one thing to organize my storage; it's another to re-categorize my kitchen and "accidentally" rearrange my closet.

So, just minutes before she dropped me off at the airport, I delivered a pre-departure speech worthy of a courtroom drama. "Mom," I said, fixing her with my fiercest don't-even-try-it glare, "under no circumstances are you to rearrange anything in my apartment while I'm gone. Nothing. Nada. Zip." I paused, letting the weight of my words sink in. "The only place you're allowed to touch is my closet, and that's because it currently looks like the aftermath of a hurricane. Other than that, I love my studio exactly the way it is, and I don't want to come home to find everything flipped upside down."

She nodded, her expression unreadable, and I couldn't tell if she was genuinely agreeing or plotting her next move. But I didn't have time to dissect her reaction. Italy was calling, and I had gelato to eat, wine to drink, and self-discovery to pursue. As I stepped into the airport, the thrill of what lay ahead hit me like a shot of espresso. I was on the brink of an adventure that promised freedom, joy, and maybe even a little chaos.

Mom could deal with the apartment. I'd deal with Italy.

Never have I ever been to Europe. Not once. The idea of traveling internationally, let alone, felt like the kind of thing meant for braver souls—until now. Here I was, standing on the precipice of an adventure that seemed equal parts thrilling and terrifying. Freshly single, battle-scarred by life, and carrying the weight of a beast inside me—a relentless presence gnawing at my body and spirit—I had decided it was time to rewrite my story. This was my "Eat, Pray, Love" moment, but make it chaotic, messy, and unapologetically *me*.

Italy was calling, and I was answering with all the desperation of someone who needed to feel alive again. They say traveling builds character, and honestly, I was in dire need of a renovation. I didn't just want to see Italy—I wanted to *feel* it, to let its magic permeate every corner of my being. This wasn't just about pasta and piazzas (though I fully intended to drown myself in carbs); it was about healing. Deep, transformative healing that I hoped would smooth the jagged edges of my heart and remind me who I was beneath the rubble of my recent past.

This trip felt like a scene ripped straight from a movie, the kind where the protagonist escapes to a foreign country to find herself and ends up discovering far more than she bargained for. Except this wasn't a movie—it was my life. And honestly, after everything I'd been through recently, the idea of walking into a real-life screenplay felt like exactly what I needed. Italy wasn't just a destination. It was a promise. A beacon of hope. A place where I could piece myself back together.

Of course, I wasn't naive enough to think this would be smooth sailing. For starters, the beast inside me—this possession-like force wreaking havoc on my body—was determined to come along for the ride. Add to that the typical travel jitters and my knack for overthinking, and I was already battling a storm before I even left. But I was determined. If Italy was a battlefield, I was ready to fight for every ounce of peace, pleasure, and purpose it had to offer.

The plan? A red-eye flight into Paris, a quick layover, and then a two-hour hop into Italy. Easy, right? Except it wasn't. Because in true Haley fashion, things were about to get gloriously chaotic. First, the 14-hour flight. Sleep? Ha! Not even close. Instead, I threw myself into a movie marathon, devouring everything from cheesy rom-coms to gritty thrillers. It was as if I were training for my own cinematic debut, bingeing stories to fuel my imagination and distract from the fact that my nerves were doing somersaults.

By the time we landed in Paris, I was delirious, running on nothing but adrenaline and a questionable in-flight croissant. But then came the miracle: the two-hour flight from Paris to Italy. Somewhere between the cabin lights dimming and the hum of the engines, I managed to pass out completely. When I woke up, it felt like I'd been gifted a small blessing from the travel gods. Two hours of sleep might not sound like much, but to me, it was a golden ticket. I convinced myself that this accidental nap was the key to beating jet lag. If I could just push through the first day on sheer willpower and espresso, I'd sync to the Italian timezone like a pro.

As the plane descended into Italy, I stared out the window, the landscape below bathed in sunlight, and felt a strange mix of exhilaration and vulnerability. This wasn't just a trip. It was a reckoning. A chance to shed the weight of everything I'd carried for too long and rediscover the person I was meant to be. I wasn't just visiting Italy—I was surrendering to it, letting its ancient streets and storied skies hold me in a way I hadn't let myself be held in years.

I had no concrete plans, no rigid itinerary. My only goals were to immerse myself in every moment, heal from the inside out, and maybe—just maybe—fall a little bit in love with life again. Italy was waiting, its magic shimmering on the horizon. And for the first time in what felt like forever, so was I.

First stop: Florence. The moment my feet hit the ground, it felt like stepping into a dream—hot, sticky, and beautifully overwhelming. The July sun was relentless, and the air seemed to wrap itself around me like a humid blanket, but none of that mattered. My heart was racing, my mind spinning with possibilities, and every nerve ending was ready to devour Italy with all six senses. This was it—the start of my great adventure, my "Eat, Pray, Love" chapter, minus the neatly polished Julia Roberts moments and with a lot more sweat.

The excitement fizzled momentarily as I faced my first challenge: escaping the airport. Sounds easy, right? Wrong. Between the language barrier (spoiler: I never got around to learning Italian) and the absolute chaos of navigating an unfamiliar space, it felt like I'd entered a labyrinth designed specifically to break me. Six hours. *Six hours* of lugging my bags, wandering aimlessly, and trying to decode signs that might as well have been written in hieroglyphics. Every pore in my body was on overdrive, sweat pouring like I was in a marathon, and I could feel my internal beast—the one that loved to flare up at the worst possible times—starting to rear its ugly head.

I know—I'm resourceful, but this was next-level. The stress built in my chest like a ticking time bomb as I wandered in circles, drenched in sweat, muttering curse words under my breath. My body, already a reluctant travel companion, thanks to the beast of symptoms I carried, threatened to spiral out of control. I tried to stay calm, to breathe, to remind myself that this was all part of the adventure. But by hour four, I was dangerously close to tears. Dramatic, I know, but being easily irritable is a PTSD symptom. Eventually, by some divine intervention or sheer dumb luck, I stumbled into a cab. When the driver loaded my bags into the trunk, I nearly hugged him. I'd survived my first Italian challenge, albeit barely.

The cab ride gave me a chance to decompress, and when I finally arrived at my hotel, I was determined to reset the tone of the day. After freshening up, I wandered out into the golden glow of Florence, my body and soul desperate for nourishment. That's when I found it—the alleyway of my dreams. Narrow and cobblestoned, it was lined with twinkling lights, bustling tables, and the sound of clinking glasses. It was like stepping into a romantic film set, and I was the star. I picked a restaurant at random, lured by the heavenly smell of garlic and the promise of pasta that would ruin me for life.

Sitting under the stars, I ordered a bowl of fresh seafood pasta and a glass of Chianti. As I took my first bite, I swear I heard angels sing. The pasta was perfection—silky, rich, and infused with the kind of magic that only Italian grandmothers know how to summon. I savored every bite, sipping wine and soaking in the moment. I was alone but not lonely, overwhelmed but in the best possible way. This wasn't just a meal; it was a revelation. I was here. I was doing this. For the first time in forever, I felt alive.

And then, dessert. Being the self-proclaimed queen of ice cream, I'd made a solemn vow before this trip: gelato every single day. It was my sacred mission, my Italian birthright. The first scoop? Chocolate and Vanilla, naturally. As I took that first creamy, heavenly bite, I nearly wept. It was so good it felt like a spiritual experience, as though the gelato was hugging my soul. If joy could ooze out of your pores, that's exactly what was happening. I practically floated back toward my hotel, gelato-induced euphoria carrying me.

But the night wasn't over. I decided to end my first day with a visit to a wine bar near the hotel. Two glasses of local red later, I was feeling more relaxed than I had in months. It was exactly what I needed after the absolute clusterfuck of a day. Between the airport ordeal, the hotel initially trying to tell me my reservation didn't exist (rude), and the oppressive heat, I deserved this moment of indulgence.

Of course, nothing in my life is ever that smooth. Back at the hotel, tipsy and still adjusting to this whirlwind of emotions, I managed to knock over the large mirror in my room. The crash was deafening. As I stared at the shattered pieces scattered across the floor, my first thought was, *Oh great, seven years of bad luck.* But then a different thought crept in: *Maybe this is symbolic. Maybe I'm breaking apart the old, broken pieces of me to make room for something new.*

Poetic, right? Until I remembered I'd have to pay for the damages. Way to go, Haley—breaking shit on your first night in Italy. I couldn't help but laugh at the absurdity of it all. Here I was, embarking on the trip of a lifetime, and already I was creating a highlight reel of disasters. But maybe that's what this trip was supposed to be: messy, chaotic, imperfect. A real adventure.

As I crawled into bed that night, I felt the exhaustion of the day settle over me, but there was a strange sense of contentment, too. Yes, it had been a rollercoaster, but it was *my* rollercoaster. And if Florence wanted to throw a little chaos my way, I was more than ready to meet it head-on. After all, this was just the beginning.

The next morning, Florence beckoned like an irresistible whisper, and I was ready to answer the call. I woke up feeling triumphant, having successfully plunged into the Italian timezone on night one. No jet lag? Check. One less obstacle to tackle, and I felt like a travel pro—well, almost. The day ahead was brimming with possibilities, and I couldn't wait to dive in.

I packed my bags and made my way to my next destination—a hostel I'd painstakingly researched during my pre-trip planning frenzy. It was the perfect choice. As I checked in, the staff handed me a free welcome drink token, a gesture that felt both charming and well-deserved after my airport debacle. Drink in hand, I found my way to the hostel's terrace, a sun-drenched haven with views that seemed to promise, *This is going to be good.*

And it was. That's where I met Fay, a solo traveler from New Zealand, with an accent as refreshing as her energy. We struck up a conversation that quickly turned into a plan. What started as two strangers sharing stories turned into a mission: rallying as many hostel-goers as possible for a sunset adventure. By some miracle of persuasion, we managed to corral fifteen travelers from all corners of the globe. With bottles of wine clinking in our backpacks, we hiked to Piazzale Michelangelo, home to a breathtaking view of Florence and a towering replica of David.

The hike itself was a kaleidoscope of laughter, accents, and shared stories. I was the lone American in the group, surrounded by wanderers from Australia, Ireland, Germany, and beyond. Each step felt like an act of connection—bonding over the universal language of awe. When we reached the top, the city unfurled before us, bathed in hues of gold and rose as the sun dipped toward the horizon. It was the kind of moment that makes you feel infinite, like you're exactly where you're supposed to be, surrounded by strangers who suddenly feel like friends.

After the sunset painted its final masterpiece, we descended into the city, our spirits light and our stomachs growling. We ended up at a pizza spot touted as one of Florence's best. While the pizza didn't exactly live up to the hype, it didn't matter. The company, the laughter, and the energy of the night more than made up for it. It was the kind of evening that left you buzzing with gratitude.

The next day, Fay and I vowed to conquer Florence. And, of course, the day started with gelato—because what's a mission without dessert for breakfast? The pistachio scoop was life-changing, unexpectedly (I'm no fan), and set the tone for what would be an unforgettable day. As fate would have it, we'd arrived on the one magical day of the year when all museums in Florence were free. It felt like a divine invitation to see it all.

Armed with gelato-fueled determination, we began our journey. Palaces, churches, museums—we left no stone unturned. We meditated in the serene Boboli Gardens, wandered through the halls of history, and rubbed wishing statues for good luck. Somewhere along the way, we stumbled upon boutiques, ancient alleyways, and picturesque corners that demanded a thousand photos. Our steps—15,000 and counting—carried us deeper into the city's soul.

What made it even more magical was Fay herself. As we walked, I found myself opening up about the troubles I'd left behind in Los Angeles—the beast inside me, the heartbreaks, the chaos. She listened, her warmth and empathy wrapping around me like a safety net. There's something uniquely freeing about confiding in someone you've only just met. Fay was compassionate and kind, the perfect blend of stranger and confidante. Our friendship grew as naturally as the vines that seemed to climb every building in Florence.

When lunchtime rolled around, we fully embraced the Italian way—long meals, plenty of wine, and food that could make you cry. The pasta? Divine. The freshness of each bite was a revelation, a reminder that food could be healing. For someone like me, who battles a tipping celiac problem back home, this was a gift. No processed junk, no fear of consequences—just pure, authentic bliss. And with my recent weight loss leaving me thin and brittle, I treated this as both indulgence and necessity. I devoured plates of pasta guiltlessly, determined to soak in the nourishment my body craved.

By the time the sun set on our whirlwind day, we'd covered so much ground I was surprised my feet still worked. Museums, gardens, cafes, and cobblestone streets had all blurred together into one magical mosaic of

Florence. That evening, I felt like I'd truly seen the city—not just its landmarks, but its spirit.

The hostel experience itself had been a revelation. My roommates were three laid-back, adventurous women who brought a sense of camaraderie to every interaction. Some of them joined us on our escapades, adding to the tapestry of personalities that colored these days. For someone who'd never stayed in a hostel before, I couldn't have asked for a better introduction.

As I crawled into my bunk on my last night in Florence, I felt a mix of exhaustion and elation. In just a few days, I'd formed connections, eaten meals that felt like love letters, and walked streets that had witnessed centuries of history. Florence had welcomed me with open arms and a chaotic kind of grace, and I'd embraced it all in return. This wasn't just a city I'd visited—it was a place that had left its mark on me. And as I drifted off to sleep, I knew this was only the beginning.

Next stop: Tuscany. This leg of my journey was the "business" side of things—the Alexander Technique retreat. I had grand visions of peace and tranquility under the Tuscan sun, but getting there was another story entirely. After my last chaotic attempt at Italian public transport, I was determined to avoid a repeat. I gave myself ample time, armed with directions, patience, and maybe a prayer or two that getting to Tuscany would be smoother than my airport experience. Spoiler alert: it wasn't.

Navigating Tuscany's transportation options was like trying to complete a scavenger hunt blindfolded. My route involved a train, followed by not one but two different buses, as Tuscany is a collection of small towns and winding hills, far from the bustling infrastructure of Florence. It was a second chaotic mission, featuring the usual blend of language barriers and my ever-growing nerves. Thankfully, by some miracle, I managed to get to the second bus in time. That's where I met an unexpected ally—a woman also attending the retreat. Her look of relief when we discovered our shared destination was mutual; suddenly, I wasn't alone in the maze.

But here's the kicker—bless her heart, but she was entirely relying on me to navigate. While I was frantically puzzling over maps and deciphering Italian bus schedules, she seemed content to let me take the reins. My inner

Tasmanian beast was already pacing, and I didn't pause until I'd secured our way to the retreat, determined not to let any obstacle get the best of me.

We finally arrived at the "downtown" of San Gimignano—a charming, medieval hilltop village that looked like it had sprung straight from a postcard. But our journey wasn't over yet. We still needed to catch a final bus to the retreat, just three miles down the road. Easy enough, right? That's what we thought. All we had to do was wait for one of the only buses in town that could take us there. We watched for it, checked the schedule obsessively, and reassured ourselves we had everything under control. And yet, somehow, we missed it.

Cue panic mode. As the minutes ticked by, I scrambled to figure out when the next bus might arrive, only to realize it wasn't coming. We already hopped on the wrong one till we jumped off and made our way back. The small town had an equally small transportation schedule, and the bus service had simply… stopped. My heart sank as we waited in vain, the hours slipping by as our hopes dimmed. With check-in time looming, my companion and I tried everything we could think of—talking to locals, checking if a taxi was available—but it was hopeless. Apparently, taxis were just as elusive as buses in these parts, and every option seemed to evaporate as soon as we asked about it.

Finally, after nearly five hours of waiting and plotting, I made a desperate call to the retreat organizer, Michael Frederick. When he picked up, his voice was like a balm to my frazzled nerves. Calm, kind, and unshakably reassuring, he promised to find us a way. And true to his word, he worked a miracle, arranging a personal ride to rescue us. I'm not sure how he pulled it off, but he did, and it felt like he was some benevolent saint sent just for us.

By the time our ride showed up, the rain had begun to pour, as if the universe was testing just how far my patience could stretch. But in that moment, drenched and exhausted, I couldn't have cared less. We'd made it. Tuscany was within reach, and Michael's kindness had saved us from what could have been a night stranded in the middle of nowhere.

As we drove the last few miles to the retreat, I looked out at the misty hills and rolling vineyards, feeling a strange blend of exhaustion and gratitude.

Yes, the journey had been a disaster, but there was something beautifully humbling about it, too. Tuscany was making me work for this peace, stripping away my usual comforts and reminding me of the kindness of strangers and the resilience hidden in the most chaotic of days. And if this journey was any indication of what lay ahead, I knew the retreat would be more transformative than I'd ever imagined.

Arriving at the retreat was like exhaling after holding my breath for far too long. Six days in a serene Tuscan villa, with nothing to worry about—no transport headaches, no over-scheduled agendas, not even the task of finding food. Everything I could possibly need was here, wrapped up in the gentle embrace of the Italian countryside. It felt as if life itself had granted me a reprieve, a gift of peace that stretched out as far as the olive groves below.

The villa was straight out of a storybook, with its timeless Tuscan architecture—a rustic yet elegant masterpiece perched high on a hill, overlooking miles of rolling vineyards and cypress-lined roads. The moment I saw it, my heart filled with gratitude. This place didn't just look like paradise; it *felt* like it. Stone staircases led down to a pool, perfect for a lazy afternoon swim, while an open-air restaurant stood nearby, its tables ready to host long, laughter-filled meals. Every corner of this villa carried a certain soul, an energy that whispered of centuries past and the promise of transformation.

Initially, I was supposed to share a room with a fellow student, but she hadn't been able to renew her passport in time. As I checked in, Michael, the retreat organizer and possibly the sweetest man alive, noticed my look of *what now?* He took it upon himself to work a little magic. With a bit of negotiation, he managed to score me the entire room to myself, an unexpected gift of privacy in this beautiful place. I'd pay a small additional fee, but honestly, I would have paid double for the privilege. Michael, ever the generous soul, even praised my determination in fast-tracking my own passport and hinted that this was his way of giving me a "well-deserved win." It felt like the universe was smiling down on me.

The retreat officially began with our first group gathering, a warm and slightly eclectic mix of introductions. There were ten of us women, most older than me, each drawn here by a different reason, a different story. Most of the women were mothers, each hoping to manage or alleviate some form of chronic pain or stress. A few, like myself, were from the acting studio, pursuing the Alexander Technique for its potential to unlock new depths in performance. Being the youngest, I felt like the little sister, or daughter, in a group of wise, world-traveled women.

Then, the teachers introduced themselves. Michael, our host and leader, exuded a gentle wisdom, the kind that instantly made you feel safe. He shared his journey of teaching the Alexander Technique around the world, weaving retreats like this one into the fabric of his life. Next was John, an English actor with a sharp wit and a knack for storytelling. He'd flown in to share his extensive experience in using this technique on stage, bringing his distinctly British charm to the group. Then there was Silvia, a graceful Italian yogi, with an energy so calm, you could practically feel your blood pressure drop just by standing near her. She would be guiding us through the technique's yoga applications, merging mindfulness with movement. The fourth instructor, Sabine, had traveled across continents to share her insights. Together, they formed a powerhouse team, each bringing a unique perspective to our journey.

But what, exactly, is the Alexander Technique? It's more than an exercise regimen or a quick-fix health hack; it's a philosophy, a gentle reprogramming of how we move and exist in our own bodies. It teaches us to shed the unconscious habits that make us rigid, unbalanced, or even prone to pain. It's a method of reconnecting with our bodies on a deeper level, a way of observing and shifting our movements toward a natural, graceful harmony. For actors, it's invaluable, helping us refine our movement, control our breath, and carry a powerful presence on stage. But it's also a gift for anyone—musicians, athletes, those with chronic pain, or simply anyone looking to feel more aligned with themselves.

The schedule was laid out in all its intensity, a six-day immersion that promised to push us mentally, emotionally, and physically. From 7 a.m. to 7 p.m., we would be diving headfirst into classes that ranged from yoga and breathwork to walking techniques and vocal exercises. They'd even included a session on "sitting," which I found oddly fascinating. Each class was meticulously designed to enhance our self-awareness and reconnect us with the subtleties of our movements—training us to listen to our bodies in a way that most of us had forgotten.

In between our classes, there were generous breaks for meals, each one prepared with care and designed to refuel us without that post-meal sluggishness. And, as a sweet nod to Italian tradition, every day included a midday *siesta*. Not just a lunch break, but an invitation to truly rest—nap if we wanted to, or just lounge in the villa, savoring that sense of timelessness that Tuscany seemed to radiate. It was a refreshing reminder that here, life didn't revolve around hustle and hurry; here, time flowed differently.

As I looked over the schedule, my heart fluttered with excitement. This was going to be more than a retreat; it was going to be a journey inward, a chance to rediscover parts of myself I'd buried under stress and obligations. I didn't have to worry about transportation, grocery lists, emails, or phone calls. I could completely surrender to the rhythm of this place, to the teachings, and to my own unfolding experience.

This villa on a hill, with its sun-drenched terrace and charming quirks, was the perfect setting for everything I'd come here to do. Over the next six days, I would let go of everything I knew and open myself to everything I didn't. I had no idea what transformations lay in wait, but I was ready to find out.

The first official day of the retreat began at dawn with a 7 a.m. yoga session, guided by the serene yet formidable Silvia. She floated around the room like some kind of yoga goddess, her movements both powerful and fluid. Yoga was an entirely new world for me—my "practice" amounted to a few random classes here and there, more of a novelty than anything serious. Yet here, in this quiet Italian villa bathed in morning light, yoga felt different. I could almost feel the tension melting from my body with each stretch and twist, the perfect balm for the turmoil I'd been carrying with me. The practice was gentle but deep, like a quiet invitation to let go. I could feel my body resisting at first, but then, slowly, I began to sink into it, hoping it would tame the beast that had been raging within.

The rest of the day unfolded like a carefully choreographed dance, each class designed to guide us closer to understanding the Alexander Technique.

We moved from breathwork to posture correction, from walking techniques to vocal exercises, all interwoven with a subtle philosophy of self-awareness that I found both challenging and intriguing. By the end of the day, I was exhausted—physically, mentally, and even emotionally spent. My muscles ached from head to toe, and my brain was buzzing with all I'd learned. Yet, despite the fatigue, a quiet satisfaction settled over me, a sense of accomplishment.

That evening, the other women and I gathered in the common room, a cozy haven filled with plush sofas and warm lighting. We laughed, swapped stories of our day, and bonded over our mutual exhaustion. It felt a bit like summer camp—if summer camp included relentless self-discovery. We weren't complaining, though; we were grateful to be here, fully immersed in the experience. But as we sat there, sipping tea and stretching out sore limbs, another thought began to creep into our minds—a thought that brought a sparkle to our eyes and a bit of rebellion to our hearts.

Just fifteen minutes away, waiting patiently for our arrival, was the ancient town of San Gimignano. The historic medieval gem we'd glimpsed on our journey in, with its towering stone spires and narrow, winding streets, beckoned to us like a siren's call. Known as the "Medieval Manhattan" for its skyscraping towers, this town had stood since the 11th century, once home to noble families and wealthy merchants who erected the towers as symbols of power and prestige. The thought of walking through that history, of touching walls that had witnessed centuries of life, was almost irresistible.

We committed to attending our classes diligently, every breath and movement made with focus. But in between the postures and the breathing techniques, our minds wandered. We were here for self-improvement, sure, but we were also in Tuscany—a place that felt like the world's most beautiful dream. And, as dreams go, we weren't about to miss out on exploring it. By the end of that second day, we looked at each other, our eyes gleaming with a shared, unspoken decision. It was time for a little adventure.

In a perfectly coordinated act of harmless rebellion, we decided to sneak away. Like mischievous schoolgirls, we tiptoed down the villa's stone corridors and slipped out into the dusky evening, our laughter hushed and conspiratorial. We were making a break for freedom, Tuscany-style. The short ride into San Gimignano felt like a journey into another time, the countryside giving way to ancient stone walls and cobbled streets that seemed to glow under the setting sun. The town was even more magical up close, a pocket of medieval splendor caught in amber. The narrow streets wound between towering structures, each turn revealing hidden treasures—small shops filled with hand-crafted trinkets, bustling cafes serving espresso and wine, and the scent of lavender and wood smoke lingering in the air.

That evening, we wandered San Gimignano's quiet alleys, browsing in little shops, sampling wines from local vineyards, and marveling at the timeless beauty around us. We stopped at a small wine bar tucked into a side street, where we ordered glasses of Chianti and toasted to our little adventure. Each sip was like tasting the heart of Tuscany itself, full-bodied and rich with history, and we let ourselves sink into the moment, free from the constraints of schedules and classes. We weren't just tourists; we were participants in the ancient, slow-paced rhythm of this town.

And so, our secret ritual began. Not once, but twice, we sneaked off like errant schoolgirls, each time with a different crew of retreat friends, each time with a new layer of adventure. We shopped to our hearts' content, gathering mementos of our forbidden outings. One evening, we treated ourselves to an extravagant dinner at a hidden gem of a restaurant. The waiter brought us course after course of fresh pasta, fragrant truffle, and creamy gelato, each dish more decadent than the last. We dined like queens, savoring each bite, each laugh, each secret shared over candlelight.

By the time we made our way back to the villa, our hearts were full and our spirits high, each of us feeling like we'd stolen a piece of Tuscany to keep for ourselves. These stolen moments in San Gimignano weren't just detours from our retreat; they were transformative in their own way. In those hidden, ancient streets, we rediscovered parts of ourselves—the adventurous, playful parts that sometimes got lost in the day-to-day shuffle of life.

As the days went by, our bond grew deeper, and our mischievous jaunts added a magical, rebellious layer to our experience. Tuscany had become more than a setting; it had woven itself into our souls. We came here to learn the Alexander Technique, to heal, to grow—but what we discovered was even more profound. In the quiet sanctuary of the villa, and in the cobbled streets of San Gimignano, we were learning to reclaim parts of ourselves, to embrace joy and spontaneity, and to carry a bit of Tuscany's magic within us, no matter where we went next.

Continuing with the classes was like stepping into a kaleidoscope of discovery—every session a new angle, a fresh lens on how my body and mind could work together. The variety was thrilling in its own way, each class offering a piece of the puzzle I hadn't even realized I was trying to solve. From posture adjustments to walking techniques, it was as if my body was a symphony I'd been playing out of tune, and now, slowly, I was learning how to conduct it properly. For someone who suddenly felt like a Tasmanian devil in human form—spinning, frantic, chaotic—this retreat was a strange and welcome grounding force. To my surprise, I got through the first day without unraveling. A small miracle, honestly.

Reverse back to Day Two. It started innocently enough, with another early morning yoga session led by Silvia. Every day, she switched up the style of yoga, keeping us guessing and engaged. I was starting to get the hang of it—stretching, breathing, flowing from one pose to the next. But then, out of nowhere, it happened. She instructed us into a deep back-twist, and as I twisted my body, something shifted. Something cracked open—not physically, but emotionally.

A sensation shot through me like lightning, striking something deep and hidden. Tears began streaming down my face before I even knew what was happening. It wasn't the kind of quiet, graceful crying you see in movies. It was raw, guttural, an uncontrollable wave of grief that I didn't even know I'd been carrying. My chest tightened as if all the pain I'd buried had decided to erupt at once. I wanted to scream, to let it out fully, but this was yoga. Screaming wasn't exactly part of the flow.

So I cried—no, I *sobbed*—my way through the rest of the class. It wasn't graceful, and it certainly wasn't pretty, but it felt necessary. That twist had unearthed something I'd kept locked away, and in that moment, I had no choice but to let it go. Silvia didn't acknowledge my tears, and for that, I was grateful. She simply carried on, her calm presence a steady anchor in the storm I was weathering.

There was, however, one constant struggle with yoga that wasn't as poetic: the floor. Our mats were thin, and the cold, hard tiles beneath them might as well have been made of concrete. My body, already fragile from being unhealthily thin, felt every sharp edge of that unforgiving surface. No amount of blankets or extra layers could cushion my bony frame, and by the end of each session, my tailbone felt bruised, my lower back aching in protest. But I pushed through, determined to show up for myself, even if it meant enduring a little discomfort.

Later that day, I stepped into my first breathwork class, buzzing with curiosity. I'd heard whispers about how powerful breathwork could be, and I was eager to experience it for myself. The teacher, with a voice as soothing as a lullaby, explained that this session would involve a series of chants designed to align the chakras. *Chakras?* The word floated in my mind like an undefined concept, something I'd heard in passing but never truly understood. Still, I was all in.

At first, the chants felt a little awkward. I fumbled through the low, resonant tones, unsure if I was doing it "right." But as we progressed, something shifted. Each chant created a vibration inside me, subtle at first, then stronger. It was as if my body was a musical instrument, and each sound was tuning it, aligning it. By the time we reached the final sequence, where all the chakras were meant to align, the sensations in my body were nothing short of electric.

And then, just like during yoga, the tears came. But this time, they weren't tears of grief or pain. They were tears of release, of wonder, of awe. It felt as though something deep within me had clicked into place, a missing piece I hadn't even realized was lost. The vibrations from the chanting had unlocked something profound, something powerful, and as the tears streamed down my face, I wasn't embarrassed or ashamed. I was overwhelmed with gratitude.

By the end of the session, I sat there, wiping my cheeks and trying to process what had just happened. It felt like my body had been holding onto my story—one of pain, resistance, and survival—and in that moment, it had finally found its voice. I didn't just cry; I *exhaled*, releasing years of tension and buried emotion in a single breath. I walked out of that class feeling lighter, freer, almost reborn.

That night, as I lay in bed, I couldn't stop replaying the day in my mind. The back-twist that broke me open, the chants that pieced me back together—these weren't just classes; they were transformations. And as terrifying as it was to confront these raw, unfiltered parts of myself, I knew I was exactly where I needed to be. This wasn't just a retreat; it was a reckoning. And I was ready for whatever came next.

The loaded schedule, the relentless ache in my bones, and the whirlwind of emotions made the days blur together. Step by step, I struggled to recall exactly when and where certain moments happened, but one thing I do remember vividly—crying. A lot of crying. It felt like every class unlocked something raw inside me, and no matter how strong my willpower was, I *just couldn't stop* the tears from pouring down my face. They weren't graceful tears either—these were the kind that left my cheeks blotchy, my throat tight, and my breath uneven. It was as if my body had decided that this retreat was its opportunity to purge years of unspoken pain, and it wasn't taking "no" for an answer.

At first, I tried to hold it together, thinking, *I can't cry in every single class, can I?* But the tears came anyway—unstoppable, unapologetic, a force of nature I couldn't tame. I became the girl who cried in class, and before long, all ten of the mothers in our group started approaching me with a mix of concern and maternal instinct. They came with warm hugs, soft smiles, and whispered reassurances, wrapping me in a cocoon of care that I didn't know I needed. While part of me felt a bit pathetic for being the walking, weeping basket case of the retreat, another part of me was deeply touched by their kindness.

It was crazy, honestly. I'd cry during yoga, tears streaming down as I tried to hold a pose. I'd cry during breathwork, my sobs interrupting the calm chants. I'd cry during posture correction classes, feeling the weight of the years I'd spent carrying myself wrong—both physically and emotionally. My tears felt like their own kind of practice, something unplanned but strangely necessary. I hadn't anticipated this level of vulnerability, but I believed, deep down, that it was needed.

What I didn't want, though, was for it to happen *in class*, in front of these wonderful new friends I was trying to bond with. I worried that my constant crying might overshadow the real connections I was forming or make others uncomfortable. But every time I began to feel embarrassed, someone would extend a gesture of love—a hand on my shoulder, a knowing glance, or a shared laugh about how the retreat was breaking us all open in different ways. It reminded me that I wasn't alone in this, even if my tears seemed more frequent than anyone else's.

I decided not to shame myself for what I was feeling. Instead, I surrendered to it. If this retreat was about transformation, then maybe this was how mine had to look—messy, tear-soaked, and utterly human. With each tear, I felt like I was shedding something old, something heavy I didn't want to carry anymore. The pain needed to come out, and if that meant crying through yoga poses or breathwork chants, so be it.

I threw myself into every session with a mix of determination and exhaustion. Yoga styles continued to shift, each one stretching me in ways I hadn't expected—both physically and emotionally. Breathwork became a space where I learned to embrace the vibrations running through me, even when they felt overwhelming. Walking techniques made me aware of how much tension I carried in every step, and sitting posture exercises revealed how tightly I'd been gripping onto things I didn't need to hold. It was fascinating, transformative, and yes, absolutely draining.

How am I supposed to explain what I don't even understand myself? There's this wild, Tasmanian devil thrashing inside me, tearing me apart from the inside out. It's like a relentless storm, an untamed beast that's taken control of my body, dragging me through each day as if I were just a passenger. I'm shedding weight, I'm jumpy, jittery, irritable—a hair's breadth away from a breakdown at any given moment. My mind is drowned in the fog of PTSD symptoms, an invisible weight pressing down on me, keeping me in a state of high alert, where even the smallest thing can make me feel like the ground is falling out beneath me.

What makes it worse is that I have no idea what to call it. No language for the madness that's keeping me up at night and driving me through my days. It's just there, always, like some silent tormentor. How do I even begin to tell anyone about this when I can't make sense of it myself? The truth is, it feels safer to keep it all bottled up. There's a strange kind of power in privacy, in convincing yourself that you're strong enough to tackle the demons alone. So, I did exactly that—kept it private, sealed it off, figuring I'd wrestle with it quietly and somehow, someday, come out on the other side.

But even iron will crack under enough pressure. Here at the retreat, surrounded by people searching for their own peace, I found myself drawn to three particular women. There was something about them—maybe a gentle openness or a quiet strength—that made me feel a little less guarded. They became my inner circle, the only ones I allowed close enough to catch a glimpse of the chaos swirling inside me. I didn't say much, just let slip fragments, pieces of my struggle, testing the waters.

And, to my surprise, they didn't turn away. They didn't try to fix it, or even push me to explain further. They simply listened, holding the space with a kindness so steady it felt like an anchor. Their quiet presence was like a balm, a silent assurance that I didn't have to carry all of this alone—not in that moment. I didn't need to explain every gritty detail to be understood. I didn't need to have all the answers to be accepted.

These three women—without even knowing the full extent of the storm inside me—had given me a place to rest, if only for a moment. They'd shown me that I could share a bit of my burden without losing control, without feeling weak. And in that small act of trust, I felt a crack in the armor I'd kept up for so long, the faintest sense of relief. Maybe this, I thought, is how healing begins: with the smallest act of letting go, and the quiet, unexpected kindness of a few strangers turned friends.

I wanted to be stronger. I wanted to show up as this poised, composed version of myself, absorbing the lessons and bonding effortlessly with everyone around me. But the reality was that I was raw. I was unraveling. And somehow, that was okay. These women—these incredible, motherly souls—reminded me that strength isn't always about holding it together. Sometimes, it's about letting yourself fall apart, trusting that you'll be caught by the love and understanding of those around you.

By the end of each day, I felt like a wrung-out sponge—emotionally spent but also strangely lighter. The tears didn't stop, but I stopped fearing them. They became part of my retreat experience, a language my body was using to say what my words couldn't. Painful as it was, I knew I was doing the work. As I wiped my cheeks for what felt like the hundredth time, I realized: This wasn't just crying. *This was healing*

Chapter 22

Escape Room: Italian edition

As the days unfolded at the retreat, there was one moment that etched itself into my memory—a comedy of errors wrapped in a personal horror show that I will never, *ever* forget. It started innocently enough, as these things often do. I was moving from one class to the next, with only five precious minutes in between, and decided to make a quick restroom stop. It was just ten feet away, so no big deal, right? Famous last words.

Let me set the scene: the bathroom was… unique. Picture a cramped space that barely fit two sinks that could fit two humans standing shoulder to shoulder. To the left and right were two doors, each leading to a stall so small you'd think it was designed for contortionists. Inside each stall, there was just enough room for a toilet and one person to sit—no windows, no ventilation, no wiggle room. Minimalism at its finest. But hey, it worked. Or so I thought.

I stepped into one of the stalls, handled my business, and reached for the door to leave. That's when it happened. The doorknob didn't budge. I jiggled it again, harder this time. Nothing. *Okay, no big deal*, I thought. *This isn't my first locked door. It just needs a little… finesse.* Spoiler alert: finesse didn't work. I yanked, twisted, and pulled, my annoyance growing with each passing second. The door refused to move. I was trapped.

Cue the panic. I knocked on the door, calling out, "Scusi! Scusi!" My voice echoed in the claustrophobic space, but there was no answer. I knocked louder, shouting, "HELP!" Still nothing. Apparently, the Tuscany walls were thick enough to muffle my pleas for rescue—or maybe everyone was too engrossed in class to notice. Either way, I was on my own. I sat back down on the toilet lid, my heart pounding as I tried to think.

Alright, Haley, I told myself. *This is a perfect opportunity to practice the Alexander Technique. Breathe. Ground yourself. You've got this.* And for a moment, I did. I closed my eyes, focused on my breath, and felt a brief wave of calm. But then, the reality of my situation came crashing back. *What if no one finds me? What if I'm stuck here for hours? I need fresh air!* My heart raced, the walls seemed to shrink, and I could feel the first tendrils of claustrophobia creeping in.

For fifteen agonizing minutes, I cycled through this rollercoaster of emotions—calming myself with deep breaths one moment, spiraling into panic the next. My tears started falling, hot and unrelenting, and I could feel the weight of my anxiety crashing down like a tidal wave. I wasn't just trapped physically—I was trapped emotionally, too, drowning in the chaos of my own thoughts.

Then it hit me: *Michael!* Sweet, dependable Michael. Surely, he could help. I grabbed my phone and called him, praying he'd answer. No dice—straight to voicemail. Fantastic. My one lifeline wasn't picking up. But then, I remembered the villa's front desk number. Desperate, I called, and to my immense relief, the receptionist answered. "I'm stuck in the bathroom," I blurted out, my voice shaky but firm. She promised to send someone immediately.

Within minutes, I heard footsteps and voices outside. *Finally, I'm getting out!* I thought. But when they tried the master key, it didn't work. My hope crumbled. They left to grab tools and returned armed with forks, knives, and other random objects, shoving them into the lock in a desperate attempt to free me. It was a valiant effort, but the door refused to budge. I could hear their frustration mounting as they left again to regroup. Meanwhile, I was still inside, hyperventilating and trying not to scream. *Is this how it ends? Trapped in a Tuscan bathroom stall?*

After what felt like an eternity, almost an hour later, they returned with reinforcements, and through some combination of brute force and ingenuity, they finally got the door open. The moment I stepped out, the cool air hit my face, and I almost cried with relief. I stumbled out like a prisoner of war, my face blotchy, my body trembling. Stacy, one of my closest retreat friends, spotted me immediately. "Where were you?!" she asked, her voice a mix of concern and confusion. "Locked in the bathroom," I said, barely able to process the words myself. Her wide-eyed expression said it all.

I skipped the next class. I couldn't face another confined space or another wave of anxiety—not yet. Instead, I made my way outside, found a quiet spot near the villa, and let the fresh air wash over me. I focused on my breathing, using every grounding technique I'd learned to calm the storm inside. But even with the air and the silence, I couldn't shake the lingering fear. That tiny stall had imprinted itself on me, leaving behind a newfound claustrophobia I hadn't known I carried.

So, I did the only thing that made sense: I grabbed my towel, went to the pool, and let myself *chill the fuck out*. The anxiety didn't disappear, but it softened, and for the first time that day, I felt like I could breathe again.

Looking back, I can almost laugh at the absurdity of it all—the forks, the failed keys, the dramatic rescue. Almost. But in that moment, it wasn't funny. It was terrifying, humbling, and strangely transformative. That tiny bathroom stall had taught me something I hadn't expected: the importance of surrendering. Of letting others help. Of realizing that sometimes, no matter how much you try to ground yourself, it's okay to fall apart. And when you finally step out into the light, you learn that you're stronger than you thought. The Alexander Technique was my guide.

I slipped into my bikini, the warm Tuscan sun already kissing my shoulders as I made my way down the villa's winding stone staircase. The pool was tucked into the hillside, surrounded by vineyards that seemed to stretch forever, their neat rows rolling into the hazy horizon. The landscape was impossibly beautiful, like something from a postcard, and I couldn't help but feel grateful for this little slice of paradise. After the chaos and terror of being trapped in that bathroom stall earlier, I needed this. Desperately.

The pool area was quiet and tranquil. A mother and her child left shortly after I arrived, leaving me completely alone with the stunning view and the kind of peace I'd been craving. I sprawled onto a lounger, letting my body sink into the cushion as the sunlight washed over me. This was it—my moment to exhale, to let the tension melt away. For the first time in days, I felt myself relaxing. The vines swayed gently in the breeze, the birds sang lazily, and for a few blissful moments, everything was still.

And then, out of nowhere, it hit me. A crushing tightness gripped my chest, like an invisible hand squeezing the air out of my lungs. My eyes flew open, panic surging through me as I tried to take a breath—any breath—but nothing came. My throat felt like it was closing, and my heart was pounding in my ears. My mind raced: *Am I having a heart attack? Am I dying?* I shot up from the lounger, tossing and turning in a frantic attempt to find air, clawing at my chest as if I could pull the panic out by force.

But nothing worked. My breath came in shallow, broken gasps, and the more I struggled, the worse it got. My thoughts spiraled as the world tilted around me, and I realized, with a sinking dread, that this wasn't something physical—it was a full-blown panic attack. I'd never experienced one before, and it felt like the ground had disappeared beneath me, leaving me flailing in freefall. Alone by the pool, with no one to comfort or save me, I was utterly consumed by the fear that I might not make it out of this.

After what felt like an eternity, the tightness in my chest began to ease. My frantic gasps turned into shallow, shaky breaths, and the terror started to loosen its grip. I collapsed back onto the lounger, my body trembling, my energy completely drained. I felt hollowed out, fragile, like a broken vase held together by sheer willpower. Vulnerable didn't even begin to describe it. I sat there, staring at the vineyards, trying to anchor myself back to reality.

Thankfully, it was still siesta time, so I had a cushion of time before the next class. Eventually, I gathered the strength to climb the stairs back to the villa, one shaky step at a time. By the time I reached the lunch area, others were beginning to trickle in, their conversations light and easy—a stark contrast to the storm I'd just survived. I found a quiet table by myself, trying to process what had just happened, still feeling the ghost of the panic lingering in my chest.

That's when she appeared. A woman I hadn't seen before glided over and took the seat across from me. She had an ethereal presence—calm, radiant, and deeply grounding, like the human embodiment of sunlight after a storm. Her name was Michaela, and she introduced herself with a gentle smile. She wasn't part of our group, I realized, but as we began talking, she explained that she was a yogi master visiting the retreat at Michael Frederick's invitation. He was considering bringing her on board for future retreats.

There was something magnetic about her—an energy that made you feel seen without judgment. As we talked, she studied me quietly, her kind eyes almost reading my soul. Then, out of nowhere, she said something like, "Your heart feels heavy. You're carrying so much pain." And even more—practically reading me like a book. Her words hit me like a lightning bolt. How could she possibly know? I hadn't told her anything, hadn't even hinted at the chaos inside me. Yet somehow, she saw right through my walls.

Her insight disarmed me, and before I knew it, I was spilling everything—the beast inside me, the anxiety, the weight of my struggles, even my battle with cancer. Michaela listened with an openness that made it easy to be vulnerable. She didn't try to fix me or offer empty platitudes. Instead, she offered something extraordinary: an invitation to attend a yoga retreat designed specifically for cancer patients.

The retreat, she explained, was a deeply immersive program that studied the effects of yoga on rare cancers while providing patients with tools to heal physically and emotionally. There was one catch—I'd need to be a Level Two yogi to qualify. But Michaela, with her calm confidence, offered to train me personally. She had connections that could secure my spot for free, a gift she presented as if it were the most natural thing in the world.

I was floored. This wasn't just an opportunity—it was a lifeline, a chance to dig deeper into my healing in ways I hadn't even considered. Stacy, my sweet Scottish mom-friend, overheard part of the conversation and later pulled me aside, insisting she'd pay for Michaela's help if it meant I could go. Her generosity made my heart swell, her belief in me a balm to the vulnerability I'd been feeling all day.

Michaela and I talked for a long time, and I felt an undeniable pull toward her. She wasn't just a teacher—she was a guide, a light in the storm, someone who could see what I couldn't and offer a way forward. The retreat, scheduled just a month after I'd return home, sounded like exactly what I needed. But life has a way of complicating even the most beautiful dreams. The retreat coincided with the final week of my first Meisner year—the culmination of everything I'd worked so hard for. Missing it wasn't an option, and as much as I wanted to say yes to Michaela's offer, I knew it wasn't the right time.

Still, the fact that she believed in me enough to offer such a gift meant everything. Even if I couldn't take her up on it, the connection we'd formed felt like a blessing in itself. As she walked away, I felt an overwhelming sense of gratitude. Michaela had reminded me that even in the darkest moments, there are people who see us, who believe in us, and who light the way forward. And that, I realized, was a gift I could carry with me—no matter where my journey took me next.

There are experiences that simply *belong* to Tuscany, things you can't leave without doing—and wine tasting tops the list. Surrounded by vineyards that stretched as far as the eye could see, the idea of sneaking away for an afternoon of wine tasting was too delicious to resist. By the end of the retreat, we'd all been through so much—emotions unraveled, bodies stretched, and souls bared—that we needed a way to celebrate and breathe together, away from the structured classes and carefully crafted schedules.

And so, like a band of giggling schoolgirls up to no good, we hatched our plan. We pooled together a group of the boldest women, called up a taxi, and told our driver to take us on a tour of his favorite vineyards. By this point, we were a sisterhood. A group of women, from all walks of life, constantly in each other's orbits through our shared classes. It was impossible *not* to bond. We'd become a patchwork family, and while I found myself closest to the three young moms—Stacy, Jenny, and Allie—there was a spirit of warmth, support, and understanding that wove all of us together.

The taxi wound through the sun-drenched countryside, taking us past vineyards as golden as they were endless. Each stop was like stepping into another world, with sprawling rows of vines stretching beneath wide-open skies. Our first stop was a family-owned vineyard where the owner himself poured us glasses of their finest Brunello di Montalcino, his accent thick and his smile wide as he shared stories of his family's history with the land. We clinked glasses, savoring the bold, earthy notes, letting each sip melt away our worries.

With each vineyard, each new glass, our laughter grew louder, and our steps grew lighter. We went from curious tasters to outright revelers, joyfully embracing the moment. At one point, we found ourselves running through the vines, heels kicked off, hair wild, our laughter echoing over the hills. The sight of us must have been ridiculous—grown women letting loose like kids on summer break—but in that moment, it felt like pure freedom. The kind of joy that comes from knowing you're exactly where you're meant to be.

After a few more stops, with cheeks flushed from the wine and endless laughter, we collapsed onto a sunny patio for yet another round. The wine had worked its magic, softening our defenses and coaxing out stories we hadn't shared yet. Girl talk, right, we began opening up about past loves, heartbreaks, and struggles we'd been through. I found myself talking about Grey Knight, about the toxic whirlwind of that relationship, the highs and lows that had left me raw and searching for answers. It felt strange and freeing to speak about him here, in Tuscany, with these women who'd become confidantes.

That's when one of the women—a sharp-witted divorce attorney—leaned in, her gaze serious but warm. "You should read *Women Who Love Psychopaths* by Sandra L. Brown," she said, her words slow and deliberate, each one landing like a revelation. "You'd be surprised how many women find themselves in these relationships." There are patterns to it, a reason you felt so pulled to him. *Understanding that can change everything*, I thought.

Her words sank in, deeper than any I'd heard in a long time. It wasn't just a suggestion—it was like she was handing me a key to a door I hadn't known existed. Could it really be that there was a way to understand the madness I'd endured with Grey Knight? A reason that could explain the magnetic pull, the pain, the rollercoaster of it all? Suddenly, the idea of reading that book felt like a lifeline, a way to unravel the mystery of what I'd been through and to find clarity, maybe even closure.

The sun dipped lower, casting a warm, amber glow over the vineyards, and I felt something shift within me—a spark of determination, of purpose. I knew that as soon as I was back home, I'd hunt down a copy of that book. I'd read every word, study every insight, and see if it could shed light on the darkness I'd been carrying. The promise of understanding, of discovering why I'd been pulled into Grey Knight's world, was irresistible.

As we piled back into the taxi, our laughter echoing through the open windows, I felt a quiet peace settle over me. This day, this adventure, wasn't just a wine tour—it was a journey of release, a moment to lay down burdens and revel in the beauty of life. Back at the villa, we stumbled out of the taxi, shoes in hand, cheeks sore from smiling, filled with stories, secrets, and new perspectives.

And that night, as I lay in bed, I felt a sense of closure I hadn't anticipated. Tuscany had given me so much more than I'd expected: new friendships, new dreams, and maybe, just maybe, a path toward healing. The adventure wasn't just about the wine—it was about letting go, laughing until it hurt, and finding a new chapter waiting to be written. The book recommendation might have been a small moment, but it was a beacon, a promise that I could understand myself in a way I never had before. And as I drifted off to sleep, I knew that Tuscany had changed me in ways I was only beginning to understand.

As the six-day intensive drew to a close, Michael gathered us for a final announcement, his voice filled with warmth and pride. "Tomorrow night," he said, "we'll celebrate the course with a five-course dinner." Dress up and meet at the restaurant. Let's end this retreat in style. A ripple of excitement moved through the group. After the sweat, tears, and breakthroughs we'd all experienced, a grand meal felt like the perfect punctuation to our journey.

The Alexander Technique had been a lifeline for me—timely, transformative, and utterly necessary. It gave me tools I hadn't known I needed, tools that had become armor against the chaos swirling inside me. Breathwork to quiet the storms, yoga to anchor my body, posture techniques to remind me I could stand tall, even when the world felt like it was crumbling. It wasn't just an intellectual or physical exercise; it was a reawakening of the connection between my mind and body. With this beast inside me—this untamable, thrashing energy—I felt like I'd finally been given a fighting chance to regain control. For that, I was endlessly grateful.

The last day of classes was a mix of nostalgia and pride, each session feeling heavier with the weight of knowing it was the final one. When evening arrived, we transformed from our usual disheveled, yoga-clad selves into a group of radiant dinner guests. The restaurant, tucked into the hillside, was like something out of a Tuscan dream. As the golden glow of sunset bathed the room, we gathered around the party tables, teachers and students alike, buzzing with a shared sense of accomplishment.

Wine and champagne flowed freely, glasses clinking as toasts were made. Laughter filled the room, each of us basking in the camaraderie that had grown over the week. Teachers shared heartfelt mini-speeches, their words brimming with pride for how far we'd all come. It felt like a family reunion, with everyone leaning across the table to chat, laugh, and reflect. Course after course arrived, each dish more exquisite than the last—fresh pasta, delicate risotto, roasted vegetables that tasted like sunshine. It was pure joy.

And then, the third course arrived. The server placed a bowl in front of me—three perfectly round meatballs nestled in a sea of rich marinara. My body froze. My breath caught. My entire focus narrowed to those three spheres of doom.

Meatballs.

The very word sent a chill through me. They weren't just meatballs. They were the "Meatball"—the nickname I'd given my cancer. My mind instantly spiraled back to that dark place, the surgeries, the fear, the endless uncertainty. The sight of them stirred something primal in me, a mix of rage, defiance, and deep sorrow. I glared at them with such intensity it felt like my stare might set them on fire.

Stacy, sitting beside me, caught my expression and knew immediately what was going on. "Oh no," she said softly, grabbing a napkin and tossing it over the bowl. "We're not doing this tonight."

I almost laughed at her protective gesture, but instead, a sudden realization hit me like lightning. *This is it.*

This was the moment I had envisioned before coming to Italy. I'd told myself that if the "Meatball"—the physical or metaphorical version—ever reappeared, I would face it head-on. I would change the narrative. Reclaim it. Rewrite the story of what it meant to me. And here it was, sitting right in front of me, like fate itself had placed it there.

"No," I said, stopping Stacy mid-motion as she reached to push the plate away. "This is meant to be."

I carefully moved the bowl aside, setting it next to me as if it were sacred. Naturally, this drew attention. Jenny and Allie, two of my closest friends from the group, leaned in, their curiosity piqued. "What's going on?" they asked, eyes darting between me and the bowl.

So, I told them. I shared my story—about the cancer, the fear, the surgery, and the name I'd given the tumor that had tried to take my life. I expected sympathy, maybe some encouraging words, but instead, Jenny's response left me speechless.

"My mom had the same tumor," she said softly, her voice trembling. "That one percent of pancreatic cancers. But by the time they found it, it had spread too far. There was nothing they could do."

Her words landed like a jab to the heart. My heart sank, a lump forming in my throat as she shared her mother's story. The same rare tumor that I'd somehow survived had taken her mother in what felt like an instant. It was the cruel reality of pancreatic cancer—silent, insidious, often undetected until it was too late.

The room around us seemed to blur as we sat there, grappling with the weight of our stories. Two women, connected by an impossibly rare diagnosis, yet separated by the razor-thin line between survival and loss. I felt an ache deep in my chest—not just for Jenny's mother, but for the fragility of life itself. How lucky was I to have caught mine in time? How wild was it that we'd found each other here, in this tiny group, across an ocean, sharing something so unimaginably specific?

As we talked, tears welled up in both of our eyes. The contrast between our stories was stark and sobering—a reminder of how precarious life can be. I couldn't help but feel bittersweet gratitude for being alive, for sitting at this table, for even having the chance to glare at a bowl of meatballs. But the guilt crept in, too—why me? Why not her mother? These were questions with no answers, only echoes of the fragile, unpredictable nature of life.

The rest of the evening felt both heavy and light, a strange mix of reflection and celebration. The teachers toasted our growth, laughter bubbled up in waves, and the wine continued to flow. The meatballs stayed beside me, untouched but no longer feared. They had become something else entirely— a symbol of resilience, a reminder of the fight I'd won, and a challenge to keep rewriting my story.

Dinner ran late, as all the best ones do. Laughter echoed through the restaurant, fueled by glasses of wine and the kind of joy that only comes from shared triumphs. We'd spent six days digging deep into ourselves, unraveling old patterns, learning, and growing—and now, we were reveling in the camaraderie forged through all that sweat, tears, and effort. By the time dessert rolled around, we were far from solemn students. Grappa and digestifs made their rounds, and soon it became a game: Who could make the most horrendous face after a sip of the fiery spirit? The results? Priceless. We clutched our sides from laughing so hard, eyes streaming, faces as red as the Chianti in our glasses.

As the group began to drift away from the table, a few of us weren't ready to let the night end. My closest partners-in-crime—Stacy, Jenny, and Allie—gathered around me, buzzing with a mix of wine and the sheer high of the evening. It was time for an after-party, our way. They already knew my story—the battle with cancer, the "Meatball" that changed my life, and the vow I'd made to reclaim the narrative. As we sat together, giggling like schoolgirls, I explained my plan for the meatballs that had made their surprise appearance at dinner.

"This is the perfect moment," I said, my voice filled with conviction. "We need to celebrate my one-year survival in the most dramatic way possible. I want to burn the meatballs."

The declaration hung in the air for a moment before erupting into a chorus of cheers. "Burn the meatballs!" Stacy cried, raising her glass like it was a battle cry. The rest of us followed suit. "Torch them!" Jenny laughed, her cheeks glowing from the wine. The mission was clear, and we were all in.

With grappa aplenty, it seemed like the obvious accelerant for our fiery plan. After all, it practically tasted like jet fuel. Yuck, no, thank you. We gathered our supplies and set up in a quiet corner, determined to turn these little spheres of marinara-soaked doom into ash. But as it turns out, burning meatballs isn't as straightforward as it sounds. Our first attempt fizzled. So did the second. And the third. We soaked them, doused them, and even whispered dramatic monologues to the universe to coax the flames into existence. Nothing worked.

As failure after failure mounted, so did our hilarity. We were laughing so hard we could barely stand. Between our increasingly wild attempts to ignite the meatballs and the absurdity of the situation, it felt like the kind of ridiculous moment you'd only see in a movie. The four of us were fully committed—stubbornly so—determined to succeed no matter how long it took.

At some point, I paused and looked around at my little makeshift sisterhood. These women, who had known me for just a week, were pouring their hearts into this goofy, symbolic mission like it was their own. And in a way, it was. The meatballs weren't just mine anymore—they represented every hardship, every fight, every moment of resilience that had brought us together over the past six days. I felt a rush of gratitude so overwhelming it almost brought me to tears.

But reality crept in—it was late, and we were getting dangerously close to waking the entire villa with our shrieks of laughter. "Alright," I said, wiping my eyes and catching my breath, "plan B. Screw the fire. Let's do something else."

We grabbed the meatballs, still stubbornly intact, and snuck down the villa's stone staircase toward the pool. Underneath the Tuscan stars, with the night wrapped around us like a soft blanket, inspiration struck. "You know what?" I said, holding up the bowl dramatically. "If we can't burn them, we'll feed them to the wildlife. Let nature devour what I couldn't. It's poetic."

The others burst into laughter, but there was something strangely fitting about the idea. And so, we documented the moment, phones out to capture this ridiculous yet profound act. I stood by the edge of the fence, holding the meatballs like an offering, thinking back on everything they represented—the fear, the pain, the fight, and the survival. My voice cracked as I shouted into the night, "Fuck you, cancer!" With all the strength in my arm, I launched the first meatball over the fence, sending it sailing into the darkness. Then the second. Then the third.

Each throw felt like an exorcism, a release of all the heaviness I'd been carrying. We laughed until our sides hurt, imagining some lucky raccoon or fox stumbling upon a midnight feast and having no idea of the symbolic weight behind it. It was silly, absurd, and perfect all at once.

As we made our way back up to the villa, breathless and exhilarated, I felt something shift inside me. I hadn't just survived cancer—I'd taken back the story, reclaimed the power it tried to steal from me. The meatballs were gone, consumed by the wild, and with them, a piece of the fear and anger I'd been holding onto.

Maybe it was the wine. Maybe it was the limoncello. Or maybe it was the collective energy of four women who had shared one of the most transformative weeks of their lives. Whatever it was, our spirits that night were untouchable—electric, magnetic, unstoppable. In just six days, we had formed a bond so tight it felt like destiny. It was as if the universe had carefully orchestrated this gathering, weaving our lives together on a little Tuscan hilltop for a purpose.

There was magic in the way we clicked, like a symphony that had been waiting for its players to arrive. We weren't just friends; we were a sisterhood. My very own "Sisterhood of the Traveling Pants," but this time with a backdrop of vineyards and ancient stone villas. These women weren't just people I'd met on a retreat; they were soulmates of a different kind—funny, brilliant, compassionate, and endlessly supportive. And as we reveled in the afterglow of dinner, I knew that this night was going to be unforgettable.

After the triumphant meatball mission (may those metaphorical cancers be forever devoured by the wildlife), I poured out my gratitude to them, barely able to find the words to express what their support had meant to me. And then, because one good idea deserves another, someone shouted, "Let's go skinny dipping!"

We didn't hesitate. It wasn't even a question. We sprinted over to the pool under the brightest full moon you could imagine, its silvery light casting everything in a surreal glow. The air was alive with our laughter as we stripped down to nothing and dove into the cool water. It was exhilarating, liberating—a joyful rebellion against everything heavy that we'd been carrying. For a moment, we were wild and free, our laughter echoing into the quiet Tuscan night.

But, of course, nothing this magical happens without a hiccup. As we splashed and laughed, I noticed a figure in the distance. "Wait... is that a man?" Allie whispered, squinting toward the shadows. "Oh my God, it's someone's husband!"

Panic set in for about five seconds, and then we all burst into laughter, diving deeper into the water as if it could somehow save us. The man, bless him, glanced up from his phone, clearly realizing he had wandered into the wrong scene, and made a hasty but calm exit. Crisis averted, and our full moons remained solely under the light of the celestial one.

The laughter didn't stop there. With three actresses in the mix, the pool quickly turned into a stage. We took on accents, created ridiculous characters, and acted out elaborate, imaginary scenarios. Someone started singing *The Little Mermaid*, and before long, we were all belting out "Part of Your World," splashing around like unhinged mermaids auditioning for Broadway. It was pure chaos—the kind that leaves your cheeks aching and your soul feeling lighter than air.

When we finally climbed out of the pool, dripping and breathless, we decided the night was far from over. We retreated indoors, careful not to wake the rest of the villa, and huddled together to keep the party alive. Music played softly as we danced barefoot, spinning and twirling as if the world outside didn't exist. And then, as if on cue, the energy shifted. The laughter softened, and the conversations turned deep.

We shared the rawest parts of ourselves—our heartbreaks, our fears, our triumphs. Tears fell as we confided in one another, peeling back the layers we'd kept hidden. These weren't just stories; they were pieces of ourselves we had never dared to share before. At that moment, our bond was sealed. This wasn't just a fun night anymore—it was sacred. A communion of kindred souls who had found each other at just the right time.

But then, as if the universe knew we needed to balance the heavy with the hilarious, someone floated the idea of finding more booze. "Let's raid the bar!" someone slurred, her giggle bubbling over. It started as a joke, but somehow, we all ended up sneaking toward the bar like a pack of giggling teenagers.

When we arrived, there was one problem: a locked gate. "No problem," Allie said confidently, eyeing the narrow gap beneath it. "I can squeeze through." She tried—and got stuck halfway through, thanks to her, well, *assets*. "Haley, you're skinnier," she said, laughing so hard she could barely get the words out. "You try!"

So, I did. I slid under the gate with a mix of determination and ridiculousness, only to stop dead in my tracks when I spotted the security camera aimed squarely at the bar. My brain went into overdrive: *Abort mission! You're not a thief! You're not a criminal!* I quickly backed out, announcing that the heist was officially canceled. We collapsed into laughter, tears streaming down our faces as we stumbled back toward the villa, empty-handed but richer in memories than we ever could have been with another bottle of wine.

By the time we finally called it a night, the first hints of dawn were creeping over the horizon. As I lay in bed, staring up at the wooden beams above me, I felt an overwhelming sense of gratitude. This night had been more than just fun—it had been transformative. It was the perfect culmination of a week that had changed me in ways I was only beginning to understand.

These women, this place, this night—it was a celebration of survival, of connection, of the kind of joy that comes when you stop holding back and let yourself truly live. Tuscany had given me more than I ever expected. It wasn't just a retreat—it was a rebirth. And this night? This ridiculous, hilarious, soul-baring, unforgettable night? It was the best way to honor that. The meatballs were gone, the moon had witnessed our rebellion, and my heart was full. What more could I have asked for?

The meatballs had become more than just a silly nickname—they were a symbol of resilience, a reminder that even the darkest chapters can end with laughter and love. It wasn't just about surviving; it was about celebrating the survival, rewriting the narrative, and knowing that I wasn't doing it alone. That night, in the heart of Tuscany, surrounded by laughter and friendship, I felt alive in a way I hadn't in years. And that was the real victory.

As I drifted off to sleep, I made a promise to myself: No matter how heavy life gets, I will keep rewriting, keep reclaiming, and keep living for the moments that make it all worth it.

And just like that, it was goodbye time—the parting of ways that no one really wanted but everyone knew had to happen. My heart ached with that bittersweet cocktail of gratitude and sadness, the kind that sneaks up on you when something truly special comes to an end. Every single person at this retreat had been a delight, but the bond I'd formed with the ladies was something extraordinary. We weren't just acquaintances who crossed paths; we were a sisterhood forged in laughter, vulnerability, and goofy personalities.

The teachers, too, were nothing short of phenomenal. But if there were a gold medal for pure sweetness and care, it would go to Michael Frederick. Michael wasn't just a teacher; he was a living embodiment of compassion and wisdom. From the moment I signed up for this retreat, he had made it his mission to check in with me—not just on logistics, but on my life, my career, and my well-being. He had a way of making you feel like the most important person in the room, and his advice for my acting career was priceless. He didn't just teach; he empowered. Saying goodbye to him felt like saying goodbye to a mentor and friend all wrapped into one.

As the villa buzzed with suitcases rolling over cobblestones and heartfelt hugs being exchanged, I discovered a serendipitous twist: Allie and Jenny were also heading to Rome. *Wait—what?!* Not only that, but their flight back to Los Angeles was just a few hours before mine. "You're coming with us," they said, grinning as if it were the most obvious solution. And honestly? It was.

I nearly fell to my knees with gratitude. My past experiences with Italian transportation had been nothing short of chaotic, ranging from missed buses to an hour-long bathroom lock-in. The idea of navigating another solo journey had me teetering on the edge of a full-blown anxiety spiral. But with Allie and Jenny, all of that stress melted away. They folded me into their plans as effortlessly as if I'd been part of them all along, and just like that, my road to Rome was set.

Stacy, my Scottish mom-friend, was headed back to her family, who were eagerly awaiting her return. Our goodbye was a long hug filled with promises. "Don't forget," she said with a wink, "my Meisner graduation is next week. I want you there." I promised her I wouldn't miss it, already envisioning her triumphant walk across that stage. Stacy had been my anchor throughout the retreat, and knowing I'd see her again soon softened the ache of parting.

The road trip to Rome with Allie and Jenny felt like an adventure in itself. Packed into the car with music blasting, windows down, and the Tuscan countryside unfurling around us, it was the kind of journey you dream about but rarely get to live. Rolling hills painted in shades of green, ancient ruins peeking through the trees, and sleepy villages tucked into the landscape—all of it passed by in a blur of beauty. It wasn't just a car ride; it was a celebration of everything we'd been through together.

When we finally arrived in Rome, the city greeted us with its intoxicating mix of chaos and grandeur. To our delight, our hotels were only a brisk walk apart, which made planning our next few days a breeze. Rome itself felt like a living museum, every cobblestone street and crumbling facade steeped in history and magic. And, oh, how we explored it!

Walking through Italy had become one of my favorite simple pleasures. There's something enchanting about the way every turn reveals a new treasure: a hidden piazza, a charming cafe, a fountain that seems to belong in a fairy tale. Rome was no exception. We wandered with no particular agenda, letting the city unfold before us like a well-kept secret.

Every corner felt like a scene from a movie. We paused to marvel at the Colosseum under the soft glow of twilight, laughed at our reflections in storefront windows, and made wishes at the Trevi Fountain, tossing coins over our shoulders with whispered hopes for the future. The simple act of being there—together, alive, surrounded by history—felt like the most profound kind of magic.

And the conversations? Oh, they were everything. Over plates of carbonara and glasses of wine, we shared our dreams, fears, and stories. These women had become more than just friends; they were mirrors reflecting back the best parts of myself, reminding me of my giddy heart, and my capacity for joy.

As we roamed the streets of Rome, I couldn't help but feel a profound sense of gratitude. For the retreat, for these women, for the serendipity that had brought us all together. Tuscany had given me tools to heal, but Rome was giving me the space to breathe and embrace the life I still had to live.

The goodbyes at the retreat had been hard, but knowing I wasn't quite finished with Allie and Jenny made it easier. We had a few more days to soak in the magic of Italy, and a few more memories to make before our paths diverged again. And as we walked those timeless streets, I realized something: this wasn't just the end of the retreat. It was the beginning of a new chapter. One filled with possibility, connection, and the kind of beauty you carry with you forever.

Rome had already wrapped itself around my heart with its timeless beauty and endless charm, and the days spent exploring its streets with my little sisterhood were unforgettable. We wandered hand in hand through cobblestone alleys, stopping for gelato at every opportunity because, let's face it, there's always room for one more scoop. Each corner held something new—a hidden fountain, a breathtaking view, or a cozy cafe that begged us to sit and savor the moment. Every laugh, every shared plate of pasta, and every "oh my God, look at that!" felt like another stitch in the tapestry of memories we were weaving together.

And just when I thought this trip couldn't get more surreal, fate threw me another curveball. My younger cousin, Claire—the one I hadn't seen in a *decade*—was going to be in Rome *at the same time*! Of all the cities in the world, of all the timing, what were the odds? The moment we realized this cosmic alignment, we made plans to meet up, giddy with disbelief. We reunited at the Trevi Fountain, the perfect backdrop for a dramatic hello. The fountain sparkled in the sunlight as we embraced, marveling at the randomness of life that had brought us together here, of all places. Claire was traveling with a big group and had to dash off quickly, but that brief reunion felt like a scene from a movie—pure serendipity.

The next day was my solo adventure, a long-awaited boat excursion to the Amalfi Coast. I'd been dreaming about this day for months, envisioning myself gliding across turquoise waters, hopping off to explore the famous coastal gems of Positano, Salerno, and Amalfi. But as prepared as I thought I was, there was one thing I hadn't accounted for: the heat.

July in southern Italy is no joke. When I stepped off the boat in Amalfi, it felt like I'd walked straight into an oven. The air was heavy with humidity, so thick it clung to my skin like a blanket. Sweat poured from *every inch* of me. My clothes stuck like a second skin, and my hair gave up any pretense of cooperation. Even the locals looked like they were wilting in the sun. It was, without question, the hottest, stickiest, sweatiest day of my life.

And yet, the Amalfi Coast was so achingly beautiful that it didn't even matter. The pastel-colored buildings perched on cliff sides, the sparkling sea stretching endlessly, the vibrant bougainvillea cascading down balconies—it was a feast for the senses. Sure, navigating the throngs of tourists felt like sliding through a human Slip 'N Slide, but there was something oddly unifying about everyone being equally drenched in sweat. We were all in this humid chaos together, and somehow, it only added to the adventure.

For the first time on my trip, I was flying solo, and I embraced it. There's a certain magic in wandering a new place alone, letting your instincts guide you. My outgoing nature ensured I never felt lonely—strangers quickly became friends as we swapped stories about our travels. But there was also a quiet joy in simply being by myself, soaking in the experience without a schedule or plan.

Amalfi was everything I'd hoped for and more. I wandered through its winding streets, ducking into charming little shops to pick up treasures for myself and gifts for my friends. Each item felt like a tiny piece of Amalfi I could take home, a reminder of this perfect day. And, of course, I couldn't leave without indulging in the region's famous limoncello. Tasting that sweet, tangy nectar felt like sipping liquid sunshine. It was a little bottle of Amalfi's essence, and I couldn't resist buying some to share back home.

As the day unfolded, I fell deeper in love with Italy. The Amalfi Coast wasn't just a destination—it was a sensory overload in the best way possible. The salt air on my skin, the dazzling colors of the cliffs and sea, the laughter of strangers-turned-friends—it all felt like a living postcard, a memory being etched into my soul with every step.

But what's an epic trip without a little chaos to keep things interesting, right? Of course, the Amalfi Coast wasn't about to let me leave without one final test of my resolve. After a day filled with beauty, sweat, and the sheer magic of exploring on my own, the universe decided to throw a curveball my way. As I made my way to the final stop of the day, something—whether it was the language barrier, a misread direction, or just plain bad luck—left me hopelessly confused about where I was supposed to meet my boat. You know, the one that was supposed to take me back to Rome.

Cue the panic.

There I was, drenched in sweat (because Amalfi had made sure no pore went unsweat that day), frantically trying to piece together the mystery of where I was meant to be. The clock was ticking, my heart was racing, and for a split second, I thought, *This is it. I'm going to live here forever. Maybe open a limoncello stand. Or marry an Italian Chef.* Honestly, not the worst fate, but definitely not the plan.

Thankfully, my outgoing nature came to the rescue. Instead of spiraling into despair, I went into problem-solving mode. If there's one thing I've learned, it's that people—especially Italians—are generally more than willing to help if you just ask. And ask, I did. I flagged down anyone and everyone who looked like they might have even the faintest clue about my boat's whereabouts. Tourists, locals, shopkeepers, a guy selling gelato—I wasn't picky.

Each interaction was a chaotic blend of broken Italian, wild hand gestures, and hopeful smiles. "Scusi! Il The tour... um, the boat! Help?" Some shrugged, most not comprehending. Eventually, after what felt like an eternity of awkward exchanges, I quickly remembered I saved the tour guide's number. The real panic began when she didn't answer after a couple of times. She finally answered and gave me the directions. I hurried and sprinted the final stretch through the sea of people, leaping onto the boat with the grace of a giraffe in heels.

I made it. Barely.

As I collapsed onto a seat, gasping for air, I couldn't help but laugh. Of course, this had happened. Of course, my idyllic day in Amalfi ended with me nearly stranded. It was chaotic, ridiculous, and oh-so-Italy. But that's the beauty of travel, isn't it? The moments that go sideways are often the ones that stick with you the most—the ones that make the best stories.

As the boat pulled away from the coast, the golden light of sunset spilling over the cliffs, I let out a sigh of relief. I was headed back to Rome, exhausted but triumphant, my bags stuffed with limoncello and souvenirs, my heart overflowing with gratitude. The chaos had tested me, but it hadn't beaten me. As I leaned back and watched the Amalfi Coast fade into the horizon, I realized that this day—this wild, messy, beautiful day—was exactly what I'd come to Italy for. To feel alive. To be challenged. To remind myself that even in the chaos, there's beauty waiting to be found.

When I returned to Rome that evening, I was a delightful mix of exhaustion and euphoria. My bags were heavier with little trinkets, my skin a couple of shades darker from the sun, and my heart impossibly fuller. Walking back to my hotel, I let the city's warm evening glow wash over me.

I had come to Italy searching for something—healing, connection, adventure—and found it in abundance. But it was more than that. Italy wasn't just a place anymore; it was a feeling, a romance, a love affair with life itself.

And that night, as I lay in bed, replaying the day's events in my mind, I couldn't stop smiling. Italy had a way of surprising me at every turn, and I never wanted it to stop. The Amalfi Coast had been a chapter in this unfolding story, but the best part? I knew there was still so much more to come.

But, as with all things, even the most magical journey must come to an end. My final day in Italy arrived, bittersweet and brimming with possibilities. In a perfect twist of fate, Claire was free from her group, and I had no plans, so we decided to spend the entire day together. It was a gift—the universe's way of giving us one last moment to reconnect, just the two of us. We met up in the heart of Rome, and from there, the city became our playground. Every fountain, every monument, every alleyway seemed to hold a story, a history we could reach out and touch. The laughter and excitement bubbled up between us as we wandered, taking in the magic of this city that was somehow big enough to hold all of our dreams yet small enough to feel like home.

It had been a decade since we'd last seen each other, a decade since she was a kid, and I was still figuring out who I was. And now, here we were, two adults meeting as equals, both with stories that had shaped us in ways we couldn't have imagined back then. Over plates of pasta and sips of Aperol spritz, we talked. We really *talked*. I shared things with her that I hadn't told many people—like my battle with cancer. She hadn't known. Seeing her face, her shock, and her empathy, brought a flood of emotions I hadn't anticipated. It was one of those rare, golden moments when time seems to melt away, and all that's left is two people, two hearts, open and honest. It was healing. It was family in its purest form, and it was another memory from Italy that I would carry with me forever.

As our day came to an end, we hugged tightly, reluctant to let go, knowing we'd be going back to our separate lives. But I knew this was just the beginning of a rekindled bond, something strong enough to withstand time and distance.

With the last few hours of my trip, I still had one more mission: a tattoo. I'd promised myself that I would leave Italy with a symbol of this journey, something etched into my skin that would remind me of everything I'd fought for, everything I'd gained, and everything I'd discovered here. I went from one shop to the next, my heart pounding with excitement and a bit of nervous energy, and finally, at the third shop, they could take me. The thrill was indescribable.

The design was simple but deeply meaningful: a delicate bow intersected with an angel wing. To me, it was a symbol of resilience, a reminder that I was a warrior guided by unseen forces, angels. It was a tribute to my survival, to the belief that my grandmother, my beloved Cookie Grandma Rita, had been my angel, watching over me, guiding me through my darkest days, and ultimately helping me beat cancer. This tattoo was more than ink on the skin—it was my story, my strength, my gratitude.

After an hour and a half, I emerged from the shop with a spring in my step and a smile that felt like it would never fade. I couldn't stop looking at it—my new tattoo, my Italian keepsake, my warrior's emblem. With every glance, it reminded me of the incredible journey I'd just lived. I had come to Italy hoping for adventure, for a change of scenery, for something I couldn't quite put into words. But I was leaving with so much more: a tattoo that would forever be my reminder of triumph, the reclamation of my cancer anniversary, the tools to elevate my acting craft, and, most importantly, a new depth of personal growth.

And, of course, the friendships—those beautiful, serendipitous connections I'd made here, friendships that felt like they'd been written into my story long before I arrived. These memories, these moments, would be woven into the fabric of who I was, keeping Italy alive within me long after I left.

As I strolled through the city one last time, soaking in the sounds of bustling piazzas, the aroma of espresso, and the laughter of strangers— something shifted inside me. I had never felt so in love with a place. Italy was no longer just a destination on the map; it was a feeling that had seeped into my bones, a romance with a life that felt fuller, richer, and brighter. For the first time, I didn't want to go home. My life in Los Angeles, my family, my friends, my sweet Mocha—they were waiting for me, but a part of me was already plotting ways to stay.

Jenny's voice echoed in my head, teasing me to "think of Mocha," and my heart pulled in two directions. *Someone ship her to me!* I thought to myself, half-joking, half-serious because a life here didn't seem out of reach. Italy had wrapped me in its warmth, its beauty, its infinite charm, and I felt as if I'd finally found a place that spoke the same language as my heart.

As I boarded my flight, I realized that Italy would never leave me. It would be in every corner of my mind, every beat of my heart, every daring decision I made from that moment on. This trip had been more than a vacation—it was a journey home to a piece of myself I hadn't known I was missing. And while I might be going back to my life in Los Angeles, Italy would stay with me, lingering in my soul like the scent of lavender and lemon, like a song I'd always hum, a place that would always be waiting, ready to welcome me back.

This thing inside me—this beast, this relentless possession—was unlike anything I'd ever faced. It was wild, unpredictable, and completely untamed, a storm that raged inside me with no end in sight. And yet, in the midst of all that chaos, Italy emerged as the antidote I didn't know I needed. It wasn't just that I fell in love with the country itself—the sweeping landscapes, the cobblestone streets, the history etched into every corner. The gelato! I fell in love with *who I was* in Italy. A braver, freer, more alive version of myself. Every single moment, even the messy, chaotic, sweaty ones, felt like a revelation.

It's impossible to put into words how much my spirit vibrated during this trip. Italy exceeded every dream, every expectation, every fleeting thought I'd had about what this journey might be. Yes, there were disasters. The terror of transportation mishaps, the near-misses, the wrong turns that had me questioning whether I'd ever make it back. But each of those challenges became part of the adventure. Each misstep only made me fall harder for this wild, unpredictable place. Italy didn't just test me—it truly remodeled me.

Of course, life has a way of keeping things complicated. Even as I soaked up the magic of Italy, there was a tether pulling at me from afar. Billy. Somehow, even across continents, he found ways to insert himself into my days. We talked a handful of times—conversations filled with his tears, his insecurities, his endless pleas for reconciliation. He'd cry, antagonize me, beg, and spin himself into a frenzy. His desperation to pull me back felt suffocating at times, a sharp contrast to the freedom I was basking in. But I didn't let it touch me, nothing past the call itself. Italy was too sacred. This was my time, and I wouldn't let anything, not even his spiraling, take it away from me.

The beast inside me was relentless. It gnawed at me and kept me restless. Sleep was a luxury I rarely managed—three to five hours at best. The combination of the creature clawing inside me, the electric thrill of being in Italy, and the insane humidity was enough to keep me wired. It was July, and Italy was hotter than I could have imagined. The humidity clung to me like a second skin, leaving me dripping and desperate for relief. But I learned to adapt. Linen dresses became my uniform, the only thing that felt breathable against my skin. Cold showers were my nightly ritual, a small act of defiance against the heat, a way to cool my body and prepare for the next day's adventures.

Despite the discomforts, the twists, and the turns, I wouldn't have changed a single moment. Italy, with all its imperfections and unpredictability, was perfect. It wasn't just a trip—it was a revelation. It was a whirlwind romance with a place and a version of myself I was just beginning to know. Every struggle, every triumph, every laugh felt like a piece of the puzzle clicking into place. Italy didn't cure the beast inside me, but it reminded me that I was stronger than it. That even in the storm, there could be beauty.

On my last night, I lay in bed, replaying it all in my mind—the sights, the sounds, the moments that took my breath away. I thought about the espresso-fueled mornings, the laughter shared over plates of pasta, and the triumph of finding my way when it felt like the world was conspiring against me. It had tested me, broken me open, and filled me with something I hadn't felt in a long time—hope.

I knew the beast and the trauma I'd left at home would be waiting for me. But I also knew I was returning as someone stronger, someone who had seen herself in a new light. Italy had shown me that even in the hardest moments, there's room for joy. That even when you're fighting to keep your head above water, there's a place for love—love for the world, for others, and for yourself.

And as the first light of dawn began to creep into my room, I whispered a quiet thank you to the country that had given me so much. Italy had wrapped me in its magic, taught me its lessons, and left me forever changed. I wasn't just leaving Italy—I was taking it with me, a part of my soul now, a part of who I would be moving forward.

Chapter 23

Excuse My French

Coming home was like stepping out of a dream and straight into a storm I'd been avoiding. Italy had been an intoxicating escape, a picturesque pause button on life's chaos, but as soon as I walked through the door, reality smacked me in the face like a cold gust of wind. The weight of everything I'd been running from came crashing back down. My little apartment wasn't just a space anymore—it was a battlefield, and I wasn't ready to fight.

Billy showed up, there was something off about him. He hovered near the door, avoiding eye contact like he'd just stumbled upon a secret he wasn't sure how to spill. His face wore the kind of expression that screamed, "You're not gonna like this," but he didn't say a word. No warning, no heads-up— just this strange, almost guilty energy radiating from him that immediately put me on edge.

Still, there was one thing I couldn't wait for: my baby girl, Mocha Bear. Let me tell you, if unconditional love had a mascot, it would be my dog. This was the longest we'd ever been apart, and her reaction was nothing short of Oscar-worthy. She greeted me with a wiggle-butt frenzy that could power a small city, smothering me in wet kisses and high-pitched squeals, the kind I only get from traveling (rarely). The world could've been burning down around us, and I wouldn't have noticed. That kind of love? It makes your soul feel alive.

But as Mocha settled into her post-reunion nap, I finally looked around—and something was off. You know that eerie sensation when something familiar feels *wrong*? That's what hit me. My safe haven, my carefully curated oasis of calm, had been rearranged like a dollhouse. Before I could fully process it, my mom, with her ever-cheerful tone, said something that stopped me cold.

"Let me give you a tour of your apartment," she announced, beaming as if she were unveiling a luxury penthouse.

A *tour*? Of *my* apartment? I blinked at her, stunned. But she wasn't joking. Like a realtor selling a listing, she began guiding me through the space, pointing out where she'd rearranged my belongings, moved storage around, and even reorganized my bathroom. It was like waking up in someone else's home but wearing your own pajamas. I half-expected her to hand me a brochure—I felt lost in my own space.

Mom's voice faded into the background as I froze, feeling the pressure build. For weeks, I'd been navigating this constant irritability, a simmering undercurrent of anxiety just waiting for a reason to erupt. And now? It was ready to blow.

On the outside, I kept it together, nodding and murmuring "hmm" at appropriate intervals. Inside, I was a volcano. A dormant Mount Vesuvius waking up with a vengeance. The audacity, the *gall*, to touch my things—my sanctuary—without asking. I felt the pressure building, a boiling kettle ready to scream, and I knew I had to get out before I exploded. So, the moment her "tour" ended, I bolted.

Billy, my impromptu getaway car disguised as a human. He waited for me outside, and we walked to grab some food. I thought the fresh air would help. I thought wrong. The second we left the building, it hit me: a full-blown panic attack. My chest tightened, my hands shook, and tears—hot, unrelenting tears—streamed down my face. It felt like the weight of the entire world was pressing on my chest, squeezing out every ounce of composure I had left.

When it finally subsided, I knew what I had to do. This wasn't just about my apartment or my closet; this was years—decades—of boundaries being bulldozed and feelings being ignored. And now? Now I was done staying silent.

And boy, was my gut right. Turns out, he knew. HE KNEW! He knew exactly what my mom had done to my apartment while I was gone, and instead of giving me so much as a gentle nudge to prepare myself, he just let me walk straight into the ambush. I mean, really? Was this some kind of conspiracy? A tag-team effort to blindside me? It wasn't cute, let me tell you that much. It wasn't funny or charming—it was *fishy*, and it irritated the hell out of me.

"Seriously, Billy?" I snapped once the truth came out. "You could've warned me! You *knew* I was going to lose it."

He shrugged, all nonchalant, which somehow made it worse. "I figured it'd be better coming from her."

Oh, *fantastic*. Just let the grenade explode in my lap, why don't you? To say I was annoyed would be an understatement. I told him, straight up, that I was going to lay down the law with my mom. This wasn't just a casual chat; this was me setting my first real boundary with her—a line in the sand I'd never dared to draw before. And Billy, of all people, should've known how delicate this was. He'd seen it firsthand—how fragile I'd been, how the smallest thing could set off my PTSD symptoms like fireworks on the Fourth of July. And yet, he stayed quiet.

After lunch, I thanked Billy for the distraction but told him I needed to handle this alone. Back in the apartment, the tension between my mom and me was palpable, like static electricity waiting for a spark. She must have sensed it, too, because her smile faltered when I walked in.

"Mom," I started, my voice trembling but steady. "We need to talk."

And then, the dam broke. Everything I'd been holding in for years came pouring out—the anger, the frustration, the hurt. I told her how her actions, both past and present, had made me feel invisible. I explained how I'd set boundaries—not to punish her, but to protect myself—and how she'd crossed them.

"Mom, I'm not mad about the apartment," I said, my voice cracking. "I'm mad because it feels like you don't respect me. Like my feelings don't matter."

She tried to respond, but her words were laced with defensiveness. "I was just trying to help," she said, over and over again, as if that excused everything. I took a deep breath, steadying myself.

"Can you just listen? Please? I don't need you to fix it or justify it. I just need you to hear me and validate how I feel."

I told her how, despite everything, I didn't regret the past because it shaped me into who I am—a person I'm proud of. But I also made it clear that pride doesn't erase pain. I approached her from every angle I could think of, trying to make her understand. But after what felt like hours, I realized she just wasn't capable of meeting me where I needed her to be. And that was its own heartbreak.

Still, I was proud of myself. For the first time, I stood my ground. I spoke my truth—gently angry, but honestly and vulnerably. That alone felt like a victory.

Finally, drained and needing to end this on a lighter note, I grabbed the bottle of limoncello I'd brought back from Italy. "Let's toast," I said with a small smile. She raised her glass hesitantly, and we clinked them together. It wasn't the resolution I'd dreamed of, but it was something. A tiny olive branch in a forest of unresolved emotions.

As I sipped the sweet, lemony liqueur, I realized something important: healing isn't neat. It's not a Hallmark movie with a perfect resolution. It's messy and painful and sometimes incomplete. But it's worth fighting for. Even if it takes a lifetime.

Walking into my apartment that day was like stepping into someone else's home. My once-familiar space, the place that was supposed to be my sanctuary, now felt like an alien landscape. It wasn't just rearranged; it was a bit *unrecognizable*. It made my skin crawl. My mom had gone full Marie Kondo on my life without even asking if I wanted it—and spoiler alert, I didn't. For the next few days, I was like a lost tourist in my own apartment, constantly asking her where things were.

"Mom, where are my shoes? Where's my blow dryer? Where's the basket that used to be here?"

Her answers, cheerful and oblivious, only made me angrier. "Oh, I thought it looked better there!" or "I moved it; it fits best like this" I could feel my anxiety escalating with every passing moment. It was like the walls were closing in on me, the air getting thinner. I couldn't breathe. I was suffocating in what was supposed to be my safe place.

Finally, mercifully, she left. And the second I dropped her off at the airport, it was like the apartment itself exhaled, releasing all the tension it had been holding onto alongside me. I wasted no time. With a vengeance, I set to work undoing everything she'd done. I moved my clothes back to where they belonged, reorganized every drawer, and reclaimed every inch of my space like it was a battle I was born to fight.

But I didn't stop there. No, I went further. I decided to switch things up even more—not to erase the chaos she'd caused, but to reclaim the space as my own, on *my* terms. Don't get me wrong—some ideas were great enough to keep, but still. I was reinventing my sanctuary to match this new version of me—the one who'd just survived Italy, panic attacks, and a mother-induced emotional rollercoaster.

And you know what? It felt good. It felt empowering. For the first time in weeks, I felt like I was standing my ground, like I was taking back control of my life, one bookshelf and throw pillow at a time.

As I stepped back to admire my work, a sly smile crept across my face. This wasn't just a home anymore; this was a declaration. A *wink* to the universe that said, "I'm here. I'm adapting. I'm fighting back."

And slowly, step by step, I began to sink into the realization that this was my battlefield. My fight. My space to heal and rebuild. No one was going to rearrange my life without my permission ever again.

The next battle hit me like a bad plot twist: an allergic reaction that decided to crash my farewell tour as I left Italy. I woke up with lips so puffy they could've starred in their own Botox commercial, "When Lips Attack." Swollen, alien, and *wrong*. It wasn't just vanity—I knew something was seriously off. This wasn't the glamorous jet-set vibe I wanted to bring home. So, as soon as I landed, I made a beeline for the doctor, expecting a quick diagnosis, maybe a prescription, and voilà, life would return to normal. Spoiler: That's not what happened.

The visit started predictably enough. I checked in, got called back for the usual weigh-in and blood pressure check, and waited for the inevitable doctorly wisdom. But when the nurse wrapped that blood pressure cuff around my arm, her face morphed into something straight out of a medical drama. Worry, confusion, maybe even panic—it was all there, written across her expression in bold type.

"Is everything okay?" I asked, my own anxiety already revving its engines.

She didn't answer. Instead, she slapped a wristband on me that read "FRAGILE." Fragile? Like a porcelain teacup? I laughed nervously, hoping for clarification, but nope—she already sent me out the door. Now I wasn't just worried about my lips; I was spiraling into a full-blown existential crisis.

By the time the doctor strolled in, I'd convinced myself I was moments away from starring in a "Medical Mysteries" episode. I wasted no time bringing up my lips. "So, about this allergic reaction…" I started, pointing dramatically at my pout.

The doctor glanced at me, gave a cursory nod, and said, "You're dehydrated," as if that explained everything. Then, without so much as a transition, they whisked me off to an EKG to check my heart. Wait, what? I was here for swollen lips, not a deep dive into my cardiovascular system! It felt like the plot had veered off-course, and I was just along for the ride.

As the EKG machine beeped and whirred, the questions started. Not about my lips, but about *me.* "How's your mental health? Are you under stress? Any recent changes in your physical health?"

Oh, you mean aside from feeling like I'm living inside a blender set to "chaos mode"? I opened up, pouring out a story that felt equal parts surreal and horrifying. I told them about the relentless panic attacks—these Tasmanian devil-like storms of fear that hijacked my body. About how I'd dropped weight and eating had become a battle I rarely won. Can't gain weight nor keep it on. About how it felt like some raging beast had taken over my body, leaving me trapped, terrified, and helpless.

The doctor's face said it all: this wasn't normal. It wasn't just dehydration or stress—it was a full-scale meltdown of my mind and body. He leaned in, his tone serious. "I think you need to see a psychiatrist. The sooner, the better."

Walking out of that appointment felt like stepping into another dimension. I'd gone in for a swollen lip and left with the weight of a mental health intervention pressing down on me. It was like my life had been flipped upside-down, and I was being forced to look at pieces of myself I didn't want to see. But I scheduled the psychiatrist appointment because, honestly, I didn't know what else to do.

When the day arrived, I sat in the waiting room feeling like a character in someone else's story. The psychiatrist was kind but direct, wasting no time making their case. "You need medication," they said. "An anti-anxiety or antidepressant could make a world of difference."

I wanted to believe them. I really did. But as they spoke, my gut kept tugging at me, whispering, *This isn't your answer.* I'd heard stories—some hopeful, others cautionary—about medication. I didn't want to depend on pills to function, to make it through the day. My intuition, faint but insistent, told me this was a storm I had to weather on my own terms.

"Thank you," I said finally, "but I think this is temporary. I need to find another way."

They looked at me with concern, but I held my ground. I wasn't dismissing their advice; I was simply listening to the part of me that believed I could fight this beast without a prescription. Deep down, beneath the panic, beneath the exhaustion, was a flicker of strength. It wasn't loud or confident, but it was there.

Walking out of that office, I felt a mix of emotions—fear, determination, and something bordering on hope. The doctor's urgency had rattled me and made me realize just how far I'd fallen into this chaotic spiral. My body was screaming for help, and I could no longer ignore it.

But this wasn't going to be my forever. No matter how long it took, no matter how hard it was, I would fight. I would dig deep, confront the beast head-on, and claw my way back to the person I wanted to be. Because if there's one thing I've learned about myself, it's that I may be fragile, but I am not breakable.

Shortly after I returned home, Halle, my acting-class partner-in-crime, came to visit. She wasn't just a friend; she had become my lifeline in a chaotic sea of self-discovery. Halle was that rare kind of person you meet and instantly connect with, like some cosmic force had arranged for our paths to cross. She was energetic, witty, and carried this effortless Boston charm that made her feel like family—my little sister from another life. When she showed up at my doorstep, suitcase in hand and her usual bright smile plastered on her face, I felt equal parts thrilled and *mortified.*

When she arrived, dragging her suitcase into my chaotic little studio, I was hit with an odd mix of emotions—embarrassment and panic battling for dominance. My life was an absolute wreck—emotionally, mentally, and yes, physically. I was panicked, embarrassed, and wholly unprepared to let someone witness me like this. But Halle had a way of making herself at home, flopping onto my bed as if to say, "We're doing this, sister, whether you're ready or not."

Meanwhile, on the fringes of my life, Billy was circling like a vulture. He had a brilliant idea: we'd "step into the arena" to hash out our relationship issues—a gladiatorial showdown of feelings. According to him, this was the "last chance" to save us, and he insisted we face it head-on. His urgency only amplified my dread. My body wasn't ready to talk, to fight, or to feel. It had already turned against me, hijacked by PTSD that left me incapable of engaging, let alone mending a broken relationship.

Still, I caved. I let Halle take over my studio while Mocha and I moved in with Billy for what promised to be a final emotional reckoning. It was a recipe for disaster, but I convinced myself that showing up was half the battle. Turns out, showing up wasn't even close enough.

Billy's strategy was a mix of love-bombing and relentless pressure, and while it might have worked on another day, in another lifetime, it hit me like a freight train in my fragile state. Instead of opening up, my body shut down. Every fiber of my being screamed, *Get out. Protect yourself.* I couldn't think clearly. I couldn't breathe. All I knew was that his energy was too much, too heavy, too suffocating for me to bear.

And then it happened—the moment that would sear itself into my memory like a scar. We were alone, standing in his bedroom. He stood in front of me, his hands trailing down my stomach, attempting to spark intimacy. In another version of us, this might have worked. But this wasn't that version.

What happened next was nothing short of primal. His touch triggered something deep and feral in me, a full-body panic so consuming it felt like I'd been transported to another plane of existence. My chest tightened, my skin turned clammy, and my pulse raced like a drumline on overdrive. My body turned to frost, every muscle locked in place. It was the kind of terror people describe when they're staring down danger—fight or flight, except my body chose *neither*. I was a statue of fear.

As his hands lingered, the sensation amplified. A suffocating wave of dread washed over me, and in that moment, I wasn't standing in Billy's bedroom anymore. I was trapped somewhere dark and inescapable, convinced I was about to be attacked. My rational mind knew I was safe, but my body? My body had other plans.

Finally, the paralysis broke. I shoved him away, tears spilling down my face as I collapsed into a fit of uncontrollable sobbing. It wasn't just fear—it was survival, raw and visceral. It felt like my body was exorcising years of buried trauma in one horrific, humiliating instant. Billy stood there, confused and likely hurt, but I couldn't explain it to him. I couldn't even explain it to myself. All I knew was that this moment wasn't just the end of our relationship—it was the beginning of something much bigger.

In that moment, clarity arrived like a bolt of lightning. I couldn't keep doing this. Billy and I were over—*had been over*—if I was being honest with myself. I'd known for months that he wasn't my person. The signs were there, clear as day, but I'd ignored them, hoping things might magically fix themselves. But magic doesn't work that way. Love doesn't work that way. And this—whatever this was—definitely didn't work that way.

After that night, I made the call. Billy had to go, for good this time. But as much as I wanted to be angry with him, I couldn't. Not entirely. Because, in his own twisted way, Billy had been a catalyst. His relentless presence, his toxic pressure, had forced me to confront the trauma I'd been burying for years. He was the trigger that blew the lid off my tightly sealed emotional trauma box, and while the aftermath was excruciating, it was also necessary.

So, Billy, this is my goodbye. If I could tell him one last thing: Thank you for the lessons I didn't want but desperately needed. Thank you for showing me my own limits, for pushing me to the breaking point so I could finally start to heal. You were a mirror, reflecting all the parts of myself I'd been too afraid to face. And now, because of you, I have no choice but to look. I wouldn't be in this horrific, agonizing, but desperately necessary stage of healing if it wasn't for you.

You were a lesson I needed to learn. And for that, I let you go. But as I do, I also let in gratitude—for the pain, for the clarity, and for the hope that this, too, will lead me to the other side. Thank you for being the trigger that pushed me onto this healing path. It's ugly and painful, but it's mine—and I wouldn't trade it for anything.

The first year of the Meisner program was like stepping into a storm you don't realize you've been craving until it's swirling all around you. It wasn't just an acting class; it was a baptism, a stripping away of everything false to uncover what lay beneath. The focus was on repetition, improvisation, and emotional preparation—all deceptively simple terms for something that turned my life inside out. These weren't just techniques for acting; they were tools for being, for *feeling* in ways I'd forgotten were possible.

At first, it started slow, like dipping a toe into cold water. Repetition exercises forced us to be present, to listen deeply, and to respond authentically without overthinking. It was maddening, yet hypnotic, a dance between instinct and intention. But then came improv, and suddenly, the water wasn't just cold—it was a tidal wave. Twice a week, we performed unscripted scenes born from our own imagination, vulnerability, and truth.

There was no hiding, no safety net. You either leapt or stayed on the shore, watching everyone else soar.

And leap I did.

With each improv, I felt something inside me stir, awaken, crack open. My imagination, dormant for so long, came roaring back to life, spilling out like confetti from a burst balloon. Vulnerability, that terrifying thing Anne spoke of on day one, stopped feeling like a risk and started feeling like a superpower. It wasn't just my acting that grew—it was *me*. Week by week, I could feel the layers peeling away, those metaphorical onion skins Anne had promised would shed. She wasn't lying. I was shedding, and what lay underneath was real and unfiltered.

But the stakes were high. Every scene had to be rooted in either the best day or the worst day of our lives—holding the weight of the world on our shoulders, and let me tell you, the emotional rollercoaster of that twice-a-week routine was no joke. One moment, I was reliving a joy so pure it made my heart swell; the next, I was drowning in despair so deep it stole my breath. Twice a week, I cried—no, *purged*—tears. It wasn't a gentle cry; it was guttural, soul-cleansing, the kind of release that leaves you hollow and whole all at once.

There were days I walked out of class utterly drained, my energy spent, and my emotions wrung dry. And yet, as the year progressed, I noticed something miraculous: recovery became easier. Thanks to emotional preparation, I learned how to step in and out of intense emotions with precision and grace. I could summon grief, rage, joy, or love on command, and then let it go just as quickly. It was like learning to dance with my emotions instead of being dragged around by them.

Anger, in particular, became my focus. For most of my life, anger had been this foreign, unwieldy thing I didn't know how to hold. I'd always been too soft, too quick to smooth things over rather than stand my ground. But something shifted in February, and suddenly, anger was no longer a stranger—it was that guest crashing through my door. At first, it terrified me. My body didn't know how to process it; every flicker of rage felt like an explosion. But I was determined to understand it, to tame it, and to turn it into something constructive.

So, I wrote myself into circumstances that demanded anger. I gave myself scenarios where I had to shout, fight, and claw my way through emotional barriers I didn't even know were there. And slowly, anger became less of a beast and more of an ally. It was no longer something to fear—it was something to *use*. If I was going to be an actor, I needed to know how to wield every emotion in my arsenal, and anger became my greatest teacher.

This first year wasn't just about acting—it was about transformation. Every note from Anne, every moment of applause, every piercing critique carved me into someone I barely recognized but deeply admired. Acting became my sanctuary, my mirror, my therapy. It wasn't just a craft; it was a way of rediscovering myself, of peeling back the layers to reveal truths I'd buried long ago.

In class, we were the writers of our own stories, crafting improv scenarios that pulled from the deepest wells of our lives. And for me, Grey Knight became a recurring character. I used him as a muse, channeling the heartbreak, the longing, the love, and the devastation he had left in his wake. Each scene gave me a safe space to process what he'd done to me, to take control of the emotions he'd once wielded like weapons. It wasn't about revenge; it was about reclaiming my power.

Grey Knight became my alchemy. His ghost haunted my performances, lending them a depth and rawness I didn't know I possessed. Through him, I found a way to turn pain into art, to transform my heartbreak into something beautiful. It was messy, it was therapeutic, and it was magic.

As the year came to an end, I looked back at the journey and felt nothing but gratitude. Meisner hadn't just taught me to act—it had taught me to *feel*. To live. To embrace vulnerability, not as a weakness, but as the most profound strength I had. It gave me permission to be messy, to cry, to rage, to love, and to be human in the fullest, most honest way possible.

Year one was a storm, but it was the kind of storm that clears the sky and leaves the air feeling fresh and alive. It stripped me bare, only to rebuild me stronger, freer, and more open. As I stepped into year two, I knew one thing for certain: I wasn't the same person who had walked through those doors on the first day. I was something new—something whole.

When I think of Anne, my Meisner teacher, I see more than a mentor. She's a force, a character, a whirlwind of inspiration, and—oddly enough—a reincarnation of my Cookie Grandma Rita. It's not a passing resemblance; it's the *essence* of her. From the very first day of class, Anne radiated the same warmth, sharp wit, and quiet resilience that made Grandma Rita unforgettable. The way she carried herself, the twinkle in her eye when she cracked a joke, the no-nonsense attitude—it all felt like a cosmic wink from the universe.

As the weeks passed, Anne kept proving me right. Every class is the highlight of my week, and as I grow to spend time with her, I'm more sure that I'd stumbled into the best impulsive decision of my life. This program wasn't just a challenge—it was a lifeline, a place where I could shed my layers and rebuild, and Anne was the guide I didn't know I needed. Strict rules and all, I embraced it. "The industry's cutthroat," she'd remind us, her tone leaving no room for debate. Tardiness was a capital offense, and she was serious about it—get kicked out once, and good luck coming back. But punctuality wasn't a problem for me. I'm a 15-minute-early type of person, and my neurotic earliness gave me precious one-on-one moments with her before class. Those quiet minutes became my secret treasure, moments where she poured her wisdom into me without the hum of the room.

Anne was vibrant and alive in a way most people can only dream of. She was a firecracker, bursting with stories that could send us from belly laughs to jaw-dropping awe in seconds. Her lectures were an adventure, starting with a point about acting, veering wildly into tales from her past, the state of the film industry, or a news story she'd read that morning, and somehow, she'd circle back like an expert tightrope walker finding her balance.

Her "French tongue" added to the charm. She'd curse unapologetically, then immediately follow it up with, "Excuse my French," a twinkle in her eye. "Never in a fucking million years—excuse my French," was practically her catchphrase. Her laugh—a little squeaky, undeniably infectious—was the soundtrack of our class. You couldn't help but laugh with her. It wasn't forced or rehearsed; it was joy, pure and simple.

But make no mistake, Anne wasn't all laughs and lightness. She had a tough-love streak that could knock the wind out of you. On her harder days, she'd snap at us, her passion spilling over in sharp bursts. "I've worked three jobs, had two scene partners, and I didn't miss a single rehearsal. I don't want excuses!" she'd bark, her voice tinged with a fiery determination. But even then, you could feel the love underneath it. She wanted us to succeed—not for her, but for ourselves. She believed in us, even when we didn't believe in ourselves, and that belief pushed us to rise to her level.

Anne wasn't just our teacher; she was a study in resilience. She worked relentlessly, juggling classes, private tutoring for Hollywood's elite, and her beloved "dog babies" waiting for her at home. She rarely took a day off, and while she kept her personal life guarded, you could feel the depth of her experiences in every word she spoke. She wasn't just teaching us how to act; she was teaching us how to live.

One of my most vulnerable moments with Anne came during an improv class, one of the first. I had written a scene about cancer—a deeply personal choice I hoped would help me heal while still honing my craft. When Anne called, "And cut," the tears I'd been holding back broke free, pouring out of me like a flood. After class, I shared my story with her—my battle with cancer, my recovery, and the ever-present shadow of surveillance scans. Anne listened intently, her face a mix of compassion and professionalism. Then, with a kindness that felt like a hug and a boundary all at once, she said, "Don't use cancer again. It's too fresh, too close to home."

She was right, of course. And in that moment, I saw the depth of her care—not just for my growth as an actor, but for my well-being as a person. It was this balance of empathy and structure that made Anne such a magnetic force.

Every class was an emotional rollercoaster. One moment, you'd be laughing at a comedic improv; the next, you'd be tearing up through a scene so raw it felt like you were peeling away pieces of your soul. Failure was part of the process—happy accidents—and they were just as valuable as the triumphs. "There's always room for improvement," she'd remind us, even when she applauded our progress.

Anne challenged me like no one else ever had. She pushed me to my limits, not just as an actor but as a person. And I thrived on it. Her constructive criticism was gold, each word a seed I planted and nurtured until it grew into something stronger, more refined. By the end of the year, I felt transformed, not just in my craft but in my understanding of myself.

At the end of the year, we sat down for a one-on-one meeting—a teacher-student conference that felt more intimate than any parent-teacher meeting I'd ever experienced. Anne's feedback was thoughtful, honest, and full of surprises. She saw things in me I hadn't even noticed, and hearing her reflections filled me with a deep sense of pride and gratitude.

Toward the end of the meeting, I couldn't hold back any longer. "You remind me so much of my Cookie Grandma Rita," I blurted out, laughing nervously. "I hope that's not weird."

Her eyes lit up, her face breaking into that signature smile. "No! That makes me feel special," she said, her voice full of warmth.

And in that moment, I felt the weight of how lucky I was to have Anne as my guide through this wild, transformative year. She wasn't just a teacher; she was a light, a mirror, and a force of nature. I love you, Anne. Here's to you, to your magic, and to the journey ahead.

The final verdict came in from my case with Aflac, and the news hit me like a sucker punch: they were terminating me. The silver lining? They'd allow me to keep my newly earned license. But that small concession did little to dull the sting. The decision left me feeling raw, as if all the work I'd done to outrun my ugly past had been dragged into the light, kicking and screaming. It was a stark, bitter reminder of what it feels like to have your mistakes shadow you, a faint taste of what life must be like for those carrying the weight of a criminal record.

What caught me off guard the most was that I hadn't anticipated this at all. I'd foolishly believed my record would be confined to Wisconsin, hidden neatly behind state lines. Turns out, I was wrong. My optimism had been misplaced, and reality had other plans. Still, I wasn't about to let this derail me. No way. If one door slammed in my face, I'd just kick down another. My shiny new life and health insurance license weren't going to waste.

A little backstory here: one of my best friends, Troy, and I had shared a dream of breaking into this industry. We'd both studied and passed our licensing exams at the same time, cheering each other on from our respective corners. When I found myself jobless and at a crossroads, Troy was the first person I turned to. I poured out my frustrations, venting about Aflac's decision, and without hesitation, he recommended I meet his new boss, Hannah.

Hannah was the powerhouse leading World Financial Group, a finance firm Troy had been raving about recently. He assured me she was sharp, driven, and exactly the kind of person who might take a chance on me despite my record. So, I swallowed my nerves, prepped my resume, and reached out.

The interview with Hannah felt electric. She was as impressive as Troy had promised—confident, inspiring, and full of energy that made you want to sit up straighter and get to work. She didn't hesitate. She hired me on the spot. Just like that, I was on the brink of what felt like a brand-new chapter. The position was remote, offered a solid income potential, and was worlds away from the grueling restaurant grind I'd been stuck in for far too long. It felt like a game-changer, a golden ticket to the kind of career I'd been dreaming about. My excitement was through the roof.

But there was a hitch. A big one.

I knew I couldn't dive into this new role without coming clean, so I sat down with Hannah and confessed the truth about my misdemeanors. My heart pounded as I spoke, my voice tinged with vulnerability. I fully expected the other shoe to drop, for her to take back the offer or politely show me the door. But Hannah surprised me. She listened, nodded, and then said something that made me want to cry: she believed in me. Not just in my potential, but in my ability to rise above my past and thrive.

Her faith in me lit a fire. It gave me the courage to tackle the next hurdle: working with the Department of Insurance to address the restrictions on my record. It wasn't going to be easy, but with Hannah in my corner, I felt like I could take on anything.

The job started with weekly meetings, part training and part inspiration, featuring motivational speakers who had already made their mark in the business. It was a slow build at first—no big payouts until you closed a client—but the energy in those meetings was infectious. I soaked up every word, every strategy, every story of success. These weren't just meetings; they were fuel.

I dove in headfirst, determined to make this opportunity count. This was more than just a career shift—it was a lifeline, a chance to rewrite my story on my terms. And for the first time in a long time, I felt like I wasn't just running from my past. I was building a future worth running toward.

Let me tell you about Troy—a man who walked into my life at the worst possible time and somehow managed to stick around long enough to become one of the most important people in it. It all started during the "high drama era" of my relationship with Grey Knight, a time when everything was combustible, including my sanity. Troy entered the picture unassumingly, at precisely the wrong (or maybe the right?) moment, and our story kicked off in the most absurd way possible: I stole his seat.

Yes, *stole it*. Not exactly the kind of meet-cute you'd write in a rom-com, but that's us—chaos from the start. At the time, I was in full-on fighting mode with Grey Knight, a walking storm cloud of anger and defiance. Troy, innocent bystander that he was, had no idea what he was getting into. Grey Knight's paranoia immediately painted Troy as a threat, but the truth? Troy wasn't a threat to anyone. He was a breath of fresh air in the middle of my emotional hurricane.

Over time, Troy and I built something special, even as my relationship with Grey Knight crumbled. He became the steady voice in the background, a witness to the toxicity I was drowning in. There were moments when life pulled us apart, gaps where we drifted, but somehow, we always found our way back. When I moved back to California, we rekindled effortlessly, as if no time had passed. Even when I lived in San Diego, we'd find ways to see each other. And when that wasn't possible, we leaned on our signature long phone calls—marathon sessions where we'd talk about everything and nothing until the early hours of the morning.

Those conversations were magic. They flowed so naturally we'd lose track of time, bouncing from topic to topic, laughing until our stomachs hurt, or diving into deep, soul-searching discussions. I like to think that Troy has been my ride-or-die, the one person I could be *fully* myself with—silly, serious, ridiculous—it didn't matter. He accepted me in every form, and for someone who spent years feeling like I had to guard myself, that was priceless.

Troy wasn't just a friend; he was *the friend*. The one you call when your world is falling apart—or when he needed a ride home from nasal surgery. Yep, that happened. He needed help, and I didn't think twice. I picked him up, got him food, made sure he was comfortable, and didn't let him lift a finger. When he got sick during the height of COVID, I double-masked and delivered tea to his doorstep, determined to make sure he was taken care of. But the thing is, he's done the same for me—time and time again. That's just who we are for each other.

What sets our friendship apart is the transparency, the brutal honesty that never comes from a place of malice, only love. We call each other out, we push each other, but it's always rooted in care. It's a kind of connection I didn't have much of in my life, and it's why I think of him as one of my closest friends. Over the years, when I struggled to feel authentic in other relationships, Troy was the one person I didn't have to filter myself for. With him, I could just *be*.

Another thing about Troy? The man is a hustler to the core. I know my work ethic is pretty strong, but his is on steroids—he won't quit. One of the hardest workers I've ever met. We're cut from the same cloth when it comes to work ethic, and that's part of what bonded us so deeply. Troy's work ethic is unmatched—he's wickedly smart, self-taught, and relentless in his pursuit of success. Take stocks, for example. Troy didn't just dabble in trading; he mastered it. He became so skilled that people started asking him to manage their portfolios, offering him commissions for his expertise. And that's just the tip of the iceberg. He's been working on creating an app, staying up until 7 a.m. every night, researching, coding, and perfecting his vision.

To me, Troy isn't just a friend—I think of him as a mentor, someone who inspires me to aim higher and think bigger. Knowing how much I thrive on intellectual conversations, it's no surprise I was never bored in his company. We'd talk about everything—business, life, the universe—and it was always engaging, always uplifting. Whether we were cracking up over something absurd or brainstorming about future plans, time with Troy was never wasted.

Now, we've reached an exciting new chapter: working together at a financial firm. After years of being there for each other, cheering each other on from the sidelines, we're finally teaming up. The thought of combining our shared determination, grit, and mutual respect is nothing short of exhilarating. We've both been through our fair share of hardships, but those experiences only made us more resilient.

Troy and I are the kind of hustlers who don't just survive—we thrive. And now, with this opportunity in front of us, I can't wait to see where our hard work takes us. One thing's for sure: We'll do it the only way we know how—together, with a mix of relentless ambition, contagious laughter, and conversations that never seem to end.

Another pivotal shift in my life was my relationship with Natasha. Moving out of our shared apartment felt like hitting the reset button, a chance to breathe and let the dust settle before figuring out if our friendship could be salvaged. I'd hoped a little space would bring clarity, that the tension that had built up between us might dissipate. So, cautiously optimistic, I reached out to reconnect. What I didn't expect was to get a different "version" of Natasha every time I saw her, like flipping through the pages of a book where the plot kept changing.

One day, she'd show up energetic and goofy, perfectly matching my vibe. It was like stepping into a time machine and being transported back to the early days of our friendship when things were easy, carefree, and uncomplicated. Those moments reminded me of why I'd loved her so much, why I'd fought so hard to keep us together. We'd laugh, we'd be silly, and for a brief moment, I'd think, *This is it. We're getting back to us.*

Then, there was the time after I got back from Italy. That Natasha was almost unrecognizable—calm, serene, the *most* zen I'd ever seen her. It was downright unsettling. She didn't complain about a single thing. Not one. I sat there, blinking in disbelief, wondering what alien had abducted my friend. She explained that she'd been gifted a Reiki session for her birthday, and apparently, it had changed her life. She spoke about energy healing with a sense of peace I envied. For the first time in a long time, she seemed light, untethered. And me? I was intrigued. My life felt heavy, chaotic, and here was Natasha, glowing with a tranquility that practically demanded curiosity. *Maybe I should try it, too,* I thought.

But those moments were rare. Too rare. More often than not, when I saw Natasha, she felt miles away—even when she was sitting right in front of me. She'd dive into endless venting sessions, unloading all her frustrations, and I'd listen, truly listen, because that's what friends do. But when it was my turn to share, to open up about my life, it was like talking to a mannequin. She'd stare through me, her eyes blank and detached, as if I were some ghost floating in and out of her consciousness.

The worst moments were when she tried to fake it. She'd throw out half-hearted responses that didn't even match what I was saying, and I'd sit there, watching the trainwreck in slow motion, thinking, *Is this what I deserve? To be this unseen?* It was like she'd put up a wall, one I had no hope of climbing, and I was left standing on the other side, waving my arms in vain.

Thank you, Meisner program, for giving me the clarity to spot this. The program had sharpened my emotional radar, making it painfully obvious when someone wasn't present, wasn't truly *listening*. And Natasha? She wasn't. She was a million miles away, and the more I saw it, the more it drained me.

I gave it about five chances. Five separate occasions to see if things could be different, if our friendship could breathe easier now that we weren't living together. Each time, I left feeling emptier than the last. That final meeting, though, was the breaking point. I had gone in hopeful, thinking maybe this time would be different, but it wasn't. The truth hit me like a brick:

my own growth had created a gap too wide for us to bridge. The things I had once ignored, once tolerated, now screamed for my attention. Her lack of engagement wasn't just disappointing—it was almost unbearable.

I realized something brutally honest: I had come to know Natasha too well. I'd seen the cracks in the foundation, and there was no unseeing them. There was no way to rebuild. No matter how much I wanted to, I couldn't forget the ways she made me feel invisible, the ways she drained rather than fueled me. It was time to let go.

It wasn't easy to walk away. Cutting ties never is. But I knew deep down that Natasha wasn't the kind of person I wanted in my life anymore. As much as I wished I could rewrite our story with a happier ending, I couldn't ignore the reality. Letting go wasn't just a choice—it was a necessity.

Oddly enough, I'm grateful for the experience. The Meisner program didn't just teach me how to act—it taught me how to see people clearly, to understand dynamics, and to recognize when someone isn't meant to be part of your journey anymore. It elevated my people skills to an almost surgical level, giving me the tools to navigate relationships with both clarity and compassion.

Natasha was a chapter in my life—a complicated, messy, and at times beautiful chapter. And while that chapter is now closed, I'm grateful for what it taught me. Not every friendship is meant to last forever, but every one of them leaves you with lessons. And this one? This was my lesson in letting go with grace.

Chapter 24

Pain Has a Passport

My "Eat, Pray, Love" adventure through Italy was supposed to be a dreamy escape—a whirlwind of picturesque landscapes, transformative experiences, and soul-healing moments. And while it delivered all of that and more, it also turned into something far deeper, far messier, and far more raw than I could have imagined. Italy didn't just show me its beauty; it exposed the jagged edges of my soul and forced me to confront them. It was a journey of duality, where every moment of bliss was shadowed by a storm brewing inside me.

On one hand, there were the highs that felt almost too magical to be real. Gazing at the intricate details of Michelangelo's David, I marveled at how something so perfect could be created by human hands. The Amalfi Coast dazzled me with its cascading cliffs and turquoise waters, a postcard come to life. And the food? Every bite of gelato, every swirl of pasta, every sip of wine felt like a love letter to my taste buds. I laughed so hard with new friends that I forgot, for a moment, about the weight I was carrying. For those fleeting moments, I felt light, free, alive.

But then there was the other side—the darker, heavier counterpart to all that joy. Like the time the boat on the Amalfi Coast almost left without me, my heart pounding as I ran, panic gripping my chest like a vise. Or the chaos of train stations, where the foreign signs and bustling crowds turned into a cacophony that left me dizzy and breathless. Italy's magic didn't make the Tasmanian devil inside me disappear. If anything, it brought it to the surface, demanding to be faced.

And then there was the Alexander Technique, my unexpected lifeline. I'd signed up for it as a way to add to my craft, but it turned out to be so much more than that. It became a secret weapon against the chaos inside me, a set of tools I didn't know I needed. Every practice session was like taking a tiny step toward grounding myself, like reclaiming a piece of my sanity from the relentless storm. It wasn't perfect, and it wasn't easy, but it was something—an anchor in the midst of a tempest.

Coming home from Italy felt like stepping off the edge of a cliff. Italy had been my mirror, reflecting the truth I could no longer ignore: I was housing a beast within me. This wasn't just trauma quietly lurking in the shadows. This was a raging, wicked possession that had taken root deep in my bones, and it was no longer content to sit silently. It screamed, it shook, it demanded to be seen.

After dealing with a few practicalities upon my return—those mundane tasks that make you feel like a functional adult—I knew it was time to face the wildfire head-on. No more running, no more burying, no more pretending it wasn't there. I was ready to confront this beast in the rawest, most vulnerable way possible. It was terrifying, sure, but also liberating in its own twisted way.

I didn't care how long it would take or how messy it would get. This wasn't a battle I could walk away from—it was *the* battle, the one I'd been avoiding for years. The trauma box I'd always wondered about had finally been cracked open, and what spilled out was nothing short of a full-blown disaster. My body, my mind, everything was screaming with urgency, demanding attention I could no longer deny. It was like carrying a volcano inside me, erupting at the most inconvenient times, reminding me that this wasn't something I could suppress any longer.

But here's the thing: I wasn't afraid anymore. Italy had changed me. It had shown me beauty and chaos, peace and panic, and it had handed me the tools I needed to start taming this beast. The Alexander Technique wasn't just for acting—it was for survival. For healing. For finding a way to live with the storm inside me until I could finally calm it.

So, I stepped into the fire, ready to face whatever came next. I didn't have all the answers, and I didn't know how long it would take, but I knew this much: the healing I'd been avoiding for years could no longer wait. The fight was here, and I was ready to meet it. No matter how disruptive, no matter how messy, no matter how painful.

Italy had been the beginning—a spark that lit the flame. Now, it was up to me to turn that flame into something transformative. To tame the beast. To reclaim myself. To finally heal.

From the moment I broke up with Billy, it was as though I had lit a match and dropped it onto a pile of dormant explosives. He was the trigger, the spark that ignited a trauma bomb buried so deeply inside me I didn't even realize it was there. Once the explosion began, there was no turning it off, no escaping the storm. The symptoms arrived in waves, each one more relentless than the last until I was left gasping for air, desperately trying to make sense of the chaos within me.

First, it was the weight. Ten pounds disappeared as if my body was physically shedding the burden of everything I had been holding onto for far too long. Then came the PTSD, creeping in like a shadow, subtle at first but quickly growing into a full-blown monster. My first panic attack in Italy— trapped in a bathroom so small the walls felt like they were closing in—was just the beginning. That panic didn't stay in Italy. No, it packed itself into my suitcase and came home with me, where it grew sharper, angrier, and more unyielding.

Italy had changed me; I could feel it in my bones. It had cracked me open in the most profound ways, showing me beauty, purpose, and the beginnings of healing. But coming home made one thing clear: the beast inside me wasn't done with me yet. If anything, it had been biding its time, waiting to unleash its full fury.

PTSD, as I quickly learned, is a master of ambush. It doesn't announce itself politely or ask for permission. It slams into you from every direction, turning your mind and body into battlegrounds. For me, it showed up in nightmares—relentless, vivid reminders of Grey Knight and the chaos we had lived through. It invaded my waking hours, too, with flashbacks so vivid they made the present feel like a cruel hallucination. Memories I thought I had buried forever came flooding back, clawing their way to the surface with a ferocity I couldn't control. And worst of all, it dragged me into a constant state of fear, like I was a prey animal waiting for the next predator to strike.

From the outside, I must have looked like a walking disaster—a fragile, trembling bundle of nerves barely keeping it together. My health was a delicate house of cards, ready to crumble at the slightest breeze. Panic attacks felt inevitable, lurking around every corner. One morning, I spent the entire day running to the bathroom, violently dry heaving even though the only thing in my stomach was coffee. My body was in full revolt, purging something I couldn't see, couldn't name, but could *feel.*

In my desperation to understand, I developed a theory: maybe my body was replaying the physical trauma of heroin withdrawal. Maybe this was PTSD's way of revisiting that pain, forcing me to relive it in another form. I don't know if I'm right, but it's the only explanation that made sense to me.

Just another day in the ongoing circus that is my life, where chaos isn't an occasional visitor—it's a permanent resident. Frantic energy buzzed around me like an invisible storm cloud, my mind juggling a dozen things at once while my body operated on autopilot, locked in survival mode.

I spotted a car parallel parking along the curb—a perfectly normal, uneventful sight. I clocked it, calculated my next move, and, feeling particularly strategic, decided now was the perfect time to dart across the street—plenty of room, no interference with his parking masterpiece. Flawless timing. Precision execution.

Or so I thought.

Because just as I made my move, for reasons known only to him and the ever-mischievous universe, this man decided to throw it into reverse. And not just a slight, cautious adjustment—oh, no. He *gunned* it. Rolled a solid ten feet straight into me.

Yes, into me.

The sheer audacity of physics in that moment was almost impressive. The worst and best timing, colliding all at once—literally.

Before I could react, *bam*, he hit me. Not hard, but enough to rattle me. And what did I do? Did I yell? Bang on the car? Demand an apology? No, of course not. I apologized. "Sorry!" Like I had somehow inconvenienced *him*.

And just like that, it was like I handed him a golden ticket to drive off guilt-free. He sped away without so much as a second glance, leaving me standing there on the curb, mouth agape, trying to piece together what had just happened.

As I walked away, still vibrating with anxiety, a cocktail of confusion and overwhelm washed over me. I replayed the scene in my head on a loop, each time trying to make sense of it. Had that really just happened? Did I somehow *deserve* to get hit? Was it my fault for running there, existing in his trajectory? Then, it hit me—again, no pun intended. *He hit me.* No mirror check, no awareness, just pure carelessness.

Later, I laughed at myself. Who apologizes for getting hit? Next time, I'm standing my ground—and keeping my "sorrys" to myself. Lesson learned.

What I do know is that the old me—the one who once lived with lucid dreams that felt like wild, magical adventures—was gone. My dreams were now erased, replaced with a blank void or relentless nightmares. Even when I wasn't asleep, my body lived in constant turmoil, a Tasmanian devil whirling inside me, refusing to let me rest. Eating felt like a chore. Sitting in stillness was unbearable. Even breathing felt like an impossible task.

The worst part? I felt completely disconnected from myself. My body and mind no longer felt like mine; they were occupied by this uncontrollable beast, and I had no idea how to fight it. But in the chaos, I began to sense something deeper—a purpose beneath the pain. The more I reflected, the more I realized this wasn't about Billy or even Grey Knight. It wasn't just about heroin, or the trauma we endured together. This was everything—every hurtful emotion, every painful memory, every suppressed thought I had ever buried. It was a lifetime of suppression finally demanding to be seen.

I started to piece it together, thread by thread. Suppression had been my superpower for so long, the thing that kept me functioning, kept me alive. But now, it had turned on me. And in the quiet moments of reflection, I thought to myself, *I didn't give Grey Knight all of me just to be left with nothing.* This pain had to mean something. It couldn't just consume me. It had to fuel me.

I'm going to take this pain and turn it into something beautiful, I thought. I'm going to fight for the light inside me, no matter how small or dim it feels right now.

This wasn't just a fight for survival—it was a fight for myself. For the authentic, unguarded, resilient version of me, I had always longed to be. I've worked too damn hard to stay alive to let the beast win now. If there's one thing I know, it's that I'm a fighter. I've survived heartbreak, addiction, and chaos, and I'm still here. Plus, the two near-death experiences! This? This is just another battle.

It's messy. It's exhausting. It's the hardest thing I've ever done. But I'm ready. I'm ready to face the beast, to dig deep, to find the pieces of myself I've been missing and put them back together. I'm ready to love myself—not in spite of the chaos, but because of it.

This is where the healing begins. This is where I find myself.

Billy *finally* detached himself from me. Finally. The cord was cut, the weight was lifted, and the storm he brought into my life began to dissipate. It felt like freedom—a long-overdue liberation from the constant triggers he stirred up in me. Every time he was around, he was like a live wire, jolting my PTSD into overdrive, bringing back the haunting shadows of Grey Knight. I'd made it abundantly clear to him, over and over, that the dynamic of a relationship—boyfriend and girlfriend—wasn't just unwelcome, it was dangerous for me. It made my symptoms worse. It threw gasoline on a fire I was already struggling to contain. What I wanted—what I *needed*—was to be alone.

Alone sounded heavenly. Alone meant no distractions, no pressure, and no one to see the chaos I'd become. My body, my mind—they were unrecognizable. I was constantly teetering on the edge of fear, my moods swinging like an unhinged pendulum, my reactions exaggerated and volatile. I was an emotional tornado, and for the first time in my life, I actually felt embarrassed to be around people. *Me? Embarrassed?* It was almost laughable because that's never been me, not ever. But this—this mess—I didn't want anyone to see it.

What I wanted was isolation, not as an escape but as a way to face myself. I needed to dissect everything, pull it all apart, and figure out how to put myself back together. I knew this about myself: I do my best work and think best when I'm alone. I'm not afraid of my own company, and I knew this battle was one I had to navigate on my own. What had happened with Grey Knight was just the final blow in a long series of buried hurts and unresolved pain. It was the cherry on top of years of wounds I'd patched over but never healed. And now, with everything unraveling at once, I felt more than done. I felt ready. Ready for real, lasting change.

The doctors, of course, had their opinions. Anti-anxiety meds, antidepressants—solutions that were handed to me like Band-Aids for a wound that was gaping and raw. But I refused. No amount of convincing could make me believe that pills were the answer. This wasn't something I wanted to numb; it was something I needed to *feel*—all of it. As messy and overwhelming as it was, I wanted to face it head-on. There was a voice inside me, faint but steady, whispering over and over, *This is only temporary, Haley. You've got this.* I clung to that voice, cheering myself on with every shaky step forward.

Maybe what I needed was a shake-up, something new to spark a sense of magic as I worked through the pain. So, I started exploring. The Alexander Technique, for one, had already proven transformative. It wasn't just about breathwork or body alignment; it was about finding stability in the storm. Yoga became another tool, a way to reconnect with my body when it felt like a stranger. And then there was Meisner—a year of stripping down my defenses and rebuilding myself from the inside out. That work had sewn itself into the fabric of my being, and it felt like the foundation I needed to dive deeper into.

Other ideas floated into my mind, too. Natasha's post-Reiki glow still haunted me, in the best way. She'd been so calm, so serene, so unlike her usual self, that it felt like a neon sign flashing "TRY THIS." And the book *Women Who Love Psychopaths*? Just the title alone was enough to pull me in. I wanted to understand my past, my choices, and, most importantly, myself. Every new curiosity felt like a tiny light in the darkness, guiding me toward something I couldn't yet name.

This new chapter of my life was born from pain—messy, soul-crushing, earth-shattering pain—but it also felt like an opportunity. For the first time, I felt the urgency to truly love myself. Not in the superficial, self-care-on-Sundays way, but in the deep, transformative way that requires you to sit with your shadows and befriend them. My dad's voice echoed in my mind, a mantra he'd repeated so many times during my childhood: "Love yourself, because you're all you truly have." Back then, it felt like a cliché. Now, it felt like a lifeline.

I decided then and there that every ounce of love I'd poured into others, every bit of energy I'd given away, was going to be redirected to myself. It wasn't selfish—it was survival. I needed to take care of myself, to nurture the parts of myself I'd ignored for too long. That also meant forgiving myself. Forgiving myself for the choices I'd made, for the situations I'd stayed in, for the pain I'd carried for years. I realized I'd been using Grey Knight as a scapegoat, blaming him for everything because it was easier than looking inward. But blaming him hadn't gotten me anywhere. It had only kept me stuck, a prisoner of the victim mindset I so desperately wanted to escape. That's not who I *want* to be.

I'm done being a victim. I want my power back. I want to reclaim my life, my heart, my soul. This isn't about surviving anymore—it's about thriving. It's about loving myself enough to fight for the light inside me, no matter how dark it feels right now.

This is the moment. My moment. The time to pour love into myself, to forgive myself, to fight for myself. It's not going to be easy—it's already messy as hell—but I know one thing for sure: *I'm worth the fight.*

Through every yoga and breathwork class in Italy, I felt the faintest spark flicker inside me—a whisper of a soul I hadn't connected with in years. It's almost laughable now, how lost I'd been, how estranged I felt from my own body, as if I'd been evicted and left to wander aimlessly while this broken shell carried on without me. Reconnecting with my spirit wasn't just a desire; it was a lifeline. And in those quiet moments of movement and breath, I felt something awaken—a glimmer of hope, a thread to follow.

But reconnecting wasn't simple, and it wasn't easy. Beyond my work schedule and any obligatory appearances, I made a deliberate decision to isolate myself. Not because I wanted to escape the world but because I needed to face myself. I needed to sit in silence and dive into the cavern of my mind. What I found wasn't peace. My thoughts weren't just racing—they were whirling, relentless, and chaotic, matching the physical turmoil within me. It was as if my body and mind were working together in a manic symphony, a Tasmanian devil spinning out of control, leaving tremors in my bones and turbulence in my chest.

Strangely enough, my overthinking wasn't the usual brand of self-doubt or negativity. This time, it was purposeful, sharp, and almost... elegant. After positive affirmations and some rewiring, my thoughts moved with a precision that felt tailored to my pain, navigating through the wreckage of my past like a well-trained surgeon. Every relationship, every hurt, every unresolved wound—my mind turned them over with care, examining each one under a microscope. It was instinctive, like I was wielding an innate weapon designed to tackle my demons head-on.

But let me tell you, facing your demons isn't a walk in the park. It's suffocating. Exhausting. Some days, it felt like I was clawing at the edges of my own sanity. I cried so hard I thought I might shatter. The tears weren't delicate or cinematic; they were raw, primal, and relentless. I'd cry until my chest heaved, my breath caught in my throat, and my body begged for rest. But the tears didn't stop. They didn't need a reason. They poured from a well so deep I wasn't sure I'd ever reach the bottom.

Amidst all the chaos, I found myself drawn to forgiveness—specifically, forgiving myself. It was a concept that had always felt foreign, almost laughably idealistic. Loving myself? Forgiving myself? Where was I even supposed to start? So, I started simply. I repeated the words like a mantra: "I forgive you, Haley. I FORGIVE MYSELF." At first, it felt hollow, like trying to fill a chasm with a teaspoon. But I kept going, saying it with as much love and intention as I could muster.

And then something shifted. The words began to carry weight. They weren't just sounds anymore—they were anchors. I started adding specifics.

"I forgive myself for staying too long. I forgive myself for the choices I didn't know how to make. I forgive myself for hurting myself when I didn't know another way." Each sentence felt like a key, unlocking parts of me that had been chained shut for years. The tears came harder, but they felt lighter, as if each one was carrying away a piece of the burden I'd been shouldering for far too long.

One afternoon, as I lay in bed letting the tears flow yet again, something extraordinary happened. In the midst of my wailing, I caught a glimpse of Cookie Grandma Rita's spirit. Her face appeared so vividly before me; I froze, my breath caught in my throat. It wasn't a fleeting thought or a blurred memory; it was her, unmistakably her. I hadn't seen her like that before—not in spirit. And yet there she was, clear as day, radiating the same warmth and comfort she always had in life.

The moment stopped me in my tracks. My tears dried instantly, replaced by an overwhelming sense of peace and calm. It was wild, surreal, and utterly beautiful. I hadn't dreamed of her in years, and I hadn't expected to see her in this way. But there she was, my angel, reminding me that I wasn't alone. Her presence felt like a gift, a gentle reminder that even in my darkest moments, I was being watched over.

No sugarcoating it—I cried every single day for three months after coming home from Italy. Not the quiet, delicate kind of crying, but the soul-wrenching, face-contorting kind of tears that leave you breathless and depleted. It was relentless, and yet it was necessary. Every tear felt like a release, a step closer to healing. Italy had cracked me wide open, exposing all the wounds I'd hidden away, and now it was up to me to tend to them. It wasn't pretty, and it certainly wasn't easy, but piece by piece, tear by tear, I began to rebuild. Slowly, painfully, beautifully.

You see, my emotions have a one-size-fits-all outlet: tears. It doesn't matter if I'm devastated, furious, or over the moon with joy—my body seems to believe the answer is always the same. Sadness? Cue the silent, heart-wrenching sobs. Anger? Here come the explosive, fiery tears that make me look anything but intimidating. Even laughter isn't safe; I'll laugh so hard that tears stream down my face, leaving me a mess of giggles and a snotty nose.

But here's the thing: My tears aren't a weakness; they're my truth. They're my emotions refusing to stay locked inside, spilling out in their purest form. And while it's not always convenient—or attractive—it's honest. In a world that often feels guarded, I'll take being someone who feels too much over someone who feels nothing at all. My tears remind me I'm alive, messy, and beautiful as that may be.

During this chaotic yet transformative chapter of my life, I found myself drawn to the idea of Reiki like a moth to a flickering flame. My research had already planted the seed of curiosity, but the desperation to heal—to *really* heal—was what pushed me to take the leap. I stumbled across a Reiki master from New England who had made Los Angeles his home. Something about his energy felt promising, like he was exactly who I needed to meet at exactly the right time.

From the moment we met, he was a breath of fresh air. Calm and collected, but with radiating energy and full of wild stories that instantly piqued my interest—crazy emergency surgical experience involving cancer, spiritual awakenings, and a legacy of Reiki passed down from his father, the original "OG" master. He told me how his journey began at the age of three, learning from his father, and how he'd carried that sacred knowledge ever since. His words painted a vivid picture of someone deeply attuned to the energy that I so desperately wanted to harness.

I opened up about what I'd been going through, this manic storm that had consumed me for months. He listened without judgment, nodding like he understood every word. I was anxious, excited, and—let's be honest—terrified. To calm my nerves, I hit my weed vape before the session, praying it would relax me enough to fully experience what Reiki had to offer. Spoiler alert: It didn't help. But I lay down on the table anyway, determined to embrace whatever was coming.

The session required me to fall into a deep meditative state, which felt about as achievable as climbing Mount Everest in flip-flops. But somehow, as the Reiki master moved his hands over my chakras, my mind began to quiet. When he placed his hands on my stomach—right above the scar left by my cancer surgery—the real magic began.

Suddenly, it was as though a projector had been switched on in my mind. A vivid movie of my cancer journey unfolded before me, pulling me into its raw, unfiltered reality. I saw everything—the fear, the fragility, the sheer weight of how close I'd come to the edge of death. But amidst the darkness, there was light. I saw the moments where angels must have been guiding me, their unseen hands steering me toward discovery and toward survival. It was both gut-wrenching and beautiful, a stark reminder of how fragile life is and how fiercely I'd fought to hold onto it.

Tears began to flow, silently at first, but they carried a depth I'd never felt before. These weren't just tears of pain; they were tears of release, of acknowledgment, of gratitude for having made it through something so monumental. By the time the session ended, I felt… lighter. My body, which had been a battlefield of tension and chaos for months, was suddenly calm. I felt peace—actual peace—blooming in places I thought were long abandoned.

It wasn't a complete transformation, but it was a start. And for that, I was overwhelmingly grateful. That one session cracked open a door I'd been too afraid to face, allowing me to finally begin processing the hard truth I'd avoided for so long: I had cancer. I survived. And now, it was time to heal.

But one session wasn't enough. Healing isn't a one-time event; it's a process, a journey. Hungry for more, I decided to explore other avenues. Soundbaths quickly became my next obsession, and oh, what an obsession it was. These weren't just relaxing; they were cathartic. I'd arrive early, positioning myself as close as possible to the crystal bowls so their vibrations could ripple through me like waves crashing against a stubborn shoreline. Rainsticks, chimes, and gongs created an otherworldly symphony that seemed to resonate with my very soul.

Every soundbath was like an emotional exorcism. As the vibrations moved through my body, they unlocked deep-seated pain and memories I hadn't realized I was still holding onto. The tears came fast and hard, every single time. It wasn't pretty—imagine a grown woman sobbing uncontrollably in the middle of a serene, candlelit studio—but it was necessary. Each session felt like a release, as if the sound waves were dragging the toxins out of my body, one tear at a time. And when it was over, I'd walk out feeling like a million bucks, transformed, rejuvenated, and just a little bit more whole.

Music became another unexpected lifeline. I clung to country songs that felt like they'd been written for me—songs about heartbreak, loss, and resilience. I'd put them on repeat, singing every lyric with a fervor that bordered on desperation, as if the words themselves could carry me through the growing pains. Tarot cards also found their way into my routine, offering insights that felt eerily accurate and pushing me to confront the parts of myself I'd been too scared to face.

Of course, my trusty weed vape was never far from reach. At first, I thought marijuana would be my savior, the thing that could calm my frazzled nerves. But I quickly learned that my usual Sativa strain was only making things worse, sending my symptoms spiraling out of control. So, reluctantly, I switched to Indica—a strain I'd always avoided because it made me feel like I was sinking into a black hole. Under the circumstances, though, it made sense. Indica's depressant effects were supposed to soothe me, and while it didn't always work, I gave it a fair shot.

Meanwhile, my nicotine addiction naturally began to fade. I'd been vaping less and less, realizing it wasn't doing me any favors in this circumstance. It was a small victory, but a victory nonetheless.

With every Reiki session, every soundbath, every song, and Tarot reading, I felt myself inching closer to the light. Healing was messy, unpredictable, and often excruciating, but I was finally on the path. I was purging the pain, releasing the toxicity, and finding my way back to myself. Slowly but surely, I was beginning to believe that peace wasn't just a fantasy— it was a destination I could reach.

Panic attacks barged into my life like an uninvited guest who just wouldn't leave. They didn't knock; they didn't announce themselves. They just took over, wrecking my peace and planting chaos in its place. It felt like living in a constant state of free fall—frantic, disoriented, like someone who snorted an entire caterpillar of cocaine. My body was a ticking time bomb, always seconds away from detonation. Every moment felt like teetering on the edge of something I couldn't stop, couldn't control.

After Italy, the panic attacks came with a vengeance. That first episode in the claustrophobic bathroom wasn't just a fluke—it was the opening act of a performance I never auditioned for. At first, I thought it was manageable in a "dip your toes in the water" kind of way. But then the current pulled me under, dragging me into a riptide of anxiety. They began striking randomly, as if my body had a mischievous little gremlin inside, deciding to wreak havoc whenever it felt like it. Trigger or no trigger, it didn't matter. My body had become its own cruel master, and I was a victim trapped inside, powerless to fight back.

The unpredictability was the worst part. Some days I couldn't leave the house, too afraid of when the next wave would hit. Some work days were out of the question—I couldn't trust my body to behave long enough to even show up. Panic attacks are a monster, plain and simple. They wrap their icy claws around your chest, squeezing so hard it feels like your lungs might collapse. Breathing becomes a battle, and just when you think it can't get worse, the rest of your body decides to join in. Muscles lock up, nerves tingle like static electricity, and a chilling, paralyzing stiffness spreads through you, freezing you in place. It's like being turned to stone, except every ounce of fear is still coursing through your veins.

I had to make the tough call to quit my second job after eight months. It wasn't just the growing annoyance—it was the anxiety, spiraling into full-blown panic attacks. They toyed with my schedule and my money like it was a game, leaving me constantly scrambling.

Then came the whispers, swirling like smoke—rumors of shady business practices. At first, I brushed them off as gossip, but the truth hit like a punch to the gut. The fire was real, and I wasn't about to get burned.

It all clicked. Staying wasn't an option; my peace was worth more than their paycheck. Sometimes, you have to walk away from the mess before it drags you under.

But here's the thing about panic attacks—they don't just hit your body; they mess with your mind. They make you doubt yourself and make you feel weak, broken, and incapable. And in the midst of all that, you have to somehow convince yourself to *breathe*.

Breathwork became my lifeline. Those tools I'd learned in Italy—the Alexander Technique, the focus on controlled, intentional breathing—were all I had to hold onto. It didn't matter if I was driving, sitting alone, or pacing my living room like a caged animal—I clung to my breath like a rope in a storm. And in those fleeting moments, it worked. It calmed the wildfire roaring through my chest, just enough to make me feel like I had a sliver of control.

But when I wasn't actively practicing breathwork, the fear crept back in. The fear of the next attack, the fear of being consumed by it. It was relentless. A part of me felt like I was in a boxing ring with my own body, constantly dodging punches I couldn't see coming.

Some days, it felt like I was barely surviving. But even in the thick of it, even when my body betrayed me, I kept showing up for myself. Breath by breath, I fought to steady the chaos. And though I didn't win, I never stopped trying. Because that's the thing about panic—it makes you feel like you're drowning, but deep down, there's always a part of you that's still fighting for air.

Somewhere along this chapter—after Italy, after the high of adventure and freedom—reality came crashing down in the form of a single soul-crushing realization: my insurance had terminated me. *Just like that.* No warning, no mercy, just a cold, impersonal notice that left me stranded without coverage.

Health, for me, is non-negotiable. It's not just a necessity—it's a lifeline, a non-stop, ever-present fear humming in the background of my life. Cancer saw to that. Three months. That's all it took for my body to turn into a battleground, for my perspective on survival to be forever rewritten. So, losing my insurance? It wasn't just inconvenient—it was *terrifying*.

And with it went my specialty prescription, the one thing my body needed to process food properly—food, something I needed more than ever to get back to a healthy weight. No pills meant my system was thrown into chaos. Anxiety skyrocketed. Panic attacks multiplied. I still remember the exact day I swallowed my last pill, hoping I could figure something out before my body noticed. Spoiler alert: My body noticed.

Whether it was withdrawal, the stress, or some sick joke courtesy of the universe, the moment my prescription ran out, the anxiety hit me like hellfire. Not just a fleeting, heart-racing moment—an all-day, teetering-on-the-edge, can't-catch-my-breath, trapped-in-my-own-body kind of panic attack.

Desperate, I called Troy—the one person I knew could either talk me down or at least make me laugh in the middle of my meltdown. He stayed on the phone for hours, unwavering, his voice the only thing keeping me tethered while he went into full rescue mode. Together, we called every pharmacy in the city, chasing down any possible way to get my prescription out-of-pocket.

The verdict? Over a thousand dollars for one bottle. Hot. Damn. That's insane.

Troy didn't flinch. He was relentless, dialing up every CVS, Walgreens, and back-alley apothecary he could find, refusing to accept defeat. And even though, in the end, it was a total fail, it didn't feel like one. Because just having him on the other end of that call, fighting alongside me, making me laugh through my panic, meant everything.

I kept digging deeper into my relentless mission to heal, exploring every tool in my arsenal: sound baths, meditations, books, breathwork, journaling my past like a detective piecing together a crime scene, and crying as if tears alone could wash away the pain. Healing, it turned out, wasn't a one-size-fits-all solution. It was messy and layered, and I was determined to peel back each layer, no matter how raw it made me feel. That's when the craving hit—I needed another Reiki session.

This time, I wanted to try someone new, someone different. So, naturally, I turned to Groupon. Yes, Groupon. Laugh if you will, but there's something magical about scoring a bargain for what could potentially be a life-altering experience. I found a Reiki master in Torrance offering sessions for a fraction of the usual cost. Was it unconventional? Sure. But I'm a sucker for a deal, and honestly, it felt like fate was nudging me in his direction. I booked the session, and just like that, the excitement began to bubble.

Carlos greeted me with a presence so calm and grounding that it felt like stepping into a sanctuary. He was warm and welcoming, and before we even began, he walked me through the philosophy of Reiki in a way that was both poetic and practical. He told me stories about his years of experience, about clients who had walked in broken and left healed—some after just one session, others after a few. He even shared that he'd been teaching Reiki for decades, helping others tap into their healing potential. His voice, his energy, and everything about him reassured me that I was in good hands.

When we finally moved to the treatment room, it was like stepping into a cocoon of serenity. Soft light bathed the room, and harmonious soundbath music played in the background, creating an atmosphere so soothing I felt my tension start to melt away. Carlos had thought of everything—propping my legs for ultimate comfort, tucking me in under a cozy blanket, and guiding me into a meditative state with his gentle voice. I could feel myself sinking into the bed, my body softening as my spirit began to rest.

As the session progressed, Carlos placed his hands over my chakras, one by one, moving through each energy point with care. I fell deeper and deeper into the meditation until I felt like I wasn't even in my body anymore. Then, the tears started—silent, unbidden, and entirely necessary. Again. They poured from me like a flood, carrying with them pieces of the pain and toxicity I had been holding onto for far too long.

And then, something extraordinary happened. When he placed his hands behind my neck and gently lifted my head, I was transported. In front of me appeared a blinding, radiant light—a light so pure and mesmerizing it felt like it was calling me in. I wanted to move toward it, to cross into whatever peaceful realm it promised, but I couldn't. A powerful, unseen force held me back, tethering me in place.

The sensation was like something out of a sci-fi movie, the kind of moment where the protagonist is on the brink of stepping into a portal but is caught in a struggle with the gravitational pull of two worlds. My entire being felt like it was vibrating, caught in a tug-of-war between the light and the force holding me back. It was surreal, like the most vivid dream you've ever had but experienced while completely awake.

When the session ended, I woke up feeling like I'd been through a cosmic battle and somehow came out the other side. My body felt lighter, my mind calmer, and my spirit… freer. Like, woah. *WOW*. Carlos and I sat down afterward to talk about what I'd experienced, and as I described the tears, the light, and the force pulling at me, I could see his eyes light up with understanding.

It was the wildest thing I'd ever experienced, but it was also profoundly healing. That session didn't fix everything—it wasn't a magical cure—but it cracked open something inside me. It gave me a glimpse of what was possible, of the peace that might be waiting for me if I kept moving forward. And for the first time in a long time, I felt a spark of hope.

As I spilled everything to Carlos—the tears, the vision, the tug-of-war between the light and the force holding me back—my intuition wasn't just whispering; it was screaming at full volume: *You need to do it again. You have to cross into the light.* It was as if the experience had planted a seed, and now my soul was begging for the next chapter. I tucked that thought away, knowing I wasn't quite done with this journey.

Our conversation shifted, and before I knew it, Carlos dropped a bombshell that left me reeling. He mentioned a book—*Women Who Love Psychopaths*. I nearly choked. *What?!* The same book my divorce attorney had recommended just recently? The one I'd just bought for myself? The synchronicity of it all gave me chills. I felt like the universe was winking at me, nudging me to pay attention.

And then Carlos, with his calm, knowing demeanor, added another layer to the revelation. He explained how, in his experience, many women who endure deeply toxic or abusive relationships often end up having their gallbladders removed. He believed that heartbreak—especially the kind that comes from being a victim of emotional or physical abuse—can manifest physically, sometimes with startling precision.

I was floored. My brain went into overdrive as I told him about Grey Knight, about my cancer surgery, and how the surgeons had removed my gallbladder during the process. Was this why? Could this theory—this connection between love, heartbreak, and physical trauma—actually explain it? The more I thought about it, the more it made sense. My gallbladder, my heartbreak, my survival—it all felt intertwined in a way I couldn't fully comprehend but also couldn't dismiss.

By the end of our conversation, I was vibrating with curiosity, revelation, and a touch of exhaustion. Carlos wrapped up by recommending a detox bath to help enhance the healing process. It sounded nice in theory, but by the time I got home, I was *done*. I barely had the energy to stand, let alone draw a bath. My body, mind, and spirit felt like they'd been wrung out and hung up to dry. For someone who prides herself on resilience, I was thoroughly humbled.

And then, the detox hit me. Two hours after leaving Carlos, I found myself sprinting to the bathroom and calling out of work. Every hour. On the hour. It was like clockwork, a relentless purge that left no corner of my body untouched. By nightfall, it wasn't just inconvenient—it was *comical*. I messaged Carlos, half-panicked and half-laughing, asking if this was normal. His response? "Oh, yes! That's the detox phase!"

Ah, *that* kind of detox. Got it.

What followed was a marathon I hadn't known I signed up for. My body went through a full-on evacuation, leaving me drained yet strangely… lighter. The purge carried on for days, but so did something else. Beneath the physical exhaustion, I felt the most profound sense of peace I'd ever known.

And I mean *ever*.

I'm not talking about the kind of peace you feel after a good nap or a relaxing day at the beach. This was something deeper, purer—a calm that radiated from my very core. My mind was quiet for the first time in months, maybe years. My body, though still recovering, felt weightless, as if I'd shed more than just toxins. And my spirit? My spirit was *soaring*.

It wasn't just internal. I could *see* it, too. I caught my reflection in the mirror and barely recognized myself. I was glowing—radiating a light from within that felt otherworldly. I looked like I'd been kissed by the universe, shining brighter than any diamond, exuding a warmth that wasn't just visible but palpable. I felt untouchable, like nothing in the world could tarnish this newfound solitude and serenity.

For those few days, I floated on clouds. Music sounded sweeter, food tasted richer, and even the little annoyances of life couldn't touch me. If you'd seen me, you might've thought I was on something—some magical, hallucinogenic journey. But no. This was all me, *all natural*, all Reiki.

And while the glow didn't last forever, its impact did. That session was a turning point, a pivotal curve on my healing path. It didn't just show me what was possible—it made me believe in the process. For the first time in what felt like forever, I wasn't just existing. I was living. Thriving. And in those fleeting days of pure bliss, I caught a glimpse of what healing really looked like, what peace really felt like.

It was proof that my soul was still capable of shining, even after everything. And for the first time, I knew I was on the right path.

Of course, that conversation with Carlos about *Women Who Love Psychopaths* lit a fire in my soul—a relentless need to know more, to understand everything. I was wired, buzzing with curiosity, but the thought of sitting down to actually *read* the book? That felt like an Olympic-level feat my brain wasn't prepared for. Concentration and I had been strangers lately. No matter how hard I tried to reel it in, my mind was like a browser with twenty-seven tabs open, half of them frozen, the other half playing some chaotic background music I couldn't mute.

I'd managed to dabble in a few self-help books along the way—little lifelines that helped pry my mind and heart open just enough to breathe. But still, focus wasn't coming to me the way it used to. I wasn't the same sharp, locked-in version of myself, and honestly? It was frustrating as hell.

So, naturally, the universe—or, let's be real, Instagram's creepy algorithmic wizardry—decided to step in. Because, of course, it did. Right on cue.

Smartass phone. Always listening.

Suddenly, my feed was an endless scroll of philosophers, motivational speakers, and experts breaking down the psychology of toxic relationships. It was as though Instagram had heard my inner cries for guidance. The term "psychopath," I quickly learned from the book, was an umbrella for a spectrum of toxic behaviors—narcissists, manipulators, emotional vampires, you name it. Every post seemed tailored to my exact journey, dissecting love, heartbreak, and healing in ways that hit painfully close to home.

And, oh, did it hit. Hard. Watching those videos sent me spiraling into a fresh wave of grief over Grey Knight. It was like reliving the breakup all over again, but this time with a sharp lens of clarity. I wasn't just mourning him; I was mourning the *me* I had lost in the process. Yet, amidst the pain, those videos were my guides, gently nudging me to heal, grow, and move on. They peeled back layers I hadn't even realized were there, forcing me to confront the patterns in my past relationships—the lies I ignored, the red flags I excused, the ways I'd lost myself while trying to save someone else.

Then came the content on narcissists. It was like a masterclass in heartbreak, and I was glued to my screen, devouring every nugget of insight. The psychology behind it all fascinated me. I started to see the monster I'd been entangled with in Grey Knight and, scarily enough, the pieces of myself I'd unknowingly offered up to him. Narcissists, manipulators, and psychopaths weren't just toxic partners—they were architects of destruction, building intricate traps designed to pull you in and keep you there.

Narcissists, in particular, were experts at the game. Their charisma? Magnetic. Their charm? Irresistible. They lured you in with dazzling illusions, painting themselves as the hero of your story while carefully ensuring they were always at the center of it. They preyed on empaths—people like me— because we were the perfect fuel for their fragile egos. They gaslit, blame-shifted, and withheld affection with surgical precision, keeping you perpetually unsure of your reality and craving their approval. A relationship with a narcissist isn't just toxic—it's like chasing a mirage. What you think is real is never actually there.

Then there are the manipulators. They didn't operate in the spotlight; they thrived in the shadows. Subtle, calculating, and insidiously effective, they used guilt, kindness, and loyalty as weapons, slowly eroding your confidence and making you question your instincts. They didn't need to dominate outright—they thrived on the quiet control they exerted over your every thought, decision, and emotion.

And then, at the darkest end of the spectrum, were the psychopaths. Cold, calculating predators. They were charmers, yes, but their charm was a weapon, a means to an end. They mirrored your desires, your values, your very soul, crafting an eerie connection that felt too good to be true. And once they had your trust, the mask fell away. Love-bombing became devaluation, adoration turned to contempt, and you were left grappling with the hollow shell of someone you thought you knew. Psychopaths don't just break hearts—they dismantle identities.

I couldn't stop watching, couldn't stop learning. The patterns became clear, the tools they used chillingly familiar: gaslighting to distort your reality, love-bombing to lure you in, triangulation to sow chaos, and devaluation to strip away your self-worth. It wasn't just a relationship; it was a psychological warzone. These insights hit me like a ton of bricks. *This was my life.* I saw it all so clearly now—the traps, the manipulation, the way I'd been twisted into someone I didn't even recognize.

But knowledge is power, right? Anne embedded that in my brain! Naming their tactics felt like reclaiming a piece of myself, like holding a map that could guide me out of the labyrinth I'd been trapped in for so long. The more I learned, the more I realized how vital it was to bring this to light and connect the dots of my past. Toxic relationships, especially with narcissists or psychopaths, aren't just personal struggles—they're epidemics of emotional and psychological abuse that so many people don't recognize until it's too late.

And let's be real, women are often the primary targets. With our nurturing tendencies and empathetic hearts, we're prime candidates for their games. They exploit our kindness, twisting it into a tool to keep us trapped. And the hardest part? Once you're under their spell, the truth becomes nearly impossible to see. Escaping feels like trying to climb out of quicksand while they're standing on your shoulders.

I've heard that it takes an average of *seven attempts* for someone to leave a toxic, abusive partner. Seven times of leaving and going back before they finally break free. That statistic gutted me. I knew how hard it was to walk away, how easy it was to get sucked back into their promises, their love-bombing, their carefully crafted lies.

Another gut-punch moment came when I flipped over the book *Women Who Love Psychopaths* and let my eyes fall on one of the first sentences. There it was, staring back at me like a cruel joke: *"One in 100 persons or 13 million people in the United States, have no conscience, are cunning, impulsive and manipulative, and pathological liars—known as psychopathy."*

It felt like the universe itself was pulling no punches, handing me the brutal statistics in black and white. One in 100? That's not rare—that's unsettlingly common. Suddenly, the odds didn't feel so far-fetched, and the weight of my reality hit even harder. It was as though the book was holding up a mirror I wasn't quite ready to face.

So, if sharing my story, my mistakes, my heartbreak, and my hard-earned lessons can help someone else avoid that cycle—or escape it—I'll shout it from the rooftops. Don't wait to recognize the signs. Learn them now. Arm yourself with knowledge so that if someone like Grey Knight walks into your life, you can spot the danger before it's too late. And if you're already caught in their web, know this: The greatest escape you'll ever make is the one where you save yourself.

As my knowledge deepened, the world of red flags didn't just become clear—it became a field of flashing neon signs, impossible to ignore. Each discovery felt like a puzzle piece snapping into place, forming a picture of all the things I hadn't seen before but now couldn't unsee. What I learned wasn't just about *them*—the toxic ones who had wreaked havoc on my peace—but also about *me*. My blind spots. My patterns. My complicity in allowing others to chip away at my boundaries.

It was humbling, to say the least, but it was also empowering. For every toxic behavior I identified, every manipulative tactic I uncovered, I found another reason to forgive myself. And, oh, how I needed that forgiveness. I needed it like a parched traveler stumbling upon an oasis in the desert. Because when I really let myself sit with the memories—the flashbacks to fights, the cutting words, the suffocating anger—I saw all the ways I had allowed others to control my peace, my boundaries, and my worth.

I replayed those moments in my mind, the ones that left invisible scars on my soul. The shouting matches that drained me to my core. The silences that screamed louder than any argument. The subtle ways I had contorted myself into smaller, more palatable versions of me, just to avoid conflict or keep someone else comfortable. I connected the dots, one by one, until the tangled mess of my past relationships began to make a twisted kind of sense.

The clarity was both painful and illuminating. For the first time, I wasn't just looking at what they had done wrong—I was looking at the cracks in my own foundation. The moments I'd ignored my gut because it was easier to believe a lie. The times I'd let someone else's chaos seep into my life because I was too scared to shut the door. And yet, even in the midst of all that self-reckoning, I found grace. I forgave myself for not knowing better, for staying when I should've left, for trying to fix what was never mine to fix.

But here's the thing: this wasn't just about romantic relationships. As I followed the trail of red flags, I saw how the same patterns had crept into my friendships, too. The one-sidedness, the emotional dumping, the lack of reciprocity—it was all there, clear as day. Some friendships had crumbled because of my own blind loyalty, my unwillingness to see when someone was taking more than they were giving. Others fell apart because I let unresolved tensions fester until they became unfixable.

It was a bittersweet realization. On one hand, I grieved the connections I'd lost, the friendships I'd held onto for far too long or let slip away. But on the other hand, I felt a flicker of freedom. I wasn't blind anymore. I could see the patterns, the dynamics, the warning signs—and that knowledge was power.

It wasn't just about spotting red flags in others; it was about reclaiming the parts of myself I had given away. It was about learning to trust my gut, to protect my peace like it was sacred, and to say no without guilt or apology. And, most importantly, it was about forgiving myself—not as a way to excuse the past but as a way to honor my growth.

I realized that forgiveness wasn't just about letting go of the pain; it was about making room for something better. It was about saying to myself, *You didn't know then, but you know now. You're learning, and that's enough.* It was about choosing to move forward with eyes wide open, ready to build the kind of life—and relationships—that I deserved. And that, to me, felt like the greatest victory of all.

It hit me like a slap I wasn't ready for—a little birdie, out of the blue, chirped the words that would change everything: "Natasha is a narcissist." My jaw didn't just drop; it practically hit the floor. For a moment, my brain short-circuited, caught between disbelief and denial. Natasha? A narcissist? No, that couldn't be right. Labeling anyone as a narcissist feels heavy, but labeling a woman—a friend? That felt impossible. And yet, as those words settled into my mind, they unlocked something. Suddenly, everything about her behavior, everything I'd overlooked, came into focus.

It was as if someone had handed me a flashlight in the middle of a dark maze. The signs were everywhere, glaringly obvious now that I knew what to look for. The way she carried herself, the way she interacted with others—it all screamed narcissist. Women can be narcissists, too. Of course, they can. But the realization still cut me deep. I didn't *want* it to be true, but once I saw it, I couldn't unsee it.

Looking back, it was clear my subconscious had been trying to warn me for ages. There was a reason I'd felt myself pulling away from her, distancing myself without fully understanding why. And when I replayed the dynamics of her relationships—especially with her ex-boyfriends—it was undeniable. They were the sweetest, kindest empaths you could imagine, and she had chewed them up and spit them out, one by one.

Ezekiel stood out the most. I'd watched him crumble under the weight of her manipulation, his emotions spiraling into a state of despair that didn't even seem real. He became a version of himself I barely recognized—crippled by her toxic abilities. I had done my best to support him, to help him pick up the pieces, but it was like trying to stop a hurricane with an umbrella. Natasha's influence had wrecked him.

And then my mind went further back, tracing the patterns in my own life. Arianna—the "kind" friend who helped me move to San Diego—was another glaring example. She wasn't kind; she was calculated. The way she deliberately disrupted my peace, the little digs she threw in under the guise of concern, the constant devaluation—it was all so clear now. She thrived on control, on planting tiny seeds of doubt in my mind and watching them grow.

This wasn't about attacking these people or playing the blame game; it was about awareness. It was about finally understanding the truth of what I'd been living through and putting the pieces together. This wasn't just random bad luck in friendships or relationships—this was a pattern, one I could now name and navigate.

Diving into the world of narcissists, manipulators, and all the other traits that fall under the giant, ugly umbrella of "psychopaths" wasn't just eye-opening—it was empowering. It was like someone had handed me a decoder ring for human behavior, and suddenly, everything made sense. Their charm, their tactics, their ability to twist reality—it was all laid bare, and with that knowledge came a newfound strength.

Once you learn to see the red flags, they're impossible to ignore. And for the first time, I didn't just feel like a victim of circumstance. I felt equipped. Armed. Ready. My instincts sharpened, my perspective shifted, and I started spotting toxic traits like a trained detective. Every interaction became an opportunity to apply what I'd learned, to protect myself before someone could cross a boundary or siphon my energy.

But here's the catch: it hurts to see people clearly. It hurt to admit that Natasha wasn't just difficult; she was toxic. It stung to realize Arianna's kindness came with strings attached. There's even more I have not mentioned. But even in the pain, there was liberation. The truth gave me permission to step away, to stop internalizing their actions as reflections of my own worth.

And now? I feel like a completely different person. Knowledge is power, and this knowledge? It's become *my armor*. I no longer feel blind or naive; I feel capable. Capable of spotting red flags before they take root, capable of setting boundaries that protect my peace, and, most importantly, capable of forgiving myself for the times I didn't know better.

This journey isn't about bitterness or vengeance—it's about reclaiming my life. And every step I take feels like a victory, a small but significant reminder that I am finally choosing myself.

Chapter 25

Plot Twist Mayhem

During the swirling chaos of my PTSD healing—a tempest of sound baths, breathwork, and endless soul excavation—I threw myself into something entirely new: a career with World Financial Group. Because, naturally, balancing deep emotional healing with a brand-new career seemed like the perfect way to *not* overwork myself (spoiler: It was anything but easy). But I was determined. This job was more than a paycheck—it was my way out of the restaurant industry, my chance to build a life that felt as free as it did ambitious. The kind of life I'd dreamed of: remote work, occasional travel, and the flexibility to finally marry stability with creativity.

Thursdays quickly became the crown jewel of my week. Why, you ask? Because those were the days when motivational speakers graced us with their wisdom. And not just *any* speakers—Marshall Faulk, the NFL legend himself, was a regular. Every Thursday, Marshall's words struck me straight in the heart, weaving inspiration into my very bones. His speeches were so powerful they sometimes left me in tears—not the ugly, overwhelmed kind, but the happy, cathartic, I'm-ready-to-take-on-the-world kind. It was like receiving a lightning bolt of energy straight from the universe. By the end of his sessions, I was buzzing with motivation, eager to crush my goals like a caffeinated superhero.

And let me tell you, I gave this job *everything*. That's just who I am—when I want something, I don't tiptoe; I cannonball. I threw myself into the work, attending trainings, diving headfirst into meetings, and devouring every bit of knowledge I could. My relentless efforts didn't go unnoticed, either. Compliments from mentors and peers became a regular occurrence, each one feeding my hunger to prove that I belonged in this role. I was on fire, burning with the kind of passion that makes the impossible feel entirely doable.

This wasn't just a job to me—it was a lifeline. A bridge to the entrepreneurial lifestyle I'd always envisioned. Work from home, calling my own shots, and still having the freedom to chase my dreams in entertainment? It was like someone had handed me the blueprint for the perfect life. My ambitions felt limitless, and for the first time in a long time, I saw a future that didn't feel suffocating.

But the cherry on top of this ambitious sundae was working with Troy. If there was anyone in my life who could match my relentless drive, it was him. Troy wasn't just a friend; he was my partner in crime, my creative co-pilot. We had always shared a deep understanding of what it meant to hustle, to dream big, and to pour ourselves into something with everything we had. Now, we had the chance to do it together.

Working with Troy felt as natural as breathing. We brainstormed ideas effortlessly, bouncing thoughts back and forth like a finely tuned machine. Between cracking jokes, sharing deep emotional insights, and debating strategies, we turned every workday into a mix of productivity and camaraderie. Our long-standing tradition of marathon phone calls—those ridiculously long conversations that veered from the profound to the absurd—now had an exciting new layer of shared purpose. And with this job, we had even more reasons to see each other, to connect, and to grow both as friends and as colleagues.

The job wasn't just a distraction from my healing journey—it became part of it. It grounded me in a way I hadn't expected, giving me something to focus on when the weight of my emotions felt unbearable. Balancing my mental health with this new career was no easy feat—there were days when it felt like juggling fire while riding a unicycle—but it gave me purpose. Between Marshall Faulk's wisdom, Troy's partnership, Hannah's guidance, and my own unrelenting determination, I found myself building something that felt bigger than a job. I was building a life. A life that didn't just revolve around surviving but dared to dream of thriving. And for the first time in what felt like forever, I believed that was possible.

For training and growth, I'd been inviting people into my financial world, encouraging them to learn how to take control of their money and build something meaningful. Ezekiel was the first to say yes. He jumped in, eager to learn, and loved it so much he didn't just want to learn—he wanted to be part of it. Watching him light up with excitement made me realize how much this new chapter could change not only my life but the lives of others. When Ezekiel officially joined the team, our friendship found a new groove, deepening in ways I hadn't anticipated.

Mixing business with friendship is a risky cocktail, but for us, it worked. Training Ezekiel felt natural, and spending more time together brought us closer than we'd been in years. But there was an elephant in the room— Natasha's shadow still loomed over us. I'd seen what she'd done to him, and I knew rebuilding trust would take time. The wounds she left behind were still raw for both of us.

To his credit, Ezekiel didn't sweep it under the rug. He brought it up himself, apologizing with a level of vulnerability I hadn't seen from him before. It wasn't just words; it was genuine, heartfelt, and emotional. That apology cracked something open between us, making space for healing to begin. Slowly but surely, we rebuilt our friendship, brick by brick.

The Ezekiel I was reconnecting with wasn't the same person Natasha had shattered. He'd done the hard work to heal—maybe not perfectly, but with intention. I could see it in the way he carried himself, the strength he'd found in his growth. And honestly? I'd grown, too. So, here we were, two people who had been through the wringer, finding our way back to a friendship that felt stronger than ever.

The best part? Natasha wasn't there to meddle anymore. Without her toxicity poisoning the well, we could finally let our connection flourish. From the beginning, we'd known we had something special, a genuine bond that had survived so much. Now, free from her influence, we could lean into that connection fully. Our conversations became longer, more open, and more frequent. We laughed, strategized, and shared in ways that felt effortless. It was like rediscovering a favorite song you hadn't heard in years but still knew all the words to.

But as we grew closer, Ezekiel began revealing the truths Natasha had kept hidden. Each revelation was like a brick being tossed at my feet, heavy and jarring.

The Costa Rica incident hit hardest. Natasha had agreed to watch Mocha while I was away, but instead of keeping her word, she'd pawned the responsibility off on Ezekiel without telling me. And then, to add insult to injury, she'd turned around and guilt-tripped me, saying I should have paid her for the care she hadn't even provided. I was floored. The audacity of it all was enough to make my head spin.

But that was just the beginning. Ezekiel shared how she'd sneak him over to our place whenever I was at work, her motives murky at best. Then there was the time she "disappeared" because she tested positive for COVID and wanted to protect me. Turns out, she stayed at Ezekiel's place despite knowing he was COVID-free—because, of course, her comfort took priority over anyone else's health.

The lies kept unraveling, one after another. All the gifts Ezekiel had bought her, the ways she manipulated him, the attempts to drive a wedge between us—all because of her own insecurities. It was as if she thrived on sowing chaos, keeping us divided, so she could maintain control. By the time Ezekiel finished sharing, I wasn't even shocked anymore. The pattern was clear: Natasha was a master manipulator, and her web of deceit stretched farther than I'd ever imagined.

Hearing these stories wasn't just painful—it was validating. Every instinct I'd ignored, every uneasy feeling I'd brushed aside, was suddenly confirmed. Natasha wasn't the person I thought she was. The friend I'd trusted like a sister had been wearing a mask all along, and now that it had slipped, I could finally see her for what she truly was.

It's a strange mix of emotions to discover the truth about someone you once loved as family. On one hand, it's heartbreaking to realize the relationship was never as genuine as you believed. On the other hand, it's liberating. Each lie Ezekiel revealed felt like a chain breaking, freeing me from the weight of her toxicity.

The more I learned, the more grateful I became—for the clarity, for the distance, and for the people who remained in my life, unmasked and authentic. Natasha may have deceived me, but she didn't win. If anything, she gave me the gift of understanding what I *don't* want in my life. And now, with that knowledge, I can move forward lighter, stronger, and surrounded by connections that are as real as I am.

After months of relentless emails, endless forms, and pouring my soul into every word, I was in the fight of my life. Battling the Department of Insurance felt like trying to scale a wall with no rope—frustrating, exhausting, and riddled with uncertainty. I was pleading for redemption, asking them to look beyond the blemishes on my record and see the person I'd worked tirelessly to become. I wanted them to see me, not just the mistakes I'd left behind.

The waiting? Agonizing. Each day stretched longer than the last, filled with whispered prayers and flickers of hope. And then the answer finally arrived, dressed in an unassuming email that might as well have been a grenade. My license would carry a restriction, they said. A bold, unforgiving line, drawn between me and the dream I'd poured my heart into.

That email drained the color from my world. Everything I'd envisioned—this new career, this fresh start, this escape from my past—washed away in an instant. My hope didn't just waver; it nosedived. I felt like a runner who'd trained for a marathon, only to be told I couldn't cross the starting line. The sting was unbearable. I wanted this so badly. I'd pictured the life it would give me, the doors it would open, and to have it snatched away felt deeply personal.

But bless Hannah—my mentor, my cheerleader, my beacon of sanity in this storm. "This isn't the end for you!" she told me, her voice full of unwavering belief. She saw what I couldn't in that moment: my resilience, my potential, my unrelenting drive. Her words planted a tiny seed of hope, just enough to keep me from drowning completely. I clung to her encouragement like a lifeboat.

Still, I knew what had to be done. If I wanted this dream to come to life, I needed to tackle the elephant in the room: my record. It was the one thing standing between me and the life I'd worked so hard to build. So, I rolled up my sleeves and dove headfirst into research. Attorneys were an option, sure, but I stumbled across something even better: CleanSlate, a pro bono organization based in Wisconsin that specialized in record expungement. It felt like a gift from the universe, a small yet significant crack in the door I was determined to kick open.

When CleanSlate approved my application, it was like a weight lifted off my shoulders. I immediately got to work on the paperwork, meticulously filling out each section like my future depended on it—because it did. But I wasn't about to stop at the bare minimum. Oh no, I wanted to knock this out of the park. I decided to include character letters and heartfelt testimonials from the people who truly knew me. If I was going to plead my case, I wanted it to be as ironclad as possible.

I reached out to friends, family, mentors—anyone who could speak to the person I am today. Asking people to write about me felt vulnerable, like standing naked under a spotlight, but I knew it was necessary. The process became almost cathartic, a way to reflect on how far I'd come and the connections I'd built along the way.

Each letter that came in felt like a big warm hug, a reminder that I wasn't alone in this fight. They spoke of my work ethic, my resilience, my growth—and, most importantly, my heart. The very thing that my record couldn't show. These letters weren't just about convincing a court; they were about reclaiming my story and rewriting the narrative that had followed me.

Sure, the road ahead felt daunting, but for the first time in a while, I felt something new: determination, hope, and a quiet confidence that I wasn't just fighting for a career. I was fighting for *me*. For the life I deserved. For the chance to finally break free from the weight of my past.

And trust me, I wasn't going down without a fight.

It wasn't all storms and shadows during those months of healing. Amidst the chaos, there were rays of light—moments that reminded me that life, despite its relentless challenges, still had beauty to offer. My work as a model and actor began picking up pace, offering a lifeline that felt like the universe giving me a much-needed nudge. Booking after booking came through, each one breathing fresh energy into my spirit.

One assignment even took me to San Diego, which turned into more than just a job—it was a reunion. I got to see one of my best friends, Anthony, and meet his new girlfriend. Let me tell you, I adore her. She's perfect for him! My heart dances for him having her in his life. Seeing Anthony again was like revisiting an old song that still makes you dance, and spending time with them left me walking on air. It was simple, sweet, and exactly what my soul needed.

Around the same time, I decided to update my portfolio with Kevin, one of my favorite photographers. Kevin and I have this unspoken creative chemistry; every session with him feels like catching lightning in a bottle. We don't just shoot photos—we create magic. I always leave our shoots with cheeks sore from smiling and a heart bursting with pride over what we've captured.

But this shoot was different. This one carried weight. For weeks leading up to it, I'd been mentally preparing for something bold, something vulnerable. It was my first shoot since my surgery. For so long, my scar—the long, vertical reminder of my battle with cancer—had been something I hid, unsure of how to embrace it. But not anymore. I wanted this shoot to be about *owning it*.

Kevin had known me for years, so opening up to him about my journey felt natural. I told him I wanted to celebrate my survival, to wear my scar like a medal. When we met at the location, we brainstormed ideas, but as always, the real magic happened in the moment. I climbed onto a large rock, draped in a shawl, cowboy boots grounding me, and my stomach exposed. This was it—*the shot*. I wasn't posing for anyone else. This was, for me, a declaration of strength, resilience, and empowerment.

Snap. The moment froze in time, and when I saw the photo, I could hardly believe it. We'd nailed it. If you flip to the back of this book, you'll see it—the scar, the boots, the quiet defiance in my stance. It's not meant to be seductive or flashy; it's raw, honest, and deeply personal. A visual reminder of everything I've endured and conquered. And now you know why it's there.

Mocha's career in the film industry was gaining momentum, and watching her stack commercials and print gigs alongside me was nothing short of inspiring. We were like two dreamers carving out our paths, fueled by ambition and a shared determination to make it.

Enter Ezekiel, a photographer and videographer with an eye for magic. He offered to take new professional shots of us—partly for fun, partly to update our portfolios. By the end of the day, we had shots that didn't just look good—they felt authentic, like tiny declarations of who we'd become.

All these photoshoots were the perfect opportunities for me, as I desperately needed to update my portfolio. To top it off, I scheduled new headshots. My last ones no longer felt like me—I'd lost weight, gained perspective, and evolved. It was time for my photos to reflect that.

These photos weren't just for auditions or portfolios; they were about staying relevant, showing growth, and preparing for the next big step. Whether it was launching my website or simply owning my current image, it felt empowering to see myself through the lens—stronger, sharper, and ready to conquer whatever came next.

I discovered a little trick for taming my anxiety—no prescriptions, no hormonal chaos, none of that. Forget the anti-anxiety meds; I went straight for the underrated heroes: vitamin D and magnesium citrate.

They're supposed to be the magical duo for calming nerves, and let me tell you, I jumped on that bandwagon fast. Did it work? Honestly, it felt like it. Day by day, the suffocating grip of anxiety started to ease, like a knot slowly unraveling. Maybe it wasn't magic, but it sure felt like it.

Life wasn't done throwing little gifts my way. I surprised my dad with a quick trip to Northern California for his birthday. His face lit up when I showed up, and for a few days, it felt like all the heaviness in my life had taken a backseat. Then came the call from my car dealership. They offered me an upgrade to a new model, and I saw my chance to make a clean break. My condition was simple: the lease had to be in my name alone. No co-signers, no lingering ties to Natasha. They agreed, and just like that, I drove away in a brand-new HRV Sport. Sexy grey colored with a matte finish—I was happy stepping into my dog-mom vehicle. Wind in my hair and music blasting, I felt untethered, truly free. It wasn't just a car—it was independence, a fresh start on wheels.

And as if the universe wasn't done yet, it handed me another gift. During one of my marathon calls with Troy—our usual blend of chaotic banter, deep life talks, and wildly random tangents—I told him about my goal of building a website to level up my brand. It was a small dream but one I'd been quietly manifesting. I'd been updating my portfolio with this exact intention, but before I could make any real plans, a project through Casting Networks landed in my lap. They offered to build me a free actor website. Manifestation at its finest.

In no time, I had a sleek, professional website up and running. Designed just for me.

Each of these moments—the reunion with Anthony, the empowering shoot with Kevin, all the bookings, the freedom of my new car, and the unexpected gift of the website—felt like little victories. They were reminders that even in the darkest seasons, life has a way of surprising you, of offering glimmers of hope and reasons to keep going. And for the first time in a long time, I let myself celebrate those wins.

I've come to believe that these victorious moments—the bursts of joy that ignite my heart like fireworks—are anything but random. They're the natural result of the work I've poured into myself, the tireless effort of peeling back old layers, healing deep scars, and choosing gratitude as my compass.

My intuition didn't arrive all at once—it flickered, small and fleeting, like a candle in the wind. At first, it was subtle, easy to brush off, but over time, it grew, strengthening like a muscle I didn't realize I was training. Eventually, it stopped feeling like a quiet whisper and started feeling like a superpower— one that, when I honored it, never led me astray.

I would listen. Sit with the message. Let it settle. And then, I'd move forward in whatever way felt right. But the moment I ignored my intuition— the infamous *criminal activity era*—was when I learned just how brutal the consequences could be. Ignoring that inner voice cost me everything. And in the end, I learned the hard way: if you don't listen, life will make sure you do. That lesson hit like a freight train when I found myself convicted of a crime I didn't commit.

But here's the thing—pain, when you let it, *transforms you.* The moment I turned inward, when I stopped running from myself and started loving who I actually was, everything shifted. My relationships deepened, my world expanded, and I began to trust myself in ways I never had before.

And then something even more powerful happened. When I focused on *gratitude*, when I connected deeply with my soul, the universe seemed to tilt in my favor. The whispers became louder, the signs clearer, like a secret language between me and fate itself. As I clawed my way out of the darkness I once feared, I finally understood—this wasn't luck.

The good things in my life weren't random. They were the rewards of alignment. Of showing up for myself. Of realizing that when you nurture your inner world, the outer world has no choice but to rise and meet you.

By November, life felt like one long, unending test of endurance. PTSD was still my relentless shadow, panic attacks lurking just out of sight like unwelcome guests refusing to leave. The Tasmanian devil inside me hadn't exactly lost its grip, though the outbursts were less frequent now. And the weight I'd lost? It was still missing in action. I threw everything at my body— pizzas, pasta, even baguettes smothered in butter, carbs on top of carbs. I didn't care if I was flirting with celiac disease; I just wanted to fill out my frame again. But no matter what I ate, the scale refused to budge. Healing isn't linear, they say. *They weren't kidding.*

Every morning, like clockwork, my alarm went off at 7 a.m., and the day began the same way: Mocha, my fur baby, hogging the majority of my pillows as if she owned them. Four for her, two for me—because, let's face it, she deserves it. Little pillow princess. The moment I opened my eyes, she'd spring to life, showering me with her signature good-morning kisses. It was our ritual, her way of saying, *"Good Morning, Mom! Let's take on the day!"* But one morning, everything changed.

When I woke up, Mocha didn't move. She didn't wiggle or nuzzle or kiss me. She just lay there, stiff and distant, her eyes vacant. My heart sank like a stone. Something was wrong—*really* wrong. My mind went into overdrive as I frantically Googled her symptoms, convincing myself to stay calm. "I'll monitor her," I told myself, even though my gut screamed at me to do more. No matter how much I tried to excite her—treats, toys, silly voices—she didn't flinch. Her eyes had this haunting emptiness, and I couldn't take it. Tears welled up, and before I knew it, I was sobbing. Not the quiet, graceful kind of crying, but the full-body, hyperventilating kind that shakes you to your core.

I could feel the panic building like a tidal wave, threatening to sweep me under. Desperate to calm myself, I grabbed my headphones and searched for a soundbath on YouTube. I sprawled out on the bed, letting the gentle vibrations wash over me, willing them to drown out the storm in my chest. For 45 agonizing minutes, I couldn't relax, my mind fighting against the soothing tones as I couldn't help but stress about my baby. But then, as if the universe finally took pity on me, the magic kicked in. My breathing slowed, my tears dried, and I felt… steady. Not great, but steady enough to handle whatever came next.

When I finally emerged from two hours of deep meditation, it felt as though I'd wrung every drop of anguish from my soul. The weight of watching Mocha suffer had lifted, leaving me refreshed and renewed—strong enough to face her pain without crumbling under the weight of my own emotions. It was as if I'd pressed reset on my spirit, giving me the clarity and resilience to monitor her with a steady heart and a clear mind.

That fragile peace shattered the moment I looked at Mocha again. She was still the same—lifeless, her spirit seemingly trapped in some invisible grip. My newfound calm unraveled like a loose thread, and I knew I couldn't wait another second. Scooping her up in my arms, I rushed to the vet, my heart pounding with every mile. The fear was suffocating, but my determination was louder.

When we arrived, I was met with something unexpected: laughter. The vet observed Mocha for a moment and chuckled, almost mockingly, as if I'd dragged her in for no reason. "She's jumping around just fine," they said, waving off my panic. But I knew better. Her sudden burst of energy wasn't proof she was okay—it was trauma. Mocha was terrified of the vet, her fear rooted in a terrible experience at a different clinic years ago. Her trembling and nervous energy didn't mean she was healed; it meant she was scared out of her mind.

Still, they humored me enough to run some tests and monitor her for hours while I sat in the waiting room, a mess of nerves and worry. Every minute felt like an eternity. I cycled through fear, guilt, and helplessness, my mind looping through worst-case scenarios. When the vet finally came out, his words were dismissive enough to sting. "She's perfect," he announced, as if my concern was nothing more than paranoia, as if I were just another hysterical dog mom.

His nonchalance felt like a slap to the face. My gut screamed that he was wrong, but I had nothing to fight him with. With tears streaming down my face and my heart heavy, I drove home feeling utterly defeated. Mocha may have looked "perfect" to him, but I knew my baby better than anyone. Something wasn't right, and I wasn't about to let this go.

The next day, still unsettled, I sought a second opinion at another vet further away. This time, they confirmed what I already knew: Mocha had a minor spinal injury. My poor girl had been in pain, hiding it as best as she could. Dogs are like that—stoic little warriors who won't show they're hurting until it's unbearable. But I knew. I *always* knew.

We started her on pain meds, switched her to a senior-friendly diet, and added pet-safe CBD to help her relax. Watching her try to play, only to let out a yelp when she twisted the wrong way, broke my heart over and over again. For two long months, she endured strict rest—no running, no jumping, no fun. It was miserable for her, and equally heartbreaking for me.

And then, as if the saga couldn't get more ridiculous, her regular vet called a month later with "an update." Apparently, they'd overlooked bacteria in her urine during the initial checkup. Cue my fury. I saw red. I was boiling. How dare they dismiss her pain and take my money, only to circle back with this information *after* the fact? I unleashed my anger over the phone, and when the vet hung up on me, I didn't even care. Mocha isn't just a pet—she's my *baby*. My heart in a dog form. And they had let us both down.

But after two months of careful healing, something amazing happened. Mocha didn't just recover—she came back to life with a vengeance. She was like a puppy all over again, bouncing around with so much energy it was almost overwhelming. Her spirit was wild and untamed, like she was making up for all the time she'd spent resting. Seeing her so full of life, so unapologetically joyful, filled me with a sense of relief and happiness I hadn't felt in months.

Her journey mirrored my own in so many ways. We were both battling through pain, both finding our way back to ourselves. Watching her heal reminded me that even the toughest storms eventually pass. And when they do? The sun feels that much brighter. Mocha's resilience became my anchor, her joy my guide. And every time I see her zooming around with that spark in her eyes, I'm reminded of what it means to fight for the life you deserve.

A few months back, I decided to take another step in reclaiming my life by switching to a new gym. Cutting ties with Billy wasn't just about emotional detachment—it was about scrubbing every trace of him from my world, starting with the spaces we'd once shared. For me, breakups are about creating distance in every way possible, a ritual of rebuilding. Grey Knight had been the exception—a breakup so monumental it deserved its own anthem—but this was about moving forward.

The new gym was like a breath of fresh air: new machines, new energy, new possibilities. And then, out of nowhere, a face from the past emerged—Dameon. It took me a moment to place him, but then it hit me: I'd seen him before, years ago, back when I was working out with Grey Knight at Gold's Gym in Venice. Attraction was flickering, too. The recognition sparked something bold in me, and I made the first move, walking up to introduce myself. "Hey, I think I remember you from Gold's," I said, casually confident. He responded like a deer in headlights. To my delight, I was right.

The very next day, Dameon came over to where I was stretching, his presence as natural as if we'd planned it. He plopped down beside me, chatty and outgoing, and started a conversation that caught me completely off guard. His energy was magnetic, and before I knew it, we'd planned to work out together. As if that wasn't already exciting, he upped the ante by suggesting brunch afterward. A workout and brunch? My kind of first date.

From that point on, our paths kept crossing. We weren't just gym buddies—we started seeing each other outside the gym, too. Dameon didn't waste time being anything less than brutally honest, which I respected. He told me he was recently separated from his wife and that his situation was, in his words, "complicated." Not exactly music to my ears, and certainly not what I wanted to hear. I wasn't exactly seeking a relationship—I was still reeling from my own—but his candor shifted my focus. Instead of dreaming up what could be, I guarded my heart, determined to proceed with caution.

And yet, there was something about him. From the very first conversation, Dameon lit a spark in me that I hadn't felt in ages. Maybe it was the breath of fresh air I desperately needed, or maybe I was genuinely intrigued. Either way, he was hard to ignore. He was this lively, magnetic force that drew me in, his energy infectious. Spending time with him felt like diving into a McDonald's ball pit—pure, unfiltered fun that made me forget everything else.

He brought out a side of me I hadn't seen in months, maybe years. The carefree, laughing version of myself that had been buried under layers of pain and self-doubt. Dameon reminded me how to play, how to let go, how to find joy in the little things. Our conversations were effortless, flowing as if we'd been friends forever. He made me laugh until my cheeks ached, something I hadn't realized I'd been missing.

And then, just as quickly as it began, it came to an end. After a whirlwind few weeks of workouts, brunches, and laughter, Dameon told me he wanted to reconcile with his wife. Respectfully, I stepped back. It was the right thing to do, but that didn't make it any less painful.

I found myself grappling with emotions I hadn't seen coming—like a sneak attack from my own heart. After months of crying, unpacking my demons, and sifting through the wreckage of my past, here comes this man— lighting me up, making me feel alive again—only to vanish just as quickly. And damn, did it sting. More than I wanted to admit.

I took one look at myself and thought, *Oh, I'm in trouble.* I hadn't planned on catching feelings, *definitely* not this fast, and *absolutely* not with this kind of intensity. But there it was, pulling me in like a riptide I had no desire to fight. Reckless? Maybe. But wasn't I just stepping into my new era? Emerging from the wreckage, spreading my wings, stepping into the light? And then—boom— he appears, right in the middle of my rebirth, amplifying every last spark.

But instead of drowning in the ache of his absence, I reframed it. Maybe this wasn't heartache. Maybe it was a test. Could I stay friends with him? Keep my guard up, protect my heart? Could I let myself enjoy what we had without unraveling in the aftermath? The old me might have spiraled. But this new me—the one clawing her way to the surface—wanted to find out.

Dameon was like a spark in the darkness, a reminder that even amidst the chaos, there was still light in me waiting to be rekindled. He showed me what I wanted, what I deserved, and what I wasn't willing to compromise on anymore. And for that, I was grateful. Even if our time was brief, it was a chapter worth writing—a moment that reminded me I'm still capable of joy, connection, and hope.

Shortly after the whirlwind of Mocha's alarming vet saga, life handed me a welcome distraction—the start of the second year in the Meisner program. Cue the confetti cannons, because this wasn't just another year of acting class. Oh, no. According to Anne, this was *the* year—the fun year, the transformative year. "This is where the magic happens," she'd say, her voice practically vibrating with excitement, hands gesturing wildly as if conjuring invisible characters from thin air. "You've spent the first year stripping yourself down to the bare bones, peeling back those layers of protection and pretense. Now, we build. Now, we *play*."

And boy, was I ready for some play. After months of emotional chaos, panic attacks, and wrestling my own demons, the thought of diving headfirst into the world of character development felt like a dramatic makeover. One I was more than ready for. Finally, I could step out of my own turbulent story and into someone else's—an escape and a challenge wrapped into one.

Walking into that studio again felt like coming home. The smell of the space—some strange mix of old carpet floors and fresh ambition—was oddly comforting. The chairs arranged in audience fashion, the walls that had witnessed countless emotional breakthroughs, and Anne's infectious presence were all familiar sights that grounded me.

This year wasn't just about acting; it was about becoming. Becoming more fearless, more creative, and more open to the infinite possibilities of human expression. It wasn't just about learning how to cry on cue or deliver a monologue; it was about finding the soul of a character and making it your own. Anne called it "living truthfully under imaginary circumstances." I called it magic.

And my classmates? They were no longer just fellow students; there was an expansion of the tribe, comrades in this wild, vulnerable, unpredictable journey. Each one of them brought something unique to the table, and just being around them made me want to be better—not to outshine them, but to shine alongside them. We were all there for the same reason: to dig deep, to create, to connect.

Anne had warned us that this year would demand everything we had and then some. "Character development isn't about pretending," she'd said. "It's about truth—raw, messy, beautiful truth. You have to find the heartbeat of your character and sync it with your own."

The thought thrilled me and terrified me in equal measure. I'd spent so much time peeling back my own layers—confronting pain, grief, and fears I'd buried deep. Now, I was tasked with layering someone else's experiences over my own, with finding a way to let their story live within me. It was daunting, yes, but it was also exhilarating.

And Anne's guidance? Unmatched. She had this incredible ability to balance encouragement with brutal honesty. One minute she'd be clapping her hands and shouting, "Yes! That's it!" and the next, she'd be peering at you with those sharp, knowing eyes, saying, "But you're still holding back. Let's go deeper." She pushed us, but she did it with so much love and care that you wanted to push yourself even harder.

Each class was a revelation. We laughed, we cried, we failed spectacularly, and then we picked ourselves up and tried again. The studio became a playground of possibilities, a safe haven where we could stretch our creativity to the limits. Every exercise, every scene, every note from Anne felt like a step closer to not just becoming a better actor, but becoming a fuller, braver version of myself.

This was the space where the magic happened. The kind of magic that wasn't about perfection but about discovery. And for me, it was about rediscovery—of the joy, the creativity, the freedom I thought I'd lost somewhere along the way. For a few hours each week, I wasn't the girl battling PTSD or crying over a vet bill—I was whoever I wanted to be, whoever the story needed me to be. The second year was a chance to polish the craft I loved, to stretch beyond what I thought I was capable of, and to lose myself in the beauty of the work. It was exactly what I needed, and I couldn't wait to dive in.

November came crashing down like an unexpected tidal wave, leaving me gasping for air. A few days before my first hangout with Dameon, life threw a curveball I couldn't have prepared for. It was a quiet night at work, the kind where you scroll social media for a little mindless distraction. That's when I saw it—a message request from a faceless account. No posts, no profile picture, just a name I didn't recognize.

The message read:

"Hi Haley, I see you know Eric. Have you spoken to him recently? I have some news I would like to share with you."

Curiosity quickly turned into dread. My fingers hovered over the screen, reluctant yet compelled to reply. *What could this possibly be about?* I typed back, asking what was going on, bracing myself for an answer.

"He passed away this morning."

Those words hit me like a freight train. I froze, unable to breathe, my mind racing to catch up with the weight of what I'd just read. The sender—someone claiming to be his ex-wife and the mother of his children—followed up with a long message explaining everything. But I barely saw the words. My vision blurred as my emotions surged like a dam about to break.

Desperate for confirmation, I immediately reached out to Corey, our mutual friend and former roommate from my time in San Diego. Corey had been one of Eric's closest friends for over a decade, the kind of bond that made me certain he'd know the truth. My message to him was shaky and short: "Is it true?"

His response came swiftly, brutally:

"Yes. He committed suicide."

The air drained from my lungs. My stomach twisted into knots as grief clawed its way through me. Tears welled up, hot and unrelenting, until I couldn't hold them back any longer. Right there at work, in the middle of everything, I broke. Tears streamed down my face as I tried to stifle the sobs threatening to escape. My body betrayed me, giving in to the raw devastation.

I was furious. Furious that I had to hear this from his ex-wife, a woman who had emotionally derailed him in so many ways. Furious that it had come to this—*suicide*. Eric, my friend, my chosen family, had been consumed by darkness so heavy that he couldn't find his way out.

Eric and I had stayed in touch after I moved back to LA. Over the past few months, he'd confided in me about the turmoil he was facing. Corey and his new wife had made his life unbearable, throwing accusations and insults his way and bullying him to the point where he felt like a stranger in his own home. He told me he needed to move out, that the toxicity in those walls was suffocating him. I tried to be there for him, offering whatever support I could from a distance, but it clearly wasn't enough.

Eric had always been sensitive, a deep thinker who carried his emotions like a second skin. He adored Corey's children, spending hours playing with them, but the new wife was a tornado of chaos. From the moment I met her, I knew she was trouble. Her erratic behavior, her manipulative tendencies— it was all too much for someone like Eric, who felt everything so deeply. She pushed him into a corner, and that corner became his prison.

Hearing the news shattered me. Eric wasn't just a friend; he was family. As roommates, we'd grown close in a way that felt almost sibling-like. He was the annoying older brother figure I never knew I needed, and I, the little sister he loved to tease. We shared so much—laughter, late-night conversations, ridiculous jokes. He was the person who always kept you on your toes with dad jokes and just simply, wonderful company.

But now he was gone.

I left work early, barely holding myself together long enough to get home. As soon as I walked through the door, the floodgates opened, and I collapsed onto my bed, sobbing so hard it felt like my chest might cave in.

The heartbreak was suffocating. I cried through the weekend, replaying every memory, every conversation, every laugh we'd ever shared.

Losing Eric to suicide was unlike any pain I'd ever felt. It wasn't just the loss—it was the *why*. The knowledge that he'd been pushed to this point by people who should have been his safe haven, that the weight of their cruelty had been too much for his gentle soul to bear.

Rest in peace, Eric Stubbs. You were one of the good ones, a light in the lives of everyone lucky enough to know you. I'll carry you with me forever—in the laughter, in the memories, in the space you'll always hold in my heart. Love you, buddy. You're free now.

Closing out 2023 felt like stepping off a battlefield, bruised but victorious, with the kind of pride that only comes from fighting tooth and nail for yourself. December arrived quietly, like a soft sigh after a year of chaos, and brought with it some unexpected gifts. The first? The scale tipped up five pounds—a number that might sound insignificant to anyone else, but to me, it was monumental. After months of battling my own body, watching it waste away as I struggled to eat, that small gain felt like reclaiming lost ground. It wasn't just weight; it was hope, a whisper that my body was finally ready to meet me halfway.

Even more miraculous? It had been weeks since my last panic attack. That Tasmanian devil inside me, the one that spun and clawed and sent me into a spiral of fear, seemed to be loosening its grip. My breaths felt fuller, smoother—like my lungs were finally learning to relax again. I clung to those moments of calm like a lifeline, refusing to let go of the slivers of normalcy that had begun to return.

This one particular night began like so many others. A little after 11 p.m., Mocha, my ever-loyal companion, gave me her patented *"Let's go, Mom"* look. It was time for her nightly potty break, the kind that usually involves a peaceful stroll to her favorite spot near the next building over. The air was crisp, the stars twinkling just enough to make me feel like I was living in a postcard.

But peace has a funny way of flipping on you.

As Mocha sniffed around, tail wagging in her usual pre-potty routine, she suddenly froze. Her small frame tensed, and a growl bubbled up from deep within her little doggy soul. Then, out of nowhere, she erupted into a barking fit so ferocious you'd think she was auditioning for Guard Dog of the Year.

I glanced around, my heart thudding like a drumline. "What is it, baby?" I whispered, scanning the shadows. My logical brain tried to assure me it was probably just a raccoon or an overambitious squirrel. But then I saw it—or, rather, *him.*

A figure moved, not gracefully, but deliberately—a man, dressed in all black, leaping off the second-story balcony of the building across from us. He hit the ground with an unsettling ease, like someone who's done this before. Hood up, face masked, curly hair spilling out to conceal what little remained visible, and a backpack strapped to his shoulders, he looked like the love child of a ninja and a poorly planned heist movie.

My instinctive reaction? "Oh, I'm sorry! I didn't see you!" Because, you know, *apologizing to suspicious strangers leaping from balconies* is a perfectly rational response in a potential crime scene.

But as the words left my mouth, something primal stirred in me. My awkward politeness morphed into laser-focused awareness. The fight-or-flight switch inside me flipped—not to flight, but to *fight.* I turned, planted my feet, and locked eyes with him, my inner hawk fully activated.

He started walking away, but not without noticing my unwavering gaze. I tracked his every move like a predator sizing up its prey. He tried to act nonchalant, even walking backward for a moment, his eyes meeting mine as if to gauge whether I was just a concerned dog mom or someone ready to rain hellfire if necessary.

Spoiler alert: I was both.

I stood my ground, unblinking, until he finally disappeared into the shadows down the street. My heart was pounding, but I didn't move. I didn't want him to know where I lived. If this guy was trouble—and let's face it, people dressed like that at midnight usually are—I wasn't about to lead him to my front door.

When I finally got home, adrenaline still coursing through my veins, I picked up the phone and called the non-emergency number. Calmly, I recounted what I'd seen, choosing to stay anonymous. Within minutes, the sound of helicopter blades ripped through the quiet night. It was oddly satisfying to think those searchlights were for him, scouring the streets to find out what the hell he was up to. I hoped they caught him, or at least scared him enough to rethink his life choices.

After the call, I sat down to process everything. My hands were shaking, but not from fear—no, this was something else entirely. For months, I'd been trapped in the suffocating grip of PTSD, drowning in a sea of victimhood. Trauma had made me feel small, powerless, and broken. But that night? That night, I didn't crumble. I didn't freeze.

Instead, I stood tall, stared danger straight in the eye, and let it know I wasn't backing down. Sure, hindsight made me realize how risky it all was—what if he'd had a weapon? What if he'd come at me? But he didn't. And in that moment, I felt invincible, like the universe had orchestrated this bizarre encounter just to show me how far I'd come.

It was a pivotal moment in my healing journey, a reminder that I'm no longer the woman who lets fear dictate her life. I didn't need visible armor to be strong; my strength was rooted deep within me, silent but unshakable. That night, I wasn't just a dog mom walking her pup. I was a warrior, armed with nothing but instinct and an unrelenting will to fight back against the darkness—both external and internal.

The man in black may have fled into the night, but I stayed, grounded and victorious. In the end, it wasn't just about reporting suspicious activity or hoping justice would be served. It was about reclaiming a piece of myself I thought I'd lost forever. That night, under the hum of helicopters and the glow of a streetlight, I realized something monumental: I am no longer a victim. I am the storm.

Acting class, as always, was my sanctuary. It wasn't just a place to work on my craft—it was a lifeboat, a space where I could channel everything I was going through into something tangible. Every emotion I'd bottled up, every ounce of turmoil I carried, found its way into my performances. Anne's voice echoed in my mind: "Use it. All of it." And I did. I poured my heart into every scene, every character, until the pain didn't feel quite so heavy anymore. Acting became my alchemy, a way to turn grief into art.

December wasn't without its challenges, though. My mom came to visit before Christmas, and while I was excited to see her, I also braced myself for the emotional tightrope I always seemed to walk around her. Our relationship had shifted since Italy—I'd let go of a lot of old baggage, but that didn't mean everything was suddenly perfect. Still, I'd made a conscious decision to love her as she was, without expecting her to be anything more or less. We had a lovely time, but her presence, as always, stirred something in me. My anxiety crept back in, and before I knew it, I was vaping more than I had in months. Progress, I reminded myself, isn't always linear.

Dameon had come and gone like a flash of lightning—brief, intense, and gone before I could even process it. I wasn't going to let his sudden exit rattle me, though. Instead, fate stepped in with perfect timing. Out of the blue, a director I'd worked with back in San Diego reached out. His offer? A free sound bath session at Equinox. It was like the universe handing me a warm blanket and saying, *You need this.* And it was exactly what I needed.

The session was transcendent. As the vibrations washed over me, I felt the heaviness in my chest start to dissolve. Afterward, the director, Anthony, and I caught up, and he threw out an idea that floored me: He'd pay for my Equinox membership if I agreed to train with him and network at the gym, which was practically a hub for Hollywood connections. It was a win-win— a chance to leave behind the gym where I'd always run into Dameon and step into a space brimming with possibility. I said yes without hesitation.

If it weren't for this Equinox deal, I'd have vanished from this place like smoke in the wind. Running into Dameon every other day is like being caught in an endless loop of déjà vu—except instead of a fleeting familiarity, it's the slow, gnawing itch of irritation that refuses to fade. The thought of returning to Gold's Gym—*The Mecca*—has been circling my mind like a shark sensing blood in the water. That place was a temple of transformation, a raw, unfiltered crucible of sweat, steel, and spirit. Grey Knight and I worshipped there. No gym has ever come close to matching its wild, unbound energy— it was untamed, electric, alive. It wasn't just a place to work out; it was a battleground where you fought yourself and came out sharper, harder, and somehow hungrier than before. I could almost hear the clang of metal plates echoing like war drums, feel the pulse of music vibrating through my bones, and see the faces of strangers-turned-allies locked in their own quiet wars. Yeah, I missed that. I missed *me* in that space. No glossy, eucalyptus-scented 'wellness club' could ever replicate that kind of magic.

Then came the cherry on top: my first-ever rave. One of my "Powerpuff Girls" invited me, and I thought, *Why not?* After everything I'd been through, I deserved a night to just let go. And let go, I did. We danced like maniacs, the music coursing through us like pure adrenaline, our laughter echoing over the bass. For one night, I wasn't the girl battling PTSD or navigating heartbreak—I was just *alive*. It was a euphoric, glittering send-off to a year that had tried its hardest to break me.

As the clock ticked closer to midnight on December 31st, I couldn't help but reflect on how far I'd come. This year had been brutal, raw, and relentless, but it had also been transformative. The scars were there, sure, but so were the victories. I wasn't just closing out 2023—I was stepping into 2024 stronger, lighter, and ready to keep fighting for the version of myself I was slowly but surely becoming. And that was worth celebrating.

Chapter 26

Whispers from the Universe

Before the whirlwind of 2023 officially wound down, life decided to toss me a plot twist—a glittering, audacious challenge wrapped in the faintest glimmer of destiny. It wasn't just an opportunity; it was an invitation to take my chaos and heartbreak, my survival and resilience, and turn it into something extraordinary. It was as if the universe whispered in my ear, *Buckle up, Haley. This one's yours.*

It started with an audition notice. There it was, blinking at me from my casting network like a neon sign: "Seeking women with crazy, traumatic life stories to share." Practically screaming my name. *Me, me, me!* I thought, a mix of nerves and excitement bubbling up. My life had been a rollercoaster on steroids, complete with screaming drops, loop-de-loops, and moments where I was sure the whole thing was about to crash. If anyone could take on this call, it was me.

For days, I couldn't stop obsessing over it. *This is mine. I need this. Ask me to audition, universe—I dare you.* And just like that, the universe obliged. The call came, and on the other end was a warm, steady voice. She explained the project, invited me to share a brief summary of my story, and gave me permission to lay bare my soul in a way I hadn't done before.

A *brief* summary? Ha! Where could I even start? My life wasn't just a story—it was an epic saga of love, loss, madness, and moments that still make me think, *Wait… did that actually happen?* But I dug deep, peeled back the layers, and told her. As I spoke, tears fell—mine and hers. We connected over shared pain, kindred chaos, and the raw beauty of survival. By the end of the call, I had been officially selected as one of 100 women sponsored to write and publish a book. The project is called "100 Voices of Women."

Let me tell you, I could've fainted. The thrill, the disbelief, the *holy-shit-this-is-actually-happening* moment hit me like a tidal wave. I had dreamt of this for years but never quite dared to believe it could come true.

Here's the thing: this wasn't a brand-new idea. Years earlier, after limping back to Los Angeles from the whole burglary-conviction fiasco, I'd thrown out a half-serious, half-desperate thought to Isaiah: "I should write a book about my life." It felt like one of those sarcastic quips you tossed into the ether, only this one lingered. The idea stuck.

Every time my life took another wild turn, it whispered louder, *Write me down.* But back then, I wasn't ready. My story wasn't ready. Or maybe I was just too tangled up in the chaos to see it clearly. Life kept delivering me fresh chapters, twist after twist, until I started to feel like the heroine of a never-ending drama—a Netflix series with no season finale in sight.

By the end of last year, though, the stars finally aligned. The timing felt close enough to right—well, almost. Because here's the truth: revisiting your past isn't for the faint of heart. It's like willingly walking back into a burning building, knowing every scar and blister you earned the first time is waiting to greet you again. Grey Knight was the fire I was most afraid to face. Our story, with all its pain and madness, felt like an emotional landmine. I knew the book had to start with him, but the thought of reliving it?

It was like swallowing glass.

Then there was the nagging voice of doubt. Who was I to write a book? I wasn't a writer—I was just a girl who'd survived some crazy stuff. I didn't even *like* writing, let alone feel capable of pouring my life onto paper. But something deeper, something stubborn and wild and unyielding, refused to let me walk away from this.

This is your moment, I told myself. *You've been manifesting this for years. You can do this. It's calling your name.* December became a month of mental war games. Every day, I wrestled with self-doubt and fear, but I also started to dream. What if my story could help someone else? What if my pain could turn into someone else's light?

By the time the new year rolled around, I finally started writing. I wasn't just writing this book for me—I was writing it for everyone who's ever felt broken, lost, or like life was conspiring against them. I was writing for the ones who laugh through their tears, who fall but always get back up. My story is messy and raw, full of heartbreak and humor, but it's also proof that survival is beautiful.

And the magic of it all? This opportunity found *me*. It fell into my lap as if the universe had been listening all along, waiting for the perfect moment to nudge me forward.

So here I am, pouring my soul into every word, every page, every punctuation mark. Vulnerable, terrified, but brimming with hope. This isn't just a book—it's my heart, my truth, my offering to the world. And I promise you, I'm giving it everything I've got.

When the clock struck midnight on January 1, 2024, it wasn't a new year—it was a resurrection. Imagine a tidal wave of light and energy washing over your soul, sweeping away every trace of fear, anxiety, and trauma that once held you captive. That's exactly how it felt. Every lingering shadow of PTSD, every tremor of anxiety, and every chaotic thought that had once spiraled through my mind like a Tasmanian devil was gone. Evaporated. Like it had never been there to begin with. What remained was something I'd been searching for my entire life: *peace*.

But this wasn't just peace. This was a rebirth. This was a metamorphosis. It was like the universe itself reached down and whispered, *Welcome home, Haley. You've arrived.* For years, I had fought to unlock the woman I always knew was buried deep within me. My higher self. The version of me I'd catch glimpses of in my dreams and my quiet moments. And now, as 2024 dawned, I wasn't just dreaming of her anymore—I *was* her.

My body, this temple I had spent years neglecting, punishing, and ultimately rebuilding, felt like it had come alive. It wasn't just a vessel anymore; it was a sanctuary. I could feel it radiating joy, harmony, and a kind of magic I didn't even know was possible. My mind, my ever-busy, ever-critical mind, was quiet for the first time in years. In its place was clarity and strength—pure, unshakable strength. I had done the heavy lifting. I had forgiven. I had released. I had learned. I had grown. I had transmuted my pain into power, my scars into stars.

I felt like an alchemist, turning the base metal of my trauma into the gold of enlightenment. I wasn't just living—I was thriving. For the first time in my life, I wasn't chasing potential; I was embodying it. I wasn't a seeker anymore—I was found.

And let me tell you, this version of me? She was ready to *write*.

The PTSD chapter of my life wasn't just over—it was buried. I felt it deep in my soul, the way you feel the shift in the air when a storm passes. It was time to close that heavy book and open a brand-new one. Writing wasn't just an idea anymore; it was a calling. And now, I had the strength to answer it.

But this rebirth wasn't just happening on the inside. It was spilling over into every corner of my life—my career, my relationships, my creative fire. Everything felt brighter, bigger, more alive. The universe wasn't just smiling at me; it was cheering me on.

Take my acting career, for instance. The moment the new year arrived, it was like someone flipped a switch, and suddenly I was flooded with opportunities. Auditions came flying at me so fast that I barely had time to catch my breath. Seven or eight a week? It was a sprint, but I was ready for it. Every morning, I'd wake up, coffee in hand, script in the other, and dive into another world.

Los Angeles is a battlefield for actors, a city brimming with talent and ambition, but for once, I wasn't intimidated. I had my rhythm down. I'd step into each audition, pour my heart into the role, and then—let it go. Because here's the thing: in this industry, rejection is part of the game. Most of the time, you don't even get a "thanks, but no thanks." You just move on. But I didn't care. Each audition felt like a win in itself. It was a chance to grow, to practice, to be seen. And who knows? Maybe the casting directors who didn't call me back this time would remember me for a future role.

With every audition, I felt stronger. The Meisner acting program I'd thrown myself into the year before had sharpened my skills and given me tools I didn't even know I needed. I could feel the difference in my craft, in the way I approached every character. Even when I didn't land a role, I felt the thrill of stepping into someone else's shoes, of exploring lives so different from my own. Acting wasn't just a job—it was a form of alchemy in itself, turning words on a page into living, breathing truth.

By the time January ended, I felt like I was on fire—in the best possible way. Even a single audition could send me soaring, so imagine the joy of seven or eight a week. My heart was practically doing cartwheels. Each opportunity, each script, and each moment in front of the camera felt like another step toward something extraordinary.

But here's the most beautiful part: this wasn't just about acting. It wasn't just about my book. It wasn't even just about me. It was about becoming the woman I had always dreamed of being—the woman who doesn't just survive but thrives. The woman who takes everything life throws at her and turns it into something beautiful, something magical, something worth sharing with the world.

So, here I am, glowing, thriving, and utterly alive. 2024 isn't just a new year—it's the year of Haley—*reborn*. And trust me, this phoenix is just getting started.

Jumping into writing about Grey Knight was like stepping into a time machine set to every emotional high and low of my life. I had no idea what the process would do to me. I knew it would be cathartic, maybe even healing in a way, but I hadn't braced myself for the full spectrum of emotions that came crashing in like a tidal wave. Writing about him wasn't just telling a story—it was reliving it.

When I started recounting how we met, how I fell for him—oh, how I *fell*—it felt like falling all over again. Each word brought those memories to life. The butterflies in my stomach weren't just from recollection; they were real, fluttering wildly as if no time had passed. I was back in those first days when love was new, intoxicating, and perfect. I could see his smile, hear his laugh, feel the warmth of his touch. It was so vivid I had to stop typing just to breathe it all in.

And the tears? Oh, they came too. Happy ones. I cried for the beauty of those moments, for the way he made me feel like the most cherished person on earth. I cried for the version of myself who believed in a love so pure, so untouchable. For a while, writing about those golden memories felt like floating on a cloud of joy, wrapped in the comforting glow of what once was.

But, as with all love stories, the plot thickened—and then unraveled.

When I reached the chapters where things began to crack, it was like watching a train wreck in slow motion, knowing I couldn't stop it. Writing about the fights, the cruelty, and the monstrous abuse felt like peeling off scabs I thought had healed. The pain wasn't just emotional; it was physical. My chest tightened, my hands trembled, and my heart broke all over again. I wasn't just remembering—it was like I was *there*, back in those moments, feeling the sharp sting of his words and the suffocating weight of his presence.

Even my friends could see the toll it was taking. One of my closest girlfriends—one of the "Powerpuff Girls," as we call ourselves—called me out one day while we were hanging out. "You're somewhere else," she said, her eyes narrowing in concern. And she was right. I wasn't fully present. I was lost in the labyrinth of my memories, stuck reliving the happiest and most devastating moments of my life on a loop. Going through the breakup *all over again*.

Writing about the good times with Grey Knight was bittersweet. It filled me with gratitude for the love we once shared, for the magic of our connection when it was still whole. But it also broke me because I knew how the story ended. Every sweet memory was shadowed by what came next: the fights, the heartbreak, the unbearable nights where I felt like I was disappearing under the weight of it all.

As I typed out the darker moments, I felt a shift in my spirit. The love I had relived just paragraphs earlier seemed so far away, replaced by the familiar ache of betrayal and the sting of being so deeply hurt by someone I once trusted with everything. It wasn't just the memories themselves—it was the rawness of confronting them. It was realizing how much of myself I had lost in those years and how hard I had fought to find her again.

But as much as it hurt, I couldn't stop. Writing wasn't just about recounting my past—it was about reclaiming it. Every tear I shed while reliving the joy was a reminder of what I'd loved, and every sob that escaped while reliving the pain was proof of how much I'd survived.

It's strange how writing can hold such duality. One moment I'd be laughing through my tears, grateful for the lessons love had taught me. The next, I'd be crumpled in my chair, feeling the weight of those lessons all over again. But that's the beauty of storytelling, isn't it? It lets us hold space for both the light and the dark, for the love and the loss.

What I've realized is this: writing about Grey Knight isn't just about him. It's about me. It's about understanding who I was when I loved him and who I've become after walking away. It's about forgiving the girl who stayed too long and celebrating the woman who finally found the strength to leave.

Yes, writing about him broke me in ways I wasn't expecting. Very confusing to my heart as well. But it also reminded me of my own resilience. Of my capacity to love deeply and to heal even deeper. And maybe that's the real story here—not just about the man who broke my heart but about the woman who put it back together.

It didn't take long for Dameon to come crawling back, his life in shambles after a failed attempt to patch things up with his ex-wife. The divorce papers were practically inked, and there he was, knocking at the door of my life like a stray cat looking for shelter. But I wasn't about to just roll out the welcome mat. Oh no. This time, I played it cool—detached, aloof, even a little distant. Sure, we could be friends, but if he thought he could simply waltz back into my heart like a returning war hero, he had another thing coming.

Our relationship became something of a messy mosaic—sporadic meetups, sprinkled with plenty of space. Picture a book where you only read random chapters. Some pages were thrilling; others were blank, ghosted by silence. It was inconsistent, unpredictable, and maddeningly addictive. Dameon had this infuriating way of being just present enough to stir the pot but never enough to serve the meal. And somehow, I convinced myself this erratic connection was a golden opportunity to practice the art of emotional detachment.

Every time Dameon showed up, it felt like stepping onto a carnival ride with no safety bar. And, oh, was it a ride—sometimes too wild for my own good. His humor wasn't just funny; it was magnetic. The kind of humor that hits you like a shot of tequila—bold, intoxicating, and just a little bit dangerous. You know you shouldn't have too much, but it's so good you convince yourself, *Just one more won't hurt.* Spoiler alert: It always hurts.

The man had the stamina of an Energizer Bunny on a sugar rush, and somehow, he pulled me right into his current. I'm no stranger to energy; I thrive on it. *I am it.* But with him, it was different. His boundless imagination made even the most mundane moments feel like a movie montage. It was like finding a dance partner who never missed a beat.

I live for that kind of entertainment. I *need* it. Call it what you want— restlessness, short attention span, a chronic need for stimulation—but I crave it like oxygen. The mundane bores me, and the predictable lulls me to sleep. Dameon was none of those things. He was a living, breathing adventure. Every conversation with him was an open invitation to ride shotgun on a road trip with no map. No destination. Just vibes.

But here's the catch: adventures aren't always sustainable. Fun has a way of blurring reality, and Dameon's availability was like a desert mirage. Close enough to tempt you, gone the second you reached for it. I knew better than to fall for it, but knowing and doing are two very different things. So, we danced that exhausting dance—him leaning in, me pulling away—or vice versa— both of us pretending it wasn't a game we'd played before. After every high, I'd call a timeout, coaching myself like a player on the bench. *Girl, stop. He's going through a divorce.* This isn't going to end well…

I *knew* I should pace myself. I told myself I would. I even played it cool—purposely holding back, resisting the urge to dig into those deep, soul-searching conversations that would fast-track our connection. I didn't even reach out first, a rare feat for someone like me when attraction is involved. But with him? Moderation was a myth.

He pulled something out of me I hadn't felt in a long time—the unfiltered, reckless joy of my inner child. The kind of laughter that left my cheeks aching, my stomach sore, and my soul lighter than it had been in ages. For someone like me—easily bored, always chasing the next thrill—he was intoxicating. The perfect cocktail of mystery, excitement, and just enough chaos to keep me coming back for more.

But at the end of the day, I knew. I always knew. Fun can be addictive, but it's not the same as fulfillment. My heart's no fragile antique, but I'm not about to lend it out like a library book with no return date. I'm a lot of things—adventurous, restless, even a little reckless at times—but I'm not careless. When it comes to love, I've learned that being entertained is easy. But being seen? That's rare. And I'd rather be alone than be somebody's occasional amusement.

So, I pulled back, untangling myself from the invisible strings I swore I wasn't tied to. It hurt like hell. But I'd rather walk away with my pride intact than wait around hoping a mirage turns into water.

Yet, no matter how hard I tried to keep it casual, something inside me began to shift. Slowly, without my permission, I started to feel something. I'd catch myself smiling when his name lit up my phone or replaying memories in my head during quiet moments. Ways to make me smile at the thought of him. *Damn it, Haley*, I'd think, *you're slipping*. The clues were there—subtle but persistent, like a song slightly out of tune or a sweater that looked cozy but itched like hell the second you put it on. But my heart, ever the hopeless optimist, chose to hum along anyway.

I have to say *"luckily"*—and I use that word with the kind of self-awareness that makes you laugh through clenched teeth—Dameon wasn't without his flaws. His inconsistency, his baggage (because let's be honest, fresh-out-of-a-marriage is its own genre of chaos), and his habit of showing up when it suited *him*—it was all just enough to keep my walls standing strong, my feet planted firmly on the ground, and my heart safely tucked behind an ironclad lock.

That's why I say *luckily*. Because seeing the flaws early was my saving grace, my reminder to keep my expectations in check, to not let myself fall into something with no one there to catch me. And yet—because the universe loves a good plot twist—the cruel joke was that, for the first time in a long time, I actually *wanted* someone. Not just in a fleeting, surface-level way, but in that *deep, I want to know every inch of your mind* kind of way. That *undeniable pull* toward connection, toward discovery, toward craving something *real*.

But here's the truth: universal timing wasn't on our side. *At all.* There was no way this could work—not when he was carrying the weight of a crumbling marriage while I was standing on the other side of the spectrum, single, healing, and stepping into the best version of myself. And now that *she's* here—the woman I've fought to become—she's hopeful. Hopeful that when love *does* find her again, it will be steady, intentional, and entirely hers.

So, I put him in a category all his own. He became my "What If," my living, breathing experiment in emotional restraint. I let myself enjoy his company without surrendering my soul. Every laugh, every lingering glance, every touch was a test of my ability to stay in control. Could I care for someone without falling apart? Could I hold on to my independence while still letting someone in? Dameon became my teacher, though he never knew it.

Balancing acting class and my serving job was already a juggling act worthy of Cirque du Soleil. But then, just to spice things up, my new fitness regime with Anthony, the self-proclaimed gym guru who had more quirks than a Wes Anderson movie. Our sessions at Equinox started as casual training, I thought, but quickly turned into a full-blown production. Picture this: every squat, lunge, and deadlift is captured on video, complete with impromptu podcast-style conversations. If I didn't know better, I'd think he was training me for a reality show rather than actual fitness.

It didn't take long for my well-honed people-reading skills to kick in: *this guy was an odd duck.* I mean, where do I even start? First, there was the unsolicited generosity—he insisted on paying for my $300 monthly gym membership, which, let's be real, is red flag material in itself. Then there was his claim to be a full-time director and photographer, though his work screamed amateur hour to me. And the pièce de résistance? His permanent crystal-blue contact lenses, giving him an uncanny valley vibe that I couldn't shake. Add to that his insistence on being straight while his Instagram posts and body language suggested otherwise, and, well, let's just say the math wasn't matching.

It wasn't his sexuality that bothered me—it was the inauthenticity. He radiated "fake news" vibes, from his overly curated social media to his starstruck reactions every time we saw a celebrity at the gym. (Will Ferrell, for instance, caused a near meltdown.) He'd pressure me to approach them, but honestly? I wasn't about to interrupt someone's sacred gym time—something I hold dear myself. Anthony, on the other hand, seemed to live for the "fake it till you make it" motto, and I had to admit, he was fully committed.

Despite my reservations, I kept him at a healthy arm's length. But that didn't stop the absurdities. After every session, he'd insist on taking posed photos of us like we were bodybuilders preparing for the cover of *Flex* magazine. The catch? He'd slap on filters so intense they turned my bare-faced, gym-grungy self into a cartoonish nightmare—duck lips, overdone makeup, the whole clown car. It became a running joke until I finally snapped: "Anthony, I look like a wax doll melted in the sun. Please stop."

Then there was his workout philosophy. Fresh off a body physique competition win, Anthony acted like the messiah of fitness. He was *obsessed* with glutes. And sure, I appreciated the results—I mean, who doesn't want a sculpted peach? But it quickly became clear that his focus was one-dimensional. I wanted to be strong all over, but Anthony had other plans. Upper body? Skimmed by. Core? Barely touched. Legs? Glutes, glutes, and more glutes.

The kicker? His meal plan. Knowing my cancer journey and the fact that my stomach was half its original size, he still pushed a diet plan that included *seven cups of rice a day*. For whom, Anthony? A linebacker? Needless to say, I ditched his advice and stuck to my own plan, which focused on nutrient-dense, protein-packed, small meals that wouldn't leave me nauseous.

Still, I couldn't deny the progress. My body was toning beautifully, and yes, my peach was thriving. But after two months, I started to feel my upper body strength slipping, and that was unacceptable. As a gym unicorn—someone who thrives on sweat, weights, and the grind—neglecting the rest of my body felt like a betrayal. So, I started sneaking in secret workouts, reclaiming the balance I craved.

And then, out of nowhere, came *the message.* A stranger slid into my DMs with a warning so ominous it could have been the opening scene of a thriller.

"Hi Haley, I trust you'll understand my intentions here and respect my anonymity. Please share this with anyone you think should see it, but do not reveal I contacted you."

Attached was a YouTube link, a small stack of news articles, and a summary that left me reeling. Anthony Perlas, my quirky gym buddy, was not just odd—he was dangerous. A self-proclaimed Neo-Nazi, a Scientology infiltrator, a blackmailer of models, and the mastermind behind a bizarre blog about the Latin Mass Society. A predator.

Cue the stomach drop.

I watched the YouTube video with a mix of horror and *I-knew-it* validation. Every red flag I'd picked up on suddenly made sense. He wasn't just an odd duck; he was a full-blown *cuckoo bird.* The irony wasn't lost on me, either—just days earlier, we'd had a heated debate about Scientology. I had ripped it to shreds with facts and documentaries, while he defended it with suspicious casualness. Little did I know he'd been neck-deep in it for years.

I went into escape mode immediately. I texted Anthony that I was "sick" and avoided him like the plague while strategizing my exit. I started gym-hopping to different Equinox locations, my head on a swivel, ready to bolt if I saw him. Then, I scheduled an urgent meeting with a gym manager to plead my case.

Luckily, the manager was a woman—someone who didn't need much convincing once I explained my fears. Armed with my best acting skills, I laid it all out, and she gave me the perfect out: a doctor's note. Within days, I was free from both the contract and the nightmare.

To the anonymous stranger who reached out to warn me: Thank you. You saved me from what could have been a much darker story. Anthony's true nature was worse than I could have imagined, but I'm grateful for the lesson. Trust your gut. Odd ducks might seem harmless at first, but sometimes, they're hiding something far more sinister under the surface.

And as for Anthony? Let's just say my peach looks even better without him.

After the dust settled on the whole Anthony saga and I'd successfully terminated my Equinox contract, I found myself deep in reflection. Life, as it so often does, had handed me yet another pop quiz, and this one came with a sinister twist. It felt like the universe was leaning in, arms crossed, asking, *So, Haley, you've studied narcissists, manipulators, and psychopaths. But what will you do when one lands in your orbit?*

Apparently, I'd do what I always do: stay calm, think on my feet, and find a way out without breaking a sweat. Well, maybe a little sweat—it *was* a gym, after all.

Looking back, the red flags had been there all along, waving like they were auditioning for a Broadway musical. Anthony wasn't overtly dangerous, but he was manipulative in the most textbook way. A charming oddball with a flair for deception, he had wrapped me in his web without me even realizing it. But here's the thing about webs—they're no match for a sharp knife. And this time, I had one.

Exiting the situation felt like defusing a bomb. I stayed calm, played it cool, and slid out of his life like butter on a hot skillet. No drama, no confrontation—just a clean break. And Anthony? He didn't even flinch. Whether it was my strategic retreat or sheer luck, he let me go without a fight. I'd never been so relieved to cut ties in my life.

But the universe wasn't done with its lesson. A few days later, I had a conversation with the boxing coach at Equinox, someone I'd casually been working with. Over a casual chat, I dropped the Anthony story as a kind of "by the way, watch out for this guy" warning. His response stopped me in my tracks. "Oh, I know," he said. "That's actually why I reached out to you in the first place. I'd heard the rumors and wanted to make sure you were okay. You seemed different than the rest of his *type*."

Cue the shiver down my spine. It was one thing to trust my instincts but to have them confirmed so blatantly was equal parts validating and chilling. Anthony wasn't just a quirky gym buddy—he was the real deal in all the wrong ways. And while nothing terrible had happened, the mere fact that I'd been orbiting someone so toxic was enough to make my skin crawl.

Here's the thing: When you've spent years fighting your way back from heartbreak, trauma, and life's most brutal curveballs, you start to think you've built an impenetrable fortress around yourself. You learn the signs, you set the boundaries, and you assume you're invincible. But life, as it loves to remind us, will always find a way to test you.

This wasn't just about Anthony. It was about *me*. It was about proving to myself that I could spot the signs, trust my gut, and extricate myself before things got messy. It was a reminder that strength isn't just about surviving the storm—it's about knowing when to walk away before it even begins to rain.

And you know what? I'm proud of myself. I didn't just slip out of Anthony's orbit—I shattered the gravitational pull. I didn't tiptoe around his manipulations; I sliced through them with the sharp edge of self-awareness. And while I can't say the experience was fun, it was a damn good reminder of how far I've come.

The universe sent me a narcissistic oddball in a gym full of mirrors, and I passed the test with flying colors. Anthony may have been a small chapter in my story, but the lessons I learned from him? Those are going in bold print. Every knot I untie, every toxic tie I cut, is another step toward the life I'm building—a life where my instincts are sharp, my boundaries are firm, and my sense of self is stronger than ever.

So, here's to trusting your gut, staying grounded, and remembering that even the oddest ducks have something to teach us. As for Anthony? He can keep his web—I'll take my wings, thank you very much.

I didn't just rejoin Gold's Gym—*I reclaimed it.* The Mecca. The one place where I feel most alive, where grit and glory collide beneath a sea of iron and sweat. It wasn't just a gym; it was my sanctuary, my stage, my battlefield.

But it was also *our* gym—mine and Grey Knight's. Every inch of it held echoes of us: stolen glances between sets, silent competitions, and the quiet hum of familiarity. Walking back through those doors felt like stepping into a time capsule where every weight rack, every bench, and every mirror still remembered us.

And yet, the thrill of returning was undeniable. My heart pulsed with the kind of excitement reserved for homecomings and grand openings. This was my playground, my proving ground—and I belonged here as much as the clanging of weights belonged to the air. Memories of *us* didn't matter anymore. This time, it was just *me*.

Every step I took felt like a reclamation, every rep a reminder of my power. Grey Knight may have shared this space with me once, but now? Every mirror reflected only *me*.

Oh, but the universe wasn't done with me yet. No, it decided to crank up the chaos, throw in a Grade-A psychopath, and see just how much I'd learned about boundaries, self-preservation, and, apparently, dealing with madness.

It all started with one of my best friends—let's call him "J" to protect his privacy. J had been in a relationship for about a year, and to call it toxic would be the understatement of the century. Every time he got a moment alone, he'd call me, his voice tight with frustration or pain, venting about the absolute circus his girlfriend had turned his life into. Physical outbursts, alcohol and drug abuse, mind games that could make a chess grandmaster blush—it was all there.

"She's a psychopath," he said once, and I didn't even blink. The evidence was mounting.

As J described her behavior in detail, my protectiveness kicked in hard. I'd been in his shoes before—with Grey Knight—and hearing the similarities lit a fire in me. I used my past as a map, pointing out the red flags and begging him to leave before she completely dismantled his life. "Run, J. *Run like hell*," I'd say, my voice shaking with the kind of passion only someone who's been through the same hell can muster. But no matter how much I tried, I could tell he wasn't ready to leave. Not yet.

Then came that night.

I was enjoying a quiet evening of writing, completely absorbed in my work, when J called. From the moment I heard his voice, I knew something was horribly wrong. He sounded shaken, vulnerable in a way I'd never heard before. He told me she had violently attacked him, leaving him with a concussion, and now he was sitting at the police station, waiting to file a report.

"She beat me up," he said, his voice cracking. "The proof is all over my face."

My heart raced. Anger boiled inside me, so hot I could barely think. How dare someone do this to my friend? How *dare* she? I wanted to scream, but I held it together, focusing instead on guiding him through the next steps. "Tell them everything," I urged. "Show them the proof, all the messages, everything." J was brilliant–he documented everything about her that *screamed* psychopath.

After we hung up, I couldn't sit still. There was no way I was going to let him handle this alone, especially in his condition. I offered to come to support him, and he accepted. Rushing out the door, I drove to the police station, my mind a storm of anger and worry.

When I arrived, I asked to see him, only to be told, "He's in a cell."

Wait. What?

My heart dropped like a stone. J, the victim, was behind bars? I stood there in disbelief, a mix of helplessness and rage bubbling up inside me. I couldn't save him. I couldn't do anything to help, and it crushed me. I drove home in a fog, crying myself to sleep that night.

The next morning, I dragged myself to acting class, but my head was still at the police station. I asked Anne, my teacher, to excuse me, and thankfully she understood. Sitting through the four-hour class was torture; I couldn't focus on anything but J, watching my phone like a hawk for any update.

Finally, the text came: "I'm out."

When he finally called, relief washed over me. But as he explained what had happened, my relief turned to disbelief. His now ex-girlfriend—the same woman who had assaulted him—had called the cops first, filing false allegations. Then, in the ultimate act of gaslighting, she showed up at the station to *ask the officers to drop the charges she'd just filed.*

I mean, how do you even process that level of psychotic behavior?

But the nightmare didn't stop there. A few weeks later, J called with news that made my blood run cold: she'd transferred to my restaurant. Yes, *my* workplace.

"Are you fucking kidding me?" I practically yelled into the phone.

This was the same woman who had once called me from J's phone to scream at me, harass me, and now I'd have to see her at work? The thought made my stomach churn. What if she recognized my voice or pieced together who I was from my contact photo? Psychopaths are nothing if not clever.

I wasn't taking any chances. I filed a statement with HR, laying everything out to protect myself. My boss, bless her, was on my side and adjusted the schedule to ensure our paths never crossed. A few weeks later, she resigned, and I finally breathed a sigh of relief.

But of course, the universe wasn't done yet. J called again, this time to tell me she'd taken his phone, gotten my number, and was convinced I was having a secret romance with him. (Spoiler alert: I wasn't.) She started texting me wild, unhinged messages, but I didn't engage. I blocked her, ignored her, and started carrying a personal alarm, just in case.

It was a nightmare—one I didn't sign up for but somehow got dragged into anyway.

Looking back, though, the experience was oddly healing. It felt like watching a version of my past unfold through someone else's life. J's story mirrored mine in so many ways, and I tried my hardest to help him see the truth before it destroyed him. It wasn't easy—there were moments of tension between us—but in the end, he got out.

And that's what matters most.

As for our friendship? I haven't heard from him in months. But I like to think he's out there, healing, rebuilding himself, finding his way back to peace. And when he's ready, I know he'll come back. Until then, I'll carry this lesson with me: even in the chaos, even when life pulls you into someone else's storm, you have the power to protect yourself, to stay grounded, and to walk away stronger than before.

Not long after that hurricane tore through my life, leaving its chaotic aftermath in my heart, another storm gathered on the horizon. This time, the turbulence wasn't born of romance or personal heartbreak—it was conjured by the unlikeliest source: the *"Powerpuff Girls."* What began as an unexpected whirlwind of camaraderie and sisterhood unraveled into a soap opera I couldn't have scripted if I tried.

I won't bore you with the gritty details—there's enough drama in the world—but let's just say accusations were hurled like confetti at a messy party, and I found myself dodging their sharp edges. They bullied me, questioned my intentions, and stirred a pot that boiled over before I even realized the heat had been turned up. Suddenly, my emotional strength felt like it was hanging on by a thread. I was caught in the nonsensical tides of "she said, she said," where no one was entirely innocent, yet everyone carried a torch of righteousness.

The twist? These weren't just acquaintances or fleeting companions. These were my people. My *only* female best friends at the time. Two women I loved fiercely and uniquely, each with her own vibrant personality, forming a trio that felt like magic. Together, we were unstoppable—or so I thought. So, when the cracks began to show, it felt personal. No—it felt *surgical.* These weren't just friendships; they were lifelines, and losing them carved out a deeper wound than I'd like to admit.

The drama came and went in the blink of an eye, but its impact lingered. Our friendships weren't repaired. Instead, they quietly dissolved into memories I replayed over and over, trying to figure out where it all went wrong. Eventually, I made peace with the idea that maybe these relationships were never meant to last forever. Maybe they were the kind of friendships that burn bright and fast, teaching you lessons you didn't know you needed before they fizzle out.

That's the thing about healing—it rewires your lens on life. When the dust settles, you start to see things differently. Those two women taught me so much about the beauty and power of female friendship. They showed me how much I crave it, and how deeply I value the ability to lean on someone who just *gets* me. And even though our time together ended, I came away with a clearer sense of what I need and deserve in my relationships.

But make no mistake—healing isn't a graceful waltz through enlightenment. It's ugly. Messy. Painful. I grieved those friendships deeply. First, there was "J," my best friend, who vanished into the ether, leaving a hole in my life. Then came the "Powerpuff Girls" saga, and suddenly, I felt like the universe was stripping me bare, peeling away every layer of companionship I'd invested in and built.

Yet, as painful as it was, it forced me to confront the truth: not every relationship is meant to last. Not every bond is built to withstand the test of time. And sometimes, walking away isn't a failure—it's an act of self-preservation. I began to let other relationships fall away, too, relationships that felt lopsided or unreciprocated. Because here's the thing: I've learned to value *me*. I've taught myself to love myself, flaws and all. And when you know your worth, you stop settling for breadcrumbs.

I've become ruthless in the best way. If someone takes my kindness, my loyalty, or my effort for granted, I won't argue. I won't scream or beg for change. I'll simply pack my bags and leave. Not in anger, but in quiet, unshakable certainty. If you can't meet me halfway, you're not coming along for the ride. Period.

Here's the beauty of that realization: It's made me a woman who stands alone, tall and unafraid. A woman with no friends or a very small circle isn't lonely—she's liberated. My confidence doesn't come from the number of people I surround myself with; it comes from within. I don't need an entourage to feel valued. I've learned that quality will always trump quantity. Every. Single. Time.

I'm not here for fake friendships or drama disguised as connection. I've walked away from the noise, from the betrayal, from the superficial nonsense. And in doing so, I've found peace. I've created a life that feels serene and grounded, a life where I don't need to perform or compete for approval.

The friends I do hold close now? They're rare treasures. They've weathered storms with me, earned my trust, and proven their loyalty in ways words can't capture. I'd rather have one of those friends than a hundred whose loyalty only exists in sunny weather. And if that means standing alone, so be it. Because I've realized something beautiful in this journey: standing alone doesn't mean you're lonely. It means you're free.

The darkest chapters of my life weren't just painful—they were transformative. They cracked me wide open, shattered everything I thought I knew about myself, and then demanded I rebuild. And I did. Brick by agonizing brick. What I didn't realize at the time was that those cracks were the birthplace of my strongest self. It turns out, the soul shines brightest when it's forged in fire.

It's funny—my dad always used to say, "Love yourself. You are all you have." Back then, it felt like a cold, distant truth, like being told to tread water in the middle of an ocean. Now? It's my mantra. Because he was right. When the dust settles, when the people you leaned on have vanished, you realize you've been your own lifeboat all along. I've embraced that truth, and it's set me free.

For years, I confused solitude with loneliness. I clung to people, seeking validation, desperate to fill a void I didn't understand. But now, solitude isn't something I fear—it's something I crave. My own company is a treasure. I've fallen deeply, wildly, unapologetically in love with myself, flaws and all. The traumas that once felt like anchors dragging me under have become treasures I carry proudly. They're the glittering proof of everything I've endured—and everything I've overcome.

Reframing those traumas *as gifts* wasn't easy, though. Let's be real: No one wants to unwrap heartbreak, betrayal, or rejection. But I've realized they were never there to break me—they were there to shape me. Without those moments, I wouldn't be the fiercely resilient, unapologetically powerful woman I am today. Those experiences gave me the wisdom I could never have learned from a self-help book or a TED Talk. They handed me a mirror and forced me to confront every part of myself—the good, the bad, and the parts I was too scared to look at before.

The toxic talk, the chaos, the doubt—it all drove me back to my soul. And when I say I've reconnected with myself, I mean it in the deepest, most profound way. I dove headfirst into psychology, spirituality, and everything in between. I learned how to listen to that quiet, unwavering voice inside me. The one that whispers, *You are enough.* The one that reminds me that my peace is priceless.

And let me tell you, it's dangerous to be this healed. Dangerous in the best way. Because now? No one can drag me back into the unhealed version of myself. You could try, but you'd fail. I've worked *so* hard to climb out of the trenches of my trauma, to battle my demons, and to become the best, strongest, most radiant version of myself. I'm not about to let anyone undo that work. If you want to be in my life, you better have something real to offer. Your presence needs to *add* to my peace because—spoiler alert—my peace is your competition. Not another person. Not some external source. Just me, sitting in my own calm, loving my own company.

I don't entertain manipulation anymore. I see through the pity parties, the emotional bait, the guilt trips. You think throwing your trauma at my feet will make me bend? Think again. I'm not cold—I'm compassionate—but that compassion starts with me. I've learned to recognize when someone's pain is a tool for control, and I won't fall for it. Your trauma is not a free pass to disrupt my sanctuary.

That's the thing about boundaries: They're not walls to keep people out; they're gates to protect what's sacred. And what's sacred to me is my peace, my joy, my growth. I've worked too damn hard to let anyone trample over that. If you think I'll compromise my boundaries for your convenience, you don't know me. My peace isn't negotiable.

The fear of rejection? Gone. The desperation for approval? Evaporated. The lies I used to tell myself—that my worth was tied to someone else's happiness—have been rewritten. I'm the author of my story now, and I refuse to give anyone the pen.

The result? A woman who is dangerous in her clarity. Dangerous in her strength. Dangerous because she knows her worth and will not lower herself to match anyone else's dysfunction. I don't need a crowd to feel validated. I don't need a partner to feel whole. I've built something far better than any fleeting relationship—I've built a fortress of peace within myself, and it's impenetrable.

So, if you want to be in my life, you better bring something extraordinary to the table. Your presence has to be better than my solitude, because here's the truth: I will never sacrifice my peace for someone else's chaos again. Standing alone doesn't make me lonely—it makes me free. And freedom? Freedom is the ultimate flex.

Chapter 27

Spiritual Wi-Fi

Another pearl of wisdom Marshall Faulk gifted me was his philosophy on the five "C's" of life—the kinds of people you need in your corner. *The Comforter, The Confronter, The Challenger, The Counselor, and The Celebrator.* At first, it sounded like a motivational poster waiting to happen, but as I let it sink in, I realized it wasn't just advice—it was alchemy. These roles weren't just about other people; they were invitations to reflect on the dynamics I was cultivating in my life. It was like holding a mirror up to my relationships and seeing them with fresh eyes. And boy, some of those reflections were as beautiful as a sunrise; others, well… let's just say they needed some polishing.

I wove this newfound perspective into the patchwork of what I'd learned from spirituality, psychology, and good ol' life lessons. It was a game-changer. Friendship stopped being a word I threw around casually and became something I revered. It's funny how life works, though. Just when I started grasping the true meaning of connection, I lost three people who had been pillars in my world. The ache was raw, a jagged edge in my heart. There's still a little light of hope flickering for J to come back into my orbit one day, but even if that doesn't happen, those losses carved space in me for growth and new doors.

Here's the truth about healing—it's not a fairy tale with a neat "happily ever after." It's more like climbing a spiral staircase. Just when you think you're reaching the top, you realize there's another turn, another step, another challenge. The universe has a wicked sense of humor, doesn't it? It'll throw a curveball at you the moment you think you've mastered the game. And that's where the magic lies: Healing isn't about "getting over" things; it's about weaving those lessons into the fabric of who you are.

Of course, change didn't come without its growing pains. There were disagreements, friction, and even moments where it felt like friendships might crumble under the pressure of my evolution. But something incredible happened: we faced the hard stuff together. We talked, really talked, and worked through it like adults who cared more about the bond than the bickering. And when we did, those friendships became stronger than ever— a testament to the sacredness of connection when nurtured with honesty and love.

Now, I cherish my relationships with the reverence they deserve. I've learned to celebrate the kaleidoscope of colors people bring into my life— their brilliance, their shadows, and everything in between. Because life isn't about perfection; it's about depth. And if you're lucky, you'll find people who make your soul feel at home, no matter how messy the journey gets.

So, here I am—scarred, healed, growing, and still throwing confetti wherever I go. Life is wild and unpredictable, but it's also breathtakingly beautiful when you walk through it with an open heart, a steady mind, and a dash of glittery chaos.

As I moved forward, I found myself naturally attuned to the energy of others. It wasn't something I consciously decided to do—it just happened, like flipping a switch I didn't even know was there. I started noticing how people made me feel, how their presence either lit me up or drained me dry. With every step deeper into my healing journey, my perspective shifted. I rewired my brain in ways that left me both amazed and, at times, overwhelmed. Blessings, especially those wrapped in good people, became a little harder to accept. Maybe it's because when you start seeing the world for what it truly is, it's impossible to unsee. The good shines brighter, yes, but so do the shadows.

Let me be blunt—I've run out of patience for drama, idiocy, and fakery. My standards are sky-high now, a direct result of the soul-deep work I've done. And while that's something to celebrate, it also means I've embraced solitude in ways I never expected. My inner circle has become less of a crowd and more of a sacred space—a private garden I fiercely protect. I'll hold space for those who meet me where I'm at, but I've got no room for sinkers. You know the type—people who drag you down with their chaos, negativity, or lack of self-awareness. I just can't. Life is too short to keep pretending to swim with anchors tied to your ankles.

And here's the thing: I can't fake it anymore, even if I wanted to. The days of grinning and bearing it are behind me. If someone lacks empathy, if they spin lies like cotton candy or can't see the difference between right and wrong, I sense it instantly. It's like my intuition got a software upgrade, and now I catch onto lies and games before they've even fully formed. This ability feels like both a superpower and a curse. On the one hand, I'm grateful—it saves me from a lot of nonsense. But on the other hand, it's made my world a little lonelier. True friendships are rare when you see people with crystal-clear clarity.

Don't get me wrong—I'm not judgmental. If anything, I respect the hell out of where people are on their own journeys. Healing isn't linear, and everyone's timeline is different. But once you've done the work yourself—once you've clawed your way through the muck and found your light—it changes you. You start noticing who's still wandering in their shadows, and though you wish them well, you can't dim your shine just to make them comfortable. It's not arrogance; it's self-preservation.

The truth is, I've always felt like I didn't belong. Like I was the piece of the puzzle that never quite fit. Now, I see that standing apart isn't a weakness; it's a power. With everything I've been through, every wild twist and turn of my life, I've become fearless. Stronger than ever, mentally and emotionally. I don't crave the crowd. I don't need to blend in. Instead, I embrace the boldness of standing out, of carving my own unique path.

It's funny how life chisels you, isn't it? Like a sculptor with a hammer and chisel, it chips away at the parts of you that no longer serve. Every heartbreak, every setback, every hard-earned victory has shaped me into someone who walks taller, thinks sharper, and feels deeper. And yes, it's isolating at times. But solitude, I've learned, isn't emptiness. It's space. Space to grow, to breathe, to bloom into the kind of person who no longer fears standing alone.

And so, I stand—unapologetic and unshakable. My crazy, chaotic, beautiful life has turned me into a person who can weather any storm and laugh in its face. My energy is sacred, my time is precious, and my circle is tiny but mighty. I don't need to fit in when I was born to stand out. And that, my friend, is freedom—glorious, unfiltered freedom. It's not just about surviving life; it's about thriving in its messiest, most magnificent moments.

Acting this year has been nothing short of a whirlwind—thrilling, exhausting, and oddly poetic as the days inch closer to July. The deeper I dive into my craft, the more challenging it becomes, like peeling back layers of myself I didn't even know were there. It's exhilarating, yes, but also a little terrifying. And yet, the universe has this wild way of throwing me exactly what I need, even when I'm not ready for it.

Take one of my recent class projects: a scene from the 1960s play *The Hustler*. I was cast as Sarah, the girlfriend of Eddie, the pool hustler himself. On the surface, it was just another assignment—a chance to stretch my acting muscles. But the second I started digging into the relationship between Sarah and Eddie, it hit me like a freight train. Their dynamic? It was *too* familiar, almost like a mirror reflecting the tumultuous relationship I had with Grey Knight.

Here's where it gets even crazier: at the same time I was embodying Sarah's heartbreak in class, I was pouring my own pain into the pages of my book, writing about the abuse I'd lived through with Grey Knight. Talk about emotional whiplash. Every rehearsal felt like reopening old wounds, while every writing session felt like stitching them back together. It was a dizzying dance between the past and the present, art and reality. Some days, I felt like I was drowning in it all. But somehow, I kept going, leaning into the chaos instead of running from it.

And then there's Anne—my acting coach and, quite possibly, a modern-day sorceress. She has this uncanny ability to assign scenes that resonate so deeply with her students that it's almost spooky. I mean, come on—what are the odds she'd hand me *this* scene at *this* exact moment in my life? My classmates and I joke that she has a sixth sense, like she's channeling some cosmic force to push us toward the lessons we need to learn. Magic or not, it's one of the reasons I've grown so much as an actor this year.

Outside of class, life has been equally electric. Auditions are rolling in, and commercial bookings are stacking up. But here's the twist: The real star of the show this year isn't me—it's my four-legged diva, Mocha. Yep, my baby girl has decided to take Hollywood by storm, and honestly, I'm just here to carry her treats, cheer her on, and train her from take to take.

It all started when we booked a few commercials together through one studio. Next thing I know, the director is obsessed with her—like full-on fanboy status—and now she's their go-to for all things dog-related. Watching her on set is pure magic. She hits her marks like a seasoned pro, soaking up the attention and wagging her tail like she knows she's the main character. And at the end of the day, she crashes in the car, completely wiped out, surrounded by whatever gourmet treats she's been spoiled with that day. It's honestly the cutest thing ever.

Some days, Mocha gets booked without me, and I can't help but laugh. My dog is officially out-earning me, and I'm not even mad about it. If anything, it feels like she's paying me back for all those bougie Farmer's Dog meals and her ever-expanding toy collection. It's a little humbling when your dog becomes the breadwinner, but hey, life's full of surprises, right?

What I love most, though, is sharing those on-set moments with her. We're a team, and watching her thrive in her spotlight is one of the greatest joys of my life. It's funny how life works—how the universe sneaks in these unexpected blessings, like a nudge reminding you that joy can coexist with the grind. Between Mocha's bookings and my own acting projects, we've built this quirky little partnership. She's the diva, I'm the proud stage mom, and together, we're carving out our own version of success.

Meanwhile, I'm still pouring my heart into this book, channeling all the highs and lows, the triumphs and tears, into something that feels raw and real. Balancing writing, acting, and Mocha's growing stardom is a circus, but it's *our* circus, and I wouldn't trade it for anything. Life right now is a wild, chaotic, beautiful ride, and as long as I've got my craft, my words, and my furry co-star by my side, I know I'm exactly where I'm meant to be.

This year, I set my sights on another bucket list adventure: the Tough Mudder. I'd heard stories—mud-soaked warriors trudging through ten miles of chaos, fifteen obstacles testing their limits, the kind of challenge that's equal parts insane and exhilarating. Naturally, I thought, *Sign me up!* Originally, the plan was to tackle it with one of the "Powerpuff Girls," one of my closest friends. But by the time race day rolled around, our friendship had already sunk into the metaphorical mud. So, there we were at the starting line—me with my game face on, her with… well, awkward vibes. The tension was a little thick, but I refused to let it derail me. This was *my* journey, and I was about to own it.

The morning air in the San Bernardino mountains was a brisk 50 degrees, biting enough to make you question your life choices but energizing enough to keep you moving. The starting point was a mess of mud and anticipation, and as the whistle blew, I surged forward. This wasn't just a race—it was a test, a warrior's rite of passage, and I was ready to conquer it.

Did I prepare? Ha! That's cute. My training was just my regular gym routine—weights, strength training, and cardio avoidance like it was a bad ex. Yet, as I took off, something primal awoke inside me. It was like a hidden beast had been waiting for this exact moment. I shot out of the crowd so fast it was just me and two others leading the pack, mud flying in our wake. I didn't stop, didn't look back, and, frankly, I didn't even recognize myself. By mile three, I'd caught up to and started passing the group ahead of mine. Who was this untamed, unstoppable version of me? I had no clue, but I liked her.

The trail was unforgiving—steep, slippery, and downright relentless. Forget the picturesque hiking paths of LA. These were mountains with a grudge. And then the obstacles began. First up, a classic: army crawling under barbed wire through thick, cold mud. Glamorous? Not even a little. Tough? Not so much. Empowering? Yeah, didn't get hooked! Then came the uphill battle—literally—a steep, muddy incline covered with a heavy net that pinned me down. I had to wait for someone to catch up so we could strategize our escape. It was a humbling reminder: sometimes, even warriors need allies.

That theme carried through the course. At one point, we had to navigate ten-foot muddy pits filled with freezing water. The only way out? Team up with strangers. Boost them up, cheerleader style, and then scramble up yourself with a helping hand from whoever was already at the top. Rinse and repeat—six grueling times. It was messy, chaotic, and weirdly heartwarming.

One of the wildest challenges was the human pyramid. Picture this: a diagonal, 15-foot slippery wall, and the only way to conquer it is by stacking bodies on bodies. Watching others try—and repeatedly fail—was both hilarious and nerve-wracking. When my turn came, I somehow channeled my inner Spider-Man, climbing over the pile of human limbs with surprising grace. At the top, I stayed to lend a hand to those struggling below, because if this course taught me anything, it's that we rise by lifting others—literally.

And then there was the water. Oh, the *water*. Every few obstacles seemed to involve plunging into ice-cold pools that felt like tiny Arctic hells. One particular obstacle required crawling on your stomach to avoid dangling electric wires above the water. It was so cold that my body went into full-on convulsions, shaking like I'd been tossed into a freezer. By the halfway mark, I was waddling like a penguin, my legs threatening to give out. At one point, I was so delirious a kind stranger had to redirect me back to the course. Still, I pressed on. Giving up was not an option.

That said, there was one obstacle I skipped: the infamous ice bath. When I saw it looming near the end of the course, my body screamed *nope*. I was already on the edge, shivering uncontrollably, and I knew diving into that icy abyss might just be the end of me. Sometimes, survival means knowing your limits, and that was mine.

When I finally crossed the finish line, it wasn't with a triumphant sprint but a wobbly, bruised, penguin-like shuffle. Three and a half hours, over 1,500 calories burned, elbows and knees decorated with fresh battle scars, but no blood spilled nor electrocutions—what a win. The sense of accomplishment was overwhelming. I'd done it. By myself. For myself.

The Tough Mudder wasn't just a physical challenge; it was a mental and emotional reckoning. It tested every ounce of my grit, resilience, and determination. It was messy, brutal, and beautiful all at once. And as I stood there, mud-caked and exhausted, I realized this wasn't just about crossing the finish line. It was about proving to myself that I could face the messy, steep, cold, chaotic obstacles of life and come out stronger. That's the real victory.

As my writing journey deepened, I finally reached the chapter I had been both dreading and anticipating: the moment heroin crept into my life. Reliving the tumultuous love story with Grey Knight—if you call it *true* love—had already tested every ounce of my emotional strength. Writing about his monstrous behavior was like trying to tame a hurricane. But this? This was the storm's eye. Writing about heroin addiction felt like peeling back the final, raw layer of skin to expose a wound that had barely begun to heal.

The hardest part wasn't just the emotions; it was the silence of my own mind. Two years of my life—two of the darkest, most chaotic years—had vanished from my memory. Entire chapters gone, as if someone had taken an eraser to my history. Trauma does that, I suppose. Maybe my subconscious locked those memories away for safekeeping, or maybe it decided I was better off without them. Either way, the blank spaces were maddening. How could I write the story of my addiction when I didn't even have the words to describe it?

And yet, the universe, with its twisted sense of timing, handed me a gift wrapped in pain: the surge of PTSD. Memories I thought were buried forever came flooding back, ugly and relentless. It was brutal, but also exactly what I needed to break through the fog. My saving grace in this emotional excavation? Music. I curated a playlist of songs that had been the soundtrack to my life in Wisconsin during the peak of my addiction. These were songs I had avoided for years, their opening notes capable of triggering an avalanche of heartache and grief. But now, I pressed play and let them take me back.

Walking Mocha became my ritual. I'd lace up my shoes, pop in my earbuds, and blast that playlist as we made our way through the neighborhood. With every step, the music tugged at the locked doors of my subconscious, coaxing the memories out. The lyrics, the melodies—they were like breadcrumbs leading me through the labyrinth of my past. It worked, but it was devastating. Each walk felt like stepping onto a battlefield, with emotions I thought I'd buried rising to meet me.

The moments before heroin were already a storm of confusion and heartbreak. But writing about the drug itself? That was something else entirely. It wasn't just painful; it was surreal. Yet, as I sat down to write about the introduction of heroin into my life, a strange calm settled over me. For the first time in this entire process, I felt... content. Not happy, not unbothered, but at peace. Writing about everything else had been like ripping open old wounds, but this felt different—like facing a monster I had already defeated. I only managed to write a little that day, but it was a start.

The tools I gained from acting class, especially in emotional preparation, became my quiet superpower in writing. Learning to flip emotions on and off like a stage light didn't just stay on the set—it rooted itself deep in my subconscious.

When I hit the hardest stretch of the writing process, I didn't crumble. I leaned in, channeling each emotion as if it were a role to play. Grief, rage, hope—they weren't obstacles; they were cast members. I embodied them fully, then called "cut" when the scene was done. What once felt like an uncontrollable flood of feelings became a symphony I could conduct. Acting didn't just teach me how to perform—it taught me how to master my own heart on the page.

Then came the next day—the pink moon, the new moon. A celestial event is said to stir up trauma while offering the promise of renewal. If that wasn't a cosmic metaphor for what I was going through, I didn't know what was. I woke up feeling it—a tightness in my chest, the unmistakable edge of a panic attack creeping in. It was like being dragged under by a wave, gasping for air while the ocean refused to let go. I thought I was past this. I thought panic attacks were ghosts I'd already exorcised. But here they were again, clawing at me.

That day, I surrendered completely. I canceled every plan, shut out the world, and let myself unravel. The tears came in uncontrollable waves, the kind that leave you raw and empty, but also strangely lighter. It was terrifying, suffocating. I honestly didn't think I'd make it through the day without falling apart completely. But somehow, I did.

When the chokehold of a panic attack started to tighten, I reached for a familiar remedy—Troy. He had a way of cutting through the suffocating fog, turning my spiraling body into a playground of distraction. Laughter, wit, mischief—he wielded them like weapons, and for a while, they worked. But this time, his advice hit differently.

"Turn the pain into pleasure," he said, his voice dripping with suggestion. Bold? Absolutely. Unorthodox? Without question. But the idea rooted itself in my mind, seductive in its simplicity. If pain could be rewritten, why not give it a different ending?

Enter Dameon. Pediatric doctor by day, master of playful seduction by night. Medical expertise *and* romantic finesse? He was the obvious choice. One call was all it took. No questions, no delays—he was at my door like a superhero in scrubs, ready to save the day.

Dameon had a way of commanding a room, his presence both grounding and electric. His playful charm softened the edges of my panic, his steady hands pulling me back from the ledge without me even realizing it. His words, his touch, his teasing grin—all of it worked in perfect harmony. The suffocation loosened, the ache dulled, and suddenly, I wasn't drowning anymore. Not fully healed, but no longer gasping for air.

Sometimes, relief doesn't come in the form of stillness. Sometimes, it's wild and unorthodox—a dance with fire instead of a retreat from it. And if Dameon was leading? I wasn't about to miss a single step.

The next morning, something shifted. The storm had passed, and in its wake, there was a fragile stillness—a sense that maybe, just maybe, the worst was behind me. The pink moon had done its work, forcing me to face the pain so I could begin anew. It wasn't a grand, cinematic transformation, but it was enough. A flicker of hope, a whisper of resilience.

Months later, I can look back on that day with gratitude, as strange as it sounds. That panic attack episode? It was the last one. The pink moon, with all its chaos and clarity, marked the end of one chapter and the beginning of another. Writing about heroin, facing the memories, enduring the tidal wave of emotions—it was all part of the journey. It reminded me that healing is *far* from linear. It's messy, it's relentless, and it's damn hard. But sometimes, you have to walk through the fire to emerge stronger. And for the first time in a long time, I felt ready to keep walking. Ready to face whatever was next. Ready to write the rest of my story.

They say when one door closes, another opens. I've always clung to that idea like a lifeline, hoping it would soften the ache of losing people I once held close. Over time, though, I realized that the beauty of life isn't just in the doors that open—it's in the spaces in between. The quiet, messy moments when things fall apart, leaving you raw and vulnerable, but also wide open to receive new blessings. I stopped resisting the crumbling and embraced it instead. And just when I thought I'd settled into this quieter chapter, the universe surprised me, as it always does, in the form of an ordinary day at work.

It started so simply, the kind of shift that blended into a blur of tables and orders. My first table of the day was two guys around my age. Nothing unusual. Or so I thought. But as I approached, one of them caught my attention—his energy was like a gravitational pull. His name was Rich, and let me tell you, the man was pure charisma wrapped in a human form. Outgoing, smile stamped on his face, and unapologetically loud, Rich radiated a kind of joy that you couldn't ignore even if you tried. He was planning a bachelor party for his best friend, scribbling notes on the back of a menu while talking a mile a minute.

The more I interacted with their table, the more drawn in I felt. Rich's voice carried across the restaurant, an enthusiastic, booming energy that somehow didn't feel overbearing but magnetic. There was something about him—something I couldn't quite put my finger on. Then, in the middle of one of our casual exchanges, he dropped a bombshell: He'd had a *near-death experience*.

It was like my soul jolted awake. My breath caught, and before I could stop myself, I blurted out, "Me too!" I hadn't met anyone who had crossed that line between life and whatever lies beyond, and my curiosity flared like wildfire. We dove into it immediately, sharing bits and pieces of our experiences. He spoke with such openness, and his story lit a spark in me I hadn't felt in a long time. Somehow, the conversation meandered into astrology, moon phases, and healing—a perfect cosmic trifecta. The recent pink moon, in particular, had been heavy on my mind. I told him about how I'd spent that day wrestling with a near-panic attack, and to my surprise, he didn't just listen—he got it. He *really* got it.

There was a connection between us I couldn't ignore, something deeper than just small talk over a meal. It felt as if the universe had orchestrated this meeting, aligning the stars just so. By the end of their meal, I knew I couldn't leave it there. We exchanged contacts, and within a week, plans were made to meet again and share our stories properly.

When the day came, I brought Mocha along. She's my little anchor, my furry partner in all things new and intimidating. We met at a restaurant, and from the moment we sat down, the conversation was electric. Rich opened up about his near-death experience, and I was utterly captivated. He described floating toward a bright light, weightless and free, only to wake up in his own body with a renewed determination to change his life. At the time, he was overweight and unhealthy, but that moment sparked something in him. He committed to turning it all around, and his transformation wasn't just personal—it became *his purpose*.

Rich's journey led to the creation of his meal-prep business, Sugarfree Rich. The meals he used to lose weight became the cornerstone of his thriving company, helping others on their health journeys. Now, five years in, he's a success story that feels straight out of a movie—his life a testament to resilience, purpose, and universal alignment. Listening to him, I couldn't help but feel in awe. His story wasn't just inspiring; it was magical. The way the universe seemed to guide him, placing the right opportunities in his path, was nothing short of miraculous.

When it was my turn to share, I laid it all out. The near-death experiences, the heartbreak, the healing, the writing of this very book—it all poured out. And the way he listened, with genuine interest and understanding, was unlike anything I'd experienced. There's something indescribable about connecting with someone who *gets it*, not just on a surface level but deep down, in the marrow of their being.

We talked for hours, well past the restaurant's closing time, completely lost in each other's stories. It wasn't just a conversation; it was a moment suspended in time, a rare connection that felt divinely orchestrated. By the end of the night, I didn't feel like I'd made a friend. It was something much bigger than that. It was as if we'd known each other in another life, as if the universe had conspired to cross our paths for a reason.

Rich didn't just open a door for me that day—he shattered a wall I didn't even know I'd built. His story, his energy, his presence—all of it reminded me of the beauty of connection, the kind that transcends the ordinary. And for the first time in a long time, I felt like I wasn't walking this journey alone.

Just as one door quietly creaked shut—the slow, inevitable fade of my friendship with the "Powerpuff Girls"—another one swung open. And through it walked Aire. Yes, like a breath of fresh air, and trust me, I needed one.

Let's rewind for a second. She drifted into my life right around the time I started this book, as if the universe had tagged her in like a much-needed plot twist. How did we meet? Well, she reached out to me—two strangers connected by the shared chaos of becoming first-time authors in 100 Voices of Women. We were both blindly stumbling through this literary battlefield, grappling with the art of storytelling while trying to silence the ever-lurking imposter syndrome.

I welcomed the connection with open arms. Writing a book is an untamed beast, and Aire and I quickly realized we were in the same arena, armed with nothing but our words and a shared determination not to let it devour us. We became each other's accountability partners, trading doubts for pep talks and long-winded voice notes for deep Saturday writing sessions. Our battlefield? A little hidden-gem coffee shop market—a sanctuary tucked away from the noise of the world. Our oasis.

There, between the aroma of fresh espresso and the sound of keys clicking against our laptops, we wrote, unraveled, and rebuilt. We weren't just writing books; we were writing ourselves into existence—one vulnerable, soul-baring word at a time.

As I approached the final chapters of writing about my heroin addiction, I felt like I was trudging through emotional quicksand. Every word, every memory, was like peeling back layers of my soul, only to find fresh wounds waiting underneath. It was brutal, but it was also necessary—part of the catharsis I'd promised myself when I set out on this journey.

Writing about heroin addiction wasn't just heavy—it was *soul-crushing*. Reliving the darkest parts of my life—the addiction, the chaos, the fallout— had drained every ounce of my energy. Digging for details, trying to remember the moments my brain had mercifully erased, felt like running a marathon on a broken leg. My subconscious waved the white flag before I even realized a battle had begun. Suddenly, I was in full shutdown mode. Not a quick nap, not a lazy day, but a complete and utter *power down*. One month bled into the next, and before I knew it, six weeks had passed. At first, I didn't understand. Why was I so drained? Why did my energy vanish like smoke after a fire? I wasn't just tired—I was *depleted*. Bone-deep exhaustion that no amount of sleep could fix.

Then, like a flicker of light in a dark tunnel, the clarity hit me. My mind had been wading through megaloads of trauma, reliving it all on the page. Every word I wrote carved through old wounds I thought had scarred over. My body knew what my mind refused to admit: I needed *rest*. Real, sacred, unbothered rest.

Giving myself permission to slow down felt unnatural—like asking the Energizer Bunny to just *sit still for a second*. But grace found me. I stopped fighting the stillness and let it wash over me. I realized that rest wasn't laziness. It was *recovery*. It was *necessary*. My body wasn't betraying me—it was *saving me*. Sometimes, the bravest thing you can do is *stop moving*.

The process was so draining that by the time my birthday crept closer, I could feel my spirit curling inward. The thought of celebrating felt foreign, almost laughable. For the first time ever, I didn't want to celebrate my birthday. Not a party, not a dinner, not even a casual toast with friends. I even ignored calls from my closest circle, needing silence more than connection. All I wanted was to retreat into solitude, to gather the pieces of myself that had scattered across the pages of my book.

And yet, the universe had its own plans. Two unexpected moments gave my quiet birthday a glimmer of light. The first was a surprise from Ezekiel, who managed to gift me something I'd been wanting for weeks: a tattoo. With his endless connections in the tattoo world, he somehow scored me a complimentary session with a talented artist. I'd had the phrase *"with Grace"* on my mind for a long time, a mantra that had carried me through the turbulence of life lately. In soft teal ink, those words now sit on the inside of my right forearm—a permanent reminder to give myself grace through every hardship, every misstep, every climb back to the surface. The moment the tattoo was finished, I felt a quiet kind of peace, like I'd etched my own survival story into my skin.

The second surprise came in the form of Halle, my adopted little sister in spirit. She flew in the weekend before my birthday, completely unprompted, to spend time with me. At first, I wasn't sure I had the energy to host anyone. I was still raw from the emotional toll of writing, and having someone in my space felt daunting. But the second she walked through the door, it was as if she'd brought sunshine with her. Halle's infectious, bubbly energy was the exact medicine my soul needed.

That weekend turned into a whirlwind of joy and silliness. We laughed until our stomachs hurt, talked up ridiculous accents, and soaked up the sun at the beach. One of the highlights was electric surfboarding in Malibu with Isaiah and Rich. At one point, I was so laser-focused on chasing dolphins that I didn't even notice I'd cut my toe on the board. Leave it to Halle to swoop in like the nurturing little sister she is, patching me up without a second thought. She's the sister I never had but always wished for, and every moment with her felt like rediscovering a part of myself I thought I'd lost. Her visit wasn't planned as a birthday celebration, but it turned out to be exactly what I needed—unfiltered, uncomplicated joy.

On my actual birthday, I honored my need for quiet. It wasn't sadness or bitterness—it was peace. Just me and Mocha, my forever companion, heading to my favorite secret dog beach near Ventura. Watching her run wild, her tail wagging like she'd just won the lottery, filled me with a rare kind of contentment. That little stretch of sand has always felt sacred to me, and this year, it felt even more so. There, under the open sky, I let the ocean waves carry away the weight of the past year.

Two weeks later, it was time to celebrate Mocha's birthday—her big day that always felt more exciting than my own. As is tradition, I stacked nine burger patties from In-N-Out for her, one for each year of her incredible life. Watching her devour her "cake" with pure, unfiltered glee made me laugh out loud, the kind of belly laugh that shakes loose all the heaviness you didn't know you were holding. Each year, I snap a picture of her next to her towering burger stack, a tradition that's become one of my favorite rituals.

This year's birthday season wasn't about grand plans or flashy celebrations. It was about stillness, grace, and the quiet miracles of the people and moments that found me when I needed them most. From the ink on my arm that whispers reminders of resilience to Halle's luminous spirit reviving my joy, to Mocha's endless love reminding me of life's simplest pleasures, this year wasn't what I expected—but it was exactly what I needed. And isn't that the most beautiful kind of gift?

Rich and I didn't just become friends—we collided, like two stars drawn together by some unspoken force, our connection bursting to life with an intensity I can only describe as *cosmic*. From the moment we started hanging out, it was clear this wasn't an ordinary friendship. We didn't need extravagant plans or distractions; all it took was a drive through the city or a walk under the stars. Our conversations flowed like a river, deep and endless, to the point where we didn't even bother turning on music in the car. Why would we? The sound of our laughter and the cadence of our words were a soundtrack enough.

It felt like our souls recognized each other from another life, picking up right where they'd left off. And what struck me most was how effortlessly Rich made me feel seen—truly, deeply *understood*. That's a rare gift in this world, one I'd spent most of my life searching for. With him, it wasn't something I had to explain or justify. He just *got* me. And the craziest part? I got him, too. This mutual understanding became the foundation of something far more precious than I'd anticipated.

Our friendship blossomed with a kind of ease that felt like fate. It wasn't just about the time we spent together—it was the energy we created when we did. Both of us share a deep spirituality and an appreciation for astrology, numerology, and the subtle ways the universe speaks to us. It wasn't long before we started treating the moon like an old friend, sitting under its glow as if it were lighting our path. One night, we popped open a bottle of champagne right there under the stars, toasting to our little victories and the unshakable belief that we were on the right track.

Rich's energy was unlike anyone I'd ever met. He's deeply authentic and connected to his soul in a way that feels almost otherworldly. It's impossible not to be inspired by him. He is, without a doubt, one of the rarest and most beautiful souls I've ever encountered. And while I treasure his wisdom and authenticity, it's his laughter that has a magic all its own. When Rich laughs, it's contagious—one of those full-bodied, face-crinkling, can't-breathe kinds of laughs. And when he snorts? Forget it. Game over. We're both doubled over, clutching our stomachs, tears streaming down our faces. It's the kind of joy that makes you feel alive.

But our connection wasn't just built on laughter. It was built on dreams. From the beginning, we shared our visions for the future out loud, speaking them into existence with the kind of confidence that only comes from being fully understood. He told me about his Sugarfree Rich meal prep business, a thriving passion project born from his journey to better himself and help others do the same. And I shared my dream for this book, my mission to inspire and heal through my story. Together, we realized we were both on a path to create something meaningful, to make an impact on the world in our own unique ways.

We quietly started calling ourselves superheroes—not in the cape-wearing, world-saving sense, but in the way our near-death experiences had given us a certain spark. It sounds strange, I know, but we both believe those moments on the brink of life and death left us with something extraordinary. A kind of magic that drives us to be bigger, bolder, and braver in everything we do. Most authentic and humbly speaking, of course.

And yet, for all the depth and intensity of our conversations, there's also a lightness to our friendship that feels like a breath of fresh air. We're silly together in a way that's rare for adults. We belly-laugh until it hurts, make up ridiculous sound effects, and celebrate the smallest victories as if they were the biggest milestones. Rich's name might be literal, but it's also fitting—he's the richest friend I've ever had, not because of material wealth, but because of the joy, depth, and inspiration he brings into my life.

He proved that impact isn't measured by time—it's measured by *magnitude*. People can drift through your life for years, barely leaving a ripple. But with him, it was a tidal wave. No slow build, no gradual rise—just an undeniable force crashing into my world, leaving everything brighter, bolder, *bigger*.

It wasn't just rare—it was *revelatory*. Some people sneak into your life quietly, unnoticed, until they're gone. But he? He arrived like a plot twist you never saw coming, the kind that shifts the entire story. Our connection wasn't built on history or longevity—it was built on *truth*. Raw, unfiltered, *immediate truth*. He taught me that it's not the length of the chapter that matters—it's the weight of the words written in it.

In the short time I've known him, he's become so much more than a friend. I see Rich as one of my soulmates—not in a romantic sense, but in the way our spirits seem to have been designed to meet and uplift each other. Soulmates, I've learned, aren't confined to love stories. They're the rare connections that show up in friendships, too, and Rich is one I'll treasure forever. Our bond is a constant reminder of what's possible when two people come together with open hearts, shared dreams, and a whole lot of laughter. It's a connection that feels timeless, and one I'll hold dear for the rest of my life.

Not just Rich—but every gem in my life—holds a sacred place in my heart. It's not just space they occupy; it's a *kingdom* I protect, nourish, and treasure. They're my chosen family, the kind of people who'd show up at 3 a.m. with takeout, no questions asked, and somehow make the world feel a little less chaotic.

It's the qualities I find in my friendships that mean the most. My circle is small but unbreakable. They're not just people I call when things are good. They're the ones I call when everything's gone to hell—and they *always answer*. They're the spice rack of my life, adding flavor, color, and unpredictability to every day. Without them, my world would be grayscale, but with them? It's a feast.

I've been burned before, so when I say I'm selective, I mean it with my *whole chest*. If you're in, you're *in*. And these friends of mine? They're not going anywhere. They're my unshakable, undeniable, ride-or-die family. I'd be nothing without them, and I'm not afraid to admit it. Love isn't about luck— it's about *choice*. I chose them, and they chose me right back.

Many of the closest people in my life are men. Growing up as a daddy's girl, I've always gravitated toward the laid-back, goofy energy they bring. It's not that I don't value friendships with women, but my vibe syncs better with playful banter than with dramatic whispers. Someone once suggested it might be because I'm subconsciously seeking the bond I never had with my brother—a relationship that, for all intents and purposes, doesn't exist. And honestly? They might be right.

Male friendships feel like a breath of fresh air—simple, straightforward, and without the undercurrent of rivalry or intrigue. But don't let my easygoing nature fool you. I run these friendships with the precision of a courtroom judge: no crossed boundaries, no blurred lines. If there's an unspoken crush simmering beneath the surface, I'd rather face it head-on than endure the subtler heartbreak of female friendships gone sour. I've been there: the whispers, the drama, the trust splintering like glass. Never again.

With men, there's a refreshing clarity. Vulnerability feels safer when the stakes aren't laced with ulterior motives or hidden critiques. Sure, the occasional hiccup happens, but I've learned to hold firm to my boundaries. Through these friendships, I've found fragments of the brotherly connection I've always yearned for—a bond I'll forever treasure.

It's not about choosing one gender over another. It's about choosing peace and authenticity. These friendships, and others, bring lightness to my life, a place where I can laugh, be vulnerable, and exist without pretense. And honestly? That's the kind of connection worth holding onto.

What I've come to realize is that Marshall Faulk's five C's of life aren't set in stone—they're more like a game of musical chairs, shifting with time and circumstance. Some friendships blaze in like shooting stars, dazzling for a moment before vanishing, while others linger like an old, beloved song, playing in the background for years. I've had both, and I've learned to treasure them all—the ones that stayed, the ones that left, and even the ones that exploded in spectacular, fiery fashion. Now, as I step into this softer, more intuitive version of myself, I know some friendships will deepen, evolving into something richer, while others will quietly fade, unable to survive the woman I am becoming. And you know what? That's okay. Growth demands a little pruning.

The final days of class arrived like the closing act of a play you never wanted to end. Graduation was just around the corner, and we spent our last weeks together working on a period piece—our grand finale. This one was different, a comedy that let me shed the heavy emotional weight of past roles and step into the playful shoes of an 18th-century maid. I polished up my British accent, put on a flirty grin, and dove headfirst into the hilarity of it all. After months of peeling back my soul in gut-wrenching scenes, this was a gift. Watching my classmates shine in their own performances was equally rewarding. It wasn't just about the acting—it was about celebrating how far we'd all come together.

Graduation was set for July, a semi-formal affair at the Writers Guild in Beverly Hills, which felt as glamorous as it sounds. We were allowed only a few invitations, so I had to choose carefully. My mom wanted to come— bless her—but I decided this was a moment I needed to share with the little family I'd built here in Los Angeles. Halle flew out again to stay with me, and just knowing she'd be there already felt perfect. Thank you, Mom, for always supporting me, but this time, I wanted to keep it close to the people who had been part of my day-to-day grind.

Not everyone I invited could make it, but honestly, the ones who showed up were the ones who mattered most. Isaiah, Rich, Ezekiel (my honorary brother), Rich (my new best friend), Aire (a fellow writer on her own journey), and Jonathan (a friend who's been in my corner for three years)—they were my tribe. Having them there made the day feel even more special, and their presence was everything I needed.

That morning, Halle and I transformed the pre-graduation prep into its own celebration. We cranked up the music, sang at the top of our lungs, and danced around my apartment like two giddy kids. It was pure, unfiltered joy—

the kind you don't plan but happens when you're with someone who knows you inside and out. We slipped into our shiny gowns, strapped on our heels, and stepped out feeling like queens heading to our coronation.

When we arrived at the Writers Guild, the room buzzed with a mix of excitement and nostalgia. My classmates, radiant in their best attire, hugged and laughed, snapping pictures like paparazzi were waiting outside. There was pride in the air, but also that bittersweet ache of knowing we wouldn't be seeing each other twice a week anymore. These were the people who had seen me at my most vulnerable, who had cheered me on as I bared my soul in scene after scene. They weren't just classmates; they were family.

The ceremony itself was everything I hoped it would be. Our teachers shared heartfelt speeches, reflecting on the journeys we'd all taken and the growth they'd witnessed. The program's founder gave a moving talk that left us teary-eyed. Then came the video—a beautifully curated montage of photos and clips from our time in class. Seeing myself on screen, alongside my classmates, brought a lump to my throat. It was a moment of pure pride. I'd given everything to this program—rarely missing a class, diving into every exercise, and letting the Meisner technique seep into my bones. By graduation day, I didn't just feel like an actor—I felt *brand new*.

When they began calling names, the anticipation in the room was electric. With four classes combined, there were nearly a hundred graduates, and we waited patiently as one by one, people crossed the stage. Then, it happened. My moment. The announcer's voice boomed: "Haley MOO-zon-ic." Internally, I *lost it. MOO-zon-ic? Really?* Where on earth did they find an O in my last name? I was laughing so hard inside I almost forgot to start walking. But I composed myself, walked up to the stage, and accepted my diploma with the biggest, most genuine smile of my life.

Each teacher hugged me as I crossed the stage, but I saved the tightest squeezes for Anne Dremann and Michael Frederick. These two had changed my life in ways I couldn't have imagined when I first walked through the door two years ago. They didn't just teach me how to act—they taught me how to trust myself, how to be vulnerable, and how to find strength in my truth. As

I hugged them, I whispered my gratitude, hoping they understood just how much they meant to me.

Graduation wasn't just an ending—it was a beginning. As I stood there, surrounded by the people who mattered most, I felt ready for whatever came next. This wasn't just a milestone. It was a moment that said, *You did it. You became who you were always meant to be.*

After the ceremony, the celebrations began—the kind of magical moments that make you feel like you're living inside a dream. My arms were overflowing with bouquets, each one more beautiful than the last, sent by my mom, Isaiah, and Aire. The flowers weren't just gifts; they were tangible reminders of the love and pride surrounding me. Every petal seemed to whisper, *You did it.* My heart was bursting with gratitude and bliss, soaking in the joy of having completed what might just be the best impulsive decision of my life.

After the hugs, photos, and final goodbyes at the Writers Guild, a group of us headed out for dinner. Laughter echoed around the table, glasses clinked in celebration, and the room buzzed with the shared energy of achievement. But the night wasn't over. We moved on to Hollywood, where one of our classmates, Hunter, was performing with his band. The venue was alive with music, and before long, we were on the dance floor, losing ourselves in the rhythm. We danced like nobody was watching, the kind of carefree, joyful abandon you can only feel when you're surrounded by people who truly *appreciate you.* The night was perfect—electric and unforgettable. I couldn't have scripted it better if I tried.

Reflecting on the journey that brought me to this moment, I realized that Meisner wasn't just an acting technique for me—it was a transformation. It became my secret weapon, not only for my career but for my life. Signing up for this program had felt like a leap of faith, but it turned out to be the kind of leap that lets you soar. It didn't just teach me how to act; it taught me how to *be.* To show up in the most raw, unfiltered, present version of myself. It stripped me down to my core and rebuilt me in the best possible way.

The timing of it all was serendipitous. I was already exploring my vulnerability, peeling back layers of myself I'd long kept hidden. Meisner didn't just nudge me forward—it shoved me headfirst into the deep end, forcing me to truly *live* in the moment. It taught me to engage all six senses, to listen with my whole being, and to fully inhabit every second—whether I was crafting an imaginary scene or navigating real life.

And it didn't stay confined to the classroom. Outside of class, I found myself practicing quietly and subtly. I'd always thought I had a knack for reading people, but this program elevated that gift to a whole new level. Now, I felt like a detective of human behavior, a mastermind armed with a divine toolkit. It wasn't just acting—it was understanding people, emotions, and moments on a profoundly deeper level.

The commitment was intense. Daily homework, twice-weekly classes, and endless self-reflection pushed me to my limits. But instead of breaking me, it molded me into someone stronger, more capable, more *me*. This wasn't just about honing my craft—it was about rediscovering myself. Meisner gave me the space to break down walls I didn't even know existed, to release the pain I'd been carrying for far too long, and to channel my emotions in ways that were both cathartic and creative.

At the center of it all was Anne Dremann, the diamond of this entire experience. Anne wasn't just a teacher; she was a guide, a force of nature, a light in the dark. Her wisdom was a gift she shared generously, and her words became mantras I'll carry for the rest of my life. "Knowledge is power," she'd say, over and over, until the phrase took root in my soul. It wasn't just something she said—it was something she lived, something she inspired in all of us.

Research became the heartbeat of our second year in class, threaded into every lesson like a secret pulse. We unraveled the intricacies of impediments, unearthed the buried magic in words, and plunged headfirst into the layered worlds of plays. Somewhere in that whirlwind, I fell in love with research itself. It wasn't just about finding answers; it felt like solving a puzzle where every piece revealed something deeper and more meaningful.

Now, whenever curiosity taps me on the shoulder, I'm straight to Google—my trusty co-pilot in this chaotic quest for knowledge. Add in the psychology, philosophy, and even spirituality I've absorbed along the way, and I've basically become a human sponge. Okay, maybe not the *coolest* superpower, but hey, it works for me. My mind's this chaotic playground of questions: swinging between wild ideas, climbing toward new revelations, and sliding down endless rabbit holes of discovery.

It all started in acting class, but that spark has since turned into an unstoppable fire. It's no longer just about perfecting a craft; it's about feeding my insatiable curiosity and embracing the endless thrill of learning. Acting may have lit the match, but this passion for exploring—for peeling back layers and asking "what if?"—that's the real blaze. And honestly? I don't think I'll ever stop fanning the flames. Who would want to?

Anne's belief in me pushed me to be better, to dig deeper, and to never settle for less than my full potential. Even now, her voice echoes in my mind, urging me to keep learning, to keep growing. I dream of the day when I'll stand on a stage, accepting an award, and dedicate it to her—the woman who saw something in me I didn't even see in myself. She's etched into my heart, a *permanent* part of my story.

The night of graduation wasn't just the end of a chapter—it was the beginning of something extraordinary. As I stood there, surrounded by people I love, holding my diploma and feeling the weight of all I'd accomplished, I realized something: this wasn't just about acting. It was about growth. Healing. Transformation. Meisner didn't just change my craft—it changed *me*. And for that, I'll forever be grateful.

Closing the chapter on the acting program felt like stepping off a stage after delivering the performance of a lifetime—electric, unforgettable, and bittersweet. It wasn't just a milestone; it was a metamorphosis. I'd gone into the program unsure of myself, but I came out a completely transformed version of me, armed with tools, confidence, and a fire that felt unstoppable. It was the kind of experience that made you believe anything was possible. And as I walked away from that final day, diploma in hand, I wasn't just ready to take on the industry—I was *hungry* for it.

But alongside that excitement, the other looming chapter of my life waited for me: finishing this book.

Chapter 28

Sparks Fly

After weeks of dancing around the deeper parts of my story, I finally found the courage to jump back in. Writing about Grey Knight had felt like reliving an endless storm, each memory crashing over me like a relentless wave. But now, finally, I'd reached the halfway mark. Crossing that threshold felt like stepping into sunlight after years of rain. Writing about the time *after* Grey Knight wasn't just easier—it was liberating. The weight I'd been carrying started to lift, and for the first time, I could see the horizon clearly.

The second half of the book didn't demand the same heart-wrenching introspection, which meant I could attack it with a sharper focus and a lighter spirit. It felt less like dredging up old pain and more like piecing together a story of resilience, growth, and triumph. And, oh, how satisfying it was to feel the words flow again, like they'd been waiting for me to catch my breath and come back stronger.

Meanwhile, life outside the pages of the book was surging with momentum. Auditions kept rolling in, and the bookings started piling up like gifts I wasn't sure I'd earned but was thrilled to receive. Then came a two-week whirlwind where everything clicked. Long, exhilarating days on the set of a thriving web series pushed me to my limits in the best possible way. Every scene, every line, every take felt like a celebration of everything I'd worked so hard for in the program.

And the best part? I wasn't just another actor showing up to set—I was showing up armed with the techniques, lessons, and confidence I'd gained. Those moments of vulnerability and struggle in class had prepared me for this, and I could feel the difference. I wasn't performing anymore—I was living in my craft.

During that spree, I landed a few lead roles, which felt surreal. There's a magic to being entrusted with a lead role, to carrying a story and making it your own. It's like stepping into someone else's shoes while realizing they were made just for you. Every moment on set fueled me, reminding me why I fell in love with this chaotic, beautiful industry in the first place.

Those shoot days were a rollercoaster of early call times, long hours, and the kind of exhaustion that only comes from doing what you love. But instead of feeling drained, I felt alive. I'd come home at the end of each day, buzzing with excitement, too energized to sleep, my mind racing with gratitude for every second I got to spend doing what I loved. It was the kind of high no drug could replicate—the pure, unfiltered joy of living your dream.

As the days blurred together, I realized something profound. The girl who had walked into that acting program two years ago wasn't the same woman walking off these sets. I'd grown, evolved, and become someone I barely recognized but deeply admired. Closing the chapter on the program wasn't an ending—it was the beginning of a much bigger story. One where I was finally the lead, ready to step into the spotlight not just on screen but in my own life. And as I balanced acting, writing, and healing, I could feel the pieces falling into place. This wasn't just a moment. This was a movement— a promise to myself that the best was yet to come.

As September approached, so did a milestone that meant everything to me: the second anniversary of my cancer survival. Two years since my life had pivoted from despair to resilience, from uncertainty to a fierce determination to celebrate every moment I've been given. I knew I wanted to mark the occasion in a way that felt deeply personal, something that honored the fight and the healing. I've never been one for big parties or grand gestures, but I wanted to celebrate *me*—raw, real, and unapologetically alive.

I decided to get a tattoo: my zebra-printed cancer ribbon inked onto my left forearm. This wasn't just about aesthetics. This tattoo would be my armor, my symbol, a permanent reminder of what I'd endured and conquered. I wanted it there, visible every day, to whisper, *You made it. You're still here.* I knew the act of getting it inked would be a healing ritual, but I had no idea just how much it would stir within me.

Around this time, I was opening up more to Rich, sharing pieces of my story. When I told him about my failed attempt to ceremoniously burn the meatballs from Italy last year—a symbolic gesture to rewrite my narrative—

his eyes lit up with a mischievous glint. "Do you want to finish the job?" he asked with a grin. "I have a flamethrower." A flamethrower. *A freaking flamethrower.* I gasped, then burst into laughter, my excitement bubbling over. "YES. Absolutely YES!" Only Rich could take my half-baked ideas and turn them into grand, fiery adventures. The thought of torching that ridiculous metaphor was both hilarious and oddly poetic. Leave it to him to make my healing process feel like an action movie.

September 8th finally arrived, and I decided to start the day quietly, with gratitude. Before dawn, Ezekiel and I met up on Mulholland Drive with Mocha to watch the sunrise. The view was breathtaking, the kind that makes you feel both infinite and small at the same time. As the sky shifted from deep indigo to a palette of golds and pinks, I let myself sit in the moment, overwhelmed by how far I'd come. I thought about how rare my tumor was, how it could have been the end of me, but instead, here I was—alive, healthy, and witnessing another sunrise. I whispered a silent thank you to the universe, the stars, and whatever forces had decided, I still had chapters left to write.

Later that evening, I wanted to celebrate in a way that felt intimate yet special. I invited Rich to join me for dinner at BOA, my favorite steakhouse in Hollywood. Rich, being Rich, turned what could have been a simple meal into an unforgettable night. We laughed and talked through every second of it, our energy bouncing off each other as always. He even worked his last-minute magic, connecting me with a tattoo artist who could ink my ribbon that very night. Because, of course, Rich would make the impossible happen.

After dinner, we headed to the tattoo studio. The artist placed the stencil on my forearm, and I stared at it for a moment, knowing I was about to carry this symbol with me forever. The buzzing of the tattoo machine began, and so did something I hadn't anticipated. From the first prick of the needle, a wave of emotion surged through me—intense, unrelenting, and entirely unexpected. My forearm felt like it was on fire, but the physical sensation was nothing compared to what was happening inside. Anxiety bubbled up, nausea crept in, and I fought to stay grounded, teetering on the edge of a panic attack. I couldn't even look at the artist. I just focused on breathing, on *not spiraling.*

When the tattoo was finally finished, the storm inside me lingered. I wasn't complaining—I was proud to have the tattoo—but I hadn't expected it to feel so raw, so overwhelming. It wasn't about the pain; it was about everything the tattoo represented. The years of fear, survival, and healing condensed into this one moment—it was a lot to process. I knew it would take time to fully embrace, and I gave myself the grace to do just that.

The universe, as if sensing I needed a balance of lightness after the intensity of that night, had something magical in store for the next day. Rich, with his endless generosity and impeccable timing, invited me to tag along to the first NFL game of the season. And not just any game—it was our teams going head-to-head at Levi's Stadium, home of the 49ers. It was the perfect way to continue celebrating life.

The next morning, Rich picked me up for the road trip to the Bay Area. This was a first in our friendship—music played in the car. For three months, our drives had been soundtracked only by relentless conversation and laughter, but that day, we let a playlist sneak in—briefly, of course. It didn't last long before we fell back into our usual rhythm of ridiculous banter and nonstop chatter. The six-hour drive there and back felt like a comedy marathon, the kind of fun that leaves your cheeks sore from smiling.

At the game, I got to meet Rich's cousins, though I didn't sit with them during the game—because of rivalry boundaries, naturally. The 49ers won (cue Rich's smug grin), but the outcome didn't matter. The day was pure joy—electric energy, shared moments, and a celebration of being alive.

That weekend was a kaleidoscope of emotions—quiet gratitude, intense healing, unrestrained laughter, and pure happiness. From the sunrise on Mulholland to the buzzing tattoo needle, from a steakhouse dinner to a stadium full of cheers, it was a reminder of how full life can be when you open yourself to it. As I looked down at the fresh tattoo on my arm, tender and healing, I felt its weight—not just on my skin, but in my soul. It wasn't just an anniversary.

It was a declaration: I survived. I'm alive. And I'm not done yet.

The fun didn't stop with our whirlwind trip to the Bay Area. Not even close. Shortly after returning, Rich and I set our sights on something we'd both been curious about for a while: an event called Witality. We'd heard the buzz—people leaving in tears, purging buried emotions, even experiencing full-body jolts as if their souls were being rewired. It was said to be a powerful breathwork experience, one that could shake you to your core in the best possible way. Naturally, we were intrigued. So, we committed.

When the day came, we showed up in our comfiest sweats, ready to dive headfirst into the unknown. As Witalij Martynow, the founder of Witality, began explaining the process, Rich and I exchanged wide-eyed glances, the kind that said, *What did we just sign up for?* It sounded heavier than either of us had imagined. But that only fueled our determination. We weren't just ready for it—we wanted all of it.

To truly capture Witality, let me borrow from Witalij himself: Witality™ combines breathwork, meditation, movement, and philosophy, weaving together modern science, ancient wisdom, and indigenous teachings. The premise is simple yet profound: unprocessed emotions, chronic pain, and even childhood trauma create stuck energy in our bodies. By breathing in specific rhythms and intensities, we can release this energy, altering our state of consciousness and jumpstarting the body's natural healing process. Essentially, Witalij believes that through guided breath and movement, we can tap into our inner vitality—and let me tell you, he's not wrong.

The session was four hours long, but time felt irrelevant. It was a sound bath, a psychedelic journey, and a deep therapy mixed into one session—all while completely sober. As I settled into the rhythm of the breathwork, it felt like peeling back layers of myself. What started as a curiosity quickly became a journey into the deepest corners of my soul.

I felt my body hum with energy, as though I'd unlocked a portal to something ancient and powerful within me. At first, it was disorienting—visions flashed before my eyes, memories I didn't even know I had.

In other visions, I met every past version of myself—the shattered ones, the lost ones, the ones who didn't know how to fight back yet. One by one, I poured love into them, whispering the words they had always needed to hear: *I see you. I know you did the best you could. I'm proud of you. I love you.* And with each affirmation, I wrapped them in the warmest, tightest hug, sealing the message like a vow. It was healing across lifetimes, a soul-deep embrace that rippled through every version of me. Beautiful. Magnificent. Transformative.

The pain I thought I'd long buried rose to the surface, demanding to be felt. It wasn't just emotional—it was physical. My chest tightened, my limbs trembled, and tears poured down my face as if they'd been waiting for permission to fall. It was like my body had been storing this weight in hidden crevices, and Witality was the key that finally unlocked them.

And then, just when I thought I couldn't take any more, something shifted. The tears of pain softened into tears of relief, and then, miraculously, into tears of joy. I wasn't just crying anymore—I was *laughing*. It started as an outburst giggle, but before I knew it, I was full-on cackling, my whole body shaking with uncontrollable joy. The kind of laughter that feels like a waterfall bursting through a dam. I wasn't laughing at anything in particular—it was the pure, overwhelming release of joy. It was like my soul had found its voice, and it couldn't stop singing.

By the time the session was nearing its end, I felt something I can only describe as divine. My body was buzzing with a golden, glittering sensation, as if every cell was alive and vibrating with light. It felt like I'd stumbled upon a sacred temple within myself, a place where my soul resided in its truest, most radiant form. I wasn't just *connected* to myself—I *was* myself, fully and completely. For a moment, I saw my own power, my worth, and my potential as if I were standing outside of myself, marveling at the beauty within.

I know this probably sounds batshit crazy. Trust me, if someone had told me this story before I experienced it, I might have laughed. But if you're into spirituality—or even just open to the idea of it—you'll understand. It wasn't just breathwork. It was a portal to the kind of healing you don't even realize you need until you're in the thick of it.

But the craziest part? The aftermath. The session ended, but its effects lingered like a song that stayed with you long after the music stopped. In the days that followed, I felt like a different person. Lighter. Freer. More alive. It was as if Witality had recalibrated something inside me, aligning me with a version of myself I'd only caught glimpses of before.

Rich and I couldn't stop talking about it. It wasn't just an event—it was an *awakening*. Something we couldn't quite put into words but knew we'd carry with us forever. And as we walked away from Witality, still buzzing with the energy of what we'd just experienced, I realized something: This wasn't another step in my healing journey. It was a leap. A reminder of the power we hold within us when we're brave enough to face ourselves.

I kid you not—since the Witality event, I feel like an entirely new version of myself, one I didn't even know was waiting to emerge. It's as if a switch flipped inside me, illuminating parts of my soul I hadn't realized were still in shadow. I'm lighter, freer, glowing from the inside out with a sense of purpose that's both exhilarating and consuming. The heaviness I carried for so long has lifted, leaving behind this unshakable clarity. And that clarity? It's poured directly into my writing.

The momentum I've gained since that day is nothing short of wild. It's like the creative floodgates opened, and there's no shutting them now. My devotion to this book has become laser-focused, almost obsessive, in a way that feels both thrilling and a little terrifying. Every single day, I carve out time to write. Some days, it's a few hours of drafting new chapters; other days, it's meticulously revising old ones. But no matter what, the words keep coming. And then there are my Saturdays. Oh, Saturdays—they've become sacred. These are my marathon sessions, where I dive headfirst into my story for eight hours straight, or more, fully immersed in this world I'm creating.

But here's the thing about writing marathons: they leave you wrecked. By the time I close my laptop, my eyes are burning, my shoulders are stiff, and my head feels like it's been cracked open and poured onto the page. Even with my trusty prescription glasses and their blue light filter, the screen still takes its toll. I'll tell myself, *Okay, you're done. You've earned a break. Walk away.* But my brain? It doesn't care. The moment I step away, the ideas come rushing in—fragments of dialogue, flashes of scenes, memories I'd forgotten, all demanding to be included. It's like my book has become a living, breathing entity, and it's whispering to me constantly.

And it's relentless. I could be out with friends, trying to have a normal conversation, and suddenly a random word or gesture will spark a new idea. One moment, I'm fully present, soaking in the world around me—then, like a detective chasing a clue, I'm diving into my phone, frantically typing notes before the brilliance vanishes into the abyss of forgotten thoughts.

It's like the story won't let me go. It follows me everywhere, tugging at my sleeve, insisting I come back to the page. Even when I try to give myself a moment to just *be*, my brain keeps spinning, connecting dots and uncovering nuances I didn't see before. It's thrilling, yes, but also a little maddening.

This wild cycle has taken over my life in the most unexpected way. I've started to retreat from the world, not out of sadness or avoidance, but because my creative bubble has become my sanctuary. I'm pouring everything I have into this book, every emotion, every memory, every piece of me. And as much as I miss the simplicity of hanging out with friends without my mind wandering back to my laptop, I know this is where I'm *meant to be* right now.

It's a paradox—both a blessing and a beautifully chaotic curse. The blessing? That intoxicating, all-consuming flow, where creativity surges through me like a tidal wave, sweeping me into a world where time ceases to exist. There's magic in that kind of immersion—the kind that makes the outside world disappear, where every word feels like alchemy. The tools I've gathered from Anne's classes have only intensified that spark, turning embers into an inferno. But the curse? Oh, it's the way this obsession has devoured me whole. I sink so deep into writing that my eyes feel like they're bleeding by the end of a session, my stomach growls like an abandoned pet, and I forget the most basic human functions—like eating, drinking water, or, you know, blinking. I've become both the writer and the recluse, locked in an intoxicating, unrelenting dance with my book—one I'm not sure I'd step away from even if I could.

But the truth is, I wouldn't change it for anything. This story has become a part of me—no, it *is* me. Every word I write feels like a piece of my heart stitched onto the page, a raw and unfiltered expression of who I am. And as exhausting and all-encompassing as it can be, it's also the most fulfilling thing

I've ever done. This book isn't just a project; it's my soul in ink. And every sleepless night, every sore-eyed Saturday, every moment of solitude is worth it. Because with every page, I'm not just writing a story—I'm writing *myself* into existence.

And then came the moment—the *flamethrower moment*. Oh yes, it was as epic as it sounds. Rich and I were at the stunning Malibu house he'd rented for his family, a place straight out of a California dream. Think sweeping ocean views, salty breezes, and sunsets so vibrant they almost seemed fake. But let's be real—none of that could compete with what we were about to do.

Rich, ever the mastermind of adventure and absurdity, had prepped everything. He took two hamburger patties and smashed them into oversized meatballs—big enough to match the tumor I'd survived. The symbolism wasn't lost on me. These weren't just meatballs; they were stand-ins for my pain, my fight, my triumph. And they were about to meet a fiery end.

"Alright, here's how you use it," Rich said with the enthusiasm of a mad scientist unveiling his latest invention. He handed me the flamethrower, this massive contraption that looked like it belonged in an action movie. As I held it, I felt this rush of adrenaline, like I was about to save the world—or at least, scorch a metaphorical piece of my past.

And then, with one squeeze of the trigger, a blazing jet of fire erupted, hotter and brighter than I'd expected. The power of it was electrifying. Rich held up the pan of meatballs like a true partner in crime, steadying it while I unleashed flames onto those symbolic suckers. The sound, the heat, the sheer absurdity of the moment—it was perfect.

I couldn't stop laughing. I mean, *who does this?* Who turns their survival story into a flamethrower therapy session? But that was the beauty of it. It was ridiculous, sure, but it was also profound. With every lick of flame, I felt lighter and freer, as if I were burning away not just meat but every ounce of fear and pain that tumor had brought into my life.

And let me tell you, there's something cathartic about holding a literal flame to your metaphorical baggage. It's a kind of therapy they don't teach you in textbooks, but damn, it works. As the meatballs charred and sizzled, I couldn't help but think, *This is healing*. Messy, fiery, laugh-until-your-cheeks-hurt healing.

Of course, I didn't completely annihilate them—I'm no monster. Rich, ever the practical one, finished cooking the meatballs on a proper grill, transforming them into delicious burgers. We sat under the Malibu sky, eating our flame-kissed creations, laughing at what we'd just done. Every bite felt symbolic, like I was digesting a chapter of my life and turning it into fuel for whatever came next.

And that's the thing about healing—it doesn't always look the way you'd expect. Sometimes, it's quiet and reflective, and other times, it's holding a flamethrower in Malibu while your best friend cheers you on. Those silly, absurd moments can carry the most weight, speaking volumes about what it means to have people in your life who truly *get you*.

Rich's brilliantly ridiculous idea was a plot twist I never saw coming. In his delightfully offbeat way, he flipped the script on a story that had once felt like dead weight, handing me back the pen with a mischievous grin. It was proof that healing isn't always found in quiet introspection or profound breakthroughs—sometimes, it's wrapped in absurdity, laughter, and the kind of magic that sneaks up on you when you least expect it.

As we sat there, the stars shining above the horizon, I couldn't stop smiling. This was what it meant to be alive—to turn pain into laughter, to find joy in the chaos, and to have a friend who's willing to hold the pan while you wield the flamethrower.

Reaching the one-year mark of getting to know Dameon, I took a deliberate step back—not to retreat, but to breathe, reflect, and do what I've come to call my "love autopsy." It felt like stepping out of a storm, drenched but exhilarated, to assess the damage and marvel at the unexpected beauty that had emerged in its wake. The more I unraveled the layers of who he is, the more I glimpsed something extraordinary: potential. The kind of potential that makes your heart stutter, your imagination soar, and your playlists turn suspiciously romantic. There was a connection between us, rare and fragile, like an antique vase you're terrified to drop. I hadn't felt this way since Grey

Knight. Dameon was, quite literally, the first person to awaken that irresistible pull again—a gravity that defies logic and reason, drawing you in as if by some cosmic conspiracy.

They say we don't choose who we fall for, and with Dameon, that truth was intoxicatingly evident. It wasn't just the butterflies or the thrill of the chase; it was the quiet yearning to dismantle the fortress I'd built around myself, brick by stubborn brick, just to let him in. Yet, when he confided in me about the messiness of his life, it was like a warning bell clanging in the distance. It was my cue to armor up, to test my ability to stay detached, to play it safe. But, oh, how troubling it was. I'm the type who just *knows*, and with Dameon, my heart didn't just know—it proclaimed. This was someone worth risking it all for. Or at least, worth risking a little dignity over.

From the outset, the timing was our cruelest antagonist, a villain lurking in the shadows of our story. It forced me to fortify my defenses, to shield my heart from the chaos of mismatched circumstances. But a year of Dameon weaving in and out of my life was a test of endurance I wasn't prepared for. He had this infuriating yet endearing habit of showing up at the precise moments when my walls were most vulnerable, as if the universe itself had conspired to lay me bare. And therein lay the maddening paradox—he caught me in moments of raw openness, moments when I was simultaneously exposed and trying desperately to keep my guard intact.

Yet, those same moments were often painted with the kind of joy that makes life worth living. Laughter, the kind that feels like a secret between two souls, spilled effortlessly from his presence. Dameon was a cocktail of charm and complication—equal parts intoxicating and perplexing. He could be a gentleman, disarming me with his thoughtfulness, but the warning signs were there, subtle yet undeniable. White flags, waving like whispers in the wind and reminding me to tread carefully. Here's the truth: *I'm ready now.* Ready for a love that feels like home, not a battlefield. Ready for something enduring, something unshakeable. And I'm deserving of it, too.

Admitting it was the hardest part—I was falling for him. Slowly, but with the inevitability of a river carving its path through stone. The mere thought of him had me smiling like a teenager with a diary full of secrets. But this wasn't the reckless infatuation of my past. This was something tempered, refined by the fires of heartbreak and the hard-won lessons of healing. To find someone meaningful now, in this renewed and resilient version of myself, would be nothing short of miraculous.

Reality, however, has a way of tempering dreams. Dameon's life was, and remains, a web of complications—a breakup still echoing, a divorce not yet finalized. His world was chaos, wrapped in charm, and the timing once again stood as the immovable barrier between us. Whenever my feelings grew too strong, I'd pull away, retreating to the safety of self-preservation. But Dameon? He always found a way to bridge the gap, pulling us back together with an ease that was both maddening and magnetic.

Over the past year, our connection has been a dance—a delicate, unpredictable waltz of one step forward, one step back. Playful flirtation interwoven with profound conversations became the rhythm of our bond. And though the future remains an enigmatic question mark, one thing has become clear: knowing him has reignited a hope I thought was extinguished. It reminded me that love—or even the potential for it—is still within my grasp.

I've surprised myself with my newfound ability to detach when necessary, not out of coldness, but out of reverence for my own well-being. I guarded my heart, offering only fragments of myself, never the whole. And yet, those fragments were enough to teach me that love is still possible, even when I'd convinced myself otherwise.

Halfway through our year together, I made a quiet decision—one that felt like slipping out of my own skin. I stopped reaching out first. No more eager texts, no more playful check-ins. It was a self-imposed survival tactic, a way to keep my heart from latching on like a barnacle to a sinking ship. But I also told myself it was for the sake of keeping things light, breezy—like a summer fling that had somehow overstayed its welcome. Of course, deep down, I knew the truth: I was shielding myself from any unnecessary feelings—whether it was disappointment, frustration, or that gnawing little sting of being a little too available.

By making this quiet little pact with myself, I unknowingly set off a whole new game of push and pull between us—like some bizarre, unspoken tug-of-war where neither of us ever fully won. One minute, he'd pull me back in with just enough warmth to keep me intrigued, and the next, I'd remind myself to stay cool, detached, like a seasoned player in whatever this so-called "dating" situation was. We weren't exactly a couple, but we weren't strangers either. We were somewhere in between—circling each other like two people too stubborn to let go, yet too uncertain to hold on.

When Dameon entered my life, I was still fumbling my way through the last vestiges of a healing journey, groping for the light at the end of a long, dark tunnel. His presence, however fleeting it may ultimately be, reminded me of my capacity for joy, for spontaneity, for being unabashedly, unapologetically myself. He helped me rediscover pieces of myself I hadn't realized I'd lost—pieces I was delighted to find again.

The timing, as ironic as it seems, turned out to be a gift in disguise. It granted me the clarity to understand what I want and, more importantly, what I will no longer tolerate. I've come to appreciate Dameon for who he is at this moment, without the weight of unmet expectations or the sting of disappointment. He's been a companion, a mirror reflecting both the best parts of me and the growth still waiting to unfold.

I've come to realize that the end of one story is often the beginning of another. Somewhere out there, someone will come along who not only sparks that fire but stays to keep it burning. And until then, I'll keep standing tall, whole, and unapologetic, knowing that my journey isn't about finding someone to complete me—it's about being complete on my own. It's a quiet triumph, a promise to myself that the best chapters are still waiting to be written.

The brightest, most unwavering star in my life has always been Mocha— my angel, my confidante, my mischievous, four-legged soulmate. Yes, technically, she's a dog, but let's not get caught up in details. She's something more—part mind reader, part comedian, and entirely irreplaceable. From day one, she mastered tricks with the flair of a Broadway performer—kisses on command, twirls, and her show-stopping *Bang!* where she dramatically collapses as if I've (pretend) shot her. But loyalty? That was never a trick. It's in her bones. She's my shadow, my protector, my ride-or-die who's never needed a leash to stay by my side.

Her intuition borders on supernatural. She *knows* when I'm leaving before I do, studying my movements like an FBI profiler, sighing theatrically as she drapes herself over my suitcase in protest. The moment she sees me grab *her* things—leash, travel bag—she combusts into a dramatic mix of anxiety and excitement, belting out her own operatic performance. And if we're on the road? Ten minutes before arrival, without fail, she announces it like a canine GPS. Attention? She demands it with a royal stomp or a slow-motion paw to the face, her eyes whispering, *Submit*. And I do. Every. Single. Time. Compliments follow her like confetti, and she *knows* she's adored. Because Mocha isn't just a dog—she's an experience, a tiny force of nature wrapped in silky fur and boundless love.

Mocha was once *ours*—a piece of my past, tangled up with Grey Knight. But time unraveled that, and now she's *mine*, my greatest blessing, my North Star. She's seen me at my strongest, my most broken, my most lost, and never once wavered. When life knocked me down, she was there, licking away my tears, dropping toys at my feet like joy itself could be the antidote to heartbreak. And somehow, it was.

But don't mistake her softness for weakness—Mocha is part guardian angel, part *raging bitch* when necessary. The second Grey Knight was gone, she stepped up, taking her role as my protector *very* seriously. She's got the intelligence of a seasoned therapist and the attitude of a queen—reading me like a book, claiming my pillows as her throne, and somehow *knowing* when I'm about to leave before I even touch my keys. And don't get me started on the beach—my "sandy psycho" loses her mind at the first whiff of salt air, sprinting, digging, and throwing herself into the waves with wild, reckless joy.

Mocha is an experience. A little fairy in fur, a healer, a mind reader, my once-in-a-lifetime love. Quite literally, my shadow. And soon, she'll be inked onto my shoulder—a permanent mark of the angel who saved me, over and over again.

At long last, the day has come. The day I've fantasized about, dreaded, avoided, and circled back to a hundred times over. I'm finally quitting vaping—that seductive, poisonous little addiction that has whispered in my ear like a devil on my shoulder. For a few years now, nicotine was my constant companion, but it was never just about the vape. No, I believed it to be a connection to him—the Grey Knight. That bittersweet entanglement of love, loss, and regret wrapped itself around my addiction so tightly that quitting always felt like cutting the last string connecting me to him. And yet, I knew: If I ever wanted to be truly free, I had to let both go. And for my health and Cookie Grandma in my thoughts.

Enter "Quit With Jones," a product I stumbled upon during one of my midnight Googling sprees. The name alone made me chuckle. Back in those wild, chaotic days with him, we had a term for that itchy, desperate feeling of withdrawal: *jonesing*. So, in some twisted poetic way, it felt like the universe was in on the joke. *Alright, Jones*, I thought, *Let's do this*.

But here's where the plot twist comes in—because life with me is never just a straightforward story. As I prepared to say goodbye to my vape with Jones in my corner, something miraculous happened. A little voice inside whispered, *You don't need this. You're already done.* And for once, I listened. With every puff, I could feel myself detaching—not just from the nicotine, but from the memories, the pain, the tangled mess of emotions that came with it. It was like my higher power stepped in, waved a wand, and said, *Enough, my dear. You're ready.*

How serendipitous, right? After years of dancing with demons—some mine, some his—I'm finally cutting the music. Quitting nicotine isn't about ridding myself of a bad habit. Oh no, it's far bigger than that. It's a declaration. A roar. A phoenix rising from the ashes of heartbreak, screaming, *I am done with all of it!* The vape, the excuses, the toxic cycles. It's all over.

There's something poetic about this being the last addiction I'll ever have. Because let's be honest, I've had my fair share—addictions to people, to drugs, to feelings, to chaos. But this? This is different. This is the final boss in the game of me reclaiming my life. And I can tell you now, *I'm winning*.

As I hold this ridiculous little device in my hand for what I know will be the last time, I can't help but laugh at the irony. All those years, I thought I needed this to survive, when all I really needed was the strength to say goodbye. Goodbye to the Grey Knight. Goodbye to the crutches I leaned on for too long. Goodbye to the version of me who settled for anything less than the freedom I deserve.

So, here's to a new chapter. To fresh air and clear lungs. To mornings that don't begin with a puff of poison and nights that don't end with regret. Here's to a life where my happiness isn't tethered to anything—or anyone— but *myself*.

There's a certain electricity in the gym—a pulse, a rhythm, an unspoken camaraderie. I see the same faces, day in and day out, each person grinding away with relentless determination, chasing their own version of greatness. It's the energy I *live* for. My passion. A space where effort is currency, and sweat is proof of devotion. The gym is my happy place, my sanctuary, a world where glances turn into nods, nods into quick greetings, and eventually, new connections.

And then—there was *him*. A new presence in my orbit. It started small, the way these things often do—a passing comment, a casual compliment. "Love the bright colors you're rocking." Because, yes, colors *matter*. They have depth. And as it turns out, Eddie and I both had a knack for neon. We were beacons in a sea of black and gray gym gear, gravitating toward each other like human highlighters. But it wasn't just the bold hues we noticed about each other—it was something deeper. My intuition honed in on his energy, his spirit. He carried a resilience I recognized, like someone who had seen battle and lived to tell the tale. Strength, not just in muscle, but in soul. And I *felt* it.

Then came the details. Eddie wasn't just another fitness junkie—he was a force. A personal trainer to elite athletes, celebrities, military personnel, models, doctors, moms—hell, even other trainers. A wizard in health and nutrition, so much so that actual doctors sought his advice. But what struck me most wasn't his résumé—it was his *why*. At some point, he realized fitness alone wasn't enough. People—especially women—needed more than just a workout plan. They needed mental fortitude, emotional strength. So he dove in, headfirst, building a business, Arouse Health, where excellence wasn't just a standard—it was the only way.

And then, the kicker—the moment my gut whispered, *See? He's here for a reason.* We were mid-conversation, casual gym talk, when I dropped it: "I'm actually writing a book."

His face lit up. "No way—I just started writing one too."

What are the odds? The universe doesn't deal in coincidences, and suddenly, it all made sense. From that moment on, our conversations deepened. We started investing real time into each other, sharing stories, exchanging knowledge. And the more he spoke, the more my intuition kept nodding, whispering, *Yes. He's a good one.* His passion, his excellence, the way he approached life—it is impressive.

It didn't take long to see why we clicked—he speaks my language. The way Rich does. The way only a rare few ever have. He doesn't just observe the world; he deciphers it, picking up on energies, unspoken truths, the hidden layers most people skim past.

With a mind sharp enough to cut through illusions and a soul stitched together by self-awareness and hard-won wisdom, he's… well, evolved. Not just "reads self-help books" evolved—actually did the work, burned the old versions of himself, and rose from the ashes kind of evolved. His eyes? Microscopes into the human experience.

And somehow, I'm the latest specimen under his lens. He reads me effortlessly—like a novel he's already highlighted, dog-eared, and analyzed. Maybe it's his work with women, with mental health. Or maybe, just maybe, some people are wired to recognize each other on sight. Whatever it is, one thing's for sure—I've never felt so seen. Terrifying? A little. Magnetic? Absolutely.

And then it hit me—maybe we weren't just dropped into each other's lives for book talk. Maybe there was something more. Maybe I was supposed to hire him, work with him, let his brilliance shape the next chapter of my evolution. Because let's be real—his expertise in health and fitness, paired with that razor-sharp mind, makes him exactly the kind of person I should have in my corner. Why wouldn't I want someone like him fine-tuning this rebuilt version of me? I've already gutted the old foundation, knocked down the walls, and done the hard labor of transforming myself. But even a brand-new house needs upkeep. And with this fresh insurance policy on my life— both metaphorically and quite literally—who knows what's coming next? A renovation? An expansion? A full-blown estate upgrade? Either way, I have a feeling the blueprint just got a whole lot more interesting.

Getting my old doctor back felt like a small victory—one I desperately needed—because catching up on my health has been nothing short of feeling like a lab rat being passed from one specialist to the next. Every test, every scan, every round of bloodwork dissecting me like a science project, all in the name of making sure this body of mine is still firing on all cylinders. And let's not forget the uphill battle of getting my prescription back in my hands— because apparently, surviving cancer doesn't come with an *express pass* to basic healthcare.

After nearly a year without insurance, jumping back into this world of appointments and follow-ups felt long overdue, but necessary. And, because life loves to keep things interesting, some new results have had my stress levels clocking overtime. There are whispers of possible concerns, lingering questions, and referrals to yet another specialist, sending me deeper into the medical maze. The cycle hasn't let up, and truthfully, the whole process drags up a familiar unease in me.

Hospitals, waiting rooms, test results—I'd be lying if I said they didn't still haunt me. Cancer came crashing into my life, flipping my world upside down in just three months. That kind of trauma doesn't just disappear. But when the fear creeps in, I remind myself:

You've beaten cancer. You are deadly fear itself. You can handle anything that comes your way.

That mantra is my anchor. It grounds me. It reminds me to breathe, to let grace flow through my veins instead of panic. I won't jump to conclusions about what my doctor has hinted at—everything is still being tested—but deep down, I suspect this is just another consequence of my Whipple surgery. My body is still learning how to function without that "Meatball" that once tried to strike me out. And I'm still learning how to navigate this *new* version of myself.

But if I've survived the worst, then what's left? Nothing I can't handle.

These days, I find myself drawn to *real* people. The kind of souls that radiate authenticity—the ones who live for life's simple joys, who grind without losing their integrity, who don't bother with masks or façades. And when I find them, I make it a point to invest in them. Because genuine people? They're rare.

Souls like Eddie. And Jonathan—who, truthfully, has been in my life for a while, but our friendship deepened when I intentionally invested in it. Because when you recognize a truly good person, you don't just let that go unnoticed. I saw his kindness, his unwavering character, and the way he shows up for people, and I knew he was someone worth holding onto. That's the thing about energy—you have to nurture the connections that *feel* right. And at this stage in my life, I only have room for the ones who do.

Here's the thing about writing a book about your life—especially when your life has enough *mic drop* moments to rival an awards show—I've said it once, and I'll say it again: You *think* you've closed a chapter, tied it up with a neat little bow, and moved on. But no. That chapter isn't done with *you*.

Just like life itself, it comes knocking when you least expect it. One moment, I'm convinced I've poured every ounce of truth onto the page, and the next? Memories barge in like uninvited guests at a party, demanding their moment in the spotlight. Forgotten details, pivotal moments, emotions I thought I'd left behind—they all resurface, refusing to be ignored. So, what do I do? I sprint back to the pages, chasing down every last thread of my story, knowing that if I don't, I'll regret it.

I thought I was done—like, *done, done*. And then? Life, in all its mischievous, unpredictable wisdom, threw another plot twist my way. Thank *God* I extended my own finish line, because had I stuck to my original deadline, I would've missed capturing one of the most defining moments of my journey.

And that's just it—everything happens for a reason. Call it divine timing, call it fate, call it my angels pulling strings behind the scenes—I know the universe is always nudging me, whispering, *Wait. Not yet. There's more to say.* So, I listen. I trust. I surrender to the process. Because if there's one thing I've learned, it's this: The story isn't over until the universe says it is.

That big conversation—the kind two people usually have early on when they're intentionally dating—finally happened. *At last.*

I had reached a point of full honesty with myself. No more dancing around it. If I was going to have *this* man in my life—whatever *this* was—I had to take it seriously. I'd been dodging my own detective instincts, resisting the natural pull to dig deeper, to connect in a way that felt real. All in the name of self-preservation. A tactic I was actually *proud* of. But now? Now, I was at my wit's end. I craved meaningful connections. No more half-measures. No more lingering in the "what are we?" gray zone.

And hey, how poetic—right as the new year began. Fresh start, new energy—let's get some damn clarity. Where was this going? What were his intentions? What were *we*? The questions swirled around me, landing in conversation like confetti, only to be followed by those dreaded, weighty silences. And honestly? I was tired of feeling like a toy being picked up and put down at his convenience—especially when I *knew* how much my heart wanted to open for him.

We both deserved more than this back-and-forth momentum. I had tried to pull the trigger on him a few times already, convinced that it needed to stop. But *Relentless Dameon* wasn't having it. Instead of me "breaking up with him," he insisted we sit down and have a real conversation. Two days of unfiltered, "let's finally be real" dialogue about where we stood.

And right before we started that talk, something in me shifted. A new perspective settled in.

I'll just enjoy the hell out of this beautiful man for what he is. No expectations. No emotional deep-dives. No getting sucked in. I decided to be present, to let myself feel good in the moment, without losing myself in the possibility of something more. And just like that, I felt *free*. Because deep down, I had known from the start—this man was never truly available. But my soul? My heart? They were addicted to him anyway. The way he made me feel, the chemistry that cracked like lightning between us—*holy hell*. Big sigh.

I know life is short. And with that, I gave myself permission to try something new—to stay guarded, but present. To be authentic, but not fall. Just blissful, electric moments with someone who lights me up in a way I've only ever felt once before—with Grey Knight. And now, this was the *second* time I'd ever felt that way. How was I supposed to feel about that?

But instead of chasing a fairytale ending, instead of clinging to the idea of a serious, defined relationship, I chose something radical. Simplicity. I would enjoy this man exactly as he was. Not for what he *could* be, not for what I *hoped* he'd become, but for *who he was* in each moment we shared.

And the second I made that choice, I felt liberated. No more mental tug-of-war, no more agonizing over whether or not I should keep him in my life. I wanted him. I enjoyed him. And that was enough.

That day, we're strolling through town with Mocha, talking nonstop, peeling back even more layers, and just *being*. And just like that—like a splash of cold water to the face—I learn something I hadn't fully grasped before.

Dameon is still emotionally tied to his ex.

Not in the maybe-they'll-get-back-together way, but in the "they still have lunch, they still hang out, they still exist in each other's orbit" kind of way. A relationship in some capacity. Let's be *real*. And then, there's *me*—the one he gets to escape with, the playground he gets to run wild on.

That was the cold, hard truth I needed to hear. And digest.

It wasn't going to happen. Not the way I secretly, deep-down, *maybe* hoped it would. And even if it ever did, I had no idea how long it would take. And I wasn't waiting. Not for him. Not for anyone. In fact, I made it *clear*—

if someone comes into my life and takes me seriously the way I *deserve*, then he needs to *back off*.

He agreed. But only if he's perfect, he demanded.

Somehow, after all that truth-telling, after that jarring reality check, we still melted right back into our natural rhythm. Playful. Easy. Enjoying each other without expectation, without the weight of the conversation lingering over us.

And I realized—I had finally, *finally* taken my power back.

My energy had me floating—high on the fluffy clouds of feel-good endorphins, weightless, untouchable. For a moment, I was soaring. And then—boom—just like that, my emotions yanked me down with a force so unexpected it left me reeling.

Sadness crept in, slow but steady, settling into my mind like a storm rolling in on a clear day. And then, the thought hit me with the force of a wrecking ball: *Dameon and I will never be anything.* Not really. Not in the way my heart, deep down, had once hoped. The realization wasn't sharp or sudden— it was a slow, sinking knowing. A truth that had been lurking in the background, waiting for its moment to be acknowledged.

And you know what? It was okay.

I believe now, looking back, that my soul *needed* to hear those words spill from his lips—to let the truth hit me like a hurricane so I could finally, *finally* process it. Dameon was a *fantasy*—something I had built in my mind, something I had clung to in my heart. And that? That is not where I can afford to live.

Then, without warning, the tears came.

Not a slow trickle. Not a single, poetic drop rolling down my cheek. *No.* These were painful, gut-wrenching tears—except, strangely, I didn't even *feel* connected to them. It was as if I were watching myself from the outside, sitting in the backseat while my body broke down in front of me. My mind? Disconnected. My heart? Confused.

How? How is this man making me cry like this?

It didn't make sense. This wasn't an emotionally intimate relationship. We didn't have deep, soul-baring conversations. Our connection was playful, magnetic, full of heat—but it wasn't *that.* And yet, here I was, sitting in my car, dissolving into a puddle of tears, *alone,* and getting annoyed that I was even experiencing this in the first place.

But if there's one thing I've learned after everything I've been through, it's this: when the tears come, you let them. You don't fight them, you don't shove them down—you let them move through you.

So, I did.

I sat in the parking lot, staring blankly at the dashboard as the emotion hit me like a rogue wave—sudden, merciless, and completely uninterested in whether I was ready for it. The floodgates burst open, tears spilling faster than I could process what the hell was even happening to me. One minute, I was laughing—actually laughing—at how bizarre it felt to be experiencing this for the first time, like some kind of emotional tourist. The next, frustration clawed at my chest, leaving me breathless and annoyed at myself for not knowing how to just *be* in this moment. It was a ridiculous tug-of-war between hysteria and heartbreak, but at some point, I just gave up trying to control it. Screw it. The emotions were in charge now—I was just along for the ride.

And then, when the storm settled, I wiped my face, took a deep breath, and went on about my errands like I hadn't just had a full-on breakdown in my driver's seat. *Maybe* it was just a quick release, a short but necessary eruption.

Except—when I got home, I felt the need to reach out.

I called Aire, needing the comfort of a friend, needing to *say* out loud what had just happened, to process it outside of my own head. And the second I started talking? The tears started all over again.

This time, it wasn't just a few drops. Oh no. This was something deeper. Something primal. A dam had broken, and the pain came pouring out like a flood, relentless and raw. And the strangest part? I *still* wasn't mentally connected to them. Normally, when you cry like this, it's because you're fixated on something, because your mind has latched onto the pain and won't let go. But *this*? This was different.

This was my body releasing something buried.

And in that moment, I *knew*. Dameon had unlocked something deep inside of me—something I hadn't even realized needed to be unearthed. Something that had been sitting there, dormant, waiting for the right moment to rise to the surface.

My instinct kicked in—I had to *digest* this, *process* this, *understand* what it actually meant. Because I had never been in a dynamic like this before. A connection so strong, yet one I had intentionally kept bolted down, refusing to let myself get emotionally attached.

Because we *all* know—sexy time *does* that. It binds you in ways logic can't undo.

And honestly? I thought I had done a damn good job keeping my heart out of it. Sure, there had been moments of sadness, moments of frustration from the tug-of-war between us, but overall? I had handled this. I had given myself *grace*. I had remained *strong*.

And yet—there I was. Crying tears that weren't tied to thoughts, but to something deeper. Something unresolved.

And that? That's the part I still needed to figure out.

Maybe this was another *bomb effect*—not quite like the trauma explosion of summer 2023, but a detonation nonetheless. A smaller-scale shockwave, one I hadn't seen coming.

Had I unknowingly suppressed every feeling I had for Dameon, only for them to come bursting through the second we had that tough conversation? Had an entire *year* of unacknowledged emotions been locked away in some hidden vault inside me, waiting for the right code to be entered? And the moment he *unlocked* it—was this the tidal wave I had been avoiding?

Was this what my heart actually felt all along?

The feelings, the longing, the emotions I refused to admit or accept—they poured out of me, relentless, undeniable. And it made sense. Unlike any other time in my life, I didn't allow myself to express what I naturally would have for someone I felt so drawn to. With Dameon, I had held it all in. Shut it down. And now? Maybe my subconscious had taken matters into its own hands, throwing a flood of tears at me like, *Here, deal with this.*

It made no sense. And yet, it made *all* the sense.

I ran circles in my head, crafting theories, analyzing every layer of emotion—because there had to be an explanation, *right?* The perfect storm had formed: an intense, emotional conversation mixed with playful, electric intimacy that sent me straight over the moon.

And then—another epiphany.

Well, *no shit* I ended up in this vulnerable state. That conversation was personal. Walls came down. He asked, I answered. I asked, he answered. And before I knew it, I felt exposed. Open. Maybe *that* was the problem—diving into emotional depth with someone I had convinced myself was just for fun.

But, of course, I didn't stop there. *Oh no.*

Then came *the* moment. The thought that hit me so hard, I felt it in my bones: *I'm scared I may not find someone I'll feel this way about again.*

The second I said it—to myself, out loud—the floodgates shattered. The pain multiplied. That singular realization cracked something wide open inside me, and the tears came harder, fiercer. And once my mind *digested* that truth, the emotions just kept rolling in, wave after wave.

But then, clarity. *Finally.*

I figured it out.

My heart is special. It doesn't just skim the surface—it runs as deep as the ocean. And I know—*I know*—how rare it is for me to feel a connection this strong. So, of course, my heart is hurting. Because it's *ready* to fall in love.

And I just shot myself in the foot with this man.

The warning signs had been flashing since day one. I saw them, clear as day. And instead of protecting myself, instead of doing my heart justice by walking away when I *knew* the truth, I chose to stay. To soak up the *now* and just enjoy what we had.

Haley, you can't do this. You cannot handle something like this.

That was fair. I never tried to play this game before—because I knew myself too well to even attempt it. But here I was, tangled up in it anyway.

And then—one shift. The narrative changed.

We don't fall in love with *people*. We fall in love with the versions of *ourselves* we get to become when we're with them.

Dameon and I never had a real dating phase, never got to dive into that deep, intimate connection my soul craves. But my intuition—my always-right, frustratingly strong intuition—just *knew*. My soul *wanted* him in the worst way. Because I follow energy, I follow frequency, and his? It lit me up.

He was a rare find.

But now, I realize—it wasn't about him.

Dameon was the *catalyst*. The trigger that revealed the purest, most undeniable part of me—the *lover* in me. The part of my soul that is built to love deeply, fully, wildly. I just happened to associate it with him in this dynamic.

And that? That explains a lot.

It wasn't about losing *him*. It was about discovering *me*.

I turned to Julius—the master of psychology himself—for some much-needed, hearty advice. It wasn't even a planned intervention; life just worked its magic, and I happened to see him recently to catch up. One thing led to another, and before I knew it, I was spilling the latest saga of my life. Dameon, of course, being at the center of it.

As I unraveled my emotions to him—sharing the uncontrollable tears, the final goodbye—Julius helped me uncover something my subconscious had been desperately trying to show me. And when he laid it out for me, it struck like a bolt of lightning.

This wasn't just grief over Dameon.

This was a *pattern*. A toxic, exhausting pattern.

What if the pain I was feeling wasn't just about *him*, but about something *bigger*? Something *deeper*? What if this was my subconscious waving a giant red flag, screaming at me to pay attention?

And then it clicked.

Grey Knight and Dameon—two of the only men in my life who had this *undeniable, intoxicating* pull over me—had something huge in common. And it wasn't just their high-energy, fun-loving, goofball personalities (which, let's be real, I absolutely *adore* in a significant other). No. It was something else.

They didn't prioritize me.

They weren't fully present.

They weren't emotionally available.

HOT. DAMN.

WOW.

The pattern that has *never* served me. The one I hadn't fully seen—until *now*.

And just like that, with the weight of Dameon's farewell still lingering in my chest and the remnants of my painful, purging tears still drying on my face, I *knew*.

This pattern ends here.

Since meeting Dameon just a few months after my breakup with Billy, I had learned so much about what I lacked in my past relationship and what I crave in my future ones. With Dameon, I saw it all—green flags, red flags, neon flashing signs telling me to pay attention. I had clarity. I had awareness.

Not only was I closing the chapter on Dameon, but I was closing the *entire damn book* on this toxic, dead-end dynamic. It has officially ended.

And now? Now, I make room for something real.

Anne's voice still rings in my head: "Dig deeper!" She drilled that mantra into us, pushing every single actor to peel back the layers like an onion until we reached the *core*, the rawest truth, the real objective. "There is always a deeply rooted meaning behind everything!"

After two years under her guidance, that philosophy has become second nature to me. And thank God for that, because my mind now naturally wants to keep probing, keep searching—keep asking the hard questions until I uncover the truth.

So, here it is. The truth.

I want to be loved.

It's that simple, that deep, that fundamental. But the deeper I dig, the more I realize—I need to look back. To analyze *who* I allowed into my life, *why* I chose them, and *what* patterns have been staring me dead in the face, waiting for me to finally see them.

And now? Oh, I see them.

That craving for love? It didn't just start with past relationships. No. It goes all the way back.

At first, I thought this revelation was just about Dameon. I mean, the emotional unraveling I experienced with him was enough to make me question everything. The attraction, the intensity, the gut-punching realization that he was never truly available—it all mirrored something deeper.

This isn't just about *them*. This isn't just about my relationships.

This goes all the way back to childhood.

Just days before finalizing this book, life handed me one last, unexpected chapter—one I didn't see coming but, in some ways, always knew was unfinished. It's about my brother. I haven't mentioned him beyond Chapter One, where he existed in the landscape of my childhood. Since moving to Los Angeles, our relationship didn't just fade—it evaporated. A slow, silent disappearance that I never fully acknowledged until now. It aches to write this, to admit the sheer distance between us, but the truth is, I have a brother... and yet, at times, it feels like I don't.

His life, in my opinion, has unraveled, and with it, the gap between us has only widened. I haven't heard from him in years—not a happy birthday, not a Merry Christmas. Nothing. And yet, I still find myself caring. Maybe too much. As kids, I worried about him so deeply that it became part of my identity, a responsibility I carried like a second skin. Leaving home was, in part, a promise to myself: *Stop worrying about your brother. Let the parents do their job—not you.* So, I stepped back. I let go. But every family visit reels me right back in, the old ache surfacing, whispering, *Try again.*

And this time, I did. In the briefest, most fragile of moments, I found myself alone with him. I didn't waste it. I pressed—gently at first, then deeper—asking what was really going on with him. And more importantly, what was going on with *us*. I laid my heart bare, shared childhood wounds I had once resented him for, confessed the forgiveness I had found on my own terms. And yet, he gave me nothing. No apology. No emotion. Just an empty, indifferent response when I told him I wanted a relationship: "I don't see how that's possible."

I didn't push. Maybe I should have. Maybe I shouldn't have. But every suggestion, every small olive branch, was met with rejection. And still, through choking back tears and words that felt heavier than I ever imagined, I told him—I've never stopped worrying about you. I love you. I want the best for you. It was harder than I thought, harder than I wanted it to be, but maybe that only proves just how deeply I care. I don't want an invisible brother. I don't want this endless space between us, stretching across years like a canyon too wide to cross. I just want *something*.

But here's the thing—I can't make him meet me halfway. I can't force understanding, or connection, or even the simple acknowledgment that I exist as more than a distant memory. What I *can* do is hold onto hope. Hope that someday, something shifts. That one day, he sees me—not as a figure from his past, but as someone still here, still waiting, still believing that maybe, just maybe, we'll find our way back to each other.

King Shit's Rule

Who is *King Shit*, you ask? That would be my dad—self-appointed ruler of our family, reigning with a scepter of dad jokes and an unshakable sense of self. The nickname stuck so effortlessly that I can't even remember when it began; it just *was*, like gravity or the inevitability of him making a pun at the worst possible moment.

And what's his royal decree, you ask? *"Love yourself. You are all you have."* A simple truth, wrapped in King Shit's signature delivery—unapologetic, absolute, like a commandment etched into stone.

At first, it was just another phrase in his ever-expanding library of wisdom, something I nodded at but never truly absorbed. But life has a way of circling back, of making sure you *get* the lesson when you need it most. That mantra became my lifeline, my battle cry, my compass. *Love yourself. You are all you have.* It didn't just change my perspective—it rewrote my story, pulling me back to my *feminine nature*, to a softness I had once mistaken for weakness.

Funny how sometimes, the words you don't think you need end up saving you. Turns out, even *King Shit* drops wisdom worth engraving on your soul.

That's just a taste of how we operate. Playful, sarcastic, laced with love. The same way he's called me *Pumpkin* since the moment I entered this world, as if he knew from day one that nickname would wrap around me like a security blanket. And on one of his birthdays, I decided to make that bond permanent. I had his words—*Love you Pumpkin*—etched into my skin in his very own handwriting. A tattoo, yes, but really, it's more than that. It's a living, breathing love note. A vow that no matter where life takes me, how many years pass, or how much we both change—I'll always be his little girl. Forever under the reign of *King Shit*.

Back to childhood. My subconscious—the little girl inside me—felt the absence of the love I needed most. The love from my mother that never fully arrived. And though my father was present, his love felt… tainted. Clouded by anger.

And guess what? That same dynamic? That same push-pull of love mixed with emotional unavailability? It played out over and over again in my relationships.

But here's the thing—after *years* of healing, of working through my wounds, of facing my inner child and actually listening to what she needed— I've realized something huge.

They were doing the best they could.

Our parents—your parents, my parents—all of them. They came from a different generation, a different world entirely. One where emotions were tucked away neatly, where love sometimes looked like a roof over your head rather than words of affirmation. And sure, it's easy to get caught up in what they didn't give us, what they didn't understand, what they could have done better. But at the end of the day, they gave us life. They planted the seed, set the foundation, and no matter how imperfect their nurturing may have been, they still shaped us.

So, how could I hold onto resentment? How could I stay bitter when I know they were just doing the best they could with the tools they had? And isn't that all any of us are doing?

I may not have human kids, but make no mistake—I am Mocha's mom through and through. And let me tell you, the responsibility? It's real. I prioritize her like she's the heiress to my imaginary empire, ensuring every tail wag, belly rub, and sunset beach run is nothing short of spectacular. Because that's what she deserves. Just like my parents once poured their love and time into me, I now pour mine into her—only with significantly more toys and dramatically narrated conversations.

And in my healing, I made a choice. A hard one. Instead of carrying the weight of resentment like an overstuffed suitcase I never asked for, I chose to unpack it. I chose to forgive. Not because the past deserves a free pass, but because I deserve peace. Because my freedom, my future, isn't built on the pain of what was—it's built on the love I choose now.

Because the truth is, I may never connect with them in the deep, soul- level way my heart craves. And that's okay.

What matters now is our relationship *today*.

Holding onto resentment only blocks me from the love I want to give and receive. And if I desire unconditional love from others, then *I* must be the one to extend it first. Maybe I can't have the full-circle connection I once wished for. But what can I do? Is my best. And that is *enough*.

This journey—this unraveling of my past, my patterns, my triggers—has turned me into a full-blown detective of my own life. And what I've found? It is priceless.

Every flaw, every negative trait, every limiting behavior—I don't run from them. I *study* them. I *challenge* myself to rewrite the script. To build healthier patterns, better relationships, a stronger, wiser version of myself.

Because I want *better* for myself.

And so, I dig. I dissect. I question.

I thrive on learning—especially when it comes to *me*. It only sharpens me, as a human, as a woman, as an actor. It's a part of who I am now.

And I've come to realize—most people are terrified to face themselves like this. It's scary to meet your own darkness, to stare your demons in the face and say, *Let's go to war.*

But me?

I seek it out.

I don't just want to uncover the mess—I want to clean it up. I want to burn away what doesn't serve me and transform into something greater.

And yeah, the rollercoaster ride through healing? *Brutal.* It will drag you through the mud, make you question everything, break you down before it builds you back up.

But when you reach the other side? When you feel the shift?

It's groundbreaking.

It's a *rebirth*.

And that feeling? That glorious moment when you step into the light after walking through the fire?

It's the most magical drink of your life.

So, if you're brave enough to take the journey—I applaud you. Because on the other side of healing?

The universe rewards you.

Abundance. Peace. Harmony. Alignment.

And that's when you know—you've made it.

Writing this book has been its own rollercoaster of emotions. It feels like standing on a stage completely naked, every flaw and scar on display, while the world decides whether to clap or throw tomatoes. Vulnerability is not for the faint of heart. But it also feels like purpose. I believe we're all here for a reason, and maybe—just maybe—this is part of mine. Sharing my story feels like a way to give back to the universe that let me stay. I don't think it's my only purpose; I've got a whole bucket list of dreams waiting to be chased. But for now, this is the *one*. If my words help even one person—if they make someone feel seen, less alone, or inspired to keep fighting—then every tear I shed while writing them will have been worth it.

I see life differently now because, honestly, I shouldn't be here. I've danced with death, and somehow, I'm still on the floor. When I think back to the agony I've endured, there's a highlight reel of pain that plays in my mind. Heroin withdrawals. Cancer treatments. They were both brutal, both life-altering. And yet, when people ask me which was worse, my answer comes out faster than I can even think: *withdrawals.*

Cancer is its own beast—don't get me wrong. The physical and emotional toll of fighting it was relentless. It humbled the restless warrior in me, forced me to slow down, and made me *truly* understand the fragile miracle of my own health. The pain was a battle all on its own—a brutal, unforgiving war that cracked open my perspective on life, on fear, on *everything*.

But heroin withdrawals?

That's a pain that exists in a different realm.

It doesn't just hurt—it *destroys*. It warps time itself, stretching minutes into hours and hours into eternity. It makes you feel like you're suffocating inside your own skin, your body betraying you in ways you never thought possible. And your mind? Your mind turns into the cruelest monster you've ever met. It's like being locked in a cage with no key, no escape—except the bars? They're made of your own choices.

And yet, in the depths of that living hell, something *unexpected* happened.

Grace.

Somehow, enduring that torment cracked me wide open. It stripped me down to nothing, forced me to face myself in ways I never had before. And in those shattered pieces, I found the will to rebuild.

And Mocha? Mocha saved me.

If she hadn't been there, if I didn't have *her*, I don't know where that spark of motivation would have come from—or if it would have come at all. I've always had an inner fire, a relentless drive, but when I spiraled into the darkest version of myself, when I became someone I didn't even recognize, that fire flickered. It dimmed. And for the first time in my life, I feared it might *go out*.

But then there was Mocha.

In the middle of my personal warzone, when I had fallen so far I wasn't sure there was a way back, *she* was my light at the end of the tunnel. She wasn't just my dog—she was my anchor. My last unshaken truth. The last spark of *me* still left.

Because of her, I *wanted* to change.

She was my reminder of the person I aspired to be. The version of me I had lost but desperately needed to find again. And in the darkest moments, when it felt like there was nothing left, Mocha was still there—proof that something was worth fighting for.

And that? That was *everything*.

Those experiences—the overdoses, the cancer, the withdrawals—catapulted me into becoming someone I never thought I could be. Fearless. Unapologetically, wildly *me*. And maybe that's the whole point. Maybe I had to walk through all that fire so I could come out on the other side and tell you this: You can survive your fire, too.

If my story does anything for you—if it makes you laugh, cry, or even just pause for a moment to reflect—then I'll consider it a success. If it reminds you that you're not alone, that there's light waiting for you on the other side of your darkest days, then this book will have served its purpose.

So, here I am, alive when I shouldn't be. Writing words I hope will touch hearts and change lives. Sharing my truth, raw and unfiltered, because maybe it's what you need to hear today. And if my story does inspire you, then I'll sit here, scars and all, with a heart full of gratitude, knowing that every painful chapter of my life was worth it.

Yes, I've embarked on a journey of relentless self-discovery over the years, but June of 2023 was the true ignition point. That month, I dove headfirst into the swirling depths of self-reflection, healing, and growth. By the time I greeted 2024, I felt like a phoenix rising from its ashes—fierce, radiant, and utterly reborn. It was as if the universe whispered, "You're ready," and I stood taller, more awakened, and more connected to my essence than ever before. But let's be honest: self-reinvention is not a straight path to bliss. Life doesn't hand out cheat codes for perfection. Instead, it's full of curveballs that remind me—painfully, beautifully—that I'm still, in every fiber, achingly human.

Empathy courses through my veins, electrified by the fires I've survived. It's a double-edged gift—a superpower and an Achilles' heel. I'm wired to feel deeply, to absorb life's colors in bold, unfiltered hues. Joy, pain, wonder, grief—they all seem to land harder on my heart, like the universe chose me as its confessional. And I've learned to honor that, even when it's messy and overwhelming. There are days when the emotions swell like a tsunami, threatening to consume me whole. On those days, I surrender. I cry, I scream, I dance, or I sit in the stillness of my own soul. That release—raw and unedited—is my salvation. Trust me, there's no high like the clarity that follows an emotional storm. It's like stepping outside after the rain, the air crisp and the world anew.

One of life's cruelest teachers was suppression. For years, I buried my pain, locking it away in some deep, dark cavern of my mind, hoping it would disappear. But suppressed emotions are relentless—they demand to be felt, and for me, they erupted in the form of panic attacks that left me gasping for air, convinced my life was slipping away. If you've been there, you know it's not just fear—it's a tidal wave that engulfs every cell in your body. I thought I had conquered those demons, but as I penned the final page of my book, I felt a storm brewing. When I whispered to myself, *It's done*, I expected relief. Instead, the next day, one of those ugly panic attacks tried to blindside me. Healing, as it turns out, is definitely not a linear process. It's a spiral—each cycle bringing you closer to the core of your truth.

But here's the twist: I'm okay with that. I don't want my healing to end. The process of nurturing my soul has become my art. It's nourishing and exhilarating, like sculpting something extraordinary out of the raw clay of my being. When I look back at my journey, I'm struck by the miraculous breadcrumbs the universe left for me—my life-altering trip to Italy, the serenity I discovered at the Alexander Technique retreat, Officer Griffin's push that got me out of Wisconsin, Anthony's entering my life at divine timing, and even my mother's caregiver moments of grace. These weren't just events; they were divine nudges, guiding me to where I needed to be.

Of course, not every day is marked by such revelations. Sometimes, it's the small, mundane battles that test my resilience—a rude comment, a missed opportunity, or simply a day when nothing goes as planned. In those moments, I've learned to pause and grant myself the grace to feel. Whether it's an hour or an entire day, I'll sit with my emotions, let them stretch, and yawn until they're ready to leave. Then, when I'm ready, I take charge. Maybe I use acting techniques to channel a new mood, or I meditate to recalibrate my mind. Either way, I've developed tools to gently pull myself back into the light.

It wasn't always this way. There was a time when I let every ounce of drama and nonsense worm its way into my psyche, dragging me into spirals of overthinking. But those days are behind me. I've learned to master my thoughts and emotions, and let me tell you—it's a *superpower*. It's not magic, nor is it easy. It's a practice—deliberate, sometimes grueling, but absolutely worth it. Because waking up each day with a mind at peace and a heart unburdened? That's the real jackpot I thrive on.

By the time the sun rises on a new day, I've let it all go. A fresh start, a clean slate. It's the simplest yet most profound gift we have. Above all, I've made a vow: no more suppression, no more silence. I will live my truth—fully, fearlessly, unapologetically. It's not always pretty. It's raw, chaotic, and painfully honest. But it's mine, and that makes it beautiful.

I want to live a life so vividly decorated it looks like it was painted by the universe itself—bold, untamed, bursting with color in every shade of experience. And I don't just mean aesthetically. I mean *emotionally, spiritually, intellectually*. I want to crack myself open to every frequency of life—new sounds, big love, reckless decisions, strange adventures that make no sense at the time but turn into the best stories later. I want to walk willingly into the unknown, embrace failure like an old friend, and chase the kind of magic that most people run from.

Because what's the alternative? A grayscale existence? No *thank* you.

I am in the business of breaking barriers—within myself, within my life—shattering every limitation that tries to keep me small. I refuse to be anything less than *fully awake* in my own existence.

And if there's one thing I know for certain, it's this: our bodies *always* know before we do.

My intuition. My battle with cancer. The trauma-box explosion. The Alexander Technique retreat. Every single moment has been a masterclass in *listening*. And since stepping into my own enlightenment, I've realized how much wisdom lives in stillness, in paying attention to the whispers before they become screams.

And because I listened, I *saved* myself.

I saved myself from cancer. From forces that could've taken me out of the game entirely. I tune into energy the way a musician tunes into sound—attentive, unwavering, trusting every vibration within and around me.

And one thing I know—I will *never* stop listening.

Because it has guided me through everything.

And I trust it to guide me still.

As I type the final words of my book, I feel like I'm closing a chapter—not just in my writing, but in my soul. This process has been more than cathartic; an emotional tidal wave, crashing over me again and again, pulling memories from the depths of my heart that I didn't even know were still there. Every time I broke down, tears streaming, I'd grab Mocha and head out for another walk. She probably thought we were training for a marathon with how often we hit the pavement. It became our rhythm: write, cry, walk, repeat.

I knew writing would heal me, but I never expected how deeply it would burrow into my spirit. Each memory I've poured onto the page is like a mosaic piece in the intricate, messy, beautiful picture of my life. Healing, I've learned, is not a destination. There's no magical moment where you're *done*. It's an endless process, ebbing and flowing like the tides. And yet, standing here, I can say I've reached a place I never imagined: I've become the most authentic, unapologetic, *unfuckwithable* version of myself. That alone fills me with gratitude so profound it feels like a superpower.

Don't get me wrong—I'm far from perfect. And that's okay. I've learned to love the imperfect, messy parts of me just as much as the polished ones. I'm proud of who I've become, and I don't give a damn what anyone else thinks. Cancer, addiction, abuse—these were my crucibles, each one burning away layers of fear until I emerged stronger, bolder, and fearless. Fear? It doesn't stand a chance with me anymore.

These days, I wake up *in love* with my life. It's like I've been handed a fresh pair of eyes, and suddenly, everything is drenched in color I never noticed before. The sky isn't just blue—it's an infinite ocean of possibility.

The air isn't just air—it's a whispered reminder to *breathe*, to *be here*, to *live*. And while my body carries the battle scars of heroin addiction, abuse, heartbreak, and cancer—while I've danced on the edge of death *three* times (two overdoses and a brutal showdown with pancreatic cancer)—I carry something far more powerful than pain: *gratitude*.

Gratitude for this moment, for this breath, for this *life* I almost lost. I've learned that joy isn't some grand, elusive thing—it's tucked inside the simplest moments. It's in the way my coffee warms my hands, the way the sun kisses my skin, the way laughter sneaks up and spills out of me when I least expect it. *This* is what I fought for. And let me tell you—I do *not* waste gifts anymore. Not time. Not energy. And certainly not my peace.

That's why I guard my joy like a damn fortress. Toxic energy? *Blocked.* Emotional vampires? *Deleted.* I clawed my way out of darkness, so why the hell would I invite shadows back in? Life is too short to entertain anything—or *anyone*—that doesn't feel like sunshine on my skin. If it drains me, it's done. No second chances. No explanations. Just a quiet, unapologetic exit.

And now, standing on the other side of heartbreak, loss, and a thousand soul-shaking moments, I see myself *clearly*—maybe for the first time ever. I've fallen in love with this woman I've become—a mosaic of scars, resilience, and beauty that wasn't *given* to me, but *earned* through fire. It's like putting on glasses after years of blurred vision—suddenly, everything is *sharp*. Patterns I once ignored now flash like neon signs. Boundaries I once feared now feel like armor I wear with pride.

And speaking of the universe—I trust it. I trust it to deliver love when the time is right. Because here's the thing—if I could love the *wrong* person that deeply, imagine what it'll feel like when the *right* one arrives. That thought alone electrifies me. But here's the difference now: I don't *need* anyone to complete me. I am whole. I have learned to love my own company, to laugh with myself, to find peace in my own silence.

Do I have regrets? *Not a single one.* Would I do it all over again? *Hell no.* But am I grateful for every scar, every heartbreak, every night I thought I wouldn't survive—because they built the woman I am today? *Absolutely.*

I used to carry shame like a heavy cloak, especially about my addiction. It swallowed me, convinced me I was unworthy of redemption. But now? I've shredded that cloak and reforged it into *armor*. I *own* my story—every messy, raw, painful part of it. And this book? This is my truth, laid bare. It terrifies me, but it also *frees* me.

Despite everything—despite the betrayals, the losses, the moments that nearly shattered me—I refuse to let the world make me bitter. I choose *kindness*. I choose *light*. I scatter love like glitter, because who knows? Maybe that tiny act of grace is exactly what someone else needs to keep going. And honestly, the world could use more *confetti moments*, don't you think?

I protect my energy like it's sacred—because it *is*. Fake vibes? I see them a mile away and steer clear. My circle is small but mighty, filled with people who pour love and authenticity into my life. Whether they've been with me for decades or just a season, I treasure them. My friends are my safe place, and I hold them close.

And love? I'm *open* to it. Open to the possibility of something extraordinary, but I'll never chase it. I've outgrown the need to beg for anyone's attention or affection. If someone wants to leave, the door is wide open—no hard feelings, no looking back. I've learned to live fully in the *now*, to let stress roll off me like rain. The old me would have drowned in worry, suffocated by the weight of what I couldn't control. The new me? She only holds onto what's within her power.

The rest?

It's in the hands of the universe. And I trust it.

Grey Knight

And then, there's Grey Knight. I'll always hold a space for him in my heart. He was my teacher, my mirror, my great love, and my greatest heartbreak. What we had was a symphony of every emotion on the spectrum—blissful highs and devastating lows. I've learned that soulmates aren't just found in lovers; they're found in friends, in fleeting connections, in moments that transform us. Grey Knight was one of mine, and I'm proud of him. Proud of his sobriety, of the life he's building, of the man he's become.

When I think about Grey Knight in the grand symphony of my life, especially now as I've spilled ink recounting our tangled love story, I find myself swept into a kaleidoscope of revelation. Writing about him has been like opening a treasure chest—not of gold, but of emotions long buried, each one demanding to be acknowledged. It's as though I've been granted a backstage pass to the theater of my past, where love and loss take center stage in a performance so vivid, so chaotic, it leaves me breathless. Our story swirled with reckless abandon, a tidal wave of passion that shaped me in ways I'm only now beginning to comprehend.

In my quest to understand the layers of our connection, I stumbled upon a concept so piercingly accurate it felt like the universe handed me a key: trauma bonding. The term flared to life, casting a spotlight on the invisible threads that have tethered me to him.

My intuition wasn't just whispering—it was screaming, practically throwing confetti and blasting a megaphone in my face, giving me full permission to chase the first human I'd ever wanted with every fiber of my being. And chase him, I did. We fell into love the way you fall into the deep end of a pool—suddenly, irreversibly, with no life raft in sight. He made me believe in love at first sight, not just because of our story but because I wanted him with the kind of feverish intensity that could rewrite fate. And not just any love—the all-consuming, ride-or-die, "I love the shit out of you" kind. The kind poets romanticize and therapists warn you about.

But here's the kicker—how could it *not* be a trauma bond when the foundation of our love was tangled in the suffocating grip of his heroin addiction? We weren't just lovers; we were warriors, charging into battle with reckless devotion, shielding each other from the world while unknowingly sharpening our own destruction. Chaos became our currency, and we spent it like fools, mistaking the high stakes for depth, the struggle for destiny.

And yet, even now, I know—*I know*—Grey Knight feels this pull too. Maybe he hasn't dissected it, hasn't given it a name, but it's there. An unshakable truth. A gravity that exists between us, whether I embrace it or try to escape it.

This writing process has been less like journaling and more like alchemy. Each word, a tiny elixir, revealing hidden truths and exposing raw wounds. And the truth that shimmers brightest is this: Grey Knight is my one true, everlasting love. I poured every ounce of myself into that relationship, into him, leaving no corner of my soul untouched by his presence. He was— perhaps still is—the love of my life. Despite the years, despite the battles I've waged to let him go, my feelings for him have clung to me with the stubbornness of ivy. Every year, I've fought to tear those vines away. I've tried to summon hatred, thinking it might finally cut the tether. But hatred is a stranger to my heart, and my failure to summon it has only illuminated the depth of my love.

You might assume, given our story, that bitterness would have taken root. After all, this is the man whose love was a thread woven through some of the darkest, most harrowing chapters of my life. Yet, my inability to despise him has taught me something extraordinary. It's a testament to the love we shared—a love so profound that it transcends pain. Grey Knight set a bar so high it towers over the horizon, a standard that has reshaped how I see myself and what I seek in others. But more than that, he's shown me the resilience I never knew I possessed. Through every tear, every scar, every near-death moment, I've clawed my way back to myself. And somehow, through it all, I've kept my heart wide open, choosing faith and gratitude over the cold comfort of resentment.

So, where does this leave me? Perhaps the truth is as complex as the man himself. Our relationship defied tidy definitions, dancing on that razor-thin edge between trauma bonding and unshakable love. Grey Knight wasn't just a chapter in my life—he was an earthquake, a wildfire, a goddamn hurricane, obliterating everything in his path, including me. And yet, in the wreckage, I found something startling: the raw materials of my own rebirth.

I know, I know. It probably sounds ridiculous—me sitting here, waxing poetic about the man who not only left my heart in splinters but might have also had a hand in the tumor that became my battle with cancer. That's a theory I toy with, anyway. Science backs up the idea that our bodies hold onto trauma, twisting it into something tangible, something malignant. And if that's true, then loving Grey Knight may very well have been the most toxic addiction of my life. But here's the thing: I wouldn't change a damn second of it.

Every moment—good, bad, catastrophic—was necessary. Every tear I shed, every scar I wear, every moment of unfiltered joy, every guttural scream of agony, all of it led me here. To this moment. To this woman.

It's wild, isn't it? The way you can love someone so deeply, so fiercely, like they are your person, your twin flame, your once-in-a-lifetime, and then—what comes next? The unraveling. The aftermath. The realization that the same person who made your soul feel alive also dragged it through hell. And yet, despite the carnage, you still love them. Not just any love—the unconditional, infuriating, unfair kind that refuses to die, no matter how much logic begs it to.

And you ask yourself: *Why? Why am I wired like this? Why does my heart refuse to listen to my brain?* You tell yourself to trust that there's a reason for it, some divine, cosmic lesson buried in the ashes. But the "what-ifs" still haunt you.

What if I had said goodbye when I left that night?

What if I had turned around at the door, forced the closure I never got?

What if, instead of detoxing from him like a drug, I had let myself feel every last drop of him, just once more?

That's the thing about memories. They don't just disappear. They morph into ghosts—ones that don't haunt the places you once stood, but the spaces inside you.

And yet, despite it all, here I am. Standing in a place of acceptance. Not because I've erased him, not because I've rewritten history, but because I have learned to carry him differently. Grey Knight will always be a part of me—not as a weight dragging me down, but as a talisman, a scarred yet sacred relic of everything I have survived.

Love and loss are strange companions. They break you, rebuild you, and leave their fingerprints on your soul. Grey Knight was my chaos and my calm, my undoing and my resurrection. And for that—for all of it—I will forever be grateful.

This life of mine has been chaos and beauty, destruction and rebirth—a storm I once feared but now claim as my own. I've shattered, healed, and risen, each scar etched with resilience, each lesson a spark that reignited my fire. Grey Knight, the wreckage, the past—they don't define me. *I define me.* And by finishing this book, I'm not just telling my story—I'm closing this chapter, sealing it with truth, and leveling up for what comes next. Because this isn't the end. It's the beginning of everything.

Even if I knew the day we met you'd be the reason this heart breaks, I'd love you anyway.

About the Author

Haley Mazanec

Haley Mazanec is a fresh and powerful voice in contemporary nonfiction, captivating readers with her raw authenticity and heartfelt storytelling. In her debut autobiography, *Three Strikes Can't Take Me Out*, she shares an inspiring journey through love, heartbreak, addiction, and rebirth, offering a poignant testament to resilience and hope.

A cancer survivor with a background in acting and modeling, Haley's life is a testament to perseverance. After leaving her small hometown at twenty-one to chase her dreams in Los Angeles, she faced life's challenges head-on, transforming pain into purpose and adversity into triumph.

When she's not writing, Haley embraces an active lifestyle, staying fit at the gym, enjoying life's simple joys, and adventuring with her Australian Shepherd, Mocha. Her ability to turn life's toughest moments into lessons of strength continues to inspire her readers and those around her.

LinkedIn: https://www.linkedin.com/in/haleymazanec
Facebook: https://www.facebook.com/profile.php?id=1169208861
Instagram: https://www.instagram.com/haleymazanec/
Website: www.haleymazanec.com

Your Fight Isn't Over—Own Your Power.

The Rise Continues…If you made it to the end of this book—thank you. Truly. Thank you for walking beside me through the ashes, heartbreak, healing, and rebirth.

But this book isn't just about my story—it's about yours.

I wrote these pages so you could feel the power pulsing in your own veins. So you could see that no matter how many strikes life throws your way, you are not out. Not now. Not ever.

This is not the end—it's your beginning.

As you close this chapter, I invite you to rise into your own. I'm building something sacred: a transformational space where I guide women to awaken their feminine power from the inside out. This is a space to learn, embody, and lead from ♥ your softness, sensuality, intuition, and truth.

A sanctuary where:

- Feminine power is not only honored—but awakened.

- Healing becomes embodiment.

- Survivors step into sovereignty.

- And softness transforms into strength.

This new offering includes private and group sessions, spiritual mentorship, and soul-led guidance for women ready to shed old stories and embrace their next chapter—from woman to goddess, from broken to whole.

If you're ready to reclaim your feminine fire—or curious about becoming a founding member—visit:

www.haleymazanec.com

or connect with me on Instagram: @haleymazanec

Scan the QR code below to join the movement and get early access.

Your Fight Isn't Over—Own Your Power

If Three Strikes Can't Take Me Out stirred something in you—if you've survived heartbreak, loss, trauma, or moments that nearly broke you—I want to hear from you. I want to witness your fight.

Special thanks to the photographers who helped bring this vision to life:

Kevin Weinert — www.kevinweinert.com
Will Mac — www.willgmacneil.com

Share your story: Tag me on social @haleymazanec and use the hashtag #ThreeStrikesCantTakeMeOut to join a community of survivors, warriors, and women rewriting their narratives.

Leave a review: Your voice might be the one that helps another woman realize she's not alone. Share your thoughts on Amazon, Goodreads, or wherever you purchased this book. Your words matter.

Stay connected: For exclusive updates, behind-the-scenes looks, and all future offerings, visit www.haleymazanec.com and join the movement.

No matter what you've been through—you are not a victim.

You are a warrior.

You are a queen in the making.

And your story is far from over.

Let's keep rising.